Reprints of Economic Classics

WORK AND WEALTH

Also Published in

REPRINTS OF ECONOMIC CLASSICS

By JOHN A. HOBSON

INTERNATIONAL TRADE [1904]

PROBLEMS OF POVERTY [1889]

VEBLEN [1936]

WORK AND WEALTH [1914]

With A. F. MUMMERY

THE PHYSIOLOGY OF INDUSTRY [1889]

WORK AND WEALTH

A HUMAN VALUATION

BY

JOHN A. HOBSON

[1914]

REPRINTS OF ECONOMIC CLASSICS

AUGUSTUS M. KELLEY · PUBLISHERS
NEW YORK 1968

First Edition 1914

(New York: The Macmillan Company, 1914)

Reprinted 1968 by
AUGUSTUS M. KELLEY · PUBLISHERS
NEW YORK NEW YORK 10010
By *Arrangement With* GEORGE ALLEN & UNWIN LTD.

LIBRARY OF CONGRESS CATALOGUE CARD NUMBER

68-30527

PRINTED IN THE UNITED STATES OF AMERICA
by SENTRY PRESS, NEW YORK, N. Y. 10019

PREFACE

The goods and services that constitute our national income are valued severally and collectively with a fair amount of accuracy in terms of money. For a gold standard, though by no means perfect for the work of monetary measurement, is stable and has a single definite meaning to all men. By means of it we can estimate the rates of growth or decline in our industry, as an aggregate or in its several departments, and the quantities of output and consumption of the various products. We can compare the growth of our national wealth with that of other nations.

But how far can these measurements of concrete wealth furnish reliable information regarding the vital values, the human welfare, which all economic processes are designed to yield? Though it will be generally admitted that every increase of economic wealth is in some measure conducive to welfare, every decrease to illfare, nobody will pretend even approximately to declare what that measure is, or to lay down any explicit rules relating wealth to welfare, either for an individual or a nation. Indeed, even the general assumption that every growth of wealth enhances welfare cannot be admitted without qualification. An injurious excess of income is possible for an individual, perhaps for a nation, and the national welfare which an increased volume of wealth seems capable of yielding might be more than cancelled by a distribution which bestowed upon a few an increased share of the larger wealth, or by an aggravation of the toil of the producers.

Such obvious considerations drive us to seek some intelligible and consistent method of human valuation for economic goods and processes. To find a standard of human welfare as stable and as generally acceptable as the monetary standard is manifestly impossible. Indeed, the difficulties attending any sort of calculus of vital values might appear insuperable, were it not for one reflection. Every statesman, social reformer, philan-

v

thropist, every public-spirited citizen, does possess and apply
to the conduct of affairs some such standard or criterion as we are
seeking. Some notion or idea, more or less clear and explicit, of
the general welfare, crossed and blurred no doubt by other interests and passions, is an operative and directive influence in his
policy. Moreover, though idiosyncrasies will everywhere affect
this operative ideal, there will be found among persons of widely
different minds and dispositions a substantial body of agreement
in their meaning of human welfare. The common social environment partly evokes, partly imposes, this agreement. In fact, all
coöperative work for social progress implies the existence of some
such standard as we are seeking. The complex image of human
values which it contains is always slowly changing, and varies
somewhat among different sorts and conditions of men. But for
the interpretation of economic goods and processes it has, at any
time, a real validity. For it is anchored to certain solid foundations of human nature, the needs and functions to which, alike
in the individual and in the society, we give the term 'organic.'

Only by considering the organic nature of man and of human
society can we trace an intelligible order in the evolution of
industry. The wants of man, and therefore the economic operations serving them must be treated as organic processes. This
term, borrowed from biology, must be extended so as to cover
the entire physical and spiritual structure of human society, for
no other term is so well fitted to describe the nature of the federal
unity which society presents. The standard of values thus set
up is the current estimate of 'organic welfare.'

The justification of these terms and of this mode of human
valuation is to be found in their application to the task before
us. These tools will be found to do the work better than any
others that are available.

In seeking to translate economic values into human by reference to such a standard of organic welfare, I take as the aptest
material for experiment the aggregate of goods and services that
constitute the real income of the British nation. In order to reduce that income to terms of human welfare, I first examine
separately the economic costs of production and the economic
utilities of consumption which meet in this concrete wealth,

analysing them into human cost and human utility, the debit
and credit sides of the account of welfare. Analysis of the productive processes will, of course, disclose the fact that not all
'economic' costs have human costs attached to them, but that
human utilities of varying value inhere in many sorts of productive work. Surveying the different orders of productive
energy, from the finest arts to the lowest modes of routine toil,
we discover that any two bodies of economic wealth, possessing
the same pecuniary value, may differ enormously in the quantity
of human cost they carry. For that cost will depend upon the
nature of the work, the nature of the workers, and the distribution of the work among the workers. This line of enquiry opens
out, in form at any rate, a complete criticism of current English
industry, from the humanist standpoint. A similar analysis
applied on the consumption side resolves the economic utility
of the goods and services into human utility. Here again out
of economic utilities much human cost emerges, just as out of
economic costs much human utility. Equal quantities of income
yield in their consumption widely diverse quantities of human
utility or welfare.

Piecing together the two sides of our enquiry into the production and consumption of the income, we perceive, as might be
expected, that a sound human economy conforms to the organic
law of distribution, 'from each according to his power, to each according to his needs,' and that, precisely so far as the current
processes of economic distribution of work and of its product contravene this organic law, waste accrues and illfare displaces welfare. The economic distinction between costs and unearned surplus [1] furnishes in effect a faithful measure of the extent and forms
of divergence between the economic and the human 'law' of
distribution. For when this surplus income is traced, backward
to the human costs involved in its production, forward to the
human injuries inflicted by the excessive and bad consumption
it sustains, it is seen to be the direct efficient cause of all the
human defects in our economic system. Growing in magnitude
with the development of the modern arts of industry and commerce, it is the concrete embodiment of the social-economic

[1] This distinction is elaborated in my work, *The Industrial System* (Longmans).

problem. The absorption and utilisation of the surplus for the betterment of the working-classes and the enrichment of public life are essential conditions for the humanisation of industry.

The first half of the book is occupied with the general exposition and illustration of this method of human valuation. The second part applies the humanist principles thus established, to the discussion of some of the great practical issues of social-economic reconstruction in the fields of business and politics. The medley of overlapping conflicts between capital and labour, producer and consumer, competition and combination, the individual and society, is sifted so as to discover lines of industrial reformation based upon a conception of organic harmony. The reconstruction of the business, so as adequately to represent in its operation the respective interests of capital, ability, labour and the consumer, is seen to be the first desideratum of reform. Here, as in the wider oppositions between business and business, trade and trade, nation and nation (misconceived as economic units), the more rational standpoint of a humanist valuation suggests modes of reconcilement following an evolution of economic structure in which the corporate or coôperative spirit finds clearer and stronger expression. The most debated question, how far ordinary human nature can yield economic motives to social service strong and reliable enough to enable society to dispense with some of the incentives of competitive greed, hitherto deemed indispensable supports to industry, is discussed in several of the later chapters. The practicable limits of industrial reformation are found to depend upon the reality and importance assigned to 'the social will' as a power operative for industrial purposes, in other words upon the strength of the spiritual unity of society. A final chapter is given to a discussion of the limitations of the scientific and quantitative methods in the interpretation and direction of social-economic life. It is contended that the art of social as of individual conduct must always defy exact scientific guidance, the methods of science being incompetent closely to predict or direct the creative element in organic processes.

The processes of human valuation and judgment, therefore, whether applied to industry or to other activities and achievements, must ultimately belong to the art rather than to the science of society, the statesman and the citizen absorbing and assimilating the history of the past which science presents in its facts and laws, but using his free constructive faculty to make the history of the future. The failures of the individual statesman or citizen in the performance of this artistic work are due to the fact that a larger artist, whose performance the most enlightened individual can but slightly apprehend, viz. society itself, takes an over-ruling part in the process.

This brief presentation of the argument, dwelling unavoidably upon intellectual method, may possibly have failed to convey the intensely practical purpose which I have kept in mind throughout the preparation of the book. That purpose is to present a full and formal exposure of the inhumanity and vital waste of modern industry by the close application of the best-approved formulas of individual and social welfare, and to indicate the most hopeful measures of remedy for a society sufficiently intelligent, courageous and self-governing to apply them.

Such a work evidently presents a large front for hostile criticism. Its scope has often compelled a rigorous compression in the discussion of important controversial topics, and has precluded all entrance upon the more detailed issues in the policy of reconstruction. But I venture to hope that many readers, who may disagree with the particular valuations and interpretations offered in these chapters, will be led to accept the broader outlines of the method of human valuation here proposed, and will recognise the importance of a better application of this method in the solutions of the practical problems of economic reform.

J. A. HOBSON.

HAMPSTEAD,
January, 1914.

TABLE OF CONTENTS

xi

CHAPTER XIII

CHAPTER XIV

CHAPTER XV

CHAPTER XVI

WORK AND WEALTH

CHAPTER I

THE HUMAN STANDARD OF VALUE

§ 1. In an age when human problems of a distinctively economic character, relating to wages, hours of labour, housing, employment, taxation, insurance and kindred subjects, are pressing for separate consideration and solution, it is particularly important to enforce the need of a general survey of our economic system from the standpoint of human values. Social students, of course, are justified by considerations of intellectual economy in isolating these several problems for certain purposes of detailed enquiry. But the broader human setting, demanded for the judgment or the policy of a statesman or reformer, can never be obtained by this separatist treatment. For the interactions which relate these issues to one another are numerous and intimate. Taking as the most familiar example the groups of questions relating to the working-classes, we recognise at once how the wages, hours, regularity of employment and other considerations of labour, overlap and intertwine, while, again, the questions relating to conditions of living, such as housing, food, drink, education, recreation, facilities of transit, have similar interrelations as factors in a standard of comfort. Nor is it less evident that conditions of labour and conditions of living, taken severally and in the aggregate, interact in ways that affect the efficiency and well-being of the people.

The special and separate studies of these various problems must then, in order to be socially serviceable, be subject to the guidance and direction of some general conception which shall have regard to all sorts of economic factors and operations, assessing them by reference to some single standard of the humanly desirable. This general survey and the application of this single

1

standard of valuation are necessary alike to a scientific interpretation of the economic or industrial world and to a conscious
art of social-economic progress. They must exert a control over
the division of intellectual labour on the one hand, and over the
utilisation of such labour for social policy upon the other. The
notion that, by setting groups of students to work at gathering,
testing, measuring and tabulating crude facts, relating, say, to
infant mortality, expenditure on drink, or wages in women's
industries, valuable truths of wide application will somehow be
spontaneously generated, and that by a purely inductive process
there will come to light general laws authoritative for social
policy, is entirely destitute of foundation. The humblest grubber
among 'facts' must approach them with some equipment of
questions, hypotheses, and methods of classification, all of which
imply the acceptance of principles derived from a wider field of
thought. The same holds again of the next higher grade of students, the intellectual middlemen who utilise the 'facts' got by the
detailed workers 'at the face.' They too must bring wider principles to correlate and to interpret the results got by the humbler
workers. So at each stage of the inductive process, laws and standards derived from a higher intellectual stage are brought to bear.

Even if such studies were prompted entirely by a disinterested
desire for knowledge, it is evident that their success implies the
inspiration and application of some general ideas, which in relation to these studies are *a priori*. But regarding these studies as
designed primarily to assist the art of social policy, we must
recognise that the inner prompting motive of every question that
is put at each stage of such enquiries, the inner regulative principle of the division of labour and of the correlation of the results,
is the desire to realise some more or less clear conception of general human well-being. It must, of course, be admitted that this
procedure rests upon a sort of paradox. The general conception
of human well-being is itself vague and unsubstantial, until it
has acquired and assimilated the very sorts of knowledge the
collection of which it is here assumed to be able to direct. This
paradox, however, is familiar to all who reflect upon the progress
of knowledge in any department and for any purpose. I only
name it here in order to anticipate the objection of those dis-

posed to question the validity of assuming any sort of standard of human welfare, and to insist upon testing each economic issue upon what they call 'its own merits.' The application of a general survey and a general standard of values is none the less a logically valid and a practically useful procedure, because the new facts which its application discloses afford more fulness and exactitude to the survey, while the standard is itself made clearer and more effective thereby.

Assuming it to be admitted, then, that a human valuation of economic processes is possible and desirable, both for the enlargement of knowledge and for purposes of social policy, the questions next arise, 'How shall we conceive and describe the standard of human valuation, and how shall we apply it to the interpretation of the present economic system?'

§ 2. Before facing these questions, however, it will be well to have before our minds a clear outline picture of this economic system which we seek to value. It consists of two complex operations, constantly interacting, known as Production and Consumption of wealth. By wealth is understood all sorts of vendible goods and services. So far as material wealth is concerned, it is 'produced' by a series of processes which convert raw materials into finished goods of various sorts and sizes and dispose them in such quantities as are required, for the satisfaction of consumers or as instruments in some further process of production. Similarly, in the case of professional, official, domestic, industrial, commercial, and other personal services, which also rank as wealth,[1] a variety of productive processes go to prepare them and to place them at the disposal of consumers. The processes of production may thus be classified as extractive, manufacturing, artistic, transport, commercial, professional, domestic. Thus it is seen that the work of 'distribution' and 'exchange,'[2] sometimes distinguished from the work of production, is here included in that category.

[1] Labour employed in productive work of industry is usually excluded from the category of national 'wealth', though it is sometimes regarded as 'personal wealth'. But there is no sufficient reason for this exclusion. Any increase of the efficiency of the labour of a nation is evidently as much an increase of its total vendible resources as an increase in its instrumental capital would be.

[2] Exchange is simply an ordinary branch of production, mainly consisting of

Now, the first difficulty confronting us in our search for a human valuation of this economic system consists in the obscurity in which half this system lies. For though there is everywhere a formal recognition that consumption is the end or goal of industry, there is no admission that the arts of consumption are equally important with the arts of production and are deserving of as much attention by students or reformers of our 'economic system.' On the contrary, so absorbing are the productive processes in their claims upon the physical and mental energies of mankind, that the economic system, alike for practitioners and theorists, has almost come to be identified with these processes. This depreciation and neglect of Consumption no doubt has been natural enough. So much more conscious energy of thought and feeling, and so much more expenditure of time and effort have gone into the discovery, development and practice of the productive arts. Their practice has involved so much more publicity, so much wider and more varied intercourse, and therefore so much more organisation. Consumption, on the other hand, has been so much more passive in its character, so private and individual in the acts which comprise it, so little associated with sequences of thought or purpose, that it has hardly come to be regarded as an art. Hence, even in the more elaborate civilisations where much detailed skill and attention are devoted to the use and enjoyment of goods and services, the neglect of consumptive processes by economic science remains almost unimpaired. The arts of production remain so much more exacting in their demands upon our attention.

The early influence of this dominance of the productive standpoint in economic science has had effects upon the terminology and structure of that science which are serious obstacles to the human interpretation of industry. Unconsciously, but consistently, the early structure of the science was built with exclusive regard to the industrial or productive processes. The art out of which the science grew was concerned with the progress of agricul-

wholesale and retail trade. Distribution has, of course, another and an important economic signification, being applied to the laws determining the apportionment of the product.

ture, manufacture, and commerce, or with problems of money, taxation, and population, regarded mainly or wholly from the productive standpoint. The underlying assumption everywhere was the question, 'How will this or that policy affect the quantity of wealth produced in the country?' always with an important corollary to the effect, 'How will it affect the quantity of wealth, passing as rents, profits, interest, or wages to the several classes of the nation?' But nowhere was there any direct consideration of the arts of consumption, with one particularly instructive exception. The only bit of attention paid by our early classical economists to processes of consumption was to distinguish 'productive' from 'unproductive' consumption, that is, to suggest a valuation of consumption based entirely upon its subordination to future purposes of production. Their condemnation of luxurious expenditure and waste, alike in the wealthy and the working-classes, was not primarily directed against the loss of real enjoyment, or human well-being, or the moral degradation involved in such abuse of spending power, but against the damage to the further processes of making wealth by reducing the rate of saving or by impairing the working efficiency of labour. Though occasional considerations of a more distinctively humane or moral character entered into the tirades against luxury, or the dietetic advice offered by these economic teachers, the main trend of their reflections on the use of wealth was quite evidently dominated by considerations of increased production. This tendency further impressed itself upon the central concept of economic science, that of value, which was treated by these early makers of Political Economy exclusively from the productive standpoint of 'costs.' When, however, later theorists, beginning with Jevons in this country, sought to convert the formal goal of consumption into the real goal, by substituting 'utility' for 'cost' as the determinant of value, it might have been supposed that they would have been impelled, passing through the gateway of utility into consumption, to open up that hitherto neglected country. But no such thing has happened. While an elaborate division of intellectual labour has been applied, both to the study of the objective structure of industry, and to the psychology of the various agents of production, no corresponding studies of consumption have been made. When the products of industry pass over the retail counter, economic science almost entirely loses count of them. They pass from sight into the mysterious maw of 'the Consumer.' It has never occurred to the economist that it is just as important to have a clear and close knowledge of what happens to products when they have become consumer's goods, as it is to trace their history in the productive stages. It would, of course, be untrue to say that modern economists completely ignore methods and motives of consumption. Their studies of value and of markets compel them to direct equal attention to forces regulating Supply and Demand, and many of them assign a formal superiority to the demand for final commodities which issues from Consumers, as the regulator of the whole industrial system. But while this has evoked some interesting enquiries into quantities and modes of consumption, the main interest of these enquiries has lain, not in the light they shed upon the use and enjoyment got from consumption, but in the effects of that consumption upon demand as a factor in problems of price and of production. In a word, the economic arts of consumption still run in subordination to the arts of production, and the very nature of the interest taken in them attests their secondary place. Half of the field of economic survey important from the standpoint of human welfare thus stands unexplored or ill-explored.

§ 3. A necessary result of this identification of economic subject-matter with the productive apparatus, has been to impose upon the study of economics a distinctively mechanical character. The network of businesses and trades and processes, which constitutes industry, may indeed, by an interpretative effort of imagination, be resolved into the myriads of thoughts, desires and relations which are its spiritual texture. Every business, with its varied machinery and plant, its buildings, materials, etc., is the embodiment of conscious human effort, and the personnel of management and operatives represent a live current of volition and intelligence, directing and coöperating with it. A business, thus regarded, is a distinctively spiritual fabric. Nor is this true only of those industries employed in fashioning material goods. The complicated arrangements of communications and of commerce with their ganglia of markets, by which goods pass from one process to another and are gathered, sorted and distributed in regulated channels throughout the world of workers and consumers, represent an even more delicate adjustment of psychical activities. Economic science tends, undoubtedly, to become less material in its outlook and treatment, and to give more attention to the psychological supports of the industrial system. Not only have we many special studies of such economic questions as saving and investment, business administration and other critical operations of will and judgment, but in such works as those of M. Tarde in France, and Mr. Wicksteed in this country, we find attempts at a systematic psychological interpretation of industry. Economics, indeed, according to the latter writer, is a branch of the science of 'preferences,' the application of intelligent human volition to the satisfaction of economic wants.

And yet the science remains distinctively mechanical and unfitted for the performance of any human interpretation of industry. This is due to the failure of our psychological economists to tear themselves free from the traditions of a Political Economy which in its very structure has made man subservient to marketable wealth. The accepted conception of the Art of Political Economy is that it is directed to the production of wealth whose value is attested by the purely quantitative calculus of money, and the Science of Political Economy is virtually confined to discovering and formulating the laws for the production of such wealth. The basic concepts of Value, Cost, and Utility, are subjected to this governing presupposition. Their primary significance is a monetary one. The value of any stock of wealth is signified in money, the cost of its production, the utility of its consumption, are registered in monetary terms. The psychological researches which take place into processes of thought and desire are not regarded as having significance on their own account, but merely as means or instruments in the working of industrial processes. The study of motives, interests, and ideas in the process of invention, or in the organisation and operation of some productive work, treats these thoughts and feelings not in their full bearing upon human life, its progress or happiness, but in exclusive relation to the monetary end to which they are directed.

§ 4. It is no concern of ours to criticise this attitude in the sense of condemnation. But it is important to realise that no progress of psychological analysis will enable economic science to supply a human valuation of industry so long as all the human functions involved in economic processes are measured, assessed, and valued, according to their bearing upon the production of a 'wealth' which has no directly assignable relation to human welfare, but is estimated by a purely monetary measure. The net effect of this conception of the economic system as an elaborate arrangement of material and spiritual factors, contributing to the production and distribution of a stream of various goods valued by a monetary standard, is to leave upon the mind the impress of a distinctively mechanical apparatus. No one, for example, can read the masterly work of Mr. Wicksteed [1] without recognising that his delicate, elaborate measurements and balances of motives and preferences, while involving and implying actions that no one but man can perform, treat not only industry, but humanity itself as a psychological mechanism.

This distinctively mechanical character is inherent in the structure of an economic science based upon the subserviency of all human activities to a purely quantitative conception of wealth, and a purely monetary standard of value. This character of economic science is, of course, by no means disabling for all purposes. On the contrary, it furnishes valid instruments for the interpretation of many important groups of phenomena in the business world, and for the solution of certain problems where purely quantitative standards and methods are applicable. Indeed, the increasing devotion of economists to problems of money, price, and other definitely monetary questions, may be taken as a half-instinctive recognition of the real inadequacy of current economics for any very useful solution of those more vital problems into which closely human considerations enter as governing factors. As we proceed, we shall realise in more detail the nature of the incapacity of current economics to furnish any rules for settling issues that relate to wages, hours of labour,

[1] *The Common-sense of Political Economy.*

State interference with private industry, private property, and other human problems which are in first appearance 'economic.'

Three defects appear, then, to disqualify current economic science for the work of human valuation. First, an exaggerated stress upon production, reflected in the terminology and method of the science, with a corresponding neglect of consumption. Secondly, a standard of values which has no consistent relation to human welfare. Thirdly, a mechanical conception of the economic system, due to the treatment of every human action as a means to the production of non-humanly valued wealth.

§ 5. These warning-posts may help us to discover and to formulate an intellectual procedure more suited to our needs. A human valuation of industry will give equal attention to Production and Consumption, will express Cost and Utility in terms of human effort and satisfaction, and will substitute for the monetary standard of wealth a standard of human well-being. This assertion of vital value as the standard and criterion is, of course, no novelty. It has underlain all the more comprehensive criticisms of orthodox political economy by moralists and social reformers. By far the most brilliant and effective of these criticisms, that of John Ruskin, was expressly formulated in terms of vital value. The defects which he found in the current economic science were substantially the same as those which we have noted. His famous declaration that 'There is no wealth but life,' and his insistence that all concrete wealth or money income must be estimated in relation to the vital cost of its production and the vital utility of its consumption, is the evidently accurate standpoint for a human valuation of industry. This vital criterion he brought to bear with great skill, alike upon the processes of production and consumption, disclosing the immense discrepancies between monetary costs and human costs, monetary wealth and vital wealth. No one ever had a more vivid and comprehensive view of the essentially organic nature of the harmony of various productive activities needed for a wholesome life, and of the related harmony of uses and satisfactions on the consumptive side. His mind seized with incomparable force of vision the cardinal truth of human economics, viz. that every piece of concrete wealth must be valued in terms of the vital costs of its production and the vital uses of its consumption, and his most effective assault upon current economic theory was based upon its complete inadequacy to afford such information. But, though most of his later writings were suffused with this conception of wealth and with the double process of analysis which it involved, nowhere was that analysis systematically applied. There were brilliant excursions into the domain of labour, distinguishing the nobler and the baser sorts, those which are truly 'recreative' and those which degrade and impoverish life. There was the famous distinction between 'wealth' and 'illth,' according to the essential qualities of the goods and the sorts of persons into whose hands they pass for consumption. In the most systematic of his works, *Munera Pulveris*, he, indeed, appears at the outset to have his mind closely set upon the exact performance of the required analysis. For, defining the scope of his work, he says, 'The essential work of the political economist is to determine what are in reality useful or life-giving things, and by what degrees and kind of labour they are attainable and distributable.' [1] Then follows a clear and logical distinction between value and cost. 'Value is the life-giving power of anything; cost the quantity of labour required to produce it.' Had he proceeded to estimate 'Wealth' with equal regard to its value and its labour-cost, the latter expressed in vital terms, the scientific character of his analysis would have been preserved. But unfortunately he allowed himself to be overweighted by a sense of value which stresses 'human utility' of consumption, so that, while the 'utility' side of the equation is worked out with admirable skill, the 'cost' or labour side is slighted, and the organic relation between the two is lost sight of. The confusion wrought in the minds of readers by the failure to find in any of his works a full application of his principle has been responsible for an unjust disparagement of the truly scientific service rendered by Ruskin towards the foundation of social-economics. From a Pisgah height his mind's eye swept in quick penetrative glances over the promised land, but he did not occupy it, or furnish any clear survey.

§ 6. Our purpose here is in part to perform the task indicated by Ruskin, viz. to apply to industry the vital standard of valua-

[1] *Munera Pulveris*, § XL.

tion, or at any rate to improve the instruments of vital survey. But only, in part. For our task is in scope less comprehensive than that to which Ruskin applied himself. Though his teaching sprang originally from two related roots of emotional valuation distinctively economic in their bearings, the love of the finer sorts of human work called Art, and the reprobation of the degrading conditions of the work most of his countrymen were called upon to do, it expanded into a wider meaning of 'economy' which included not merely economic activities and economic goods, but all sorts of vital activities and goods. A criticism of current Political Economy, on the ground that it did not treat its accepted subject-matter in a vital manner, thus developed into a constructive Political Economy which not merely humanised the method but expanded the area of the science and art, so as to make it in effect a comprehensive science and art of human welfare.

Now it has always been an open question whether the makers of Political Economy were intellectually justified in severing marketable from non-marketable goods and services, and framing a separate science upon studies of the former. That marketable goods are not always separable from non-marketable, and that the economic activities of man are always inter-related with non-economic activities, are accepted truths. Ruskin's perception of the intimacy of these relations between commercial and non-commercial functions and products led him to break down the barriers set up by Economic Science, in the furtherance of an art which should set up as its goal 'the multiplication of human life at its highest standard.'

Now this enlargement may be quite legitimate. But it was evidently responsible in large measure for the failure of Ruskin to drive home the criticism directed against the current economic teaching. It was one thing to attack Political Economists for failing to take due account of human values in their treatment of processes relating to marketable wealth. It was, however, quite another to insist that the barrier between Political Economy and other social sciences and arts should be torn down, and that all phenomena of vital import should become the objects of its study. Had Ruskin been able to keep to the narrower scope, doubtless he would not have been Ruskin, but his attack on current economic theory and practice would have been vastly more effective.

This brief excursion into Ruskin's work has been necessary, first in order to make proper acknowledgement of the sound scientific instinct of this great pioneer of social thought, and, secondly, to make it clear that, while accepting his standard of valuation, we do not propose applying it outside the range of economic phenomena in the ordinary acceptation of that term. While admitting the overlapping and interaction of economic and other human functions, we shall accept the ordinary definition of the boundaries of economic studies, and shall seek to make our human survey and apply our human valuation within these limits. The extra-economic implications which the unity of life will disclose cannot, indeed, be ignored, but they will be treated as supplementary to the main purpose, that of valuing the processes directly connected with the getting and spending of money incomes.

§ 7. In setting up a vital standard of valuation, we are likely to be met with the objections that life is too vague, too changing, too incomprehensible for any standard, and that life is not valuable in itself but because of certain qualities which it may possess. Our standard must be conceived in terms of a life that is good or desirable. This consideration might evidently lead us far afield. If we are to undertake a valuation of life as a preliminary to valuing industry, it is likely that we may never approach the second undertaking. The best escape from this predicament is to start from some generally accepted concept which indicates, even if it does not express fully, the desirable in life. Such a term I take to be 'organic welfare.' Though in form a mere synonym for good life, it is by usage both more restricted and more precise. It perhaps appears to thrust into the forefront of consideration the physical basis of life. But the organic concept, when liberally interpreted and applied, carries no such restrictive implication, and its distinctively biological association should not rule it out from the work of wider valuation here required. As a provisional statement of our standard of valuation, 'organic welfare' has two advantages. In the first place,

it supplies an admittedly sound method of estimating those
physical costs and utilities with which the major part of industry
and of its product is associated. Even in the most advanced
civilisation of to-day, economic processes are primarily physical
in the efforts they evoke and in the needs they satisfy; the expenditure and recoupment of physical energy constitute the first
and most prominent aspect of industry. In tracing the origins
of human industry, we shall find this rooted in what appear as
half-instinctive animal functions for the satisfaction of 'organic'
needs, individual or racial. The primitive direction of productive effort is evidently 'organic.'

Again, the 'organic' point of view avoids two grave errors
common to the more mechanical treatment of an economic
science which has subordinated man to commercial wealth. It
insists upon regarding the productive effort which goes into any
work of production and the satisfaction which proceeds from the
consumption of any product, not as a separate cost and a separate
utility, but in their total bearing upon the life of the producer or
consumer. The mechanical separatism of the ordinary economic
view follows from a treatment in which the labour bestowed on a
product is only a 'cost' in the same sense as the raw materials
and tools employed in making it, all alike purchased as separate
commodities at a market in which they figure as fractions of a
Supply. Similarly with the ordinary economic treatment of consumption. Each consumable is regarded as yielding a quality of
utility or satisfaction valued on its own account, whereas in reality its consumable value depends upon the ways in which it affects
the entire organic process of consumption. Every speeding-up
of a machine-process, or every reduction of the hours of labour,
affects for good or evil both the economic and the human efficiency of the whole man: every rise or fall of remuneration for
his labour similarly reacts upon the standard of life. Nor is this
all. Current economic science has not only treated each cost and
each utility as a separate item or unit of economic power, it has
treated each man as two men, producer and consumer. The
acquiescence in the economic tendency towards a constantly increasing specialisation of man as producer, a constantly increasing
generalisation of man as consumer, is only intelligible upon the

supposition that the arts of production and consumption have no relation to one another.[1] The standpoint of organic welfare reduces to its natural limits this useful distinction of producer and consumer, and enables us to trace the true interactions of the two processes. In a word, it obliges us to value every act of production or consumption with regard to its aggregate effect upon the life and character of the agent.

§ 8. Finally, a 'social' interpretation of industry is not possible except by treating society as an organic structure. Whether society be regarded as an 'organism' with a life conceived as comprising and regulating the life of its individuals, in the same manner as a biological organism that of its cells, or as an 'organisation' contrived by individuals entirely for the furtherance of their private ends, it must be treated as a vital structure capable of working well or working ill. I say vital structure, not spiritual structure, for I hold the tendency to interpret social organisation exclusively in terms of ethical ends, and as existing simply for 'the realisation of an ethical order,' to be unwarranted. The men who form or constitute a Society, or who enter any sort of social organisation, enter body and soul, they carry into it the inseparable character of the organic life, with all the physical and spiritual activities and purposes it contains. Particular modes of social organisation, as, for example, a Church, may be treated as directed primarily to spiritual ends, though even there the separation is not finally valid. But society in the broader sense, even though conceived not as an 'organism' but merely as an organisation, must be regarded as existing for various sorts of human purposes. For the impulses to form societies are rooted in broad instincts of gregariousness and of sexual and racial feeling, which are best described as organic, and, though these instincts become spiritualised and rationalised with the progress of the human mind, they never cease to carry a biological import.

Even though one takes, therefore, the extremely individualistic view of Society, regarding it as nothing more than a set of arrangements for furthering the life of individual men and women,

---

[1] How potent a source of intellectual confusion this separation of producer and consumer is, may be best illustrated from the commonly accepted treatment of the theory of taxation, which regards 'consumers' as a different class of beings from 'producers' for purposes of incidence of taxes.

entirely a means or instrument for achieving the ends of 'personality,' our human valuation of industry will require consideration of its reactions upon the structure and working of these social arrangements.

But this organic treatment of Society is, of course, still more essential, if we consider society not merely as a number of men and women with social instincts and social aspects of their individual lives, but as a group-life with a collective body, a collective consciousness and will, and capable of realising a collective vital end. The disposition to convert sociology into a study, on the one hand, of social feelings in the individual man, on the other of social institutions that are only forms through which these feelings express themselves, is to my mind a wholly inadequate conception of the science of Society. The study of the social value of individual men no more constitutes sociology than the study of cell life constitutes human physiology. A recognition of the independent value of the good life of a society is essential to any science or art of Society.

To a Greek or a Roman, the idea that the city existed merely for the production of good citizens, and without an end or self of its own, would never have seemed plausible. Nor to any Christian, familiar with the idea and the sentiment of the Church as a society of religious men and women, would it occur that such Society had no life or purpose other than that contained in its individual members. Society must then be conceived, not as a set of social relations, but as a collective organism, with life, will, purpose, meaning of its own, as distinguished from the life, will, purpose, meaning, of the individual members of it. To those who boggle at the extension of the biological term 'organism' to society, asking awkward questions as to the whereabouts of the social sensorium, and the integument of a society, or whether a political, a religious, an industrial Society do not conflict and overlap, I would reply that these difficulties are such as arise whenever an extension of boundaries occurs in the intellectual world. The concept 'organism' as applied to the life of animals and vegetables, is not wholly appropriate to describe the life of a society, but it is more appropriate than any other concept, and some concept must be applied. If some qualification is desired, no objection can be raised against the term super-organism except its length. What is necessary is that some term should be used to assist the mind in realising clearly that all life proceeds by the coöperation of units working, not each for its separate self, but for a whole, and attaining their separate well-being in the proper functioning of that whole. As the structure of the organic cell, the organ, and the organism illustrate this coöperative and composite life, so with the larger groupings which we call societies. An animal organism is a society of cells.

§ 9. So far as the difficulty arising from the narrowly biological use of the term organism is concerned, that is rapidly disappearing before the advance of psychology. For modern biology is coming more and more to realise its early error in seeking to confine itself to the study of life as a merely physical phenomenon. Biology and psychology are constantly drawing into closer relations, with the result that a new science of psycho-biology is already coming into being. In building, thus far, upon a foundation of organic concepts, one is no longer properly exposed to the suspicion of ignoring or disparaging the psychical phenomena which constitute man's spiritual nature.

As biology, thus treating the entire organic nature of man, becomes an individual psycho-physics, so must sociology, treating the wider organic nature of man, become a collective psycho-physics. While then the respective importance of the welfare of the individual and of society may still be difficult to define, the admission of society as a psycho-physical structure, with human ends of its own, will involve its proper recognition in the appraisement of every sort of human value. Our task, that of devising a method of valuation of industry, will evidently demand that economic processes shall be considered, not only in their bearing upon individual lives, but in their bearing upon the welfare of society. Indeed, it is difficult to see how any reasonable person can confront the grave practical problems presented by the industrial societies of to-day, such as those contained in individual, class, sex, national differentiation of economic functions, without realising that the hypothesis of humanity as itself a collective organism can alone furnish any hope of their rational solution.

The significance of the organic conception in any human valuation of industrial acts or products is evident. It requires us to value each act or product both from the standpoint of the individual and of the society to which he belongs, and it furnishes a harmony of the two areas of interest. The baffling problems everywhere presented to thought by the apparent contradiction of the unity and the diversity of nature, the whole and the parts, the general and the particular, find their clearest practical solution in the fact and consciousness of man's social nature, his recognition that in feeling and in action he is both an individual and a member of a number of social groups, expanding in a series of concentric circles from family and city to humanity, and in dimmer outline to some larger cosmic organism.

For our economic valuation, the harmony of this narrower and wider treatment of human nature is of profound and obvious importance. It will require us, in considering the vital costs and satisfactions involved in the production and consumption of goods, to have regard to their effects, not only upon the individuals who produce and consume the goods, but upon the city, nation, or other society to which they belong. Human welfare will be not merely the welfare of human beings taken as an aggregate, but of society regarded as an organic unity. The most delicate economic and spiritual issues of adjustment will be found to relate to the provisions for harmonising the order and the growth of the narrower and the wider organisms. While, then, biology has in the past been too arrogant in pressing distinctively physical implications of the term 'organism' into the dawning science of sociology, and in distorting the true conception of social evolution by enforcing narrow interpretations of selection and survival, this is no ground for refusing to utilise the terminology which, better than any other, expresses the relations of parts to wholes in every sort of living substance.

The contradictions of Production and Consumption, Cost and Utility, Physical and Spiritual Welfare, Individual and Social Welfare, all find their likeliest mode of reconcilement and of harmony in the treatment of society as an organism.

NOTE. There are doubtless those who will remain dissatisfied with this insistence upon the extension of organism and the conception of the humanly desirable in terms of 'organic' welfare. They would insist that the conscious personality of an individual or of a society transcends organism, as the latter does mechanism, and that our standard and measure of welfare should be expressed in psychical terms of personality. This point of view has recently been concisely and powerfully restated by Dr. Haldane (*Mechanism, Life and Personality*). But though there is much to say for treating personality as the intrinsic quality of our humanist standard, I decided against the course on a balance of intellectual expediency, preferring to retain the clearness and force of the organic concept while spiritualising it to meet the requirements of ascending life.

CHAPTER II

§ 1. Although it is no part of my purpose to endeavour to set forth the facts and laws of the historical evolution of modern industry, it will be useful to make some brief allusion to the origins of industry and property, so as to give concrete meaning to the stress laid upon organic processes in our interpretation. For just in proportion as it is realised that industry has all its earliest roots in the primary organic needs of man, will assent more easily be given to the proposal to adhere to the organic conception of welfare in valuing modern economic processes.

It is not easy to ascertain where the activities which we term industrial first emerge in the evolution of organic life. Every organism selects, appropriates, and assimilates matter from its environment, in order to provide for growth or waste of tissue and energy given out in the general course of its vital processes, including the activities of procuring food, protection against organic or inorganic dangers, and the generation, rearing, and protection of offspring. Nutrition and function are the terms usually applied to describe the primary balance of the vital processes of intaking and outputting energy. The organism feeds itself in order to work. It seems at first as if we had here laid down in the origins of organic life a natural economy of production and consumption. But do the organic processes of feeding, choosing, appropriating, and assimilating food, constitute consumption, and do the other activities for which food is utilised constitute production? Reflection will show that there is very little intellectual service in pressing sharply this distinction. The active life of an organism consists in a round of nutritive, protective, generative processes, each of which, from the standpoint of individual and species, may be regarded alike as productive and consumptive. A plant drives its suckers into the soil in search of the foods it needs, disposes its leaves to utilise the light and air or for protection against the wind, assimilates its organic food by the use of its stock of chlorophyl, distributes it throughout its system for maintenance and growth, and directs that growth so as to safeguard its own existence and to provide itself with favourable opportunities of fertilisation by insect or other agencies. If due account be taken both of the cellular life within the individual and of the specific life of this plant organism, the whole of the processes or activities appears to be nutritive, each act of nutrition being associated with some other function in the evolution of the cell, the organism, the species. It would be as plausible to assert that every other function, protective, generative, or other, was undertaken for the nutrition of the individual or the species, as to assert the opposite. But, without entering into the delicate metaphysics of this question, we may confidently affirm that in this elementary organic life nutrition and function cannot be regarded as mutually exclusive processes, while the economic contrasts of production and consumption, work and enjoyment, cost and utility, have no clear application. If we approach a stage nearer to human life, we begin to find, in the life of either the lower or higher animals, some organic activities to which the term industry appears applicable. The long, arduous, complex and painful output of energy, consciously put forth by many animals in the search for food, sometimes in the storage of food, in the provision of shelter, in some instances in the use of tools or weapons, in processes of coöperation and division of labour for migration, protection, or combat, certainly approaches what we recognise as industry. It involves a painstaking interference with the materia environment for the purposive attainment of some distinct object consciously regarded as desirable, which is of the essence of industry. It may, however, be objected that such processes, though resembling human industry in the intricacy and technical skill involved, are not really purposive in the rational sense, but are merely instinctive, and that, as such, they ought to be distinguished from the rational conduct of human industry. Thus, it is contended that, though the efforts given out by many animals in procuring food, protection against enemies, or provision of shelter, formally correspond with familiar processes of human industry, the direction of instinct makes the application of this term improper.   But, as we proceed further into our psychological analysis of human work, we shall find so large an element of admitted instinct in many forms of it as to preclude us from admitting that 'rational' direction is essential to industry.   It is, therefore, permissible for us to give a provisional recognition to such animal activities as containing some, at any rate, of the essential characteristics of 'work' or 'industry.' Indeed, the evident resemblance of these regular activities of animals in seeking food, shelter and protection, to the activities of primitive man applied to the same definitely organic satisfactions, would preclude us from denying to the lower animals what we must admit in the case of men.   For, even in primitive men, possessing a certain use of tools and weapons, and a higher degree of cunning in dealing with their environment, the drive and direction of organic instincts and impulses, as distinguished from reflection and reason, appear to be hardly less dominant than in their animal kindred.   Unless we arbitrarily reserve the concepts work and industry for a higher stage of social evolution, in which some measure of settled life with tribal and personal property and calculated provision for future wants have emerged, it will be well to seek the roots of the elaborated industrial system which we wish to interpret in these rudimentary and mainly instinctive activities of animals and savage men.

§ 2. In examining these organic activities lying at the basis of human industry, we shall light at the outset upon one fact of extreme significance, viz. that to each of these organically useful efforts Nature has attached some definite physical, or psycho-physical, enjoyment.   Hunting, fighting, mating, the care and protection of the young, indeed all actions which possess what is called 'survival value' or biological utility, are endowed with a pleasure bonus as a bribe for their performance.   Nature endows most organically useful efforts with concurrent enjoyment.

But, though in these 'organic functions' many animals give out a great deal of 'laborious' effort, commingled with elements of play or of incipient art, as in the dancing, singing and decorative operations of birds, to none of them is the word 'industry' fully applicable.   We do not seem to enter the definitely economic sphere until we find animals sufficiently reasonable to interfere in a conscious way with their environment, for tolerably distant ends. For, though much industrial production and consumption will continue to be either instinctive or automatic in their operation, a growing element of conscious purpose will become essential to the ordered conduct of all industrial processes. The conscious conception of more distant ends and the growing willingness to make present sacrifices for their attainment are the plainest badges of this industrial progress. When a being is aware of these purposes he has entered a rational economy.

As this more rational economy proceeds, the marks which distinguish it from a purely instinctive organic economy become evident. The instinctive economy allows little scope for individuality of life, the dominant drive of its 'implicit' purpose is specific, i. e. subserving the maintenance and evolution of the species. The spirit of the hive in bee-life is the fullest expression of this subservience of the individual life to the corporate life and of the present generation to the series of generations constituting the specific life. But everywhere the dominion of instinct implies the absorption of the individual life in promoting the ends of the species: successful parenthood is the primary work of the individual.

It might almost be said that the dawn of reason is the dawn of selfishness. For rational economy involves a conscious realisation of the individual self, with ends of its own to be secured and with opportunities for securing them. The earliest conception of this separate self and its ends will naturally tend to be in terms of merely or mainly physical satisfaction. Thus the displacement of the instinctive by the rational economy is evidently a critical era, attended with grave risks due to the tendency towards an over-assertion of the individual self and a consequent weakening of the forces making for specific life. Man, the newly conscious individual, may perversely choose to squander organic resources 'intended' by nature for the race upon his own personal pleasures and needs. He may refuse to make as a matter of rational choice those personal efforts and sacrifices for family and race which no animal, subject to the drive of instinct, is able to 'think' of refusing. Such may be an effect of the release from the life of organic instincts. The increasing supply of foods and other sources of physical satisfaction he may apply to build up for himself a life of super-brutal hedonism.[1] For, when reason first begins to assert supremacy, it is apt to become thrall to the purely animal self. Only as this animal self becomes spiritualised and socialised, does the social race-life reassert its sway upon the higher plane of human consciousness.

§ 3. But it is of importance to realise that a first effect of reason, operating to direct the purposive activities, is to liberate the 'self' from the dominion of the specific life, and to enable it to seek and obtain separate personal satisfactions. For with this power comes the fact and the sense of 'personal property' which play so large a part in industry.

Early industry and early property are largely directed by the requirements of this dawning sense of personality. Though the origins of industry are doubtless found in the promptings of organic utility, they are not of a narrowly 'utilitarian' character. We do not find the earliest industries of man closely confined to the satisfaction of what might seem the most urgent of his organic needs, food, shelter, protection against enemies. The elements of play and ornament are so prevalent in early industries as to suggest the theory, which some anthropologists press far, that adornment for personal glory is the dominant origin of industry and property. So, for example, Bücher [2] contends that the earliest really industrial activities were a painting and tatooing of the body, and a manufacture of clothing and of other personal apparatus for purely ornamental purposes.

Even the taming of domestic animals was, he held, first undertaken for amusement or for the worship of the gods. The strong attraction of most savage or backward peoples in our day towards articles of ornament and play which afford expression to naïve personal pride, appears to support this view. Primitive man certainly does not evolve towards industrial civilisation by a logi-

---

[1] 'Ein wenig besser würd er leben
Hättst du ihm nicht den Schein des Himmels Licht gegeben
Er nennt's Vernunft und braucht's allein
Nur thierischer als jedes Thier zu sein.'

[2] *Industrial Evolution* (Bell & Co.).

cally sane economy of satisfying first his most vitally important material needs, and then building on this foundation a superstructure of conveniences, comforts and luxuries, with the various industries appertaining thereto. This economic man is nowhere found. Actual man, as many anthropologists depict him, appears to begin with the luxuries and dispenses with the conveniences.

This non-utilitarian view of the origins of industry has, however, been driven to excess. There remains a large element of truth in the proverb 'Necessity is the mother of invention.' The earliest weapons and tools, adapted from sticks and stones and other raw material, were probably forced on the dawning intelligence of man by the hard facts of his struggle with hostile nature and his search for food. Fighting, hunting, mating, were presumably his first pursuits and the early arts or industries, at any rate on the male side, would be subsidiary to these pursuits. Any organised process or handling of matter which would make him a better fighter, hunter, suitor, would be likely to emerge as a craft or industry. This explains the apparent blend of utilitarian and non-utilitarian origins. In point of fact, most of the so-called ornamental activities and products have their evident biological uses. They are not mere playthings. The adornment of the human body, the use of tatoos and masks, drums and gongs and other play-products, are partly, no doubt, for mere glory of self-assertion, itself an instinctive craving, but also for courtship, for recognition and for frightening enemies. While, then, it remains true that the sportive and artistic impulses are conspicuous in the early crafts, it is a mistake to disparage the organic utility of these processes. After man has made provision for the present necessities of the body, his superfluous energy naturally tends, either to preparatory play, the practice or imitation of biologically useful actions, or else to explorative, constructive, and decorative work in handling such materials as present themselves. This curiosity about his surroundings, and the instinctive desire to construct and arrange them for his convenience, or for the dawning æsthetic satisfaction of his senses, or to impress the female of his race, these instincts undeniably coalesce with the drive of physical necessity to force man to apply his mind to the discovery and practice of the early arts and crafts.

But, though these distinctively male modes of manipulating the environment thus possess a utilitarian aspect, they do not furnish the beginnings of the chief industries which figure in civilised life. The beginnings of manufacture and of agriculture, as regular occupations, are commonly ascribed to women and to slaves. Those who conceive of the earliest human societies as matriarchal or gynæcocentric, the women forming fixed centres of order in the home and village, owning the children and the property attached to the home, regard women both as the inventors and the practitioners of the early handicrafts, including the cultivation of the soil. The beginnings of the arts of pottery, basket-making, building, clothes-making, as well as digging, planting, milling and other processes of preparing food, were doubtless women's work in the first instance, though they were probably raised to the position of regular industries when slavery became common. It is, however, noteworthy that, even in those early handicrafts devoted to the most practical needs of life, the decorative instinct generally finds expression. Not only the weapons of the men, but the pots and pans and other domestic utensils of the women, carry carvings or mouldings, which testify to the play or art impulses. Leisure and pleasure thus appear as ingredients in the earliest industries.

To whatever source, then, we trace the origins of industry, to the use of weapons, snares and other male apparatus for the fight and hunt, to the instincts of play, imitation and adornment as modes of self-expression and of pride, or to the more distinctively utilitarian work of women and of slaves around the home, we find play or pleasure mingled with the work.

This profoundly interesting truth is attested by the long surviving presence of the song and other rhythmic activities in many forms of associated labour, as well as in the dancing which in primitive societies was an almost invariable accompaniment of all important enterprises, war, hunting and harvesting, and which still survives among us in the Harvest Home. Though in slave industries this lighter element doubtless dwindled very low, it seldom died out entirely, as the song of the galley-rowers, or of the Southern negroes in the cotton-fields, testifies. Where the handicrafts throve among free men in

Europe, everywhere the motives of play, personal pride and prowess, find liberal expression in industry.

§ 4. This slight and necessarily speculative sketch of the origin of industry is designed to enforce two facts. In the first place, we can trace in every rudimentary industry the promptings of vital utility, laying the foundations of an economy of efforts and satisfactions which furthers the organic development of the individual and the race. In the second place, we everywhere find what we call distinctively economic motives and activities almost inextricably intertwined, or even fused, with other motives and activities, sportive, artistic, religious, social and political.

To trace the history of the process by which in modern civilisation economic or industrial activities have separated themselves from other activities, assuming more and more dominance, until the Industrial System and the Business Man have become the most potent facts of life, would lie beyond our scope. Nor is it at all necessary. What is important for us to realise, however, is that this process of industrialisation, through which the civilised peoples have been passing, is beyond all question the most powerful instrument of education. It appears to have done more to rationalise and to socialise men than all the higher and more spiritual institutions of man, so far as such comparisons are possible. It has rationalised man chiefly by compelling him to exercise foresight and forethought, to subdue his will and train his active faculties to the performance of long and intrinsically disagreeable tasks, in order to realise some more and more distant object of desire, and by obliging him to recognise the rigorous laws of causation in his calculations. It has socialised him by weaving an ever more elaborate tissue of common interests between him and a growing number of his fellow men, and by compelling him to engage in closer coöperation with them for the attainment of his ends. Though this socialisation is far more advanced in objective fact than in thought and feeling, it remains true that the direct and indirect association of larger and more various bodies or men in modern industry and commerce is the first condition and the strongest stimulus to the expansion and intensification of the social will.

It is this orderly rational system of industry, employing, as it does, the organic powers of man for the satisfaction of his organic needs, that we seek to submit to valuation.

The immense variety and complexity of the arts and crafts of which such a system of human industry consists, the long interval of time which often intervenes between acts of production and of consumption, the differences of personality between those who perform the efforts of production and those who utilise or enjoy the fruits of those efforts in consumption, immensely remote as they appear from the simple organic economy of primitive man, do not escape an ultimate dependence upon organic laws and conditions. A human valuation, therefore, must insist upon expressing them in terms of organic welfare, individual and social. As human activities and enjoyments ascend in the process we term civilisation, we shall expect to find this organic life becoming more psychical, in the sense that their modes are more 'reasonable' and the emotions that attach to them are more spiritual, i. e. less directly driven by animal instincts. So too we shall expect industrial progress to contribute to a growing adjustment between the individual and the social economy, restoring under the form of reasonable social service to the more highly individualised members of a modern society an increasing measure of that subservience to the organic welfare of mankind which instinct was able to secure upon a lower plane of conscious life.

CHAPTER III

§ 1. Approaching on its concrete side the economic system the human values of which we seek to ascertain, we find it to consist in a series of productive processes bringing various goods and services into marketable shape, accompanied by a series of consumptive processes in which these goods and services are used, wasted, or otherwise disposed of by those who buy them for personal uses. The former set of processes, as we have recognised, occupy a place of so much greater prominence and publicity as virtually to absorb the science of industry or 'economics', leaving to the processes of consumption an obscure and entirely subordinate position. Our organic or human valuation starts with a protest against this assumption of inequality in the arts of production and consumption. Its interpretation of economic processes will be disposed to lay as much stress upon the history of the various commodities after they leave the shop-counter and pass into the possession of consumers as before. The human good and evil associated with economic 'wealth' must, viewed from the organic standpoint, depend as much upon the nature of its consumption as upon the nature of its production.

This consideration will determine our method of applying the human standard of values. Accepting at the outset the convenient distinction between the processes of production and consumption, we shall approach the economic system at the point where the two processes meet, that is to say where wealth emerges from the productive processes as Income, in order to pass as such into the possession of persons entitled to consume it.

To make the enquiry simpler and more easily intelligible, we will ignore for the present all the extra-national or cosmopolitan conditions of modern industry, and assume that we are dealing with a closed national system producing, distributing, and consuming the two thousand million pounds' worth of goods and services roughly estimated to constitute the current annual income of the British nation.

§ 2. Now the habit of regarding wealth and income in terms of money is so deep-seated and persistent as to make it difficult for ordinary 'business' men to realise these words in any other than a monetary sense. The ordinary mind has to break through a certain barrier of thought and feeling in order even to present to itself the significance of 'real' wages or 'real' income, as distinguished from money wages and money income. This dominion of the monetary standard is illustrated by the almost instinctive thrill of elation that is felt when we are informed that the income of the nation has risen from about £1,200,000,000 in 1870 to £2,000,000,000 in 1912.[1] So accustomed are we to regard money as the measure of the desirable, that we feel that this rise of money income must imply a corresponding rise in national welfare. It requires some effort of mind to realise even the two obviously important factors of the increase of population and the shift of prices, which, when once realised, so evidently affect the bearing of the money income upon the national welfare. Year after year trade reports and other official documents, in comparing the relative economic position of the various nations or the fluctuations of trade within a single nation, habitually encourage this misleading influence of the financial standard by publishing crude, uncorrected monetary values as if they were indicative of industrial facts, and statesmen take such figures as valid evidence on which to base a policy.

As regards the particular object of our enquiry, this obsession of the general mind by the monetary standard makes it impossible for us even to assume that all our readers attach a clear and consistent meaning to the term 'real' income. It is not quite easy at first to grasp the central and essential fact that every receipt

[1] I have taken the estimate of the total income of the nation made by Mr. Flux in his *Reports of the First Census of Production for the United Kingdom* (*1907*) as the basis for the round figures adopted here for aggregate income and for savings. As a matter of fact Mr. Flux assigns to savings a slightly higher figure and proportion of income than that taken here. But since for our purpose nothing depends upon the exactitude of the figures (and indeed Mr. Flux claims no such exactitude for his) it is more convenient for us to take the round figures of our text, though probably in both instances, i. e. aggregate income and savings, they are somewhat below the true figures for 1912.

of any sort of income, whether as wages, rent, salary, interest, profit, fees or otherwise, involves the coming into being of a bit of 'real' income in the shape of some material goods or some saleable service.[1] This fact once grasped, however, it becomes evident that the £2,000,000,000, said to be the nation's income, is merely the monetary representative of goods and services which are the net product of the economic activity of the year, the quantity of wealth produced over and above that which has gone to maintain the existing material fabric of industry. The aggregate amount of 'wealth produced' is, of course, considerably greater, for a large quantity of the productive power must continually be employed in repairing the wear and tear sustained by the material instruments of production, the land, buildings, machinery and tools and other forms of 'fixed' capital, and in replacing the raw materials and other forms of 'circulating' capital which have passed out of the productive processes into consumable goods. The net 'real' income consists of the goods and services produced over and above this provision for the maintenance of the material structure of the system.

There is, however, an important qualification to this mode of reckoning the net real income of the nation which needs mention. While the portion of the current product which goes to replace this wear and tear of land and capital is not included in the goods and services represented by the £2,000,000,000 and classed as real net income, the wear and tear or maintenance fund of labour is included in it. When consideration is taken of the distribution of what is often termed the national dividend between the respective owners of the factors of production, this anomaly is seldom borne in mind. In estimating the income of labour the replacement fund is counted; in estimating the income of land and capital it is not counted. But, illogical as this discrimina-

---

[1] There is no commoner stumbling-block to the beginner in the study of Political Economy than the fact that the income of a rich man, amounting to say £10,000, when paid away to persons who sell him goods or personal services, seems to count 'over again' as incomes of these persons. Why, they are disposed to ask, should the private secretary who receives £400 out of this £10,000 be required to pay an income-tax upon a sum which (as they say) has already paid its share as part of the £10,000? Nothing but a grasp of the fact that the secretary produces a 'real' income of 'services' corresponding to this £400 which he receives clears up the misunderstanding.

tion is, usage has so universally accepted it that it will be best for us in a work not chiefly concerned with the problems of objective distribution to give a provisional acceptance to it.

The real net income, or national dividend, corresponding to the £2,000,000,000, consists of the goods and services at the disposal of the recipients of this money income. By applying each sovereign as they received it in rent, wages, interest, profit, fees, etc., to purchase consumable goods or services, they might consume the whole of it during the current year. In that event, though provision would have been made for the bare upkeep of capital, no provision would have been made for its enlargement or improvement with a view to the future increase of production. In point of fact, that provision is made by applying a considerable portion of the net money income, say £300,000,000, to demand, not consumable goods or services, but more instruments and materials of production. As this process goes on continuously, it implies that some $3/_{20}$ of the total industrial activity of the nation is engaged in making not consumable but new capital goods.[1] This saving process has an important psychology of its own to which we shall give some attention later on. At present it need only be considered as a reduction in the net income of consumable goods and services at the disposal of a progressive community for current use and enjoyment. This wealth, actually available for current use, the food, clothing, shelter and other domestic necessaries and conveniences, the travel, information, education, recreation, professional, official and domestic services, the various sorts of material and non-material comforts and luxuries, constituting the current net real income of consumer's goods, is the primary object of our valuation. The new machines, tools, buildings, materials and other forms of capital, expressing the £300,000,000 of savings, though entering our analysis upon the costs side equally with goods used for immediate consumption, do not figure directly on the consumption side, but only indirectly in the future consumables which they assist to produce.

§ 3. But as regards the application of our analysis, it makes no

---

[1] About half of this passes under the head of over-seas investments into the industrial systems of other nations, though the interest upon this foreign capital is available for consumption in this country.

real difference whether we take the narrower connotation of the national dividend which includes only consumable goods, or the broader one which includes savings. It will no doubt easily be admitted that a merely pecuniary statement of the 'value' of this dividend conveys no reliable information as to the human or vital welfare it involves. Making due allowance for all temporal or local variations of price, the statement that the national income has doubled in the last century, or even that the income per head of the population has doubled, affords no positive proof that any increase has been made in the national welfare, much less how much increase. Unless, however, we adopt an attitude of general scepticism towards the economic structure of 'civilisation,' we may admit, with Professor Pigou,[1] a presumption that a growth of the national dividend faster than the growth of population implies some increase of welfare. But even that presumption must be qualified by the reflection that it really rests upon a view of marketable wealth which has exclusive regard to its supposed utility in consumption without any corresponding consideration of the cost of its production. A pecuniary statement of the national dividend which contained no information as to the nature of the goods and services comprising it, may be repudiated out of hand as useless for our purpose. For upon such a statement £1 'worth' of 'trade gin' has precisely the same value as £1 'worth' of 'best books' or of wholesome bread, £1 worth of handmade lace sweated out of peasant women at the cost of their eyesight has precisely the same weight in the money income of the nation as £1 worth of carpentry or of medical attendance.

§ 4. If we are to estimate the human value of a given national income, it is evident that we must secure answers to three questions. We must first learn what the concrete goods and services are which constitute the 'real' income, and then we must trace these concrete goods and services backwards through the processes of their production and forward through the processes of their consumption, in order to learn the human costs and utilities which attach to each. The amount of human wealth or 'illth' which each of these concrete 'goods' contains has, strictly speaking, no assignable relation to the money ticket put upon it when

[1] *Wealth and Welfare*, Chap. I.

it is sold. That sum of human value can only be worked out in terms of the actual processes of production and consumption through which the 'goods' pass. Some students of current political economy may perhaps be disposed to cavil at this criticism, insisting that on the average things must be sold in proportion to the painful or otherwise distasteful efforts of producing them, or in proportion to the pleasant or otherwise serviceable modes of their consumption. On the average, they will contend, a rational calculus of pleasure and pain underlies the operations of the economic system. This position, however, I claim to undermine by showing, first that this 'rational' calculus rests upon assumptions of free choice and competition which are unwarrantable, and secondly, that this rational calculus of current pleasures and pains, so far as it is operative, is not a valid criterion of human welfare as conceived in the terms of organic welfare. Our task, it must be realised, is not that of reducing monetary values, or the concrete goods to which they refer, to terms of average current desirability, but to terms of that desirability corrected so as to conform to the best-approved standard of the desirable. In a word, the defects of average current estimates and desires, in part causes, in part effects of a defective industrial economy, must themselves be valued and discounted in terms of our human ideals of individual and social life.

§ 5. With this organic standard, the nature and validity of which will become clearer with use, let us set about our task of finding methods for assessing in terms of human value the stocks of concrete goods and services which are the real net income of the nation. The human, as distinguished from the money and the 'real' dividend, will consist of the amount of vital or organic welfare conveyed in the producing and consuming processes for which this concrete income stands. What we require then is to apply some sort of calculus of human cost and human utility to these processes. Now we are confronted at the outset by the position of an economic science which conceives production entirely in terms of 'cost', consumption entirely in terms of 'utility'. Indeed, the economic doctrine of value hinges almost entirely upon this antithesis. For it is mainly owing to its 'costs' that a limit of scarcity is set on each 'supply', while it is the 'utility' accorded by consumers that gives economic force and meaning to 'demand'. Hence production is conceived as a process which rolls up costs into commodities, consumption as a process that unrolls them into utilities.

Now an organic interpretation of industry cannot accept this mode of conceiving the productive and consumptive functions. Considerations of the organic origins of industry lend no support to the assumption that production is all 'cost' and no 'utility', consumption all 'utility' and no 'cost'. On the contrary, in our human analysis of economic processes we shall rather expect to find costs and utilities, alike in their sense of pains and pleasures and of organic losses and organic gains, commingled in various degrees in all productive and consumptive processes.

Our aim will be to set out, as well as we can, reliable rules for examining the productive and consumptive history of the various sorts of concrete marketable goods so as to discover the human elements of cost and utility contained in each, and by a computation of these positives and negatives to reach some estimate of the aggregate human value contained in the several sorts of commodities which form the concrete income of the nation and in this income as a whole. Only by some such process is it possible to reach a knowledge of the real wealth of nations.

We may state the problem provisionally in three questions:

1. What are the concrete goods and services which constitute the real national income?
2. How are these goods produced?
3. How are they consumed?

But in truth the consideration of the so-called 'concrete' nature of these goods is as irrelevant to our analysis as that of the money ticket placed on them. For from the standpoint of welfare these goods are nothing but the activities of those who produce and consume them, or, if it be preferred, the human processes of production and consumption. The human meaning of any given stock of wheat in our national supply will consist of the efforts of body and mind, the thought and desire and directed skill, put into the several processes of preparing the soil, sowing, tending, reaping and marketing the wheat, undergone by the farmer in Manitoba or in Norfolk, the merchant, shipper, miller,

baker who convey it from the farm and convert it into bread, and
finally the activities of mastication, digestion and assimilation
with the accompanying satisfaction as it passes into the physical
system of the consumer. And so with every other sort of concrete marketable goods or services. From the standpoint of
human value, they are wholly resolvable into the physical and
mental activities and feelings of the human beings who produce
and consume them. It is the balance of the desirable over the
undesirable in these several activities and feelings that constitutes the human value of any stock of marketable goods. The
standard of desirability will be the conception of the organic well-
being of the society to which the individuals whose activities and
feelings are concerned belong.

Or the several stages of interpretation may be expressed as
follows. A given money income must first be resolved into the
concrete goods which it expresses: those goods must then be resolved into the various efforts of production and satisfactions of
consumption, estimated according to the current ideas and desires of the individuals who experience them: these current individual estimates of the desirable must be adjusted by reference
to an ideal standard of the socially desirable. The extent of this
latter process of adjustment will, of course, depend upon how
far the actual current ideas and feelings of individuals are kept
in essential harmony with the true standard of social well-being
by the natural evolution of an organic society.

§ 6. Our task in seeking to devise a method for the human interpretation or valuation of Industry consists then in confronting the goods which form the net consumable income of the community, and in finding answers to the two related questions:

What are the net human costs involved in their production?

What are the net human utilities involved in their consumption?

A simple sum in subtraction should then give us the result we
seek—so far as any such quantitative calculus is valid and feasible.[1]

Now though economists, of course, are well aware that many

[1] The exceedingly important question of the limits to the validity of such a
quantitative calculus is discussed in the concluding chapter.

of the processes of production contain elements of pleasure and utility to the producers, while some of the processes of consumption contain elements of pain and cost to the consumers, they have, rightly from their standpoint, ignored these qualifications in their general formulae, and have represented 'goods' from the producer's side as consisting entirely of accumulated costs, while from the consumer's side they constitute pure utility. Though our brief preliminary survey of the origins of industry indicates that no such sharp distinction between production and consumption can ultimately be maintained, and that throughout the whole continuous career of goods from cradle to grave the activities bestowed on them are composites of pleasure and pain, cost and utility, organic gain and organic loss, socially desirable and socially undesirable, it will be expedient to take our start from the commonly-accepted economic position, and to give separate consideration to the human values underlying processes of production on the one hand, processes of consumption on the other.

The general lines along which such an investigation must proceed are unmistakable.

In order to express business 'costs' in terms of human cost, we require to know three things:

1. The quality and kind of the various human efforts involved in the business 'cost'.
2. The capacities of the human beings who give out these efforts.
3. The distribution of the effort among those who give it out.

Corresponding strictly to this analysis of 'costs' of Production will be the analysis of 'utility' of Consumption. There we shall want to know:

1. The quality and kind of the satisfaction or utility yielded by the 'economic utility' that is sold to consumers.
2. The capacities of the consumers who get this 'economic utility'.
3. The distribution of the economic utility among the consuming public.

The humanist criticism of Industry is condensed into this analysis. The humanist requires that the effort expended on any sort of production shall be such as to contain a minimum of painful or injurious or otherwise undesirable activity. His complaint is that Industry, as actually organised and operated under a system which treats all forms of productive human effort as marketable goods, does not secure this human economy. The humanist requires that the persons set to give out undesirable effort, 'human cost', shall be those best capable of sustaining this loss. Weak women or children, for example, shall not be set to do work heavy or dangerous in its incidence, when strong men are available who could do it easily and safely. The humanist requires that undesirable or humanly costly work shall not merely be confined to classes of persons capable of performing it most easily and safely, but that the distribution of such effort shall, as regards length of time and intensity of pace, be such as to reduce the human cost per unit of product to a minimum. The humanist criticism of Industry upon the Costs side consists in pointing out that there is no adequately reliable or normal tendency for the business economy of costs to conform to this three-fold human economy.

Similarly, turning to the consumption side, the humanist points out: 1. That many of the 'goods' sold to consumers are inherently destitute of human utility, or, worse, are repositories of disutility; and that money values is no true key to human utility. 2. That the amount of utility or welfare to be got out of any goods depends upon the character, the natural or acquired capacity, of the particular consumers or classes of consumers into whose hands they fall. 3. That a true economy of consumption, therefore, involves their distribution among consumers in proportion to their capacity to use them for purposes of welfare. It is contended that the current working of our industrial system, on its distributive and consumptive side, makes no reliable provision for securing that the maximum of human utility shall attach to the consumption of the national income.

§ 7. To test in detail the exact validity of this humanist criticism would require us to examine the costs and the utility, economic and human, represented in each item of all the various supplies of goods and services which constitute the national income. This is manifestly impracticable. Nor is it necessary for our purpose, which is to establish a sound method of valuation rather than to endeavour to form an exact computation of the values it discloses. With this object in view it will be sufficient to direct our enquiry to the accepted classes or grades of human activities figuring as economic costs, and the corresponding classes or grades of human utilities affected by consumption.

Let us begin with the 'costs' side.

Accepting the general categories of costs of production, as rent, interest and profit, salaries and fees, wages (for all other business 'costs', as for instance, cost of material, machinery, fuel, can be resolved into these), let us consider what is the nature of the human costs for which these payments are made, in the chief orders of industry, and how these human costs are related to the economic costs.

At the outset of this enquiry, however, it will be convenient to eliminate one economic 'cost' of considerable magnitude from our consideration, viz. economic rent. For, although Nature, or the earth, may in a study of objective industry be regarded as a productive agent, yielding materials, physical energy, and special utilities, this work involves no human effort, and therefore is represented by no human cost. This statement, of course, by no means implies that human foresight and activities play no part in the effective supply of land and other natural resources. Such resources, hitherto existing outside the industrial system, are continually being discovered, brought within reach and developed by human skill and effort, while new or improved uses are continually being obtained from natural resources already within reach. In such processes of discovery and development much capital, ability, and labour, are constantly engaged, the costs of which must be defrayed. Moreover, in certain uses of land for agricultural and other purposes, provision must be made for wear and tear or replacement. But all such costs or expenses are really payments for the capital and labour employed on this work of development or upkeep. They are not payments for the use of natural resources. They are not economic rent. That business cost has no human cost attached to it. From the standpoint of the manager of a particular business the payment of rent is necessary to enable him to get the use of the land or other natural agent he requires. Where private property in land exists, the payment of such rent is legally necessary. Where the maintenance of such legal rights has enabled land values to exchange freely with other forms of wealth, a moral expediency may be claimed for the payment of rent. But no human cost corresponds to it. In the organic interpretation of industry, it figures as waste. While, therefore, due account must be taken of this division of wealth or human utilities in any final survey of our social economy, it may be dismissed from our immediate consideration.

§ 8. In order to get a clear understanding of industry regarded from the standpoint of human costs, it will be convenient to fasten our attention first on the structure and working of the single businesses which are the productive units of the system. For the business is a closer, more compact, and more intelligible structure than the trades, markets, or other larger divisions of industry. We shall, therefore, endeavour to analyse the combinations of human effort as they are expressed in the various types of business, so as to discover and to estimate the human costs that are involved.

Though the term Business, as we use it here, must be extended so as to include all sorts of centres of economic activity not commonly included, such as a school, a doctor's practice, a theatre, it will be best to take for our leading case an ordinary manufacturing business. Here are gathered into close coöperation a large number of human and non-human factors of production. The centre of the little system is the manager, employer, or director, whose ideas, desires, and purposes govern and regulate the movements of the various forms of capital and labour. This man has got together on his premises a quantity of machinery and other plant which express a complicated growth of invention running far back into the past and derived from great numbers of human brains. These machines and plant embodying these inventive ideas were made by past labour of various kinds. This manager or director, in planning the Business, chose what seemed the best apparatus for the purposes he had in mind. He induced a number of investors or capitalists to lend the money which enabled him to obtain this apparatus, and to hire the various sorts of labour power required to operate it. This labour power itself is

the product of the energies of man in the past, the direct ancestry
of the labourers who produced the beings that give forth the
labour-power, the past generations of men whose growing knowledge and practice yielded the training and the habits of industry
and of coöperation essential for the productiveness of labour in
the modern arts of industry.

Here are evidently many different sorts of human effort, some
of them physical, others intellectual, some pleasurable, others
painful, some beneficial, others detrimental, to the individuals
who give out the effort, or to society.

All of these productive energies rank in Political Economy as
'costs', and as such are remunerated out of the product. Which
of these are human 'costs' and in what sense and what degree?
Such are the questions that lie immediately before us, if we are
seeking to reduce our £2,000,000,000 to terms of human well-
being.

§ 9. In this conversion of economic into human costs we can
best begin by considering the fundamental distinction between
creation and imitation, enforced with so much penetration by the
French sociologist, M. Tarde. It is not in its primary significance a doctrine of costs, but a division of productive energy into
two classes. All social progress, indeed all social changes up-
wards or downwards, according to this theory, comes about in
the following way. Some unusually powerful, original, or enterprising person, assisted often by good fortune, makes what is
called a discovery, some true and useful way of doing things or
of thinking about things, or even of saying things. This new
truth, new phrase, new dodge, is capable of being recognised as
interesting or useful, not only by its discoverer, but by the many
who had not the wit or the courage or the luck to discover it for
themselves. By suggestion, infection, contagion, or conscious
imitation, or by any combination of those forces and habits that
constitute the social nature of man, the novelty becomes adopted
and applied by an ever-growing number of persons, over a widening area, until it becomes an accepted practice or convention of
the whole society. Every new religious or moral idea or sentiment, every scientific law, every invention in the arts of industry,
every development of a new taste, thus proceeds from one or

more special centres of original discovery, and spreads by a well-nigh automatic process of expansion or imitation.

§ 10. Now this distinction between creation and imitation, as propounded and applied by M. Tarde, is doubtless open to serious objections. The psychology of imitation is shallow, for under this single term is covered what are in reality many different actions, while the whole conception of imitation as a process is too mechanical. To some of these defects we shall refer presently. But though, regarded as an explanation of the processes of human progress, the antithesis of creation and imitation does not satisfy, it furnishes an exceedingly useful starting point towards a psychological analysis of economic processes. For in the evolution of industry it is quite evident that improvements do come about in this manner. A comparatively small number of original or curious minds invent new uses or new ways of doing things that are better than the old, or they recognise the value of new ideas which others failed to recognise, and they have the energy and enterprise to put the new ideas into operation. Many of the inventions are not good enough or big enough; only by a considerable number of little increments of novelty will a new machine, or a new process, emerge into economic vitality, or, in business language, become profitable. But where an invention or improvement has once emerged, imitation multiplies it and it passes into general use.[1]

A comparatively small number of creative or inventive minds thus undoubtedly play an exceedingly important part in the development of industry. The brief acts of thinking of a Watt,

[1] Tarde applies the same term 'imitation' to two different sorts of act. The business man or employer who recognises some improved machine or method and copies it is an imitator. Every improvement thus starting from a centre of discovery becomes diffused throughout a trade.

But the term 'imitation' is also applied to the regular work of the routine operator, who is constantly engaged in repeating some single process. Now, regarded as psychological and as economic facts, these two imitations are distinct.

The former is the adoption of a discovery involving an act of recognition and of judgment—not a purely automatic imitation—at any rate until it has become a common form in the trade. The employer who copies or adopts an improvement performs a single act—he incorporates this improvement in the technique of his mill or shop—once for all. When, however, it is said of a machine-worker that his work is imitative, something different is meant. He is continually repeating himself, each act of repetition involving less consciousness in the adaptation of means to end.

a Stevenson, a Siemens or an Edison, appear to be incomparably more productive in effect than the routine life-toil of the many thousands of workers who simply repeat hour by hour, day by day, year by year, some simple single process they have learned. It is true that invention is too narrow a term properly to express the distinction we are examining between that work which expresses the creative energy of man and that which is essentially imitative. For if a successful invention furnishes machinery or methods which thus multiply the productivity of human labour, the skilful organisation and administration of a business, the work done by the employer, has the same sort of effect. An able employer who directs his business with knowledge and foresight, gathering together just the right men, materials and machinery, producing the right goods at the right time, and marketing them properly, seems by his personal ability greatly to enlarge the valuable output of the entire business. In a big business he seems to be as productive as a thousand men.

§ 11. So a broad distinction is built up between Ability and common Labour, the creative and the merely imitative work of man. From this distinction has been drawn an ingenious defence of the current inequalities in distribution of wealth. Since all the progress of modern industry is really attributable to the ability and enterprise of a small group of inventing, organising and enterprising people, common labour being in itself no more skilful, no more productive than before, there can, it is maintained, be neither justice nor reason in the claims of labour to a larger share of that huge increase of wealth due to the ability of the few.

I do not propose just now to examine the validity of this contention. What criticism I have to offer will emerge in the course of my closer examination of the nature of industrial work. At present I will only ask readers to observe that the doctrine assumes that payment for industrial services must or ought to be determined by the productivity of those services, not by their 'cost'.

Now, our immediate enquiry, we must remember, is into human costs. And the distinction between creative and imitative work is particularly instructive in its bearing upon human costs.

For if we grade the various sorts of human effort that contribute to the production of wealth according to the amount of creative and imitative character they seem to possess, some valuable light will be thrown upon the distribution of human costs among the various classes of producers.

Leaving out of consideration Land, which, as a factor in production, involves no output of human effort, we shall find that the provision and application of all the other factors, ability, capital and labour, involve some human effort both of a creative and an imitative type and contain some elements of 'cost'.

For the purpose of this analysis I propose to classify productive activities under the following heads: Art, Invention, Professional Service, Organisation, Management, Labour, Saving. The warranty for this classification will emerge in the course of the analysis.

CHAPTER IV

§ 1. The most distinctively creative kind of human work is called art. In motive and in performance it is the freest expression of personality in work. The artist in what are termed the fine arts, e. g. as painter, poet, sculptor, musician, desires to give formal expression to some beautiful, true or otherwise desirable conception, in order either to secure for himself its fuller realisation or the satisfaction of communicating it to others. It is not, however, necessary for our purpose to enter upon the exact psychology of art motives or processes. Indeed, we are not concerned with the whole range of artistic activity. So far as the artist works simply and entirely for his own satisfaction, in order to express himself to himself, he cannot be deemed to be contributing to the economic income of the nation. For us the artist is the producer of a marketable commodity, and we are concerned to discover the 'economic' and the 'human' costs which he incurs in this capacity.

Now so far as the painter, poet, or musician works as pure artist, exercising freely his creative faculty, his economic 'costs' consist merely of his 'keep', the material and intellectual consumption necessary to support him and to feed his art. The net human costs of the creative work are nil. For though all creative work may involve some pains of travail, those pains are more than compensated by the joy that a child is born. Even if we distinguish the creative conception from the process of artistic execution, which may involve much laborious effort not interesting or desirable in itself, we must still remember that these labours are sustained and endowed with pleasurable significance as means to a clearly desired end, so that the whole activity becomes in a real sense a labour of love. In other words, the human costs are outweighed by the human utility even in the processes of production, so that the pure practice of art is a net increase of life. The artist, who, following freely his own creative bent, produces pictures, plays or novels which bring him in great gains, is thus in the position of being paid handsomely for work which is in itself a pleasure to perform and which he would do just as well if he were only paid his human 'keep'. The wasteful social economy of the ordinary process of remunerating successful artists needs no discussion. For the true art faculty resembles those processes by which Nature works in the organic world for the increase of commodities whose comparative scarcity secures for them a market value. A poet who 'does but sing because he must', and yet is paid heavily for doing so, is evidently getting the best of both worlds. Our present point, however, is that the 'economic cost' which his publisher incurs in royalties upon the sales of his poem is attended by no net 'human cost' at all, but by a positive fund of 'human utility'. And this holds of all truly creative work: the performance involves an increase of life, not that loss which is the essence of all human cost.

§ 2. I have spoken of the pure 'artist'. The artistic producer who sells his freedom to the moneyed public may incur the heaviest of human costs, the degradation of his highest quality. The temptation to incur these moral and intellectual damages is great in any nation where the dominant standard of personal success is money income and expenditure. But perhaps there is a false simplicity in the romantic view of artistic genius, which assumes that the artist and his work are necessarily degraded by inducements to work for a public, instead of working for himself alone. It may, indeed, be held that an artist who is so self-centred as to have no conscious consideration of the artistic needs and capabilities of his fellow-men, is so essentially inhuman as to be incapable of great work. The use of an art-gift for communion with others, involving some measure of conscious social direction, seems involved in the humanity of the artist. Even when that direction takes the shape of market-prices, it does not necessarily incur the violent censure bestowed by romantic persons. When a sound public taste operates, this direction may be justified. The portraits which Mr. G. F. Watts painted reluctantly for money need not be considered a waste of his powers. The nature, again, of many creative minds seems to require the application of an external stimulus to break down a certain barrier of sterile self-absorption or of diffidence, which would rob humanity of many of the fruits of genius. At any rate it need not be assumed that working for a public, or even for a market, is essentially injurious. Where the taste which operates through the demand is definitely base, and where the practice and the consciousness of having sold one's soul for money are plainly realised, no doubt can exist. But where public sympathy and appreciation, even exercised through the market, induce the artist to subordinate some of his private tastes and proclivities to the performance of work which, though of secondary interest to himself, has a sound social value, the pressure of demand may produce a larger body of real wealth at no real human cost to the producer. Very different, of course, are the instances urged with so much passionate insistence by Ruskin, where depraved public tastes, springing directly from luxury and idleness, debauch the natural talents of artists, and poison the very founts of the creative power of a nation. *Corruptio optimi pessima.* The production of base forms of art, in painting, music, the drama, literature, the plastic arts, must necessarily entail the highest human costs, the largest loss of human welfare, individual and social. For such an artist poisons not only his own soul but the social soul, adulterating the food designed to nourish the highest faculties of man.

There is, however, a sense in which it is true that every pressure of social direction or demand upon the artist impairs the creative character of his work. For such social demand rests upon a similarity of taste among the members of a public, and its satisfaction requires the artist to repeat himself. An artist, endowed by the State or some other body, might express himself in unique masterpieces, as was the case with the great artists of antiquity or of the Renaissance who were fortunate in their private or public patrons. But art, supported by numerous private purchasers, whose social standards mould their tastes to tolerably close conformity, must stoop to qualify creation by much imitative repetition. This often involves a large human cost, imposing an injurious specialisation, mannerisms or mechanical routine. This is particularly true of arts where a refractory material gives great importance to technique, and where the practice of this technique necessarily restricts the spontaneity of execution.

§ 3. The descent from Artist to the more or less mechanical producer of art-products is marked by many grades. There is the grade which does not pretend to any free exercise of the creative faculty, confining itself to interpretation or execution. This in music and in certain other fine arts is signified by adopting the French term 'artiste'. But some of this interpretative work affords large scope for truly creative work. A traditional or written drama, a score of music, or other necessarily imperfect and half-mechanical register of some great creative work, requires a constant process of re-creation by a sympathetic spirit. In such arts there is a genuinely creative coöperation between the original composer and his interpreters, the latter enjoying some real liberty of personal expression and giving merit to the performance by this union of reproductive and creative achievement. The great actor or musician may thus even come to use the work of the playwright or the composer as so much material for his own creative expression. He may even carry this to an excess, ousting his predecessor and parasitically utilising his reputation for the display of his own artistic qualities or defects. In painting and sculpture, of course, we come to a mode of skilled imitation, that of the copyist, where the free creative element is confined to far narrower limits. The main skill here is that of technical imitation, not of interpretation.

As we descend from the higher grades of distinctively creative art to these interpretative and more or less imitative grades, it will be evident that larger human 'costs' of production are apt to emerge. All imitation or repetition, either of oneself or of another, is not inhuman. There is a rhythm in the processes of organic life which even requires some repetition. But this repetition is never precise, for organic history does not exactly repeat itself. The attempt, therefore, to induce a person to perform an intricate process many times and at short intervals with great exactitude, is against humanity. It involves some physical and moral injury, a human cost. We shall consider the more serious effects of this procedure when we come to consider that work of industry most widely removed from art. In considering, however, the sub-artistic workers it will not be right to rate the human costs too high. A good deal of scope for personal satisfaction remains in many of these kinds of work. The sense of skill in overcoming difficulties, evoked wherever any intricate work is done by brain and hand, yields a vital joy. This the executant artist, even though mainly a copyist, experiences in no mean measure. It sustains a fine vitality, and, what is significant for our particular enquiry, it involves low human cost, unless the pace and strain of repetition are carried to excess. Wherever any reasonable scope for individual expression or achievement remains, though the main body of the product may be rigorously prescribed by close imitation, or ordered by mechanical contrivance, the art spirit lives and the human costs are low. The photographer, or even the skilled performer on the pianola, retains a larger measure of the nature and the satisfaction of the artist than a merely cursory consideration of his occupation would suggest.

A considerable and growing proportion of productive energy is given out in these various levels of artistic or creative work, and the proportion of the national income represented by this product is growing with fair rapidity in every modern civilised community.

§ 4. From the fine arts we proceed by an easy transition to the processes of discovery and invention which play so important a rôle in progressive industry and are leading channels of creative activity. The process of discovering a new relation between phenomena, establishing a new fact or a new law, has much in common with artistic creation. The scientific imagination is creative through its use of the existing material of knowledge to frame hypotheses. Indeed, the disinterested play of the mind in the explanation of facts by bringing them within the range of scientific laws, or, conversely, in extending the range of known laws to new groups of facts, is a process of adventure containing novelties of insight and of outlook akin to artistic production. Those philosophers, indeed, who hold that the laws of science are nothing other than the patterns which man imposes upon the phantasmagoria of experience for his own private ends, would make the whole of scientific discovery merely an art, differing from the fine arts in having utility rather than beauty for its goal. But we need not press this interpretation in order to perceive the similarity of all disinterested pursuit of knowledge to the fine arts. When a mathematician speaks of a beautiful solution to a problem, he is not using the language of hyperbole, but attesting to the presence of an æsthetic emotion attendant on the mode in which a truth is reached and stated. Modern physics is full of discoveries containing some such artistic quality, e. g. the grouping of the elements in the proportions of their atomic weight which Mendelieff established, or Sir W. Ramsay's recent discovery of the relations between helium and its chemical kindred. But one need not labour the analogy between artist and scientist. For our main enquiry is into human costs, and it will be admitted that the zest of the scientific student and the joy of discovery are emotions as vital and as valuable in themselves as the emotions of the artist. So far, then, as the scientist comes within our purview as a productive agent, his activity must rank with the artist's, as yielding more human utility than cost. It may, however, be contended that the man of science seldom, as such, enters into the field of industrial productivity, save when he adds to his scientific work the rôle of inventor. With the advent of the inventor the attainment of knowledge is bent to some purpose of industrial utility. But though some definitely gainful purpose may lurk in the inventor's mind, it does not commonly impose upon his work the distinctive costs of labour. For invention, however narrowly utilitarian in its objects and results, still remains in the realm of creation, still yields the satisfaction of a production that is interesting and elevating in itself. It seems to matter little whether the inventive process is a large bold speculative handling of some problem in which the inventor is a pioneer, or whether he is engaged upon the narrower task of bringing the past inventions of many greater minds up to the level of industrial utility by some small new economy. The process of invention carries the quality of interesting novelty which from our standpoint is the badge of creative work. We shall, doubtless, be reminded at this point that history shows the path of the inventor to be almost as hard as that of the transgressor, strewn with toil and disappointments. But though a great invention, like a great work of art, often conceals an arduous and painful gestation under the appearance of a spontaneous generation, too much must not be made of such a cost.

The training of a creative faculty, though like all training it involves an exercise and a discipline not pleasing in themselves, can, indeed, scarcely be regarded in our sense as a cost of labour. It is a furtherance and not a repression of personality: the practice it involves, the technique it imparts are not merely mechanical aptitudes, and they always carry in them the conscious hope of creative achievement. The education of artistic or inventive faculty involves no real wear and tear of human vitality beyond that physical waste which every prolonged occupation involves. Invention itself involves no cost. In none of these operations is the characteristic of labour present, the giving-out of some single sort of energy by constant repetition of identical acts in a narrow groove of endeavour. Such acts of labour are indeed inimical to invention: the act of invention comes commonly in times of leisure. It is the product more of play than of work, and the element of instinct, perhaps even of chance, is often a factor of success.

§ 5. M. Tarde, in his abrupt contrast between creation and imitation or labour, has dogmatised upon the rarity of the creative faculty, and certain other sociologists and politicians have busily engaged themselves in sowing fears lest the greed of organised labour or the rashness of socialistic legislation should, by robbing genius and ability of its proper rewards, tamper with the springs of industrial progress. Now, the important question of the economic reward of ability and genius may be deferred until we have ascertained more clearly what part these creative qualities play in all the different modes of productive energy. But the assumption that artistic and inventive faculty is exceedingly rare, because it has so seldom been displayed, must be boldly challenged. The studies of modern psychologists and educationalists refute it. On the contrary, there is reason to believe that human nature is exceedingly rich in all sorts of variations from the normal, and that very many of these variations have valuable uses, provided that suitable conditions for their discovery, training and application are present.

The notion that genius, like murder, will 'out' is a false sentimentalism. Some men of genius do, indeed, make their way in spite of adverse circumstances, forcing themselves out of the obscurity of their surroundings: they 'break their birth's invidious bar, and breast the blows of circumstance, and grasp the skirts of happy chance.' That is to say some sorts of genius are united with qualities of audacity, persistence, and luck, which enable them to win 'through'. But how many men of genius do not possess these faculties and therefore do not emerge, it is from the nature of the case impossible to learn. But it is probable that much genius, talent, and ability, capable of yielding fine social service, is lost. Indeed it is probable that many of the finest human variations, involving unusual delicacy of feeling and perhaps of physique, will by natural necessity be incapacitated for making their way and forcing recognition amid uncongenial surroundings.

It is likely that far more human genius is lost than is saved, even in the more civilised nations of to-day. For what are the conditions of the successful utilisation of genius, and for what proportion of the population are they securely attained?

Leisure is a first condition for all free and fruitful play of the mind. Very few inventions have come from workers compelled to keep their noses to the grindstone, and unable to let their eyes and thoughts play freely round the nature of their work. This is why slavery contributed so very little to the development of the industrial arts: this is why so comparatively few inventions of importance have been made by hired labourers in this and other countries. The strongest economic plea for a shorter and a lighter working-day is that it will liberate for invention and industrial progress the latent creative energy of countless workers that is stifled under the conditions of a long day's monotonous toil.

Education is the next condition. The great mass of the population in this country have no such opportunity of education as is needed to discover, stimulate, and nourish the creative faculties in art, science, and industrial invention. One need not overrate what even the best education can do for human talent of the creative order. Indeed, the education of the schools may sometimes rather injure than improve the finest faculties. But education can do one incomparable service to native genius or talent. By putting the sensitive mind of a young man or woman in contact with the innumerable waves of thought astir in the intellectual atmosphere around, it supplies the first essential of all creative activity, the fruitful union of two thoughts. Until all the new minds brought into the world are placed in such free contact with every fertilising current of thought and feeling, and enjoy free, full opportunities of knowing the best that has been thought and said in all departments of human knowledge, we cannot tell how much creative faculty perishes for lack of necessary nutriment.

§ 6. From artistic and inventive work which is essentially creative, enjoyable, vitally serviceable and costless, we proceed to review the regular skilled mental work of the professional and administrative classes.

The bulk of the productive energy classed as Ability comes under these heads.

It is evident that in most of this work the creative quality is blended in various degrees with imitation or routine. We pass from the more miraculous, interesting, and rapid modes of productive achievement to a lower level, where the expenditure of time and effort is greater and where the terms 'practice' and 'practitioner' themselves attest the more confined nature of the activities. There can be no doubt that the practice of law or medicine, even in its highest walks, involves a good deal of toilsome and almost mechanical routine, though the most successful practitioners generally shift the bulk of this burden on to the lower grades of the profession.

The practice called 'devilling' in the law illustrates my meaning. But every profession has its lower grades of routine workers, assistants, dispensers, nurses, clerks and others, whose sphere of liberty is closely circumscribed, and whose work, although involving some qualities of personal skill and responsibility, mainly consists in carrying out orders.

This consideration of the subsidiary professional services brings to light, however, a certain defect in the use of the antithesis between creation and imitation, regarded as an index of humanly desirable and humanly undesirable work.

Mere repetition or close routine is not the distinctive character of much of this work. The work of a private secretary, clerk, or other subordinate to a professional man or a high official, may contain much variety and novelty in detail or even in kind. The same may be true of the work of a valet or other personal attendant. It applies to all work which consists in carrying out another's orders. There may be plenty of variety and scope for skill in such work; in its initial stage, as conceived by the chief or employer, it may contain elements of creative energy. But the subordinate does not reap these elements of personal interest because the initiation of the process does not rest with him. The essentials of the work are imposed upon him by the intellect and will of another: neither the design nor the mode of execution is his own. Though, therefore, his work may not consist in mere routine, but may be widely varied, the fact that it is not properly 'his' work, the expression of 'his' personality, deprives it of all qualities of creation or achievement, save such fragments as adhere to the details that are 'left to him.' Such work may, indeed, be described as imitative, in that it consists in executing a design prescribed to him by another. But if the term imitation be required, as it is, to designate the sort of labour which consists in constant repetition of a single act or process, it would be better to mark this distinction between free agent and subordinate in a different way. The subordination of the secretary or the clerk involves the human cost of a surrender of his personal judgment and initiative. To the extent that he does this, he becomes an instrument of another's will. The extent to which this involves a human cost will vary greatly with the particular conditions, technical or personal. Where such subordination belongs to genuine education or apprenticeship, or where close sympathy and mutual understanding happen to exist between superior and subordinate, so that the mind of one is the mind of both, no human cost at all but a human utility may emerge. Or, in other cases, the technical nature of the work may involve the necessity of leaving to the subordinate a good deal of discretion and a correspondingly large field for personal expression. But where the subordinate becomes the mere tool of his master, a heavy cost is entailed. That cost is heavier indeed than in ordinary manual routine labour, because it involves more directly the subordination of the mind and will of the worker. Part of the distaste for domestic and other closely personal service is due to the closer bondage of the whole personality that is involved in the relation. It is not so much that the work is intrinsically dull or unpleasant as that it encroaches upon personality and inhibits initiative and achievement.

§ 7. The work of the highest, most honoured and best remunerated members of the professions retains essentially the quality of personal achievement. It consists of a number of detached and usually brief acts of intellectual skill, the formation of a judgment upon the meaning or merits of a complicated case, the presentation of that judgment in advice or argument, the bringing intellectual and moral influences to bear upon some line of conduct.

In some instances, as in the argument of a difficult case in court, or the conduct of a complicated Bill in Parliament, prolonged and arduous exertion, both mental and physical, may be involved. Even where the separate acts require no prolonged output of energy, a professional career, comprising long series of such acts, may strain or exhaust the mental and physical resources even of a strong man. Though each case will be different, and will call for qualities of personal skill and judgment, interesting and agreeable in their exercise, all will fall within the limits of a special line of practice, and this specialism will wear upon the nervous system, bringing the activity under an economy of costs. The temptations of a busy and successful professional career insidiously sap the interest and joy which attend the earlier struggle, unless a man has the rare wisdom and the strength of will to limit his amount of work and income.

What is said here of the competitive professions is in large measure applicable to the official grades of the public services. The higher sorts of official work continually involve qualities of judgment and imagination, and there is little mere repetition. As one descends to the lower official levels, the routine or repetitive element increases, until one reaches a sort of official, the liberty, initiative, skill, and interest of whose work hardly exceeds that of the ordinary machine-feeder in a factory. In all such distinctively routine work there is a heavy mental and even physical cost. But there is this distinction between the case of the official and of the professional man. The former is not subject to the constant drive of the competitive system and is usually relieved from the sense of insecurity and anxiety which wears upon the mind of most professional men.

§ 8. The psychology of the entrepreneur or business man is one of great interest and complexity. If we take the ordinary activities of the manager of a well-established business in a staple trade, they do not seem to involve much in the way of high intellectual skill, imagination, or exploit—but merely a limited amount of special trade knowledge, ordinary intelligence, and common sense. He has to perform a number of little acts of calculation and decision. What we call his character, viz. honesty, reliability, sense of responsibility, really counts for more than intellect: there is little demand for constructive or creative imagination, or for high enterprise. The conduct of such a business, even on the part of its manager, though not destitute of interesting incident, involves a good deal of dull routine and even drudgery which carries a distinct 'cost' in mental wear and tear.

The subordinate officials in such business are, of course, subjected to a closer routine, though never to a merely mechanical repetition, and their working life is less affected by hopes and fears relating to the profits or loss on the half-year's working.

But a large proportion of business men work under very different conditions from these.

Most industries to-day are subjected to rapid changes in regard to instruments and methods of work, markets for materials and for finished products, wages and conditions of employment. A keen eye for novelties, a rapid judgment, long-sighted calculation, commanding character, courage in undertaking risks—these are leading notes in the modern business life.

The business man who constructs, enlarges, and conducts a modern competitive business, performs a good many functions which call for various mental and moral qualities. He must plan the structure of his business—determine its size, the sizes and sorts of premises and plant he will require, the place which he can best occupy; he must get reliable managers and assistants, and a good supply of skilled labour of various kinds. He must watch markets and be a master of the arts of buying and selling: he must have tact in managing employees and a quick eye for improvements in methods of production and of marketing: he must be a practical financier, and must follow the course of current history so far as it affects trade prospects.

If we take the most generalised type of modern business man, the financier who directs the flow of capital into its various channels, or the capitalist who lives by managing his investments, we find the business ability in its most refined form. For these men are the general directors of economic energy, operating through joint stock enterprise.

The human costs of this work of speculation and direction are difficult to assess. Such terms as labour and industry are alien from the atmosphere of these high economic functions. At the same time the strain of excitement, and, at certain seasons, of prolonged intellectual effort and attention, the sense of responsibility for critical decisions, involve a heavy nervous wear and tear. Probably the heaviest human cost, however, is a certain moral callousness and recklessness involved in the financial struggle. For the paper symbols of industrial power, which financiers handle, are so abstract in nature and so remote from the human fates which they direct, that the chain of causation linking stocks and shares with human work and human life is seldom realised. How should the temporary holder of a block of shares in Peruvian rubber concern himself with the conditions of forced labour in the Amazon forests, or the group formed to float a foreign government loan consider the human meaning of the naval policy it is intended to finance? Except in so far as they affect the values of their holdings and the price at which they can market the shares, the human significance of the business or political enterprises which are concrete entities behind finance, has no meaning for them. These men and their economic activities are further removed from human costs and utilities than any other sort of business men. In view of the immense human consequences which follow from their conduct this aloofness is a demoralising condition.

So occult and so suspect are many of the operations of financiers as somewhat to obscure the importance of the actual economic services they render to our industrial system. General finance is the governor of the economic engine: it distributes economic power among the various industries, allocating the capital of the saving classes to road-making, irrigation, mining, the equipment of new cities, the establishment of staple manufactures, and the supply of financial resources for various purposes of government. The finest business instincts, the most rapid, accurate, and complex powers of inference and prophecy, the best balance of audacity and caution, the largest and best-informed imagination, are needed for this work of general finance. It is intensely interesting, and exerts a fascination which is traceable to a combination of appeals. The chief field for high economic adventure, it evokes most fully the combative qualities of force and cunning; it is full of hazard and fluctuation, with large, rapid gains and losses: it neither requires nor permits close personal contact with the troublesome or sordid details of industrial or commercial life.

Such is the work of the financier and the skilled investor, who found capitalistic enterprises and deal in their stocks and shares over the whole area of the industrial world. It is the most intellectual and, in one sense, the most 'moral' of business activities, involving at once the finest arts of calculation and the fullest faith in human nature.

For finance is most closely linked with credit, and credit is only the business name for faith. When people talk of finance as if it were riddled with dishonesty, facts give them the lie. The normal honesty of finance is proved by the fact that larger and larger numbers of men and women in every country of the civilised world are coming to entrust their savings more and more to men who are personal strangers, for investment in distant countries and in businesses the exact nature of which is unknown to them, and over which they cannot hope to exercise an appreciable control. The working of the machinery of modern investment by which millions of men in England, France, and Germany have sent their savings to make railways in S. America, or to open up mines in S. Africa, or to build dams in Egypt, is the largest tangible result of modern education that can be adduced.

It implies the intellectual and moral coöperation of larger numbers of distinct personalities across wider local and national barriers than has ever occurred before in the history of the world.

§ 9. A reasonable faith in the future and a willingness to run some risk are complementary motives in this growth of financial investment. They are, however, by no means confined to operations of finance. All industry involves faith and risk-taking. Every producer who acts as a free agent conceives some good object which he thinks attainable by his work. He may be mistaken, either in conceiving wrongly, or in failing to carry out his plan. His failure may be due to want of skill or knowledge, or to adverse circumstances. In primitive societies, where a man produces mostly for his own use, the risk is less. For he may be supposed to know what he wants, how much, and when he wants it. But when he makes for others, i. e. for a market, the risks are greater. For he will not know so much about the wants of other persons as about his own. It might seem as if small local markets, in which the producer dealt exclusively with neighbours, would carry the least risk, and that the risk would expand with each expansion of the market area. But this is not commonly the case. As a rule, there is less risk for the producer serving a large market, the individual members of which he does not know, than a small market of his neighbours. For the fluctuations of aggregate demand will be smaller in the larger market, and though he will know less about the individual contributions to its supply and its demand, his risk of failing to effect a sale, when he desires to do so, will usually be less. This at any rate applies to most standard trades.

Since effective access to large markets implies a fairly large business, the economy of risk becomes one of the economies of capitalism, and its calculation a chief branch of the employer's skill. The watching of the market so as to reduce the waste of misdirected production is the most delicate of the intellectual activities of most managers. It takes him outside the scope of his own business and the present process of production, to consider the whole condition of the trade in the present and the probable future. These calculations and acts of judgment issuing from the brain of business managers are the psychical aspect of the whole structure of markets and of the trade and traffic arrangements which give such unity and order as are visible in what is termed the industrial system.

Thus, not merely on the financial but on the commercial side, industry is perceived to be a great fabric of beliefs and desires. Though, as we shall recognise, in dealing with labour, and with saving, risk-taking is by no means confined to employers and entrepreneurs, its wider operations belong to the speculative skill which comes under the general head of ability of management. In the psychological interpretation of industry this function of the entrepreneur is of quite crucial significance, coöperating everywhere with the more abstract calculations of financiers in directing the amounts, kinds, and directions, of the various currents of industrial energy which move in the business world. Since it involves a constant use of the constructive imagination in the interpretation of the play of changing motives in many minds, and the forecasting of future conditions which can never be a mere repetition of the past, the 'creative' faculty obtains here its highest expression. It is not for nothing that the great modern master either of finance or industry is accredited with some quality of imaginative power akin to that of the artist. This, however, must in not a few instances imply, not merely the genius of the prophet, but that of the skilled manipulator of economic material and opportunity, who helps to secure the due fulfilment of the prophecies upon which he stakes his faith.

CHAPTER V

§ 1. The classical Political Economy of this country gave to Labour a rôle of supreme importance in the production of wealth. From Adam Smith, Ricardo, and other authoritative exponents of the new 'science' many passages can be cited to support the thesis that labourers are the only producers. Nor does it appear that in these utterances Labour was usually intended to include the services of organisation and management or other intellectual activities. Wealth is baldly attributed to Labour in the sense that the manual labour, which extracts raw materials from the earth, shapes and composes them, and carries them from one place to another, alone counts as a cost of production. It is natural enough that the scientific socialism of Europe should have accepted and enforced this doctrine. Though the more intelligent socialists and 'labour men' admit the necessary work of superintendence and other mental work as useful and productive, the materialism prevalent in the business world tends to relegate to a quite secondary place all the higher forms of intellectual and moral activity.

It was upon the whole, indeed, a sound instinct which thus led the early theorists to use language which attributed to manual labour the real burden of the 'costs' of production. For closer investigation attests the force of the distinction between the productive energy given out by the intellectual, the directing, and administrative classes on the one hand, and by the labouring-classes on the other. Moreover, the social as well as the economic cleavage is so distinctive a feature of our life that it would be inconvenient to ignore it. The cleavage will be found to correspond pretty accurately to the distinction between the creative and the imitative functions which we provisionally adopted for a starting point in our analysis.

For most of the productive energy given out by the artistic, inventive, professional, official, and managerial classes, which have passed under our survey, is seen to be in large measure creative, varied, interesting, and pleasurable.

Now in the labour of the wage-earning classes these qualities are generally lacking. Alike in motives and in methods, the contrast is clearly marked. The mind of the artist or the inventor, even of the professional man or the administrator, is occupied with the work in hand, as an object of interest and of desirable achievement. The nature of the work and the conditions of remuneration conduce to fix his immediate thoughts and feelings on the performance of his work. With the labourer it is different. The conditions of most labour are such that the labourer finds little scope for thought and emotional interest in the work itself. Its due performance is hardly an end to him, but only a means to a livelihood consisting in the consumable commodities got in payment for his labour.

But the vital distinction is in the nature and method of the work done. Whereas the artistic or inventive, or even the professional man, is constantly doing something new, the labourer continually repeats the same act or set of acts, in order to produce a number of similar products. The success of most labour consists in the exactitude and pace with which this repetition can be carried on. The machine-tender is the typical instance. To feed the same machinery with the same quantity of the same material at the same pace, so as to turn out an endless number of precisely similar articles, is the absolute antithesis of art. It is often said that the man who feeds such a machine tends to become as automatic as the machine itself. This, however, is but a half-truth. If the tender could become as automatic as the machine he tended, if he could completely mechanise a little section of his faculties, it might go easier with him. But the main trend of life in the man fights against the mechanising tendency of his work, and this struggle entails a heavy cost. For his machine imposes a repetition of the same muscular and nervous action upon a being whose muscles and nervous resources are continually changing. The machine, fed constantly with the same supply of fuel, geared up to a single constant pace of movement, forced by unchanging structure to the performance of the same operation, friction and error reduced to an almost negligible minimum, works through the longest day with a uniform expenditure of power. The machine-tender is an organism, fed at somewhat irregular intervals with different amounts and sorts of food, the assimilation of which is also discontinuous, and incapable of maintaining intact and constant in its quantity the muscular and nervous tissue and the accompanying contractions which constitute the physical supply of 'work'. This organism has also many other structures and functions, physical and mental, whose activities and needs get in the way of the automatic activity of machine-tending. Thus the worker cannot succeed in becoming altogether a machine-tending automaton. He will not always exactly repeat himself, and his attempt to do so involves two sets of organic costs or wastes, due to the fact that, though his labour tries to make him a specialised mechanism, he remains a generalised organism.

So far as labour consists in specialised routine, absorbing the main current of productive energy, it is the enemy of organic health. It is hostile in two ways, first, in denying to man opportunity for the exercise of his other productive faculties, secondly, in overtaxing and degrading by servile repetition the single faculty that is employed.

As the artist presents the supreme example of creative work, with a minimum of human costs and a maximum of human utility, so the machine-tender presents the supreme example of imitative work, with a maximum of human costs and a minimum of human utility.

§ 2. Some particular consideration of these costs of machine-tending will be the best approach to a more general survey of the human costs of labour.

The indictment of the dominion of machinery by Ruskin, Morris, and other humanist reformers, was primarily based upon the degradation of the worker's manhood by denying him the conditions of good work. 'It is a sad account,' said Ruskin, 'for a man to give of himself that he has spent his life in opening a valve, and never made anything but the eighteenth part of a pin.' But, important as is this charge of degraded and joyless work, we must begin our analysis of the costs of mechanical or factory labour at a lower level.

From the great body of the factory labour which goes to the provision of our national income, the first great human cost that emerges is the burden of injurious fatigue which results from muscular or nervous overstrain, and from the other physical and moral injuries which are the natural accompaniments of this overstrain.

Modern physiology and pathology have done much to give plain meanings to these costs. Physical fatigue is not of necessity an injury to the body, nor is all feeling of fatigue a pain. The ideally correct conduct of the organism may, indeed, appear to preserve an exact and a continuous balance between the anabolic and the catabolic, the nutrition of cell life and the expenditure in function. Sir Michael Foster gives the following classical description of this process.[1]

'Did we possess some optic aid which should overcome the grossness of our vision, so that we might watch the dance of atoms in this double process of making and unmaking in the human body, we should see the commonplace living things which are brought by the blood, and which we call the food, caught up into and made part of the molecular whorls of the living muscle, linked together for awhile in the intricate figures of the dance of life; and then we should see how, loosing hands, they slipped back into the blood, as dead, inert, used-up matter. In every tiny block of muscle there is a part which is really alive, there are parts which are becoming alive, there are parts which have been alive but are now dying or dead; there is an upward rush from the lifeless to the living, a downward rush from the living to the dead. This is always going on, whether the muscle be quiet and at rest, or whether it be active and moving. Some of the capital of living material is always being spent, changed into dead waste, some of the new food is always being raised into living capital.

'Thus nutritive materials are carried by the blood to the tissues, and the dead materials of used-up and broken-up tissues are carried away for destruction or ejection. Under normal conditions of healthy activity this metabolic balance is preserved

[1] *Weariness*, the Rede Lecture, Cambridge, 1893.

by the alternation of work and repose, the tissue and energy built up out of food during periods of rest forming a fund for expenditure during periods of work, while the same periods of rest enable the destructive and evacuative processes to get rid of any accumulation of dead tissue due to the previous period of work. Abnormally intense or unduly prolonged activity of any portion of the body uses up tissue so fast that its dead material cannot be got rid of at the proper pace. It accumulates in the blood or in the kidneys, liver or lungs, and operates as a poison throughout the whole system. Over-fatigue thus means poisoning the organism.

'The poisons are more and more heaped-up, poisoning the muscles, poisoning the brain, poisoning the heart, poisoning at last the blood itself, starting in the intricate machinery of the body new poisons in addition to themselves. The hunted hare, run to death, dies not because he is choked for want of breath, nor because his heart stands still, its store of energy having given out, but because a poisoned blood poisons his brain, poisons his whole body.' [1]

The Italian biologist Mosso has demonstrated that the depressing effect of fatigue is not confined to the local centre where it is produced, but is carried to all parts of the body. When the blood of a dog fatigued by continued running is injected into the vessels of a sound dog, the latter exhibits all the signs of fatigue. The inability of the system to dispose of the used-up tissue, which thus accumulates and poisons the system, is one injurious factor in fatigue. Another is the undue depletion of the stores of glycogen and oxygen, which the organism provides for the output of muscular activity. Glycogen is a compound of carbon, hydrogen, and oxygen made by muscle tissue out of the sugar or dextrine supplied to it by the blood. 'The stored glycogen of the muscles keeps uniting chemically with the oxygen of the blood. The glycogen is broken down into a simpler chemical form, giving off the gas carbon dioxide and other acid wastes, and releasing heat and mechanical energy in the process. With the released energy contraction of the muscles takes place and hence ultimately the industrial labour which is our special theme.' [2]

[1] Foster. Op. cit.   [2] Goldmarck, *Fatigue and Efficiency*, p. 22.

'Glycogen is, as it were, stored for use. It is always being replenished, always being depleted. . . . But when the muscle is active and contracts energetically, there is a run upon our glycogen. It is used up faster than it is built in muscle. The glycogen is spent so rapidly that there is not time for the blood-stream to bring back to the tissue the potential material for its repair.' [1] Though the liver furnishes an extra store of glycogen, this too may be depleted by undue muscular activity.

'Thus we have reached the other fundamental factor in fatigue—the consumption of the energy-yielding substance itself. Not only does tissue manufacture poison for itself in the very act of living, casting off chemical wastes into the circling bloodstream; not only are these wastes poured into the blood faster with increased exertion, clogging the muscle more and more with its own noxious products; but, finally, there is a depletion of the very material from which energy is obtained. The catabolic process is in excess of the anabolic. In exhaustion, the organism is forced literally to "use itself up".' [2]

§ 3. So much for the physiological meaning of muscular fatigue. Closely associated with muscular fatigue is nervous fatigue. For every voluntary muscular action receives its stimulus from a nervous centre. Though the nature of this nervous energy, accumulated in the central nervous system and distributed in stimuli, is not well understood, its economy is gravely disturbed by conduct involving heavy muscular fatigue, as well as by work of a mental kind involving heavy drains on its resources. A process of building up, storage, and dissipation of nerve tissue and energy-yielding material, corresponding to that which we have traced for muscle tissue, must be accepted as taking place. Fatigue of the nervous system will thus be attended by a similar accumulation of poisonous waste products, and an excessive consumption of substances needed for the maintenance of nervous activity.

Though physiologists are not agreed as to how and when fatigue acts on the nervous cells, there is no question of the reality and of the importance of this injury of excessive work to 'the administrative instrument of the individual' which 'directs,

[1] Goldmarck, p. 22.　　　　[2] Ibid, p. 23.

controls and harmonises the work of the parts of the organic machine and gives unity to the whole.'

Still confining our attention to purely physical conditions, we learn that work done in a state of muscular fatigue involves an increase of nervous effort.

'Mosso showed that a much stronger electric stimulus is required to make a wearied muscle contract than one which is rested. He devised an apparatus, the ponometer, which records the curve of nervous effort required to accomplish muscular action as fatigue increases. He showed that the nerve centres are compelled to supply an ever stronger stimulus to fatigued muscles.' [1]

Professor Treves at Turin throws further light upon the relations between the muscular and the nervous economy. It is well known that in muscular activity there is an opening period during which efficiency, or practical response to nervous stimulus, increases. Before fatigue begins to set in, the muscle appears to gain strength, its working power being actually augmented. This period of maximum efficiency continues for an appreciable time, then fatigue advances more and more until muscular contraction refuses any longer to respond to even a heightened nervous stimulus. This, of course, is also an epitome of the course of organic life itself, its rise towards maturity, its level of maximum power and its decline.

Now training or practice can notoriously affect this natural economy. The muscular system, or some part of it, can by practice accommodate itself to increasing quantities of fatigue-poisons, and can draw from the general organic fund a larger quantity of material for repair of local muscular tissue and energy. But it has long been recognised that some real dangers attach to this excessive specialisation of muscular activities. The pathological nature of over-training in athletics has its plain counterpart in industry. This, according to Professor Treves, lies in the failure of the supply of nervous energy to rise in proportion to the requirements for this higher pressure upon the muscular tissues.

'According to my experience, it has not been found that training has as favourable an effect upon [nervous] energy as upon

[1] Goldmarck, p. 33.

muscular strength. . . . This fact explains why muscular training cannot go beyond certain limits and why athletes are often broken down by the consequences of over-exertion. And this fact teaches also the practical necessity of preventing women, children, and even adult men from becoming subjected to labour, which, indeed, a gradual muscular training may make possible, but at the price of an excessive loss of nervous energy which is not betrayed by any obvious or immediate symptoms, either objective or subjective.' [1]

A series of experiments has been directed to the more detailed study of the relations between activity and repose. Their general result is to prove that muscular work, done after fatigue has set in, not only costs more nervous effort but accomplishes less work. The ergograph, an instrument for measuring work, yields ample testimony to the recuperative effect of rest taken before exhaustion is reached, on the one hand, and the rapid rate of decline in achievement when activity is continued after the fatigue point has been reached.

§ 4. To this account of the physical costs of excessive work in muscular and nervous waste must be added the greater liability to accidents and the greater susceptibility to industrial and non-industrial diseases which fatigue entails.

The statistics of industry in various countries prove that fatigue is a very important factor in industrial accidents. Though fatigue is not always proportionate to duration of work, the number of hours worked without intermission is usually a valid index of fatigue. After a long stunt of work the attention of the worker and his muscular control are both weakened. We find, therefore, a marked similarity in the curves relating accidents to hours of labour, accidents increasing progressively up to the end of the morning's work, and again in the late afternoon as the day's work draws to its close. Recent German statistics show that the highest rate of accidents is during the fourth and fifth hours of morning work.

That over-fatigue connected with industry is responsible for large numbers of nervous disorders is, of course, generally admitted. The growing prevalence of cardiac neurosis and of neu-

[1] Goldmarck, p. 37.

rasthenia in general among working-people is attested by many medical authorities, especially in occupations where long strains of attention are involved. But the general enfeeblement and

Percentage of persons killed or injured in 1907 grouped according to the number of hours the injured person had been at work on day of accident

Total Accidents 79,791

(German Insurance Reports)

loss of resistance power to disease germs of all kinds are even more injurious consequences of over-exertion. Many experiments attest the fact that fatigue reduces the power of the blood to resist bacteria and their toxic products.

§ 5. So far I have dwelt exclusively upon the physiological

nature and effects of fatigue as costs of labour. But due account
must also be taken of the psychical or conscious costs. Much
work in its initial stage contains elements of pleasurable exercise
of some human organ or faculty, and even when this pleasure has
worn off a considerable period of indifference may ensue. Though

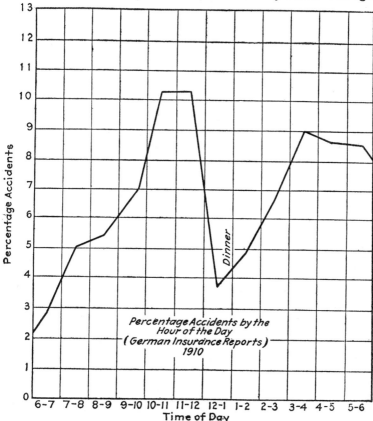

Percentage Accidents by the
Hour of the Day
(German Insurance Reports)
1910

Time of Day

boredom may set in before any strain of fatigue, the earlier period
of ennui may not entail a heavy cost. But, when fatigue advances, the irksomeness brings a growing feeling of painful effort, and a long bout of fatigue produces as its concomitant a
period of grave conscious irritation of nerves with a subsequent
period of painful collapse. Where the conditions of work are

such as to involve a daily repetition of this pain, its accumulative effect constitutes one of the heaviest of human costs, a lowering of mentality and of moral resistance closely corresponding to the decline of physical resistance. Drink and other sensational excesses are the normal reactions of this lowered morale. Thus fatigue ranks as a main determinant of the 'character' of the working-classes and has a social significance in its bearing upon order and progress not less important than its influence upon the individual organism.

§ 6. I have dwelt in some detail upon these phenomena of fatigue, because they exhibit most clearly the defects of the working life which carry heaviest human costs. These defects are excessive duration of labour, excessive specialisation, excessive repetition, excessive strain and excessive speed. Though separate for purposes of analysis, these factors closely interact. Mere duration of labour does not necessarily involve fatigue, provided it carries the elements of interest, variety, and achievement. The degree of specialisation or subdivision of labour counts on the whole more heavily. But even a high degree of specialisation is alleviated, where it contains many little changes of action or position, and affords scope for the satisfaction attending expert skill. It is the constant repetition of an identical action at a prescribed pace that brings the heaviest burden of monotony.

It is upon this combination of conditions that the first count against the dominion of machinery is based. The brief physiological consideration we have brought to bear upon the problem of fatigue gives clearer significance to monotony as a 'cost'. It implies, not merely a dull and distasteful occupation, but one which, taxing continually the same muscles and the same nerve-centres, increases the poison of fatigue. Hand labour of a narrow order, or machine-tending however light, entails this heavy cost, if maintained over a long period of time.

But where monotonous repetition is closely directed by the action of a machine, as regards its manner and its pace, there is a special nervous cost. For a hand-worker, however dull or heavy is the work, retains some slight power of varying the pace and perhaps of changing his position or mode of work. A worker who either feeds a machine or adjusts his movements in obedience to those of a machine, as for instance a cutter in the clothing trade or in shoemaking, has no such liberty. The special cost here entailed is that of trying to make an organism conform in its movements to a mechanism. Now a human being, or any other organism, has certain natural rhythms of movement for work, related to the rhythms of heart and lungs and other organic processes, and there are natural limits also to the pace at which he can efficiently, or even possibly, continue working. A machine also has rhythms and a maximum efficiency pace. But the rhythms of a machine are determined by its mechanical construction and the apparatus which furnishes its power: they are continuously uniform, and are capable of being speeded up beyond the capacity of the human tender.

A human rhythm is really labour-saving, in as much as it eases the strain to work in accordance with a natural swing. To set a man to follow the rhythm of a machine not only loses this economy, but entails an extra effort of conformity. The tendency to speed up a machine, so as to get the most out of it, is liable to take out of the machine-tender even more than he is capable of recognising in the way of nervous strain. Where considerable muscular activity is also required in following a high pace set by a machine, an appalling burden of human costs may be accumulated in a factory day.

When to such direct human costs of labour are added the risks of industrial accident or of industrial diseases, the physical injuries involved in bad atmosphere, heat, noise and other incidental pains and inconveniences which beset many branches of industry, we begin to realise with more distinctness the meaning of 'costs of labour' in the human as distinguished from the economic sense.

Later on we shall turn to consider how far the economic or monetary 'costs' correspond with these human costs.

Our present task, however, is to conduct a brief survey of general industry in order to form some idea of the magnitude of these human costs in the leading branches of production, and to consider how far they are offset or qualified by factors of human interest or utility, such as we found widely prevalent in the work of the artistic, official, and administrative classes.

CHAPTER VI

THE REIGN OF THE MACHINE

§ 1. If it were true that all the labour of the wage-earning classes which went to produce the real national income were, or tended to become, monotonous and highly specialised machine tending, the workers constantly engaged in close repetition of some single narrow automatic process, contributing to some final composite product whose form and utility had no real meaning for them, the tale of human costs would be appalling.

Fortunately this is not the whole truth about labour. Even the charge against machinery of mechanising the worker is frequently overstated. The only productive work that is entirely automatic is done by machines. For the main trend of the development of industrial machinery has been to set non-human tools and power to undertake work which man could not execute with the required regularity, exactitude, or pace, by reason of certain organic deficiencies. While, then, the sub-divided labour in most staple industries is mostly of a narrowly prescribed and routine character, it is hardly ever so completely uniform and repetitive as that done by a machine. Purely routine work, demanding no human skill or judgment is nearly always undertaken by machinery, except where human labour can be bought so cheap that it does not pay to invent and apply machinery so as to secure some slightly increased regularity or pace of output. Where, then, as in most modern factories, human labour coöperates with, tends and feeds machinery, this human labour is of a less purely repetitive character than the work done by the machines. Some portions of the labour, at any rate, contain elements of skill or judgment, and are not entirely uniform.

We can in fact distinguish many kinds and grades of human coöperation with machinery. In some of them man is the habitual servant, in others the habitual master of the machine; in others, again, the relation is more indirect or incidental. Though an increasing number of the processes in the making and moving of most forms of material goods involves the use of machinery and power, they do not involve, as is sometimes supposed, the employment of a growing proportion of the workers in the merely routine labour of tending the machines. Such a supposition, indeed, is inconsistent with the primary economy of machinery, the so-called labour-saving property. It might, indeed, be the case that the machine economy was accompanied by so vast an increase of demand for machine-made goods, that the quantity of labour required for tending the machines was greater than that formerly required for making by hand the smaller quantity. In some trades this is no doubt so, as for instance in the printing trade, and in some branches of textile industry where the home market is largely supplemented by export trade. But the displacement of machine-tenders by automatic machines is advancing in many of the highly-developed machine industries. The modern flour or paper mill, for instance, performs nearly all its feeding processes by mechanical means while in the textile trade automatic spindles and looms have reduced the number and changed the character of the work of minders. More and more of this work means bringing human elements of skill and judgment and responsibility to bear in adjusting or correcting the irregularities or errors in the operations of machinery. Machines are liable to run down, become clogged, break, or otherwise 'go wrong'. These errors they can often be made to announce by automatic signals, but human care is needed for their correction. This work, however monotonous and fatiguing to muscles or nerves, is not and cannot be entirely repetitive.

In many other processes where the machine is said to do the work, human skill and practice are required to set and to regulate the operations of the machine. The use of automatic lathes is an instance of coöperation in which some scope for human judgment remains. The metal and engineering trades are full of such instances. Though machinery is an exceedingly important and in many processes a governing factor, it cannot be said to reduce the labour that works with it to its own automatic level. On the contrary, it may be taken as generally true that, in the processes where machinery has reached its most complex development, an increased share of the labour employed in close connection with the machinery is that of the skilled engineer or fitter rather than of the mere tender. The heaviest and the most costly labour in these trades is usually found in the processes where it has not been found practicable or economical to apply machinery. Indeed, the general tendency, especially noticed in America, in the metal trades, has been to substitute for a large employment of skilled hand labour of a narrowly specialised order, a small employment of more skilled and responsible supervisors of machinery and a large employment of low-skilled manual labour in the less mechanical departments, such as furnace work and other operations preparatory to the machine processes.

§ 2. Though accurate statistics are not available, it appears that in this country the proportion of the working population employed in manufactures is not increasing, and it is more than probable that an exact analysis of the nature of the work of our factories and workshops would show that the proportion engaged in direct attendance on machinery was steadily falling.

For even in manufacture, the department of industry where machine processes have made most advance, there are many processes where hand labour is still required, in sorting and preparing materials for machinery, in performing minor processes of trimming or decoration, in putting together parts or in packing, etc. Where female labour is employed, a very large proportion of it will be found to be engaged in such processes outside the direct dominion of machinery. Though most of the distinctively human 'costs' of machine processes, the long hours, high pace, monotony of muscles and nerve strain, are usually present in such work, it is not absolutely mechanical, some slight elements of skill and volitional direction being present.

There are other restrictions upon the purely repetitive or routine character of manufacture. There is much work which no machine can be invented to do because of certain inherent elements of irregularity. Most of these are related to the organic nature of some of the materials used. Where expensive animal or vegetable products require treatment, their natural inequalities often render a purely mechanical operation impossible or wasteful. The killing, cutting, and canning processes in the meat trade, the picking, preparation and packing of fruit, many processes in the tanning and leather trade, the finer sorts of cabinet-making, are examples of this unadaptability of organic materials to purely mechanical treatment. Where very valuable inorganic materials are used in making high-grade products, similar limitations in the machine economy exist. The finest jewellery and watch-making still require the skill and judgment of the practised human hand and eye. Some of the irregularities in such processes are, indeed, so small and so uninteresting as to afford little, if any, abatement of human costs; but they remove the labour from the direct control of a machine.

A more important irregularity which restricts machinery in manufacture exists where the personal needs or taste of the consumer help to determine the nature of the process and the product. Here again we are confronted by the antagonism of mechanism and organism. For the true demand of consumers is the highest expression of the uniqueness which distinguishes the organic. As no two consumers are exactly identical in size, shape, physical or mental capacities, tastes and needs, the goods required for their consumption should exhibit similar differences. Machine economy cannot properly meet this requirement. It can only deal with consumers so far as their human nature is common: it cannot supply the needs of their individuality. So far as they are willing to sink their differences, consenting to consume large quantities of goods of identical shapes, sizes and qualities, the machine can supply them. But since no two consumers are really identical in needs and tastes, or remain quite constant in their needs and tastes, the fundamental assumption of routine-economy is opposed to the human facts.

Consumers who refuse to sink their individuality and are 'particular' in the sort of clothes they wear, the sort of houses and furniture and other goods they will consent to buy, exercise a power antagonistic to routine labour. They demand that producers shall put out the technical skill, the care, taste and judgment required to satisfy their feelings as consumers. That is to say, they demand the labour not of the routine-worker but of the craftsman, work which, though not creative in the full free ar-

tistic sense, contains distinct elements of human interest and initiative.

§ 3. The presence and the possibilities of this individuality
of labour, flowing from the educated individuality of consumers,
are a most important influence in the lightening of the human
costs of labour. At present no doubt a very small proportion of
the material goods turned out by the industrial system contains
any appreciable element of this individuality of workmanship.
It may, indeed, well appear that our recent course during the
development of the machine economy has been a retrograde one.
In the beginnings of industry it appeared as if there were more
scope for the producer's self-expression, more joy of work, more
interest in the product, even though destined for the commonest
uses. The guilds in the Middle Ages preserved not a little of this
happier spirit of craftsmanship. To those who brood upon these
visions of the past, our modern industrial development has often
seemed a crude substitution of quantity of goods for quality,
the character of labour deteriorating in the process. With the element of truth in such a judgment is mingled much falsehood.
There has never been an age or a country where the great bulk
of labour was not toilsome, painful, monotonous, and uninteresting, often degrading in its conditions. Bad as things are,
when regarded from the standpoint of a human ideal, they are
better for the majority of the workers in this and in other advanced industrial countries than ever in the past, so far as we
can reconstruct and understand that past. Machinery has rendered a great human service by taking over large masses of
heavy, dull, and degrading work. When fully developed and
harnessed to the social service of man, it should prove to be the
great liberator of his free productive tastes and faculties, performing for him the routine processes of industry so that he may
have time and energy to devote himself to activities more interesting and varied.

The uniqueness of the individual consumer has only begun to
make its impression upon industry. For it needs liberty and
education for a man to recognise this property of organic uniqueness and to insist on realising it. The first movements of conscious tastes in a nation or a class are largely imitative, taking

shape in fashions sufficiently wide-spread and uniform to lend themselves to routine mechanical production. The self-assertion of the individual is a slower fruit of culture. But, as it grows, it will offer a continually stronger opposition to the dominion of mechanical production. It will do this in two ways. In the first place, it will cause a larger proportion of demand to be directed to the classes of products, such as intellectual, æsthetic, and personal services, which are by their nature less susceptible of mechanical production. In the second place, weakening the traditional and the imitative factors in taste and demand, it will cause consumption, even of the higher forms of material commodities, to be a more accurate expression of the changing needs and tastes of the individual, stamping upon the processes of production the same impress of individuality.

But though the direct control of machinery over human labour is obstructed in the earlier extractive processes by the refractory uneven nature of materials, and in the final processes by the nature and particular requirements of consumers, its influence extends far beyond the middle processes of manufacture where its prominence is greatest. Power-driven machinery plays a larger part in agriculture every year: mining is the first of machine industries in the sense that it employs the largest amount of horse-power per man; the transport trade by sea and land is mechanised even in its minor local branches; the great public services, supplying light, water, and other common wants, are among the largest users of power-driven machinery; the greatest of our material industries which still depends mainly upon hand labour, the building and road-making group, is constantly increasing its dependence on machinery for its heavier carrying work and for the preparation of the metal, stone and woodwork it employs. When we add the growth of new large manufactures, such as chemicals and electrical apparatus, the enormous expansion of the paper and printing trades under the new mechanical conditions, the recent transference of the processes of the preparation of foods and drinks and laundry work from the private house to the factory, we shall recognise that the net influence of machinery, as determining the character of human labour, is still advancing with considerable rapidity.

§ 4. It is not easy to answer the two related questions, 'How far is machinery the master, how far the servant, of the workers who coöperate with it?' 'How far does machinery aggravate, how far lighten the human costs of labour?' Even when we compare the work of the classes most subservient to machinery, the feeders and tenders in our factories, with the domestic or earlier factory processes under hand labour, it is by no means self-evident that the net burden of the human costs has been enhanced. For, though the spinning and weaving work before the industrial revolution had certain slight elements of freedom and variety now absent, many of the hygienic conditions were far worse, the hours of labour were usually longer, and the large employment of old folk and tender children, in work nearly as unvaried as that enjoined by modern machinery, enslaved the entire life of the home and family to the narrow and precarious conditions of a small local trade. The real liberty of the worker, as regards his work, or its disposal in the market, was hardly greater than in the modern factory.

In most of the great branches of production, machinery is rather an adjunct to labour than a director. The labourer in charge of the machine tends more to the type of the engineer than to that of the feeder or mere minder. Though the mining, metal, chemical, paper, food and drink manufactures contain large quantities of machinery, a large proportion of those who have to deal with the machines are skilled manual labourers. So in the transport trade, though the displacement of the old-time sailor by the engineer and stoker, of the horse-driver by the engine-driver and the motor-man, sometimes appears to involve a degradation of labour, the issue is a doubtful one, if all the pros and cons are taken into due account. As regards the employment of machinery in the building and contracting trades, as in the mining, its first and obvious effect has been to relieve human labour from much of the heaviest muscular toil. Though most of such labour involves too slight elements of interest or skill greatly to alleviate the physical fatigue, it cannot be said that machinery has increased the burden.

CHAPTER VII

THE DISTRIBUTION OF HUMAN COSTS

§ 1. In endeavouring to estimate the human costs of labour in terms of physical wear and tear and the conscious pains and penalties entailed by the conditions under which many industrial processes are carried on, we have hitherto considered these costs as borne by workers, irrespective of age, sex, or other discriminations. But it is self-evident that a given strain upon muscles or nerves over a period of time will vary greatly, both in the organic cost and in the conscious pain which it entails, according to the strength and endurance, nervous structure, physical and moral sensitiveness, of the different sorts of workers. Indeed, a given output of productive energy will evidently entail a different human cost in every person called upon to give it out: for every difference of strength, skill, capacity and character must to some extent affect the organic burden of the task.

In endeavouring, therefore, to relate the human to the economic costs of production of any quantity of material wealth or services, it would be necessary to consider how far the conditions of employment tend to economise human costs by distributing the burden proportionately to the power to bear it. The human wastes or excessive costs, entailed by conditions of employment which impose unequal burdens upon workers with equal capacity to bear them, or which distribute the burden unequally in time over the same set of workers, alternating slack periods with periods of excessive over-time, are obvious. Unfortunately the operation of our industrial system has not hitherto taken these into sufficient account. Though the physical, moral and social injuries, due to alternating periods of over and under work, are generally admitted, the full costs of such irregularity, human and even economic, are far from being adequately realised. While some attempts at 'decasualisation' are being made, the larger

79

and more wasteful irregularities of seasonal and cyclical fluctuations are still regarded as irremediable. By the workers themselves and even by social reformers, the injury inflicted upon wages and the standard of living by irregularity of employment is appreciated far more adequately than the related injury inflicted on the physique and morale of the worker by sandwiching periods of over-exertion between intervals of idleness.

This brief survey, however, is no place for a discussion of the causes and remedies of irregular employment. It must suffice to note that over a large number of the fields of industry the excesses and defects of such irregularity prevail to an extent which adds greatly to the total human cost of the products. So far as our nation is concerned, there is no reason to hold that this waste is increasing. Evidence of hours of labour and of unemployment, indeed, appear to indicate that it is somewhat diminishing. But the unequal time-distribution of human costs must continue to rank as a great enhancement of the aggregate of such costs.

§ 2. But not less injurious than the unequal treatment of equals, is the equal treatment of unequals. The bad human economy of working immature children is a lesson which even the most 'civilised' nations have been exceedingly slow to learn. The bad human economy of working old persons of declining vigour, when able-bodied adult labour is available, is so far from being generally recognised that employers are actually commended on the ground of humanity for keeping at labour their aged employees, when younger and stronger workers are available. Fortunately, the larger provision for retiring pensions attests the growing recognition of this aggravation of the human costs of industry. In both cases alike, the employment of the young and of the old, the error arises from a short-sighted view of the interests of the single person or his single family, instead of a far-sighted view of the welfare of the community. It is often a source of immediate gain to a working-class family to put the children out to wage-earning as early as possible, and to keep old people working as long as they can get work to do. It does not pay the nation, even in the economic sense, that either of these things should be done. The case of child-labour is, of course, the more serious, in that it evidently entails not merely a wasteful strain upon feeble organisms, but an even heavier future cost in stunted growth and impaired efficiency throughout an entire life.

When the play of current economic forces places upon women work which men could perform more easily, or creates women's industries with conditions of labour involving excessive strains upon the organism, the double human costs are even heavier. For if excessive fatigue or nervous strain affects a woman as worker, the injurious costs are likely to be continued and enhanced through her capacity for motherhood. To use up or damage its women by setting them to hard wage labour in mill and workshop is probably the greatest human waste a nation could practise or permit. For some of the prevailing tendencies of modern industrialism appear to be more 'costly' in their bearing upon women than on men. In regard to factory work, and all other industrial work involving a long continuous muscular or nervous strain, or, as in shop labour with its long hours of standing, medical authorities are unanimous in holding that women suffer more than men.[1] 'If a like amount of physical toil and effort be imposed on women, they suffer to a larger degree,' states Sir W. MacCormac.[2] Statistics of employment from various countries agree in showing that the amount of morbidity, as measured by the number of days lost by illness, is greater among working-women than among working-men, and that the mortality of working-women is greater than that of working-men, notwithstanding the fact that the average life of a female is longer than that of a male. Long hours and speeding-up of machinery thus evidently inflict graver organic costs on women than on men. Where piecework is in vogue, it furnishes a stronger stimulus to over-strain in women, because the general lowness of their wage gives a larger importance to each addition.

§ 3. Thus in comparing the human costs of producing a given quantity of goods, due account must be taken of the distribution of the output of productive energy among workers of different sexes, and ages. The earlier tendency of the factory system in this country, the existing tendency in some countries, has been

[1] Cf. Goldmarck, Part II, pp. –126.
[2] *Report of the Select Committee of the House of Lords on Early Closing in Shops, 1901.*

to impose a growing of monotonous and fatiguing labour upon women and children.   At certain stages in the development of industrial machinery, this has been held to be a 'profitable' economy, and in many processes of hand labour subsidiary to the factory system it still survives.   Though legislation and other influences have done much to check the worst injuries of child employment in factories and workshops in more civilised communities, a great amount of human cost is still incurred under this head.   Child half-timers are still used in considerable numbers in textile factories, while the vast expansion of distributive work has sucked into premature wage-earning immense numbers of boys who ought to be at school.   It is probable that the net tendency of British industry in recent years has been towards a slow reduction of the more injurious and 'costly' forms of female employment.   Though an enormous number of females are engaged in work the hours and hygienic conditions of which escape legal regulation, probably a growing proportion of employed women come under an economy of shorter hours.   The drudgery of domestic service engages a less number of women, while the opening of a larger variety of employments both in manufacture and in commerce has somewhat improved their power to resist the excessive pressure of machine-conditions.   The recent organised attack upon the 'sweated industries', however, reveals the fact that at the lower level of many trades a great mass of oppressive and injurious labour is extorted from working-women.   Certain forms of new mechanical labour, not involving heavy muscular fatigue, but taxing severely the nervous system, are occupying a large number of women.   The type-writer and the telephone have not yet been brought into conformity with the demands of health.   Though machinery is generally bringing in its wake restrictions on hours of labour, the normal work-day of factory, office and shop still imposes a gravely excessive strain upon women employees.   No small proportion of this excessive cost of women's work, however, is attributable to legal, professional, or conventional restrictions, which, precluding women from entering many skilled and lucrative employments, compel them to compete in low-skilled and overstocked labour-markets. The social waste of such sex discrimination is two-fold.   Even in

trades and professions for which men have usually a greater aptitude than women, some women can perform the work better and
more easily than some men, and, if they are denied equal opportunity of access, the work is done worse or at a greater human cost.
The refusal to admit women into the learned professions upon
equal terms with men undoubtedly involves a loss to society of
some of the finest service of the human intellect, while it en-
trusts some of the skilled and responsible work, thus denied to
women, to relatively ignorant and incompetent men. The other
human cost is perhaps even heavier. For the excessive competition, to which women are thus exposed in the occupations left
to them, depresses the remuneration in most instances below
the true level of physical efficiency, induces or compels excessive
hours of labour, breaks down the health of women-workers and
injures their life.

§ 4. This general survey shows that the human 'costs' of labour are closely associated in most cases with that subdivision
and specialisation of activities which takes its extreme form in
machine tending and which conforms most closely to mere 'repetition' as distinguished from the creative branches of production. But this identification of 'repetition' and human costs
cannot be pressed into a general law. For reflection shows that
repetition or routine does not always carry cost, and that on the
other hand some labour which has considerable variety is very
costly. Healthy organic life permits, indeed requires, a certain
admixture of routine or repetition with its more creative functions. A certain amount of regular rhythmic exercise of the
same muscles and nerve-centres yields vital utility and satisfaction. In some sports this exercise may be carried so far as to
involve considerable elements of fatigue and endurance which
are offset during their occurrence by the sense of personal prowess and the interest of achievement, This sentimental zest of
endurance may notoriously be carried to extremes, injurious to
the physical organism. Moreover, a certain amount of narrow
physical routine often furnishes a relief element for the tired
nerves or brain. Digging or knitting, though intolerable as a
constant employment, may furnish by their very physical routine an organic benefit when applied as a recreation. The same,

indeed, is true of most other not too taxing forms of manual or mental routine labour, especially if they contain some obvious utility. Some slight element of skill seems needed for certain natures, but a bare uninteresting repetition commonly suffices.

Such considerations dispose of the assumption that all repetition or routine in productive work is necessarily indicative of human cost and carries no organic utility or satisfaction. It is only when repetition is extended so as to engage too large a share of the time and energy of a human being that it involves a cost.

So, on the other hand, it is not the case that all labour containing variety and opportunity for skill is costless and organically good. Take for a notable example agricultural labour. Irregularity of soil and weather, the changes and chances of animal and vegetable life, the performance of many different processes, remove such work from the category of exact routine. Yet most of the labour connected with agriculture is, under the actual conditions of its performance, heavy, dull and joyless. In each process there is usually enough repetition and monotony to inflict fatigue, and the accumulation of separate fatigues in a long day's work, unalleviated by adequate personal interest in the process or its product, makes a heavy burden of cost.

The same holds of other departments of industry where some inherent elements of skill and interest are found. The total burden of effort given out in a long day's work, continued week after week, year after year, under the conditions of wagedom, greatly outweighs these technical advantages. Duration and compulsion cancel most, though not all, of the superiority of such work over machine tending, or clerking. A little labour in any of the handicrafts, in machine-running, the management of motor-cars or boats, in gardening and other modes of agriculture, serves as a pleasant pastime when undertaken as a voluntary and occasional employment. Make it regular, continuous, compulsory, and the enjoyment soon vanishes. The very elements of interest for the casual amateur often constitute the heaviest cost for the worker who lives by doing this and nothing else. Take motor-driving for an example. The quick exercise of nerve and muscle, the keenness of eye, wrist and attention, required to drive easily, quickly and safely, amid traffic or in a tangle of roads, gives nerve and interest to driving as a recreation. But this multiplication of little strains and risks, accumulating in a long day's work, and undertaken day after day, in all conditions of health, disposition and weather, soon passes from an agreeable and stimulating exercise into a toilsome drudgery.

Consideration of the work in the distributive trades, wholesale and retail, which absorb an ever-growing proportion of our wage-earners, is most instructive for understanding the respective parts played by specialisation, duration, and compulsion in the human costs. Machinery has little direct control over the work of these clerks, warehousemen, shop-assistants, typists, etc.: their work contains constant little elements of variety in detail, and a moderate amount of it imposes no fatigue. But the scope afforded for personal skill or achievement is insufficient; most of it is unmeaning and uninteresting so far as useful results are concerned; it involves constant obedience to the orders of another; and it is unduly prolonged.

§ 5. We are now in a position to sum up the results of our general analysis of the human costs of labour, in which Tarde's distinction between creation and imitation or repetition was our starting point. So far as the merely or mainly physical costs are concerned, the muscular and nervous strain and fatigue, excessive repetition is a true description of the chief cause. Machine tending at a high pace for a long working-day is in itself the most 'costly' type of labour, and, in so far as a machine controls the sort and pace of work done by a human being, these 'costs' accumulate. But most work is not so directly controlled by machinery, and yet is so highly specialised that the routine constantly over-taxes with fatigue the muscles, nerves and attention. The duration and pace of such labour are usually such as to heap up heavy costs of physical wear and tear and of physical discomforts.

But the antithesis of creation and imitation or repetition has a different significance for the interpretation of physical costs. There it is not so much the absence of novelty involved in repetition, as the absence of personal liberty and spontaneity that counts most heavily. There are, in fact, few sorts of necessary productive labour which a man is not prepared to do for himself, with some measure of personal satisfaction, if he has within his own control the performance of this task and the result. But when another's will and purpose supersede his own, prescribing actions to be done under conditions of time, place and manner, determined by that other, this servitude to another's will is always irksome and may be degrading. The human cost of most domestic service lies largely here. The work itself has more detailed variety and interest than most, and where the housewife herself does it, it often furnishes a net fund of human satisfaction. But the moral and intellectual costs of a hired servant, compelled to obey the arbitrary and capricious orders of a mistress, and to suppress her own will, tastes and inclinations in the execution of her task, are often very heavy. In a smaller degree this applies to all wage-earners engaged in any work where scope for their free volition is technically feasible. To substitute another's will for one's own, in matters where one has a will, is always a human cost. That cost, however, need not be great. When a worker is a unit of labour in some great business, his actions conforming to rules which, however troublesome, belong to the system, the consciousness of loss of liberty is far less than when the changing will of a personal employer operating amid the details of his work is the instrument of discipline. A shop-girl in a large business has a feeling of greater independence than a domestic servant, a factory-hand than a shop-girl, while the low wage of home-workers is in part attributable to the removal of the worker from the immediate domination of the employer's will.

§ 6. In assessing the psychical elements of cost, it is well to distinguish those related to a loss of liberty, or an encroachment upon personality, from those which are the conscious results or counterparts of the physical strains. For the enlargement of certain of these psychical costs is an exceedingly important factor in what is called 'industrial unrest'. This irksomeness of narrowly specialised labour and of the 'enslaving' conditions of the ordinary working life grows with the growth of intelligence and sensibility among the working-classes. Under the older order, of accepted class distinctions and economic status, implicit obedience to the employer's will carried no conscious moral cost. A new sense of personal dignity and value has now arisen in the better educated grades of workers which interferes with arbitrary modes of discipline. When they are called upon to do work in a way which appears to them foolish, injurious, or inequitable, a sense of resentment is aroused which smoulders through the working week as a moral cost. With every widening of education there comes, moreover, a discontent not merely with the particular conditions of the labour, but with the whole system, or set of conditions, which addicts so large a proportion of their working hours and energies to the dull heavy task by which they earn their living. So too the narrow limitation in the choice of work which the local specialisation of industry involves, becomes a growing grievance. The 'conditions of labour' for themselves and others, taken as a whole, are realised as an invasion and a degradation of their humanity, offering neither stimulus nor opportunity for a man to throw 'himself' into his work. For the work only calls for a fragment of that 'self' and always the same fragment. So it is true that not only is labour divided but the labourer. And it is manifest that, so far as his organic human nature is concerned, its unused portions are destined to idleness, atrophy, and decay.

This analysis of the conditions may seldom be fully realised in the consciousness of the worker. But education has gone far enough to make them real factors of working-class discontent. They constitute a large motive in the working-class movement which we may call the revolt of the producer against the excessive human costs of his production.

This is the great and serious indictment against the economy of division of labour. Associated with it is the charge that the worker in one of these routine subdivided processes has no appreciation of the utility or social meaning of his labour. He does not himself make anything that is an object of interest to him. His contribution to the long series of productive processes that go to turn out a commodity may be very valuable. But, as he cannot from his little angle perceive the coöperative unity of the productive series, it means nothing to his intelligence or heart.

So not only does the performance of his task afford him no satisfaction, but its end or object is a matter of indifference to him. There is this vital difference between the carpenter who makes a cupboard or a door, fits it into its place and sees that it is good, and the bricklayer's labourer who merely mixes mortar and carries bricks upon a hod. A man who is not interested in his work, and does not recognise in it either beauty or utility, is degraded by that work, whether he knows it or not. When he comes to a clear consciousness of that degradation, the spiritual cost is greatly enhanced. It is true that specialisation in labour is socially useful, and that, if that specialisation does not encroach too largely upon the energy and personality of the individual worker, he is not injured but helped by the contribution to social wealth which his special work enables him to make. Larger enlightenment as to the real meaning and value of his work, and the sense of social service which should follow, may indeed be expected to reduce considerably the irksomeness of its present incidence. But it can do so only upon two conditions. In the first place, the duration and strain upon his physical and moral nature must be diminished. Secondly, the general conditions both of labour and of its remuneration must be such as to lead him to recognise that the discipline which it enjoins is conducive to a larger liberty, viz. that of willing coöperation with his fellows in the production of social welfare. As yet the attainment of these conditions has not kept pace with the new desires and aspirations which have grown so rapidly among the rank and file of workers in the advanced industrial countries. Hence a new burden of spiritual costs, expressing an increased divergence between conscious aspirations and the normal conditions of the worker's lot. The education of the town worker, the association with his fellows in large workshops, the life of the streets, the education of the school, the newspaper, the library, the club, have made him increasingly sensitive to the narrowness and degradation of excessive routine in joyless labour.

CHAPTER VIII

§ 1. So far, in discussing the human 'costs' of production, we have confined our attention to the activities of body and mind directly operative in producing marketable goods or services, grading them from the creative and generally 'costless' work of the artist and inventor to the repetitive and 'costly' work of the routine manual labourer. We now proceed to examine the human costs involved in the processes of providing the capital which coöperates with labour in the various productive operations. The economic 'costs', for which payment is made out of the product to capital, are two, risk-taking and saving. What are the human costs involved in these economic costs?

To clear the ground for this enquiry it will be well to begin by making plain the sense in which risk-taking and saving are 'productive' activities. Neither of them is 'work' in the ordinary organic sense of the application of muscle or nervous energy to the production of wealth. Both would rather be considered as activities of the human will and judgment which increase the efficiency of the directly productive operations. Their productivity may thus be regarded as indirect. But it is none the less real and important on that account. For unless there was postponement of some consumption which might have taken place, and the application of the non-consumptive goods, which this postponement enabled to come into existence, to uses involving risks of loss, 'work' would be very unproductive in comparison with what it is.

Risk-taking, the giving up of a present certain utility or satisfaction for the chance of a larger but less certain satisfaction in the future, is, we know, the essence of business enterprise. Such enterprise by no means always entails a human cost. In industry, as in all human functions, experiments, involving risk, are frequently a source of vital interest and of conscious satisfaction. There are two roots of this satisfaction, the staking of one's judgment and skill in forecasting and determining future events, and the actual joy of hazard. The former is a common trait of intelligent personality, the latter a powerful, though less general motive, involving a 'sporting' interest in life. The spirit of adventure applied to business, enhances the conscious values. Whether it be motived by some physical restlessness or by some element of faith, it must be accounted an organic good, alike as means and end. If all the risk-taking involved in current industry were of this nature, it would not then figure in our bill of human costs, but on the other side of the account. But where the conditions of actual business impose elements of risk that are either in kind or magnitude compulsory, not voluntary, not only does no satisfaction attend the taking of these risks, but considerable loss and suffering may accrue. Risks that are either great in themselves or great in relation to the capacity to bear them are frequently required by the conditions of modern business enterprise. The men who undergo these risks do not deliberately or with express intention stake their faith and foresight on a game of gain or loss, or even enter into the risks with the gambler's zest. They undergo these risks because they cannot help themselves, and the anxiety attendant on these risks is often one of the heaviest psychical and physical costs of the business man.

§ 2. In analysing risk-taking as a special cost of capital, I must guard against one misunderstanding. Risk-taking, of both sorts, humanly good and humanly bad, is not of course by any means confined to administration of capital. Everyone who, either by choice or by the necessity of his situation, devotes his personal energies to making any product for the market, or to improving some personal capacity with a view to its productive use, incurs risks. In some cases the risks may not indeed entail real human waste, as where the artist or inventor speculates with his creative faculty. Or the professional man, preparing for his career, may willingly and with zest enter a competition in which prizes are few. Men equipped with vigorous intellect and determination will get out of the struggle for professional or commercial success a satisfaction of which the risk of failure is a necessary condition. But for most men a small quantum of hazard suffices. A little risk may stimulate but a larger risk will depress efficiency. A doctor, a lawyer, an engineer is willing to put his natural and acquired ability against those of his fellows in a fair field where the chances of success are reasonably large. But when the risks are so numerous and so incalculable as they are to-day in most professional careers, the anxiety they cause must be accounted a heavy human cost. The same applies to the career of most modern business men. It also constitutes a new and growing cost of labour.

For though it may be true that the actual risks of a working life, personal or economic, are no greater than in former times, the emotional and intellectual realisation of these risks is growing. Education enables and compels the intelligent workman to understand the precarious nature of his livelihood, and his growing sensibility accumulates in 'worry'. This is certainly one of the main sources of 'industrial unrest'.

But though risk-taking thus enters as a human cost into the life of other owners of productive powers, we do right to accord it special attention in relation to the supply of capital. For in the provision of all forms of capital, and in the payment for its use, risk-taking is an element of primary importance, and, though in theory separable from the act of abstinence, postponement, or waiting, which comes into prominence as the direct psychical cost of saving, it is not separable in industrial practice.

§ 3. Let us first examine the economic costs involved in the provision of industrial capital. That process consists in making, or causing to be made, non-consumable goods, which are useful for assisting the future production of consumable goods, instead of making, or causing to be made, directly consumable goods. We need not discuss at length the shallow criticism pressed by some socialists to the effect that since labour makes all goods whether non-consumable or consumable, the only economic and human cost of providing these forms of capital is the productive energy of labour. For the decision and effort of mind or will, which determines that non-consumables shall be made instead of consumables, proceeds not from the labour employed in making them, but from the owners of income who decide to save instead of spending. This decision to save instead of spending is the economic force which causes so much of the productive power of labour to occupy itself in making non-consumables. It is of the first importance that the ordinary business man, to whom 'saving' is apt to mean putting money in a bank, or buying shares, shall realise the concrete significance of his action. What he is really doing is causing to be made and to be maintained some addition to the existing fabric of material instruments for furthering the future production of commodities. This is not, as it may at first appear, a single act of choice, the determination to use a portion of one's income, say £100, in paying men to make steel rails or to put up a factory chimney, instead of paying them to make clothes, furniture, or wine for one's current consumption. The effort of postponement, or the preference of uncertain future for certain present consumables, necessary for supplying capital, if it is an effort, is a continuous one lasting all the time the capital is in use. The critic who asks, why a single 'act of abstinence' which is past and done with should be rewarded by a perpetual payment of annual interest, fails to realise that, so far as saving involves a serviceable action of the saver, it goes on all the time that the saver lies out of the full present enjoyment of his property, i. e. as long as his savings continue to function as productive instruments.

This view, of course, by no means begs the question whether there is of necessity and always some human cost or sacrifice involved in such a process of saving. It is, indeed, clear that a good deal of capital may be supplied without any human costs either in postponement of current satisfaction or in risk-taking. The squirrel stores nuts by an organic instinct of economy against the winter, as the bear stores fat. The thrifty housewife lays up provisions by a calculation hardly less instinctive against the probable requirements of the family in the near future. The balancing of future against present satisfaction, involved in such processes, cannot be considered as involving any human cost, but rather some slight balance of utility. I am certainly in no sense the loser in that I do not lay out all my income the same day that I receive it in purchasing immediate satisfaction. Why I am not the loser is evident. The first 5 per cent of my income I can perhaps spend advantageously at once upon necessaries and comforts which contribute immediately to my welfare. But if I know the sum has got to last me for six months, it will evidently pay me in organic welfare to spread nearly all the rest in a series of expenditures over the whole period, so that I may have these necessaries and comforts all the time. If my income is no more than just sufficient to keep me in full health, i. e. in providing vital 'necessaries', organic welfare demands a quite even expenditure, entailing the proper quantity of postponement. If there is anything over for expenditure on unnecessaries, this will not be quite evenly spread over the six months. For any comforts it affords appear to bring more pleasure if enjoyed now than in three or six months' time.[1] And, besides, there is the question of uncertainty of life, upon the one hand, and the risk of being unable to get hold of the future comforts when I may want them. This depreciation of future as compared with present satisfaction and these risks will properly induce me to grade downwards the expenditure on comforts during the period in question. But in this laying out of my income, so as to secure for myself the maximum of satisfaction and utility,[2] there is no human cost or sacrifice. On the contrary, any failure to 'save' or 'postpone' might be attended by a heavy cost. Many a savage has died of starvation because he has gorged to repletion instead of storing food to tide him over till he gets possession of a new supply. Thus this simplest economy of saving, the spreading of consumption over a period of time, is evidently costless.

§ 4. Now, though the saving which consists in keeping stores of consumables for future consumption does not furnish what would be called capital, and so does not come directly within the scope of our particular enquiry into 'costs of capital,' it gives a useful test for the economy of saving under modern capitalism. The modern saver does not, indeed, usually keep in his possession for future consumption a store of consumable goods. It would

---

[1] Observe that this appearance is illusory. The maximum of organic utility would probably involve an even expenditure of all the elements of income without allowance for my preference of present over future.

[2] It may be urged that, even in respect of necessaries, there will be some discount for future as compared with present consumption. But in any class of civilised men, whose income is paid at long intervals, this discount will be very small and may be ignored.

be inconvenient to store them, many of them are by nature perishable and so incapable of storage. Besides, modern industry affords him a way of making industrial society store them for him, or, more strictly, makes it produce a constant supply of fresh consumables to which he can get access. Nay, it provides still better for his needs, for it enables him, by postponing some present consumption to which he is entitled, not merely to take out of the constant social supply the full equivalent of his postponed consumption at any time he chooses, but to receive an additional small regular claim upon other consumptive or productive goods, called interest.

This extra payment was regarded by the classical economists as a cost or price paid for an effort of abstinence. More recent economists have usually chosen to substitute for abstinence 'waiting' or some equally colourless term. But abstinence is better, for it does suggest a painful effort involving some human cost, some play of motives naturally adverse to saving which requires to be overcome by a positive economic payment. Thus, not merely the economic, but the moral or human necessity of interest is best asserted.

This abstinence or postponement of possible present consumption of commodities is admittedly the condition or even the cause of the supply of the productive instruments which increase the production of future wealth and incidentally furnish the fund out of which the interest is paid. For our present purpose, then, it makes no difference whether we look at the primitive saving which stored consumables for future use, or the modern saving which causes productive instruments to be created, applied and maintained. The question whether there are human costs of saving, and what they are, is in the last resort the same in both cases.

Out of any individual, or social, income a certain amount or proportion of saving evidently may be 'costless' in the human sense. That is to say, the person or society that saves it sustains no organic loss or injury by doing so, though he may sometimes think or feel he does. If he does so think or feel, society must set a counter-weight against this false imaginary loss, in the shape of interest. But, as we have already noted, there is a good deal of saving which represents the calculated outlay over a period of time, which the owner of an income will make in his own interest. In such cases there is no human cost, and if an economic cost (interest) is defrayed, it has no human correlative. From the standpoint of human distribution of wealth it involves a waste. The organic utility to individuals of hoarding, in order, by distributing consumption over a longer period of time, to get from it a larger aggregate of goods, will thus furnish a considerable quantity of instrumental capital to modern industry. For, only by putting the postponed consumption into the form of instrumental capital, can the savers establish the lien they want upon the future output of consumables. If all the required capital could be got by this simple play of motives, the savers balancing more useful future units of consumption against less useful present units, with due allowance for risks connected with postponement, the supply of capital would be humanly 'costless.' Though some element of risk, inherent in the proceeding, would, taken by itself, carry a cost, the superior utility attaching to the postponed units of consumption, as compared with that which the same number of units would afford when added to the consumption already provided, would offset that cost, so that the arrangement, as a whole, would be costless.

§ 5. Though the method of our analysis has obliged us to approach this problem of saving as part of our enquiry into processes of production, because it is the means by which a productive factor, viz. capital, is supplied, it appertains directly to the process of consumption, or outlay of income on consumables. As the current expenditure of any member of industrial society will be distributed among a number of different purchases, contributing by natural, conventional, or purely personal connections, towards a standard of consumption endowed with maximum utility (or what the consumer takes for such), so will it be with the distribution of expenditure over points of time. Let us elevate into a clear conscious policy of calculation what is in large measure a blind instinctive conduct, and the organic relation between the two 'economies' is apparent. It involves an intricate balancing of larger future utilities, weighted by risks, against smaller present utilities not so weighted. To take the simplest instance. If, out of an income of £600 coming in this year, I

decide to consume £500 in the current expenditure of the year
and to put aside £100 for consumption in five years' time (when
I purpose to work only half-time and earn only half my present
income), I shall have estimated that the luxuries which I could
buy this year by the sixth hundred pounds expenditure are
slightly less agreeable or 'useful' to me than the comforts purchasable by the fourth hundred pounds as visualised five years
off, with an allowance for the chance that I may then be dead, or
that I may have come into a legacy which renders this postponement of consumption unnecessary. In a word, this economic ego
must be conceived as operating by a plan of outlay which, in
regard to the disposal of the current income, has a longitude and
latitude of survey and valuation. Just as the different ingredients
of present consumption make a complex organic whole with del-
icately proportioned parts, the size and form of each dictated by
the unified conception of the current standard of comfort, so
the disposition of the income over a series of points of time in
which present values of each several consumable and of the
whole standard are compared with future values, involves the
similar application of a plan for the realisation of my economic
ideal. Though a fully rational conception and calculus, either
for the composition of current expenditure or for prospective
outlays, is very rare, some half-conscious, half-instinctive calculus of the sort must be accredited to everybody.[1] So far as it
is rightly conducted by their reasoning or just instinct, it means
that, out of all or most of the members of an industrial society,
some humanly costless saving could be got, some contribution
towards the socially desirable fund of capital.

§ 6. As, then, we have seen that a certain proportion of the
various current activities, which are directly productive in the
shape of skilled and unskilled labour of brain and hand, are
either humanly costless or carry some positive fund of human
utility, so is it also with the processes of saving and risk-taking,
which go to the supply and maintenance of capital. It is not
difficult to conceive a society in which all the saving needed for
the normal development of industry might be costless. In a
primitive society, based chiefly on agriculture and simple handi-

[1] For a discussion of the nature and limitations of this calculus see Chapter XXI.

crafts, one might find the bulk of the working population earning a secure and sufficient livelihood, but with no margin of savings for instrumental capital. The comparatively small amount of such capital as was needed might be furnished mainly or entirely from the surplus incomes of a landowning or a governing class, extracted as rent or taxes. Of course, if, as would commonly occur, such rents or taxes were extorted from the peasantry by starving them or by imposing a burden of excessive toil, the human costs of such saving would be very heavy. But where a class of feudal lords drew moderate rents and fines from their tenants, or where a governing caste, such as the Incas in ancient Peru, applied to useful public works a large share of what would be called the 'economic rent' of the country, taken in taxation, such saving need entail no human cost. Nor is such costless provision of capital necessarily confined to a society living under simple industrial conditions in which comparatively little saving can be utilised. Even in an advanced industrial society the large incessant increments of capital might be provided costlessly. For if the national dividend were not only very large but so well or equably distributed, as income, that all classes had more than enough to satisfy their current organic needs, such a society would, by a virtually automatic economy, secrete stores of capital to meet the future needs of a growing population or a rising standard of consumption, as every animal organism naturally lays up stores of fat, muscle and physical energy, for future use.

A well-ordered socialistic state, were such possible, would certainly apply the industrial forces at its disposal, so as to secure an adequate supply of costless capital. After making proper provision out of current industry for the physical and moral health of the whole population, and for normal progress in personal efficiency of work and life, it would apply the surplus of industrial energy to improving the capital fabric of industry so as to provide for the production of increasing wealth, leisure, and other opportunities in the future. The calculation, as to what proportion of current industrial energy should be thus applied to preparing future economic goods to ripen for utility at various distances of time, would of course be a delicate operation. But so far as it were correctly carried out, it would be

socially costless. For on the hypothesis that adequate provision
for current needs of individual stability and progress had been
a first charge on the industrial dividend, the postponement of
any additional consumption involved in social saving could not
rightly be regarded as involving any net human cost. For, if,
instead of the surplus being saved, it had been paid out to individual members of society for current consumption, it would
ex hypothesi be unproductive of organic welfare, being applied in
an injurious and wasteful attempt to force the pace of advances
in the current standard of living. Applying the organic metaphor, one would say that it was a natural function of an organised society to secrete capital in due quantity for its future
life.

§ 7. But how far can it be held that an industrial society like
ours is so organised as 'naturally' to secrete the 'right' quantity
of capital, to provide it in a costless way, and to distribute it
economically among its various uses? A full answer to these
questions must be deferred until our analysis of the consumption
side of the national dividend enables us to assess the human
utility of the productive work to which capital is applied. At
present we must assume the utility of the £300,000,000 of savings
applied out of the aggregate national income to the enlargement
of industry, and confine ourselves to enquiring what proportion
of this amount is likely to be 'costless' and how to estimate the
'human costs' attached to the other part. It is, of course, quite
evident that such answer as can be given is of a general and speculative nature, with no pretence at quantitative exactitude.

In considering savings with an eye to discovering the human
costs, it will be well to classify these savings under three heads.
First will come what may be termed the automatic saving of the
surplus income of the rich, that which, remaining over, after all
wants, inclusive of luxuries, are satiated, accumulates for investment. The proportion of new capital proceeding from this
source will vary with the amount and regularity of such income,
its distribution among the rich, and their attitude of mind towards the expenditure of their incomes. The automatic or spontaneous character of this saving is due to the fact that no close
relation exists between progress in industry and the evolution

of a personal standard of consumption. Sudden rapid advances of income are not usually accompanied by a corresponding pressure of new personal wants tending immediately to absorb in increasing expenditure each increase of income. Though no limit can be set upon the expenses of a luxurious standard of consumption and the vagaries of personal extravagance, expensive habits take time for their establishment, and in a progressive industrial society where skilful, or lucky, business men are making fortunes rapidly, their acquisitive power will be apt to run far ahead of their consumptive practice. Moreover, the absorption in the practice of making money evidently retards the full acquisition of habits of lavish expenditure, giving full scope to the development neither of tastes nor of opportunities. This will be particularly true of incomes growing not by regular increments but by sudden rushes. Extreme instances abound in the recent history of America. Where the quick skilful seizure of new sudden opportunities, conjoined with a general development of national resources at an abnormally rapid pace, enables a Jay Gould or a John D. Rockefeller to amass millions within a few years, a wide natural divergence is created between income and expenditure. Enormous masses of unspent income thus roll up into capital which again continually grows by the accumulation of the unspent interest it earns. Though the number of persons in this position of financial magnitude is very few, a considerable class of successful business men in America and in every advanced European country comes into the same category as regards capacity of saving. While their personal and family expenditure may be continually rising, it will tend to keep in safe adjustment to what may be termed a conservative estimate of their income. The occasional great trading coups, the enormous profits of a commercial or financial boom, will not even tend to be assimilated in expenditure.

Wherever the economic circumstances of a country are such as to throw a large proportion of the growing wealth into the hands of a class of busy rising men, by a series of great windfalls or more or less incalculable increments, the new capital flowing from these superfluous incomes will be large. Moreover, so far as it is automatic, it will have little if any regard to rate of interest, and thus to 'social demand', so far as interest can be considered a just index of social demand.[1]

Even when the element of fluctuating or fortuitous increase of income is not present, a fairly rapid advance of income, particularly where it is 'earned' and therefore carries no presumption of indefinite continuance, will ordinarily leave a considerable margin of automatic saving. This will be larger where the standard of living is already established on a high level. For though certain curious psychological traits seem to show an extraordinary concentration of personal interest in the extravagances which give personal distinction in 'society', the low pressure of organic utility, or the emergence of positive disutility inherent in many of these forms of luxury, must be considered to exercise some check. Putting the matter simply, one would say that real primary human needs are more readily assimilated in a standard of consumption than purely conventional or positively injurious modes of expenditure. So, making every allowance for the depravity of tastes and the zest for competitive extravagance, it will remain true that the classes with large incomes will tend to contribute to capital a large amount of surplus income by a process of automatic accumulation.

For such saving there is neither an economic nor a human cost involved: the interest it receives is in the economic sense as much a 'surplus' as the rent of land. Not merely is there no human cost, there is a positive human utility in such saving, for it is an instinctive rejection of the injurious effort to incorporate this surplus in a current expenditure already adequate to satisfy all felt wants, good or bad.

It is likely that a large and a growing proportion of the total volume of saving in England and in the Western world is of this order. For though it may not be generally true that the rich are growing richer and the poor poorer, it is probably true that both a larger quantity and a larger proportion of the national income are in the hands of rich and well-to-do business men whose means have been advancing faster than their expenditure.

---

[1] 'So ingrained is the habit of accumulation among the prosperous classes of modern society, that it seems to proceed irrespective of the rate of interest.' Taussig, *Principles of Economics*, Vol. II, p. 27.

§ 8. So much for the automatic saving of the rich. We have next to take into account the admittedly large contribution of the classes who in respect of income are 'middle'. This comprises the great majority of families engaged in the directive work of manufacture and commerce, and almost the whole of the upper grades of the professional and official classes in such a country as ours, as well as a considerable number of persons of moderate 'independent' means. A certain amount of conscious 'thrift' is traditional in these classes. It is by no means automatic, but involves for the most part some conscious sacrifice of current satisfaction in favour of a greater estimated future satisfaction to the saver or his family. The motives which influence such saving, alike in its amount and its application as capital, are complex and various. But the sacrifice ascribed to such saving cannot be assumed to involve any economic cost, in the sense that it requires the payment of economic interest to evoke it. Still less can it be assumed to involve a human cost. A good deal of this middle-class saving, though less automatic than the savings of the rich, is a calculated postponement of some expenditure which might purchase present comforts or luxuries, in order to make provision for the purchase of necessaries or conveniences at some future time. In a word, it is of the nature of the 'stocking' saving, which the better-to-do peasants have always practised before the opportunities of profitable and fairly safe investment were open to them. Though utilised to earn interest, the saving would be made just the same if no objective interest were attainable, provided it were tolerably secure against pillage or destruction. Risk counts for more than interest in such saving, and the bulk of the so-called interest which such savings demand, as a condition of loan or investment, is not true interest but insurance. But in practice inseparable from such saving is that undertaken with the direct object of earning interest upon the capital. A great deal of middle-class saving, and some saving of the rich class would not take place without the hope of receiving interest. If no interest were attainable, though some saving might take place, in order to provide against the possibility of a total collapse of current earning power and a consequent deprivation of the necessaries of life, there would be little disposi-

tion to give up any present free expenditure on comforts in order
to provide for future comforts which might not be wanted, or
which, in consequence of loss of savings, might not be procurable.
A positive bonus in the shape of interest seems necessary to evoke
this latter saving. The operation of this bonus as an inducement
is, however, very complex. It might appear at first sight obvious that, the larger the bonus in the shape of rate of interest,
the greater the aggregate of saving it would evoke. So far as
non-automatic saving is motived by a general desire to be better
off in the future, in order to attain a standard of consumption
and of social consideration which denote success and satisfy personal ambition, or in order to bequeath a large estate to one's
family, higher interest will tend to evoke a corresponding increase of saving in those whose current incomes enable them to
save considerable sums without encroaching upon their established standard of comfort. Young or middle-aged men, of an aspiring nature and with rising incomes, will undoubtedly save more
if they see a handsome return on their investments. But, as most
men will realise more clearly and feel more keenly these future
economic and social gains if the full fruits of such savings will be
reaped by themselves, not by their heirs, ageing men will be
likely to respond less freely to this motive. Present comfort,
security, and power, will mean more to them than a future liber-
ality of living which they can only hope to enjoy for a few years,
if at all. The amount, therefore, of the acceleration of saving
achieved by a rise of interest will depend a good deal upon the
relative importance this general desire to be better off possesses
as an inducement to save. That relative importance again will
depend a good deal upon whether the economic and social conditions of the community place considerable numbers of younger
business or professional men in a position of rising incomes and
of considerable saving power, or, on the contrary, confine such
surpluses chiefly to older men.

If, instead of taking as our motive a general desire to be better
off, we take a desire to save in order to make some limited
specific provision, as for example to buy an annuity of £100, the
effect of a higher rate of interest upon volume of saving is likely
to be different. Though it may serve to quicken in some degree

the pace at which the sum required will be amassed, it will reduce the absolute amount of saving. For when interest is higher,
the capital sum required to yield an annuity of £100 a year will
be less than before. Against this, however, must be set the fact
that, when a definite sum is needed in order to pay off some debt,
or to furnish a sufficiency for retirement, a high rate of interest
may be required in order to make this saving possible or certain.
If a man cannot save enough to attain such definite object, he
will not save at all, for an insufficient amount will be held futile;
whereas, if a rise of interest gives him a good prospect of saving
the required amount, he will put forth the effort.

§ 9. But making due allowance for counteracting motives, it
is tolerably certain that a rise of interest, showing any signs
of continuance, will stimulate an increase of 'motived' saving,
though by no means a proportionate increase. Thus it will appear that, so far as this large section of middle-class saving is
concerned, some definite measurable economic costs, in the sense
of deprivation of current consumption, are involved, requiring
compensation in the shape of interest. But the question which
concerns us is whether there are human costs corresponding to
and involved in these economic costs. In answering this question, it is not enough to point to the admitted fact that this saving involves the failure to satisfy some current desire for increased
consumption. It has to be considered whether the sacrifice of
current 'satisfaction' is really a sacrifice of welfare, either from
the standpoint of the saver, or of the society of which he is a member. For we have not taken the view that the personal transient
desires and valuations of consumers are a final criterion, either
of personal or social welfare. If then the saving evoked by paying interest merely means that certain fairly well-to-do folks abstain from comforts or luxuries, which, though agreeable and inno-
cent, carry no organic benefit, there is no human cost, or even
if there is some slight cost, it may be offset by the individual or
social benefit resulting from the postponement of consumption.
A large proportion of motived middle-class saving undoubtedly
falls within this category. But by no means all. A good deal
of lower middle-class saving eats into certain factors of humanly
serviceable expenditure, particularly expenditure in education

of the young. Frequently it injures the free life of the home by the constant pressure of niggling economies, which, though not perhaps injurious in the particular privations they impose, leave no margin for the small pleasures and amenities which have a vital value. Even though we assume that such saving brings, in the ownership of property and the interest it yields, a full vital compensation to the individual who saves, it by no means follows that it is socially justified, when a true criterion of social welfare is applied. Take for instance the saving which is diverted from expenditure on education, precluding the children from getting a university or professional training and turning them on the world to earn a living, less effectively equipped than they might have been. Society may be a heavy loser by its policy of evoking such thrift by means of interest, for it obtains a certain amount of material capital in place of the more valuable intellectual or moral capital which the money, expended upon education, might have yielded. Even regarded from the standpoint of future economic productivity, the stimulation of this sort of saving is likely to be injurious.

§ 10. Far graver importance attaches to this consideration when we approach the savings of the working-classes. The contribution made from this source to the flow of fresh capital, the £300,000,000 per annum, is evidently attended by heavy human costs. Very little of it can be regarded as the considered reasonable outlay over a long period of time of income not needed for current organically useful consumption. Most of it involves a stinting of the prime necessaries or conveniences of life, or of some rise in present expenditure which would promote the health or efficiency of the family. Almost the only saving made by ordinary wage-earners not attended by this human sacrifice is that applied by young workers, who having only themselves to keep, can afford to set aside some portion of their pay in full employment so as to furnish a future home, and to insure against a few special emergencies involving loss of earning power or expenses connected with death or sickness. Even such personally serviceable insurances the married worker can seldom properly afford. Though the narrower view of the economy of a self-sufficing family may appear to justify savings made out of a wage the entire present expenditure of which can be applied to purposes of organically useful consumption, the wider social standpoint does not endorse this policy. For a workman to pinch on housing, clothing, the education of his children, or upon wholesome recreation, in order to avoid worse pinching in some unforeseen but probable emergency, may be sound individual economy. But, unless society is unable from other resources at its disposal to provide against these emergencies of working-class life, it is an unsound social economy, involving a heavy net cost of social welfare. The issue is a very vital one. It may be stated in this concrete form. Most of the savings effected in this country out of a family income of 30/ or less per week, and much of the savings made out of a larger income when the worker's family is young, involve a sort of abstinence which is fraught with heavy net costs in the social economy. No part of the economically necessary fund of annual capital ought to be drawn from this sort of saving. It is literally a coining of human life into instrumental capital, and the degradation of the term 'thrift' in its application to such saving is a damning commentary upon the false standard of social valuation which endorses and approves the sacrifice. The great risks of loss which actually attend such saving, and the heavy expenses of the machinery of its collection and administration, aggravate the waste. If we ascribe £50,000,000 [1] out of the £300,000,000 to this class of savings, a proper social book-keeping would put the human costs of this working-class abstinence as a large offset to the net utility of the other £250,000,000. The forethought, endurance, and other real or supposed benefits to the character of the workers imputed to this 'thrift' can no more be regarded as a compensation for such social injury, than can the discipline and fortitude of soldiers be regarded as a testimony to the net human economy of war.

[1] This is most likely a gravely excessive estimate. Probably £30,000,000 or $1/_{10}$ of the national saving would be nearer the mark. Moreover, a large proportion of working-class savings is not destined to purposes of permanent investment but to provision for some early probable emergency, e. g. burial or unemployment which will cancel the saving. There exist no approximately reliable estimates of the amount of capital belonging to the working-classes. The usually accepted figure includes under the head of Post Office Savings Bank and Building Societies a large but unknown quantity of middle-class savings.

CHAPTER IX

HUMAN UTILITY OF CONSUMPTION

§ 1. When we turn to the other side of the account, the human utility which this £2,000,000,000 of goods and services represents, we enter a country which, as we have already recognised, Political Economy has hardly begun to explore. For though the trend of a large modern school of economists has been to find in consumption the *vis motrix* of all economic processes, and to bring close study to bear upon the pressure of consumers' wants as they operate through demand in the markets of commodities, this *volte face* in the theory of values does not render much assistance to our human valuation. For their analysis of demands does not help us to interpret expenditure in terms of human utility. As an instrument for such a purpose it is doubly defective. For, in the first place, it is concerned entirely with the actual felt wants and preferences which in fact determine purchases. In the second place, it takes for granted the existing distribution of incomes or consuming power, tracing the operation of this power of demand upon the actual economy of economic processes. Now these limitations, quite necessary for the purely economic interpretation, are not suited to our requirements.

The current standard of valuations and of choice cannot be taken as an adequate standard of individual or social welfare. Felt wants, and demands based on them, form no doubt some index of welfare, but an insufficient one.

A considerable proportion of the goods and services included in the real income which we are analysing must from our standpoint be classed not as wealth, but as 'illth', to adopt Ruskin's term. What proportion we should place in the category will of course depend upon the degree to which we hold that the actual evolution of the arts of consumption has been distorted from its 'natural' course. But everyone will admit that many sorts of marketable goods and services are injurious alike to the individuals who consume them and to society. A large proportion of the stimulants and drugs which absorb a growing share of income in many civilised communities, bad literature, art and recreations, the services of prostitutes and flunkeys, are conspicuous instances. Not merely does no human utility correspond to the economic utility ascribed to such goods, but there is a large positive disutility. The aggregate human value of a growing national income may easily be reduced by any increase in the proportion of expenditure upon such classes of goods, and tendencies of distribution which lead to such proportionate increase may even invalidate the assumption that social welfare upon the whole grows with the growth of the national dividend. We shall presently consider some of the factors in our social structure which bring about the development of definitely bad demands and bad products to satisfy them.

But just as we must write to the debit side of our human account a great many articles which figure on the credit side in ordinary economic book-keeping, so we shall be compelled to revise the comparative values attached to those articles which contain actual powers of human utility. A valuation which sets an equal value upon each part of a supply because it sells for the same sum cannot serve the purposes of a human valuation. For the amount of human utility, individual or social, attaching to the consumption of any stock of goods or services, must evidently depend in large degree upon who gets them and how much each consumer gets, that is to say upon their distribution.

The same goods figure as necessaries of life or as waste according to who gets them. Some quarters of the same wheat supply furnish life and working energy to labourers, other quarters pass unconsumed into the dustbins of the rich.

There is, moreover, a third consideration which counts in the process of converting economic into human values. As in the distribution of productive energy human economy requires an adjustment to the individual capacity of production, so in the distribution of consumptive utilities a corresponding regard must be paid to the natural or acquired capacity of the individual consumer. Some persons have greater natural capacity than others for the use or enjoyment of certain classes of goods, material or immaterial. An absolutely equal distribution of bread, or any other necessity of life, on a *per caput* basis, would evidently be a wasteful economy. What applies to the prime physical wants will apply more largely to the goods which supply 'higher' wants. For, as one ascends from the purely animal to the spiritual wants, the divergences in capacity of utilisation will grow. This does not necessarily imply very wide differences in the aggregate quantity of wealth which can be usefully consumed by different persons, because deficiencies in some tastes or capacities may be compensated by development of others. Moreover, the widest personal differences will usually lie outside the range of economic satisfaction. Yet even among economic consumers there will be considerable differences in the amount of organic service or satisfaction that different persons can get out of the same amount of goods. A noble work of art, as Ruskin insisted, has no value for primitive peasants without cultivated tastes. The finest library of serious literature has little value to-day in an ordinary English industrial town. But it is needless to multiply examples to illustrate the truth that the vital value got from any stock of consumable wealth must depend upon the capacity of those into whose hands it passes to make a good use of it. In other words, it depends upon how far the consumer has acquired the art of consumption. Nor is this merely a question of developing and cultivating sound tastes in a class or a people. It is often a matter of knowledge how to extract and utilise the utility which goods contain. It is sometimes pointed out that over 90 per cent of the heating power of coal burned in domestic fires is wasted. Improved grates, or the substitution of some central heating system, might stop a considerable portion of this waste, securing an increase of heating power and of its vital value out of each ton burned.

§ 2. Until we know then 'What are the concrete goods represented by the £2,000,000,000 income? How are they apportioned among different classes of the consuming public? How far are those who get these goods qualified to get the vital value out of them?' we cannot compute, even in general terms, the aggregate human utility they carry.

Our calculus of the human utility of consumption will thus in form and method closely correspond with our calculus of the human cost of production. Taking as the subject-matter of our analysis the goods and services constituting the real income of the nation, our analysis of production endeavoured to apply two criteria, one relating to the Arts of Production actually employed, the other to the Distribution of the productive efforts involved in the employment of these arts. Similarly, our analysis of consumption rests upon the application of like criteria to the Arts of Consumption and the Distribution of consuming power.

In the productive analysis, considerations of the methods of industry, in relation to the quantity of creative and imitative, interesting and repellent work, the use of machinery and subdivided labour, the elements of forethought, risk-taking, and organisation, length of the work-day, regularity of employment, apportionment of routine industry among the grades and classes of producers, are found to be the main determinants of the sum of human costs. A similar analysis, applied to the consideration of the standards and methods of consumption prevailing among the different grades and classes of consumers, and to the distribution of consuming power among these classes as to amount and regularity, will yield a sum of human utility.

But in approaching the arts of consumption, we find they have not developed in the same way as the arts of production.

Starting from primitive society with the practically self-sufficing family-group, where everybody took a hand in the different sorts of work and a share in the consumption of the different products, we find ourselves carried along a career of continual differentiation of labour not attended by any corresponding differentiation of consumption. Industry passes into large co-operative forms outside the single family, with constantly finer division of labour. But consumption is still chiefly carried on within the limit of the single family,[1] and, so far from being specialised, it becomes more generalised. This contrast of man

---

[1] Collective or coöperative consumption outside the home or family is of course increasing. Not only have we municipal supplies for public use, e. g. schools, libraries, museums, parks, baths, lighting, etc., but many forms of private expenditure of income on educational, recreative, philanthrophic and other coöperative modes of consumption.

as producer and consumer is of the first importance. Modern industrial evolution shows a man becoming narrower and more specialised on his producing side, wider and more various on his consuming side. As worker, he is confined to the constant repetition of some section of a process in the production of a single class of article. As consumer, he is in direct contact with thousands of different sorts of workers in all parts of the world, and by his various consumption applies a direct stimulus which vibrates through the whole industrial system. As producer he is 'the one', as consumer 'the many'.

This diverging tendency in the economic evolution of man has important human implications which will concern us later. At present it concerns us in its bearing upon the arts of consumption.

§ 3. The great complex unit of productive activities which engaged our attention was the Business. Productive economy, the amount of human cost involved in the production of a given quantity of goods, depended, as we saw, upon the structure and working of this Business. What is the consumptive unit that corresponds to the Business? It is the Family, or Home, regarded on its economic side. There is an economy of consumption in the family standard of life as important for social welfare as the economy of production in the Business. As the former stands towards costs of Production, so the other stands towards utility of Consumption. As the economy of Production chiefly consists in minimising cost, so the economy of Consumption should consist in maximising utility. But the standard of consumption has in modern times not been subjected to the same forces as have operated upon production. Though in the beginning, as we saw, both were natural, organic and related processes, the modern rationalisation of industry has not been accompanied by a corresponding rationalisation of consumption. Inventors and transformers of industry have not had their counterpart in consumption. A hundred times the quantity of thought and effort has gone into the recent evolution of a single industry, such as cotton or chemicals, that has gone into the improvement of consumption. It is not difficult to understand the reasons of the great conservatism of the consumptive arts. In primitive societies, where each family is a self-sufficing economic unit, or where division of labour is on the simplest lines, the industrial arts are almost as conservative as the methods of consumption. The adoption of a new way of working is nearly as difficult as the adoption of a new want. Custom rules both with an almost equal sway, though even at this stage its hold upon the organic feelings will be somewhat stronger on the consuming side, especially in matters of food and of family or tribal ritual. It will be a little easier to use a new sort of snare, or to change the shape of a pot or basket, than to take to a new headgear or a new way of cooking meat. But when the industrial arts have advanced a certain way, two forces combine to break the bond of custom and to encourage experiments and improved methods. While consumption continues to be carried on in a number of simple actions involving no considerable effort or conscious attention, industry has passed into a related series of processes of considerable duration and involving many separate acts of conscious effort and attention. The production of an article will thus present a far larger number of opportunities for change than its consumption, and there will be a greater likelihood that advantageous changes will be tried and adopted. A new idea of saving labour, the chance discovery of some new material, will be approved more readily than any suggestion for some new food or an unaccustomed article of clothing. For, in the former case, the reasoning faculty is of necessity alive and operative to some degree, and the gain of the change can be realised experimentally, while in the latter case, the reasoning faculty is hardly awake, and any novelty of consumption is apt to have an initial barrier of natural aversion to overcome.

But there is another reason for the easier progress of the productive costs. In proportion as work passes into the shape of an organised business, administered by an employer for profit, the control of any of its processes by primitive custom or taboo tends to disappear. For the rationalism involved in the profitable conduct of the business compels the employer to break any traditional barriers obstructing the adoption of profitable reforms. Though there are doubtless many reforms of the consumptive arts as humanly economical and profitable as any of the great industrial reforms, there is not the same concentrated motive of large immediately realised gains to urge their claims on any body of consumers. Not only are the gains from an improvement in production more immediate, more concrete and more impressive, but the risks and inconveniences of the change are largely borne by others than the reformer, viz. his employees, or his shareholders. The consumer, on the other hand, has himself to bear all risks and inconveniences involved in the abandonment of an old article or method of consumption, or the adoption of a new one. Finally, it must be remembered that the actual risks attending an innovation are greater for the consumer. For the modern producer is a skilled specialist in the particular art of production in which he is engaged, the consumer is an unskilled amateur in a more general art, possessing little knowledge and no effective power of organising for his self-defence.

§ 4. The fact that the monetary profit of producers is the principal determinant of most changes in the nature of consumables and the standards of consumption is one of the most serious sources of danger in the evolution of a healthy social economy. The present excessive control by the producer injures and distorts the art of consumption in three ways. 1. It imposes, maintains and fosters definitely injurious forms of consumption, the articles of 'illth'. 2. It degrades or diminishes by adulteration, or by the substitute of inferior materials or workmanship, the utility of many articles of consumption used to satisfy a genuine need. 3. It stimulates the satisfaction of some human wants and depresses the satisfaction of others, not according to their true utility, but according to the more or less profitable character of the several trades which supply these wants.

The prevalence of many of the most costly social evils of our time, war, drink, gambling, prostitution, overcrowding, is largely attributable to the fact that their material or trade appliances are sources of great private profit. Such trades are the great enemies of progress in the art of life, and the rescue of the consuming public from their grip is one of the weightiest problems of our time. Two methods of defence are suggested. One is the education and coöperation of consumers. But while education may do much to check the consumption of certain classes of 'illth', it can hardly enable the consumer to cope with the superior skill of the specialist producer by defeating the arts of adulteration and deterioration which are so profitable. Consumers' Leagues can perhaps do something to check adulteration and sweating, by the employment of skilled agents. But it will remain very difficult for any such private action to defeat the ever-changing devices of the less scrupulous firms in profitable trades. The recognition of these defects of private action causes an increased demand for public protection, by means of legislative and administrative acts of prohibition and inspection. The struggle of the State to stamp out or to regulate the trades which supply injurious or adulterated foods, drinks, and drugs, to stop gambling, prostitution, insanitary housing, and other definitely vicious businesses, is one of the greatest of modern social experiments. Though the protection of the consumer is in many cases joined with other considerations of public order, it is the inherent weakness of the consumer, when confronted by the resources of an organised group of producers, that is the primary motive of this State policy. How far the State protection is, or can be made effective, is a question too large for discussion here. It must suffice to observe that the conviction that the private interests of producers will continue to defeat all attempts at State regulation in socially 'dangerous trades' furnishes to socialism an argument on which there is a tendency to lay an ever greater stress.

§ 5. These reflections are necessary as preliminary to the consideration of the statics and dynamics of consumption in any nation or class. For they represent the most important class of disturbing influences in the evolution of standards of consumption.

Now in considering the proper mode of estimating the human utility contained in our £1,7co,ooo,ooo worth of 'consumables', we must consider, first, the validity of the standards of consumption in which they are incorporated. If we have grounds for believing that actual standards of consumption are moulded by the free pressure of healthy organic needs, evolving in a natural and rational order towards a higher human life, there will be a presumption favourable to the attribution of a high measure of human utility to the aggregate income. In this enquiry we may, therefore, best start by considering the evolution of wants and modes of satisfying them, as reactions of the half-instinctive, half-rational demands of man upon his environment. Human animals, placed in a given environment (with some power of moving into another slightly different one or of altering slightly that in which they are) develop standards of work and of consumption along the lines of 'survival value'. The earliest stages in the evolution of both standards, consumption and industry, must be directed by the conditions of the physical struggle for life. The modern historical treatment of origins applies this principle in the analysis of physical environments, in which Le Play and Buckle have done such valuable pioneer work, and which such thinkers as Professor Geddes have carried further in their schemes of regional survey.

Though the fundamental assumption which seems to underlie this method, at any rate in its fulness, viz. that there is only one sort of mankind and that all the differences which emerge in history, whether of 'racial' character or of institutions, are products of environment, is open to question,[1] the dominant part played by physical environment in determining the evolution of economic wants and satisfactions, is not disputed.

Like other animals, men must apply themselves to obtain out of the immediate physical environment the means of maintenance—the food, shelter and weapons, the primitive tools, which enable them to work and live at all. If we consider separately the consumptive side of this economy, we seem to grasp the idea of an evolution of a standard of consumption, moulded by the instinctive selection of means to satisfy organic needs of the individual and the species. The sorts of food will be those obtained by experiments upon the flora and fauna of the country, guided mainly by 'instinct', though some early conscious cunning of selection and of cultivation will serve to improve and increase the supplies. The clothing will consist of furs or plaited fibres got from the same natural supplies. The shelter will con-

---

[1] For the fullest and most recent exposition of this theory see Mr. J. M. Robertson's *The Evolution of States* (Watts & Co.).

sist of an easy adaptation of trees, caves or other protective provisions of nature. Even the early tools, weapons and domestic utensils, though admitting some more rational processes of selection and adaptation, will remain half-instinctive efforts to meet strong definite needs. So long as we are within this narrow range of primary animal wants, there is perhaps little scope for grave errors and wastes in standards of consumption. Doubtless mistakes of omission are possible, e. g. a tribe may fail to utilise some abundant natural supply of food which it is capable of assimilating. But such omissions will probably be rare, at any rate in cases where population comes to press upon the food supply, so evoking experiments in all natural resources. Grave errors of commission, e. g. the adoption of poisonous ingredients into the supply of food or other necessaries, will be impossible, so long as we are dealing with factors of consumption which have a definite survival value. This seems to apply, whether we attribute some instinctive wisdom or some more rational process of selection as the evolutionary motive. In either case we have substantial guarantees for the organic utility of most articles which enter the primitive standard of consumption. This view is, of course, quite consistent with the admission that in the detailed operation of this economy there will be a large accumulation of minor errors and wastes. The most accurate instinct affords no security against such losses: indeed the very strength of an animal instinct entails an inability of adaptation to eccentricities or irregularities of environment. No one can doubt this who watches the busy bee or the laborious ant pursuing their respective industries.

§ 6. If man had always lived either in a stationary or a very slowly changing environment, he would have remained a creature motived almost wholly by specific instincts along a fairly accurate economy of prescribed organic needs. The substitution of reason for a large part of these specific instincts was evoked by the necessity of adaptation to changes and chances of environment so large, swift or complex, that specific instincts were unfitted to cope with them. Hence the need for a general 'instinct' of high adaptive capacity, endowed with a power of central control operative through the brain. The net biological economy of this evolution of a central conscious 'control', in order to secure a better adjustment between organism and environment, carries us to a further admission regarding the organic value of the basic elements in a standard of consumption.

By the use of his brain man not merely selects from an indefinitely changing environment foods and other articles conducive to survival, but adapts the changing environment to his vital purposes. He alters the physical environment, so as to make it yield a larger quantity and variety of present and future goods, and he combines these goods into harmonious groups contributing to a 'standard' of consumption. In this adaptive and progressive economy, evolving new needs and new modes of satisfying old needs, shall we expect to find the same degree of accuracy, the same immunity from serious error as in the narrower statical economy of 'instinctive' animalism?

In the processes of adapting external nature for the provision of present, still more of future, goods, in discovering new wants and methods of satisfying them, and in assimilating the new wants in a standard of consumption, there will necessarily be larger scope for error. But so long as the inventive and progressive mind of man confines the changes, alike of industry and of consumption, to the sphere of simple material commodities having a close and important bearing upon physical survival, the limits of error and of waste must continue to be narrow. All such progress will require experimentation, and experiment implies a possibility of error. But at this early stage in the evolution of wants, any want, or any mode of supplying a want, which is definitely bad, will be curbed or stamped out by the conditions of the struggle for life. A tribe that tries hastily to incorporate a tasty poison in its diet must very soon succumb, as many modern instances of races exposed to the attraction of 'firewater' testify. Thus far it may be admitted that organic utility will assert its supremacy as a regulative force, not only in the rejection of the bad, but in the selection of the good. The low standard of consumption of a prosperous caveman or of a primitive pastoral family must conform to an economy of high utility. Not only would all his ingredients of food, clothes, shelter, firing and utensils, be closely conducive to physical survival, but they would be closely complementary to one another. This complementary structure of the standard of consumption follows from the organic nature of man. Unless all his organic needs are continuously met he perishes. While, therefore, he may know nothing of the distinctions which science later will discover in the necessary constituents of food, he must have worked out empirically a diet which will give him some sufficiently correct combination of proteids, carbohydrates and fats, and in the forms in which he can assimilate them. So also with his clothes, if he wears them. No savage could possibly adopt, for ordinary wear, costumes so wasteful and so inconvenient as flourish in civilised societies. Similarly with housing and utensils. And not only must the articles belonging to each group of wants be complementary, but the groups will themselves be complementary. The firing will have relation to the times and sorts of feeding: clothing and shelter will be allied in the protection they afford against weather and enemies: tools and weapons will be even more closely related.

Thus in the earlier evolution of wants, when changes, alike of ways of living and ways of work, are few and slow and have a close bearing on survival, a standard of consumption will have a very high organic value.

§ 7. But when man passes into a more progressive era, and a definite and fairly rapid process of civilisation begins, the brain continually devising new wants and satisfactions, we seem to lose the earlier guarantees of organic utility. When the standard of consumption incorporates increasing elements, not of necessaries but of material conveniences, comforts and luxuries, and adds to the satisfaction of physical desires that of psychical desires, how far may it not trespass outside the true economy of welfare? So long as the requirements of physical survival dominate the standard, it matters little whether animal instinct or some more rational procedure maintains the standard. But when these requirements lose control, and a standard of civilised human life contains ever larger and more numerous elements which carry little or no 'survival value', the possibilities of error and of disutility appear to multiply.

If civilisation, with its novel modes of living, be regarded as an essentially artificial process, in which considerations of organic welfare exercise no regulative influence, there seems no limit to the amount of disutility or illfare which may attach to the consumption of our national income. This appears, indeed, to be the view of some of our social critics. Even those who do not go so far as Mr. Edward Carpenter in diagnosing civilisation as a disease, yet assign to it a very wide departure from the true path of human progress. Indeed, it would be idle to deny that this income, not only in the terms of its distribution but also in its consumption, contains very large factors of waste and disutility, and that the higher, later elements carry larger possibilities of waste than the earlier.

But this admission must not lead us to conceive of the so-called 'artificial' factors in a standard of consumption as the products, either of chance, or of some normal perversity in the development of tastes which foists upon consumption elements destitute of human value.

For there are two possibilities to bear in mind. The first is that even in the higher, less material, more 'artificial' ingredients of consumption, the test of 'survival value' may still in some measure apply. A too comfortable or luxurious mode of life may impair vitality, lessen the desire or capacity of parenthood, or may introduce some inheritable defect injurious to the stock. Such results may follow, not merely from bad physical habits, but from what are commonly accounted good intellectual habits. For it is believed that the high cerebration of an intellectual life is inimical to human fertility. Again, so far as sexual attractions determine marriage and parenthood, modes of living which either impair or overlay the points of attraction will continue to be eliminated by natural selection. Habits of living, which damage either manliness or womanliness will thus continue to be curbed by Nature.

But Nature may possess another safeguard of a more general efficacy. For any intelligible theory of evolution, either of an individual organism or a species, involves the presence and operation of some central power which, working either through particular instincts, as in lower animals, or largely through a coordinating 'reason', as in man, not only conserves but develops. This organic purpose, or directive power, cannot be regarded as confined to mere physical survival, either of the individual or the species. It must also be considered as aiming at development, a fuller life for individual and species. Now the evolution of human wants and standards of consumption must be regarded as an aspect of this wider process of development. Whatever measure, then, of control be accorded to the central directive power in organic development, must operate to determine economic wants and economic standards of life. If such directive action were infallible, securing, through the central cerebral control, a completely economical policy of conservation and development, no problems of a distinctively social or moral character would arise. The existence of error, waste, sin, attests the fallibility of this directive power. Aiming to keep the individual and the species to lines of conduct that are psycho-physically beneficial, its directions are either falsified or set aside by the force of some particular impulse or emotion, usurping or defying the central authority. The liability to such error and waste appears to grow *pari passu* with organic development. As reasoning man with his more complex life has more chances of going wrong than lower animals guided by instincts along a narrow life, so with each advance in the complexity of human life these chances of error multiply. The explanation of this expanding scope for error is not that reason is an inferior instrument to instinct. Even in matters of 'life and death', with which animal nature is primarily concerned, reason must be accounted in the main an improvement upon instinct. For though a particular instinct works more easily and accurately in an absolutely uniform environment, reason deals more successfully with eccentricities and changes. Its essential quality is this superior adaptiveness. Therefore, in handling an environment, which not only is various and ever changing by its own nature, but is made more various and more changing by the interference of man, the human reason must work more successfully even for purposes of physical survival than any array of instincts could. In the struggle for a sufficient regular supply of food, or in the war against microbes, the rationalism of modern science and industry performs 'survival' work for which the exactitude of animal instinct is essentially unfitted.

The view then that error and waste necessarily increase with the development of human society is not based upon any inferiority of reason to instinct. It is due to the fact that, as humanity evolves further, a smaller proportion of its total energy is needed for mere survival, and a larger proportion is free for purposes of specific and individual progress. Now, the natural economy for survival, whether working by instinct or by reason, is far more rigorously enforced than the economy for progress. So long as the arts of industry are so crude as to absorb almost all the available work of man in provision for survival, the scope for waste is rigorously circumscribed. But as industry develops to a stage that yields a considerable 'surplus' beyond the needs for mere survival, the possibility of waste increases. For, then, it becomes possible for individuals, or groups within a community, to divert to purposes of excessive personal enjoyment the surplus of productive power which, 'economically' directed by Nature or Reason, would have served to raise the general level of well-being.

The widest aspect of this phenomenon does not concern us here. It will be the subject of later commentary. We are here concerned only to explain why it is likely that, as wealth grows, waste also will grow, and why the higher standards of comfort in a nation or a class will contain a larger proportion of socially wasteful or injurious goods. Nature's guarantee of the sound organic use of the basic constituents of a standard of consumption does not extend with the same force to the conveniences, comforts and luxuries built upon this basis. Though one need not assume that no organically sound instinct of selection or rejection operates in the adoption of new comforts or luxuries, that natural safeguard must certainly be accounted weaker and less reliable. As we study presently the actual modes by which the higher ingredients are adopted into a class standard, we shall see that this assumption is borne out by experience, and that considerations of organic welfare play a rapidly diminishing part in determining the spread of most of the higher forms of material and intellectual consumption.

CHAPTER X

§ 1. We may now apply these general considerations regarding the evolution of wants to class and individual standards of consumption. In a concrete class standard of consumption we may conveniently distinguish three determinant factors: 1st. The primary organic factor, the elements in consumption imposed by general or particular conditions of physical environment, such as soil, climate, in relation to physical needs. 2nd. The industrial factor, the modifications in organic needs due directly or indirectly to conditions of work. 3rd. The conventional factor, those elements in a standard of consumption not based directly upon considerations of physical or economic environment but imposed by social custom.

So far as the first factor is concerned, we are for the most part in the region of material necessaries in which, as we have already seen, the organic securities for human utility are strongest. Where any population has for many generations been settled in a locality, it must adapt itself in two ways to the physical conditions of that locality. Its chief constituents of food, clothing, shelter, etc. must be accommodated to all the more permanent and important conditions of soil, climate, situation and of the flora and fauna of the country. A tropical people cannot be great meat-eaters or addicted to strong drinks, though the materials for both habits may be abundant. An arctic people, on the other hand, must find in animal fats a principal food, and in the skins of animals a principal article of clothing. In a country where earthquakes frequently occur, the materials and structure of the houses must be light. In the same country the people of the mountains, the valleys, the plains, the sea-shores, will be found with necessary differences in their fundamental standard of consumption. It is, indeed, self-evident that physical environment must exercise an important selective and rejective power represented in the material standard of consumption. So far as man can modify and alter the physical environment, as by drainage, forestry, or the destruction of noxious animals or bacteria, he may to that extent release his standard of consumption for this regional control.

Primitive man, again, and even most men in comparatively advanced civilisations, are confined for the chief materials of food, shelter and other necessaries, to the resources of their country or locality. They must accommodate their digestions and their tastes to the foods that can be raised conveniently and in sufficient quantities in the neighbourhood: they must build their houses and make their domestic and other utensils out of the material products within easy reach. The early evolution of a standard of necessary consumption, working under this close economy of trial and error, appears to guarantee a free, natural, instinctive selection of organically sound consumables.

The primary physical characteristics of a country, also of course, affect with varying degrees of urgency those elements in a standard of consumption not directly endowed with strong survival value, those which we call conveniences, comforts, luxuries. The modes and materials of bodily adornment, the styles of domestic and other architecture, religious ceremonies, forms of recreation, will evidently be determined in a direct manner by climatic and other physical considerations.

Recent civilisation, with its rapid extensive spread of communications, and its equally rapid and various expansion of the arts of industry, has brought about an interference with this natural economy which has dangers as well as advantages. The swift expansion of commerce brings great quantities of foods and other consumables from remote countries, and places them at the disposal of populations under conditions which give no adequate security for organic utility of consumption. Under an economy of natural selection exotics are by right suspect, at any rate until time has tried them. The incorporation of articles such as tea and tobacco in our popular consumption has taken place under conditions which afford no proper guarantee of their individual utility, or against the bad reactions they may cause in the whole complex standards of consumption.

The back stroke of this commercial expansion is seen in such occurrences as the deforestation of great tracts of country and the alteration of the climatic character, with its effects upon the lives of the inhabitants. But though certain errors and wastes attend these processes of commercialism and industrialism, they must not be exaggerated. There is no reason to hold that mankind in general has been so deeply and firmly specialised in needs and satisfactions by local physical conditions that he cannot advantageously avail himself of the material products of a wider environment. Though the digestive and assimilative apparatus may not be so adaptable as the brain, there is no ground for holding that conformity during many generations to a particular form of diet precludes the easy adoption of exotic elements often containing better food-properties in more assimilable forms. A Chinese population, habituated to rice, can quickly respond in higher physical efficiency to a wheat diet, nor is the fact that bananas are a tropical fruit detrimental to their value as food for Londoners.

How far the purely empirical way in which foods and other elements in a necessary standard have been evolved can be advantageously corrected or supplemented by scientific tests, is a question remaining for discussion after the other factors in standards of consumption have been brought under inspection.

§ 2. Industrial conditions, themselves of course largely determined by physical environment, affect class and individual consumption in very obvious ways. Each occupation imposes on the worker, and indirectly upon all the members of his family, certain methods of living. Physiological laws prescribe many of those methods. A particular sort of output of muscular or nervous energy demands a particular sort of diet to replace the expenditure. The proper diet of an agricultural labourer, a mill operative and a miner, will have certain recognised differences. Muscular and mental, active and sedentary, monotonous and interesting work, will involve different amounts and sorts of nourishment, and different expenditures for leisure occupations. These differences will extend both to the necessaries and the higher elements in standards of consumption. Industrial requirements will stamp themselves with more or less force and exactitude upon each occupation. An analysis of budgets would show that the standard of the clergyman was not that of the merchant or even of the doctor, and that the same family income would be differently applied. The stockbroker will not live like the mill-owner, nor the journalist like the shopkeeper. So right through the various grades of workers. The skilled mechanic, the factory hand, the railway man, the clerk, the shop-assistant, the labourer, will all have their respective standards, moulded or modified by the conditions of their work: their needs and tastes for food, clothing, recreation, etc., will be affected in subtle ways by that work.

'Productive' consumption is the term given by classical political economy to that portion of consumption applied so as to maintain or improve the efficiency of labour-power in the worker and his family. Necessaries alone were held absolutely productive, conveniences and comforts were dubious, luxuries were unproductive. Regarded even from the commercial standpoint, it was a shallow analysis, confined to a present utilisation of immediately useful commodities, and ignoring the reactions upon future productivity of a rise in education and refinement. It belonged to an age before the economy of high wages or the moral stimuli of hope and an intelligent outlook upon life had won any considerable recognition as 'productive' stimuli.

But from the standpoint of our analysis the defect of this treatment is a deeper one. For us the distinction between productive and unproductive consumption is as fundamental as in the older economic theory. The difference lies in the conception of the 'product' that is to give a meaning to 'productive'. Productive consumption, according to the older economic theory, was measured by the yield of economic productivity, according to our theory by the yield of vital welfare. The two not merely are not identical, they may often be conflicting values.

A diet productive of great muscular energy for a navvy, foundryman or drayman, may produce a coarse type of animalism which precludes the formation of a higher nervous structure and the finer qualities of character that are its spiritual counterpart. The industrial conditions of many productive employments are notoriously such as to impair the physique and the muscle of the workers engaged in them, and there is no ground for assuming that the habits of consumption, conducing to increased productivity in such trades, carry any net freight of human utility.

Nor is it only in manual labour that the industrial influences moulding a standard of consumption may damage its human quality. Much sedentary intellectual work involves similarly injurious reactions upon modes of living. The physical abuses of athleticism, stimulants and drugs, are very prevalent results of disordered competition in intellectual employments. But, as bad elements in standards of expenditure, the intellectual excesses, the fatuous or degrading forms of literature, drama, art, music, which this life generates, are perhaps even more injurious. One of the heaviest human costs of an over-intellectual life today is its 'culture'.

§ 3. When we come to 'conventional' elements in standards of comfort, we enter a region which appears to admit an indefinite amount of waste and error.

The very term 'conventional', set as it is in opposition to 'natural', indeed, suggests an absence of organic utility. We hear of 'conventional necessaries' even in the lowest levels of working-class expenditure. I presume that the expenditure in beer, tobacco, upon sprees or funerals, or upon decorative clothing, would be placed in this category.

From the purely economic standpoint such expenditure has been accounted either waste, or, even worse, 'disutility .

It is often argued that a labouring family on 21s. per week could be kept in physical efficiency, if every penny were expended economically in obtaining 'organic value'. This is the ideal of a certain order of advocates of thrift and temperance. Whole generations of economists have accumulated easy virtue by preaching this rigorous economy for the working-classes. It has always seemed possible to squeeze out of the standard of any working-class enough of the conventional or superfluous to justify the opinion that most of the misery of the poor is their own fault, in the sense that; if they made a completely rational use of their wages, they could support themselves in decency. The amount spent by the workers on drink alone would, it is often contended, make ample provision against most of the worst emergencies of working-class life.

Now there are several comments to be made on this attitude towards conventional expenditure. 1. As one ascends above the primary organic needs, the evolution of desires becomes less reliable and more complicated: the element of will and choice and therefore of choosing badly, becomes larger. Some condiments are useful for assisting the digestion of primary foods, but it is easier to make mistakes in condiments than in staple foods. So with all the higher and more complex wants. As one rises above the prime requisites and conveniences, organic instincts, or tastes directly dependent on them, play a diminishing part as faithful directors of consumption. This natural guidance does not indeed disappear. The evolution of a human being with finer nervous structure, and with higher intellectual and moral needs and desires related to that structure, is a fairly continuous process. The finest and best-balanced natures thus carry into their more complex modes of satisfaction a true psycho-physical standard of utility. But it is already admitted that the liability to go wrong is far greater in those modes of expenditure which are not directly contributory to survival. This is the case, whether individual tastes or some accepted convention determines the expenditure.

This is so generally recognised that it is likely that the organic utility of personal tastes on the one hand, custom and convention on the other, has been unduly disparaged. The temper of economists in assessing values has been too short-sighted and too inelastic. A good deal of personal expenditure that is wasteful or worse when taken on its separate merits may be justified as a rude experimental process by which a person learns wisdom and finds his soul. What is true of certain freakish personal conduct is probably true also of those conventional practices, in which whole societies or classes conduct their collective experiments in the art of living.

A too rigorous economy, whether directed by instinct or reason, which should rule with minute exactitude the expenditure of individuals or societies, in order to extract from all expenditure of income the maximum of seen utilities, would be bound to sin against that law of progress which demands an adequate provision for these experimental processes in life which, taken by themselves, appear so wasteful.

Social psychology brings a more liberal and sympathetic understanding to bear upon some of the practices which to a short-sighted economist appear mere wasteful extravagance, destitute of utility and displacing some immediately serviceable consumption. Let me take some notable examples from current working-class expenditure. The lavish expenditure upon bank-holidays, in which large classes of wage-earners 'blow' a large proportion of any surplus they possess beyond the subsistence wage, is the subject of caustic criticism by thrifty middle-class folk. But may not this holiday spirit, with a certain abandon it contains, be regarded as a 'natural' and even wholesome reaction against the cramping pressure of routine industrialism and the normal rigour of a close domestic economy? It may not, indeed, be an ideally good mode of reaction, may even contain elements of positive detriment, and yet may be the vent for valuable organic instincts seeking after those qualities of freedom, joy and personal distinction that are essential to a life worth living.[1]

Or take the gravest of all defects of working-class expenditure, the drink-bill. This craving, hostile as it is to the physical and moral life of man, is not understood, and therefore cannot be effectively eradicated, unless due account is taken of certain emotional implications. The yielding to drink is not mere brutality. Brutes do not drink. It is in some part the response to an instinct to escape from the imprisonment in a narrow cramping environment which affords no scope for aspiration and achievement. It may indeed be said that the drinker does not aspire and does not achieve. He is doubtless the victim of an illusion. But it is a certain dim sense of a higher freer life that lures him on. 'Elevation' is what is sought.

> 'Kings may be blessed but Tam was glorious
> O'er a' the ills o' life victorious.'

[1] On the side of Consumption as of Production a progressive society that has not abandoned itself to excessive rationalism will recognise the desirability of keeping a scope for 'bonne chance' and 'hazard'. Cf Tarde, I., p. 130.

Or take still another item of working-class expenditure frequently condemned as a typical example of extravagance, the relatively large expense of funerals. Is this to be dismissed offhand as mere wanton waste? A more human interpretation will find in it other elements of meaning. In the ordinary life of 'the common people' there is little scope for that personal distinction which among the upper classes finds expression in so many ways. The quiet working-man or woman has never for a brief hour through a long lifetime stood out among his fellows, or gathered round him the sympathetic attention of his neighbours. Is it wholly unintelligible or regrettable that those who care for him should wish to give this narrow, thwarted, obscure personality a moment of dignity and glory? The sum of life is added up in this pomp of reckoning, and the family is gathered into a focus of neighbourly attention and good-feeling, the outward emblems of honour are displayed, and a whole range of human emotions finds expression. Such excess as exists must be understood as a natural fruit of those aspiring qualities of personality which, thwarted in their natural and healthy growth by narrowness of opportunity, crave this traditional outlet.

In fact, the more closely we study the conventional factors in consumption, the less are we able to dismiss them out of hand as mere extravagance or waste. Some organic impulse, half physical, half psychical, nearly always enters into even the least desirable elements. A margin of expenditure, either conventional or expressing individual caprice,[1] which serves to evoke pleasure, to stir interest, and above all to satisfy a sense of personal dignity, even though at the expense of some more obvious and immediate utilities, may be justified by considerations of individual and social progress.

§ 4. Such considerations must not, however, be pressed very far in the defence even of the most firmly-rooted elements of conventional consumption. For, though the deeper organic forces which work through 'natural selection' must eliminate

---

[1] Though the term 'conventional' appears formally to preclude the play of individual taste or judgment, it is in fact only in such expenditures that these qualities obtain scope for expression. For though convention prescribes the general mode of such expenditure, it leaves a far larger scope for personal choice and capricious variation than in the more necessary elements of expenditure.

the worst or most injurious modes of expenditure from the permanent standard of a race or class, it may leave elements fraught with grave danger. For neither the animal nor the spiritual nature of man is equipped with a selective apparatus for testing accurately for purposes of organic welfare the innumerable fresh applicants for 'consumption' which appear as the evolution of wants, on the one hand, and of industries upon the other, becomes more complex and more rapid. An extreme instance will enforce my meaning. To take a Red Indian or a Bantu from a natural and social environment relatively simple and staple, and to plunge him suddenly into the swirl of a modern Western city life is to court physical and moral disaster. Why? Because the pressures of animal desires or the emotions of pride and curiosity, which were regulated by effective 'taboos' in the primitive life from which he is drawn, now work their will unchecked. For the 'taboos' of civilised society are both ill-adapted to the emotional texture of his nature, and in their novelty and complexity are not adequately comprehended. But even for those born and bred in the environment of a rapidly changing civilisation there are evidently great hazards. Not only individual but widely collective experiments in novelties of consumption will often be injurious. This may be explained in the first instance as due to the perversion or defective working of the 'instincts' originally designed to protect and promote the life of the individual and the species. An animal living upon what may be termed unmodified nature is possessed of instincts which make poisonous plants or animals repellent to its taste. A man living in a highly modified environment finds such shreds of instinctive tastes as he possesses inadequate to the risk of rejecting the fabricated foods brought from remote quarters of the earth to tempt his appetite. If this holds of articles of food, where errors may be mortal and where some protection, however insufficient, is still furnished by the palate and the stomach, still more does it hold of the 'higher' tastes comparatively recently implanted in civilised man. 'Bad tastes' thus may introduce the use of books or art that disturb the mind without informing it, recreations that distract and dissipate our powers without recreating and restoring them. Nor does the 'social organism' furnish reliable checks which shall stop the spread of individual errors into conventional consumption.

§ 5. The question of individual errors and wastes in the process of evolving standards of consumption must not detain us. For though it rightly falls within the scope of a fully elaborated valuation of consumption, it must not be allowed to intrude into our more modest endeavour to discuss the several grades of wants which comprise a class standard of consumption. The relative size of the wastes or defects of the conventional factors in a class standard will not indeed depend upon the mere addition of the perversion of the separate choices of its individuals. For a convention is not produced by a mere coincidence of separate actions of individual desire.

It may be well here to revert to the distinction which we found convenient to employ in our analysis of the human value of different forms of work, viz. the distinction between creation and imitation. Here it will take shape in an enquiry as to the ways in which new wants are discovered and pass into conventional use. Let us take for an example the case of a medicine which has become a recognised remedy for a disease. Among animals or 'primitive' man the habit of eating a curative herb may be regarded as due to an organic instinct common to each member of the herd or group. Such consumption, however, would not really fall within the category of our 'conventional consumption'. It would in effect be confined to a limited number of articles containing strong elements of 'survival value', in a pre-economic period, though, as soon as tribal society began to evolve the medicine man, his prescriptions would add many elements of waste and error. But the consumables whose origin we are now considering must be regarded as involving invention or discovery, and conscious imitation or adoption by the group. Unless we suppose that the chewing of cinchona bark had a backing of instinctive adaptation, and so passed by tradition into later ages of Indian life, we must hold that the first beginnings of the use of quinine as a cure for intermittent fevers in South America were due either to chance or to early empiricism in treatment. Some person, probably enjoying distinction in his tribe, tried cinchona bark and recovered of his fever, others tried it upon this example and got benefit, and so the fame of the remedy spread first from a single centre, and afterwards from a number of other personal centres by conscious imitation. Or, similarly, take the adoption of some article of diet, such as sugar or tobacco, which is an element not of prime physical utility but of comfort or pleasure. The first men who chewed the sugar-cane, or tried the fumes of the *herba nicotina*, must be deemed to have done so 'by accident'. Liking the result, they repeated the experiment by design, and this personal habit become the customary habit of the group, moulded by a tradition continuously supported by a repetition of the feeling which attended the first chance experience.

Such accretions to a standard of consumption may be regarded as possessing guarantees of utility or safeguards against strong positive disutility in their method of adoption. They have grown into the conventional standard 'on their merits'. Those 'merits' may indeed be variously estimated from the 'organic' standpoint. Quinine has a high organic virtue, sugar perhaps an even wider but less vital virtue, while the virtue of tobacco may be purely superficial and compensated by considerable organic demerits. But both discovery and propagation have been in all these cases 'natural' and 'reasonable' processes, in the plain ordinary acceptation of these terms. Some actual utility has been discovered and recognised, and new articles thus incorporated in a standard of consumption, either for regular or special use, have at any rate satisfied a preliminary test of organic welfare.

If all new habits of consumption arose in this fashion, and the preliminary test could be considered thoroughly reliable, the economy of the evolution of standards of consumption would be a safe and sound one. This hypothesis in its very form indicates the several lines of error discernible in the actual evolution of class standards. A falsification of the standard, involving the admission of wasteful or positively noxious consumables, may arise, either in the initial stage of invention, or in the process of imitative adoption. This will occur wherever the initial or the imitative process is vitiated by an extraneous motive. A very small proportion of medicines in customary use among primitive peoples have the organic validity of quinine. Most of them are 'charms', invented by medicine men, not as the result either of a chance or planned experiment, but as the work of an imagination operating upon the lines of an empirical psychology, in which the relation of the actual or known properties of the medicine towards the disease play no appreciable part. So a whole magical pharmacopœia will be erected upon a basis of totemist and animist beliefs, mingled with circumstantial misconceptions and gratuitous fabrications, and containing no organic utility. Each addition or variant will begin as an artificial invention and will be adopted for reasons of prestige, authority or fear, carrying none of that organic confirmation which secured its position for quinine. The limit of error in such cases will be that the medicine must not frequently cause a serious and immediate aggravation of the suffering of the patient. The patent or 'conventional' medicines among civilised peoples must be considered in the main as containing a falsification of standard of the same kind, though different in degree. As the primitive medicine man, called upon to cure a fever or a drought, is primarily motived by the desire to maintain or enhance his personal or caste prestige, while the adoption of his specific into a convention is due to a wholly irrational authority or to a wholly accidental success, so is it with a large proportion of modern remedies. Even in the orthodox branches of the medical profession the process of converting vague empiricism into scientific experiment has gone such a little way as to furnish no guarantee for the full organic efficacy of many of the treatments upon which the patient public spends an increasing share of its income. But as regards the profession there is at any rate some basis of confidence in the disinterested application of science to the discovery of genuine organic utility.

In the patent medicine trade there is very little. Here we have a condition very little better than that of the power of the witch-doctor in primitive society. The maxim 'caveat emptor' carries virtually no security, for the guidance of the palate is ruled out, while the test of experience, except for purgation or for some equally simple and immediate result, is nearly worthless.

§ 6. When the invention and propagation of a mode of consumption have passed into the hands of a trade, the guarantees of organic utility, the checks against organic injury, are at their weakest. For neither process is directed, either by instinct or reason, along serviceable channels. Where the commercial motive takes the initiative, there can be no adequate security that the articles which pass as new elements into a standard of consumption shall be wealth, not illth. Where an invention is stimulated to meet a genuinely 'long-felt need', the generality and duration of that need may be a fair guarantee of utility. But this is not the case where the supply precedes and evokes the demand, the more usual case under developed commercialism. Neither in the action of the inventor, nor in the spread of the new habit of consumption, is there any safe gauge of utility. The inventor, or commercial initiator, is only concerned with the question, Can I make and sell a sufficient quantity of this article at a profit? In order to do so, it is true, he must persuade enough buyers that they 'want' the article and 'want' it more than some other articles on which they otherwise might spend their money. To unreflecting persons this, no doubt, appears a sufficient test of utility. But is it? The purchaser must be made to feel or think that the article is 'good' for him at the time when it is brought before his notice. For this purpose it must be endowed with some speciously attractive property, or recommended as possessing such a property. A cheap mercerised cotton cloth, manufactured to simulate silk, sells by its inherent superficial attraction. A new line in drapery 'pushed' into use by the repeated statement, false at the beginning, that 'it is worn', illustrates the second method. In a word, the arts of the manufacturer and of the vendor, which have no direct relation whatever to intrinsic utility, overcome and subjugate the uncertain, untrained or 'artificially' perverted taste of the consumer. Thus it arises that in a commercial society every standard of class comfort is certain to contain large ingredients of useless or noxious consumption, articles, not only bad in themselves, but often poisoning or distorting the whole standard. The arts of adulteration and of advertising are of course responsible for many of the worst instances. A skilled combination of the two processes has succeeded in cancelling the human value of a very large proportion of the new increments of money income in the lower middle and the working-classes, where a growing susceptibility to new desires is accompanied by no intelligent checks upon the play of interested suggestion as to the modes of satisfying these desires.

Where specious fabrication and strong skilled suggestion co-operate to plant new ingredients in a standard of consumption, there is thus no security as to the amount of utility or disutility attaching to the 'real income' represented by these 'goods'. But this vitiation of standards is not equally applicable to all grades of consumption, or to all classes of consumers. Some kinds of goods will be easier to falsify or to adulterate than others, some classes of consumers will be easier to 'impose upon' than others. These considerations will set limits upon the amount of waste and 'illth' contained in the goods and services which comprise our real income.

First, as to the arts of falsification. Several laws of limitation here emerge. Some materials, such as gold and rubber, have no easily procurable and cheaper substitutes for certain uses. Other goods are in some considerable degree protected from imitation and adulteration by the survival of reliable tests and tastes, touch and sight, in large numbers of consumers. This applies to simpler sorts of goods whose consumption is deepest in the standard and has a strong basis of vital utility. It will be more difficult to adulterate bread or plain sugar to any large extent than sauces or sweets: it will be easier to fake photographs than to pass off plaice for soles. But it cannot be asserted as a general truth that the necessaries are better defended against encroachments of adulteration and other modes of deception than conveniences, and conveniences than luxuries. Indeed, there are two considerations that tell the other way. A manufacturer or merchant who can palm off a cheaper substitute for some common necessary of life, or some well-established convenience, has a double temptation to do so. For, in the first place, the magnitude and reliability of the demand make the falsification unusually profitable. In the second place, so far as a large proportion of articles are concerned, he can rely upon the fact that most consumption of necessaries lies below the margin of clear attention and criticism. Except in the case of certain prime articles of diet, it is probable that a consumer is more likely to detect some change of quality in the latest luxury added to his standard than in the habitual articles of daily use, such as his shoe-leather or his soap. In fact, so well recognised is this protection afforded to the seller by the unconsciousness which habit brings to the consumer, that, in catering for quite new habits, such as cereal breakfast foods or cigarettes, the manufacturer waits until the original attractions of his goods have stamped themselves firmly in customary use, before he dares to lower the quality or reduce the quantity.

These considerations make it unlikely that we can discover a clear law expressing the injury of commercialism in terms of the greater or less organic urgency of the wants ministered to by the different orders of commodities. It will even be difficult to ascertain whether the arts of adulteration or false substitution play more havoc among the necessaries than among the luxuries of life. In neither is there any adequate safeguard for the organic worth of the articles bought and sold, though in both there must be held to be a certain presumption favourable to some organic satisfaction attending the immediate act of consumption. If a 'law' of falsification can be found at all, it is more likely to emerge from a comparative study not of necessaries, conveniences, comforts and luxuries, in a class standard, but of the various sorts of satisfactions classified in relation to the needs which underlie them. Where goods are consumed as soon as they are bought, and by some process involving a strong appeal to the senses, there is less chance for vulgar fraud than where consumption is gradual or postponed, and is not attended by any moment of vivid realisation. Other things equal, one might expect more easily to sell shoddy clothing than similarly damaged food: the adulteration of a jerry-built house is less easily detected, or less adequately reprobated, than that of a jerry-built suit of clothes.

Along similar lines we might, in considering non-material consumption, urge that there are more safeguards for utility in the expenditure upon books or music-hall performances than upon education or church membership. And in a sense this is true. If I buy a book or attend a concert, I am surer to get what I regard as a *quid pro quo* for my expenditure than in the case of a prolonged process involving many small consecutive acts.

So far as this is true, it means that relics of organic guidance are more truly operative in some kinds of satisfaction than in others, and furnish some better check upon the deception which commercialism may seek to practise. But, of course, our valuation of such checks will depend upon how far we can accept them as reliable tests, not of some short-range immediate satisfaction, but of the wider individual and social welfare. The fact that so many notoriously bad habits can be acquired by reason of an immediate 'organic' attractiveness that is a false clue to the larger welfare, must put us on our guard against accepting any easy law based on the test of 'natural' tastes.

§ 7. But, in considering the degradation of standards of consumption, it is well to bring some closer analysis to bear upon the processes of suggestion and adoption that are comprised in 'imitation'. In analysing the forms of wealth, the goods and services, which are the real income of the nation, in terms of their production, we recognised that, other things equal, the human cost of any body of that wealth varied directly with the amount of routine or purely imitative work put into it, and inversely with the amount of creative or individual work. That judgment, however, we felt bound to qualify by the consideration that a certain proportion of routine work, though in itself perhaps distasteful and uninteresting, had an organic value both for the individual and for society. How far can we apply an analogous judgment to the same body of Wealth on its consumption side? Can we assume that the utility of consumption of any given body of wealth varies directly with the amount of free personal expression which its use connotes, and inversely with the routine or conventional character it bears? Evidently not. The same analysis does not apply. The chief reason for the difference has already been indicated, by pointing out that, in a modern industrial society, each man, as producer, is highly specialised, as consumer highly generalised. The high human costs of routine work were, we saw, a direct result of this specialising process. A little routine work of several sorts, regularly practised, would involve no organic cost, and might indeed yield a fund of positive utility as a wholesome *régime* of exercise, provided it was not carried so far as to encroach upon the fund of energy needed for the performance of other special work, creative and interesting. Indeed, the usual economic justification of the excessive division of labour existing at present in advanced industrial societies is that it is essential to yield that large body of objective wealth which, by its distribution, enriches and gives variety to the consumption of all members of the society. The producer is sacrificed to the consumer, the damage done to each man in his former capacity being more than compensated by the benefits conferred upon him in his latter capacity.

The full validity of this doctrine will be considered when we gather together the two sides of our analysis and consider the inter-relations between production and consumption as an aspect of the problem of human values. At present we may begin by accepting variety of consumption as a condition in itself favourable to the maximisation of human welfare. This assumption is not, however, quite self-evident. The routine factors in a standard of consumption (and a standard *quâ* standard consists of routine), so far as they are laid down under the direction of an instinctive or a rational evolution of wants, must be regarded as containing a minimum of waste or disutility. Since they are also the foundation and the indispensable condition for all the 'higher' forms of material or non-material consumption in which the conscious personality of individuals finds expression, they may be held to contain per unit a maximum of human value. From this standpoint there would seem to emerge a law of the economy of consumption, to the effect that the maximum of social welfare would be got from a distribution of wealth which absorbed the entire product in this routine satisfaction of the common needs of life. This economy need not be conceived merely in terms of a uniform standard of material satisfactions. A wider interpretation of life and of necessaries might extend it so as to cover many higher grades of satisfaction, all the 'joys that are in widest commonalty spread.' The natural evolution of such an economy of consumption might, it is arguable, yield the greatest quantity of social welfare.

§ 8. But a high uniform level of welfare throughout society

does not exhaust the demands of human welfare. It evidently overstresses the life of the social as against the individual organism, imposing a regimen of equality which absorbs the many into the one. Now, desirous to hold the balance fair between the claims of individual personality and of society, we cannot acquiesce in an ideal of economical consumption which makes no direct provision for the former. So far, however, as the consumption of an individual is of a routine character, expressing only the needs of a human nature held in common with his fellows, it does not really express his individuality at all. The realisation of the unique values of his personality, and the conscious satisfaction that proceeds from this individual expression, can only be got by activities which lie beyond the scope of custom and convention. Though this issue has most important bearings that are outside the economic field, it is also vitally connected with the use of economic goods. For, unless a due proportion of the general income (the aggregate of goods and services) is placed at the free disposal of individuals in such forms as to nourish and stimulate the wholesome and joyous expansion of their powers, that social progress which first manifests itself in the free experimental and creative actions of individuals whose natures vary in some fine and serviceable way from the common life, will be thwarted. This brings us to a better understanding of the nature and origin of the human injury and waste contained in large sections of that conventional consumption which plays so large and so depressing a part in every class standard of comfort. Where the production of an economic society has grown so far as to yield a considerable and a growing surplus beyond that required for survival purposes, this surplus is liable to several abuses. Instead of being applied as food and stimulus to the physical and spiritual growth of individual and social life, it may be squandered, either upon excessive satisfaction of existing routine wants in any class or classes, or in the stimulation and satisfaction of more routine wants and the evolution of a complex conventional standard of consumption, containing in its new factors a diminishing amount of human utility or even an increasing amount of human costs. If the industrial structure is such that particular groups of business men can make private gains by stimulating new wasteful modes of conventional consumption, this process, as we have seen, is greatly facilitated. But, after all, the business motive is not in itself an adequate explanation. Business firms suggest new wants, but the susceptibility to such suggestions, the active imitation by which a new article passes into the conventional consumption of a group or class, requires closer consideration. Falsification of a standard can seldom be understood as a mere perversion of the free choice of individuals. A convention is not produced by a mere coincidence of separate choices. Imitation plays an important part in the contagion and infection of example. In endeavouring to assess the human utility of the consumption of wealth we see the play of several imitative forces. Current Prestige, Tradition, Authority, Fashion, Respectability supplement or often displace the play of individual taste, good or bad, in moulding a class and family standard of consumption. The psychology and sociology of these distinctively imitative forces which form or change standards are exceedingly obscure.

The merely gregarious instinct may lead to the spread in a class or group of any novelty which attracts attention and is not offensive. Where supported by any element of personal prestige, such novelty, irrespective of its real virtues or uses, may spread and become embedded in a standard of consumption. The beginnings of every fashion largely belong to this order of imitation. Some prestige is usually needed fairly to launch a new fashion; once launched it spreads mainly by 'gregariousness', the instinct to be, or look, or act, like other people. The limits of error, disutility or inconvenience, which can be set upon a novelty of fashion, appear to depend mainly upon the initial force of prestige. The King might introduce into London society a really inconvenient high hat, though the Queen perhaps could not carry a full revival of the crinoline.

Fashions change but they leave deposits of conventional expenditure behind. What is at first fashionable often remains as respectable and lives long in the conventional habits of a class. Every class standard is encrusted with little elements of dead fashion.

§ 9. But this formative influence of Prestige itself demands fuller consideration. For it not merely implants elements of expenditure in the standard of consumption, but infects the standard itself.

A true standard would rest on a basis of organic utility, expenditure being apportioned so as to promote the soundest, fullest human life. But all conventional consumption is determined largely by valuations imposed by the class possessing most prestige. It is, of course, a commonplace that fashions in dress, and in certain external modes of consumption, descend by snobbish imitation from high life through the different social strata, each class copying the class above. It is a matter of far more vital importance that religion, ethics, art, literature and the whole range of intellectual activities, manners, amusements, take their shapes and values largely by the same process of infiltration from above.

This is not the case everywhere. In many nations the distinctions of caste, class, locality or occupation, are so strong as to preclude the passage of habits of material consumption, manners, tastes and ideas, from one social stratum to another. The exclusive possession of a code of life, of language, thought and feelings by a caste or class, is itself a matter of pride, and often of legal protection. This holds not only of most Asiatic civilisations but, though less rigorously, of those European countries which have not been fully subjected to the dissolving forces of industrialism.

But in such countries as England and the United States, where the industrial arts are rapidly evolving new products and stimulating new tastes, and where at the same time the social strata present a continuous gradation with much movement from one stratum to another, the process of imitation by prestige is very rapid and general.

The actual expenditure of the income of every class in these countries is very largely determined, not by organic needs, but by imitation of the conventional consumption of the class immediately above in income or in social esteem. That conventional consumption in its turn is formed by imitation of the class above. The aristocracy, plutocracy, or class with most power or prestige, thus makes the standards for the other classes.

Now, even if it were a real aristocracy, a company of the best, it by no means follows that a standard of living good for them would be equally good for other social grades. But there would be at least a strong presumption in its favour. To copy good examples, even if the copying is defective, is an elevating practice, and in as much as the essentials of humanity are found alike in all, thoughtless imitation of one's betters might raise one's own standard. If in a society the men of light and leading occupied this place because they had discovered a genius for the art of noble living, the swift unconscious imitation of their mode of life, the morals and manners of this aristocracy, would surely be the finest schooling for the whole people: the models of the good, the true, the beautiful, which they afforded, would inform each lower grade, according to its capacity.

But where the whole forces of prestige and imitation are set on a sham aristocracy, copying as closely as possible their modes of consumption, their ways of thought and feeling, their valuations and ideals, incalculable damage and waste may ensue. For the defects in the standard of the upper few will, by imitation, be magnified as well as multiplied in the lower standards of the many. Let me illustrate.

If gambling is bad for the upper classes, its imitation becomes progressively worse as it descends, poisoning the life and consuming a larger proportion of the diminishing margin of the income of each class. If the inconvenience of decorative dress is bad for rich women, who live a life of ease and leisure, its imitation by the active housewives of the middle, and the women-workers of the lower classes, inflicts a graver disutility. For the waste of income is more injurious and the physical impediments to liberty of movement are more onerous. It is the immeasurable importance of this prestige of the upper class, percolating through all lower social grades, and imposing, not merely elements of conventional consumption, but standards and ideas of life which affect the whole mode of living, that requires us to give closer consideration to the life of the leisure class.

§ 10. Here we can find valuable aid in a remarkable book entitled *The Theory of the Leisure Class*, by Mr. Veblen, an American sociologist. Regarded as a scientific study, which it rightly claims to be, this book has two considerable defects, one of manner, one of matter. Its analysis is conducted with a half-humorous parade of pompous terminology apt to wear upon the temper of the reader. Its exaggerated stress upon a single strain of personality, as a dominant influence in the formation of habits and the direction of conduct, is a more serious blemish in a work of profound and penetrating power. But for our present purpose, that of discovering the elements of waste in national consumption, it is of first-rate importance.

Mr. Veblen's main line of argument may be summarised as follows. In primitive society war and the chase will be the chief means by which men may satisfy that craving for personal distinction and importance which is the most enduring and importunate of psychical desires. Personal prowess, mainly physical, displayed in fight or hunt, will secure leadership or ascendency in tribal life. So those trophies which attest such prowess, the skulls or scalps of enemies, the skins of slain animals, or the live possession of tame animals, will be the most highly-prized forms of property. When the capture and enslavement of enemies has taken the place of promiscuous slaughter, the size and variety of his retinue of slaves for personal service, concubinage, or merely decorative show, attest the greatness of the warrior-chief. When the industrial arts are sufficiently developed, slaves will be set to produce such other forms of property, enlarged housing, quantities of showy garments, cultivated fields, herds of cattle, as afford conspicuous evidence of the personal prowess of the chief. Glory, far more than utility or comfort, continues to be the dominant motive.

As civilisation begins to make way, the notion of what constitutes personal prowess begins to be modified. Though physical force may still remain a chief ingredient, skill and cunning, wisdom in counsel, capacity for command and law-making, come to be recognised as also giving prestige. As not only the strong man by his strength, but the cunning man by his cunning, can get that wealth or property which are the insignia of prowess, property will however still be valued by its owner mainly for the prestige it affords him among his fellows. It will still for the most part take shape in external forms of adornment or magnifi-

cence. As it develops into the culminating form of the oriental
court, the element of display will remain the paramount consideration, to which even the sense-enjoyments of the owner will be
secondary.

The effect of this early linking of property to personal prowess
will be that in the general mind of man the possession of property is honorific. It secures for its owner a presumption of personal greatness. Therefore, its possession must be kept in full
and constant evidence, especially where inheritance destroys the
direct presumption of the personal prowess of the actual owner.
Hence the two essential features of the mode of living of the dominant class or caste, ostentatious waste and conspicuous leisure.
For thus the prestige of property is best enforced. Gorgeous
palaces with luxurious grounds, magnificent banquets and enter-
tainments, extravagant refinements of sensual luxury, adornments of fabrics, jewels and articles of laborious skill, magnificent
tombs and other monuments—the elaborate parade of waste,
in order to fasten on the common imagination the sense of wonder
and of admiration of the person who could afford so lavish a
waste! The family of the rich man is chiefly valued as an instrument for making this display effective. His wife or wives
must do no work, not even copy his parasitic activities; they must
stand as open monuments of conspicuous leisure, their personal
adornments, their retinues of servants, the entire elaborate
ritual of their futile lives, must be devoted to showing how much
their possessor can afford to waste. Such was the life of the aristocracy in olden and mediæval days!

It has passed in most essentials, by tradition and imitation,
to the life of the upper class in modern civilised nations. The
modes and conceptions of personal prowess and prestige have indeed shifted. The man of business has dethroned the warrior
or the political chieftain. The typical great man of our time is
the great *entrepreneur*, the financier who directs the flow of capital and rules prices on change, the railway or shipping magnate
who plans a combine, the able and astute merchant, who controls a market, the manufacturer who conducts a great productive business, the organiser of a successful departmental store.
The personal qualities and activities involved in these tasks are

very different from those possessed by barbarian chieftains or oriental despots. Add to such men the surviving landed aristocracy of rent-receivers, and a considerable number of families that live on dividends, taking no real part in the administration of industry, and we have a synopsis of the class which to-day wields prestige. Though the elaboration of modern arts of pleasure directs a great part of the expenditure of this, our upper class, the traditional habits of ostentatious waste and conspicuous leisure as modes of glory are still paramount motives. Most rich people value riches less for the pleasures they afford than for the social consideration, the personal distinction, they procure. The craving to realise superiority over others, as attested by their servility or imitation, the power of money to make others do your will, the sense of freedom to realise every passing caprice, these remain the chief value of riches, and mould the valuations of life for the bulk of the well-to-do.

Such are the inevitable effects of easily-gotten and excessive wealth upon the possessors. So far as they operate, they induce futile extravagance in expenditure. Instead of making for utility, they make for disutility of consumption. Such is the gist of this analysis of the leisured life.

§ 11. Expenditure which is to be effectively ostentatious, so as to impress its magnificence upon the largest number of other people, cannot be directed to the satisfaction of a real personal want, even a bad want. Futility is of its essence. The very type of this expenditure is a display of fireworks: there is no other way of consuming so large a quantity of wealth in so short a time with such sensational publicity and with no enduring effect whatever. This private extravagance may perhaps be paralleled in public expenditure by the squandering of millions upon war-ships which are not needed, will never be used, and will be obsolete within a few years of their construction.

The defects which every sane social critic finds in the modes of living of the rich, their frivolity, triviality and futility, are illustrations of Mr. Veblen's thesis. Perhaps the largest complex of forms of futile waste, waste of money and of time, is contained in the performance of what, with curious aptness of phrase, are termed 'social duties', the idle round of visits, enter-tainments and functions which constitutes the 'society life'. I speak of the aptness of the term 'social duties'. This is no paradox, but merely the finest instance of that perversion of values and valuations which is inherent in the situation. For it is essential to the accuracy of this analysis that the rich members of society should regard their most futile activities as 'duties', and their small section of humanity as 'society'.

Of the expenditure which is laid out on the satisfaction of material wants, the waste or disutility will often be considerable. But Nature is strong enough to enforce some sense and moderation in the satisfaction of primary organic desires. While, therefore, there is much luxury and waste in the material standard of comfort of the rich, we do quite wrong to find in food and clothing and other material consumption our chief instances of luxury and waste. It is in the non-material expenditure that the proportion of waste or disutility is largest. The great moral law, *corruptio optimi pessima*, requires that this be so. If we seek the largest sources of injurious waste in the standard of the well-to-do classes, we shall find them in the expenditure upon recreation, education and charity.

CHAPTER XI

§ 1. It is no mere chance that makes sport the special field for the attainment and display of personal prestige among the well-to-do classes. Primitive man in his early struggle for life had to put all his powers of body and mind, all his strength and cunning, into the quick, sure, and distant discovery of beasts or other men who would destroy him. He must pursue and kill them, or successfully avoid them. He must seek out animal or vegetable foods, tracking them by signs and snares, rapid of foot, keen of eye and scent, quick, strong, and accurate of grasp. To run and spring, to climb and swim and strike and throw were necessary human accomplishments. They had a high survival value. Nature had to evolve and maintain a man who had the capacity to do these things well, and who was willing to undergo the necessary toil and pain of acquiring and exercising these arts and crafts. To ride, to shoot, to manage boats, were occupations of prime utility. Successful mating was also necessary for survival, and so the arts of courtship, dancing, music, decoration, and various displays of grace and vigour were evolved. The simple activities that were elaborated into these arts of hunting, fighting, mating, were instinctive, and strong feelings of pleasure were attached to them, as Nature's lure. When reason, or conscious cunning, came to coöperate with instinct, complicating and refining the useful arts, the specific pleasures of instinctive satisfaction were accompanied by a general sense of personal elation or pride. Now, in man, as in other animals, practice was needed for the successful performance of these useful activities. This practice takes the form of play, a more or less realistic simulation of the practices of fighting, hunting, courtship, in which, however, considerable scope exists for variations and surprises, the survival value of which is real, though indirect. Since these forms of play appeal to and exercise the same activities as are

146

involved in the serious affairs of life, the same sorts of satisfaction are attached to them. The natural meaning of play is that it is a preparation for work, i. e. for the arduous, painful, and often dangerous tasks involved in 'the struggle of life,' and the pleasure of play is the inducement to the acquisition of this useful skill.

§ 2. If this be so, it may be possible for some men to suck the pleasure from the play without performing the useful work for which it is a preparation. The play instincts can be made to yield a desirable life of interest and pleasure to any class of men who are enabled to get others to perform their share of useful work, and thus to provide them with the time, energy and material means for the elaboration of the play side of life. Such is the physical explanation of the sportsman. The play which Nature designed as means to life, he takes as an end, and lives 'a sporting life'. Some of his sports bear on the surface few signs of biological play about them. The manual and mental dexterity of such indoor games as bridge and billiards, appear quite unrelated to the arduous pursuits of mountaineering or big-game hunting. Between these two lie the great majority of active sports, such as shooting, racing, and the various games of ball. No one who analyses carefully the feelings of pleasure got from a boundary hit, a run with the ball, a neck-to-neck race, or any other athletic achievement, can doubt their nature.

Fighting, hunting, fishing, climbing, exploring, reduced to sports, contain just as much 'realism' as is needed to evoke the pleasurable excitement which sustained these skilful efforts when they belonged to the struggle for life. Some of the imitations may be so close to reality as to recall in almost its full intensity the primal thrill, as in tiger-stalking, in boxing, or rock climbing. In ball-games the fictitious circumstances call for more imagination, though the pleasure of the actual stroke is chiefly a race memory of a blow struck at an enemy, or of a blow warded off. No one can doubt the nature of the fierce pleasure of the football scrimmage with its mortal make-believe.

Although in many sports some element of physical risk is needed to sustain the realism, it is usually reduced to trifling dimensions. This is also true of the painful endurance incidental to the primitive struggle. The modern sportsman or explorer commonly devises ways of economising both his personal risk and his personal effort. Beaters find the animal or bird for him to shoot; native porters and guides carry food for him, and ease his path. His object is to secure the maximum pleasure of achievement with the minimum risk and effort. Perhaps the most highly-elaborated example is the playful revival of the migratory and exploring instincts, from the picnic to the world-tour, with the complex apparatus of pleasure-travel which occupies so large a part in the life of the well-to-do classes. The luxurious life of travel in which the motor-car, the *train de luxe*, or the yacht carries men and women from the gorgeous hotel of one beauty spot to that of another, is made pleasurable or tolerable by waking up the dim shadow of some wandering ancestor, whose hunting or pastoral habits required some satisfaction to evoke the life-preserving effort. Camping-out and caravanning are somewhat more realistic reproductions, bringing in more of the gregarious or corporate instinct of the tribe.

How subtle are the artifices by which human cunning seeks to exploit the past is best illustrated, however, in the purely spectatorial or sympathetic surroundings of sport. To play football is one remove from battle, to watch the game is two removes, to watch the "tape" or follow the scores in the newspapers is three removes. Yet millions of little thrills of satisfaction are got from this simulation of a simulated fight. Blended in various degrees with other zests, of hazard, of petty cunning, and avarice, where betting enters into sport, the sporting interest ranks highest of all in the scale of values among the able-bodied males of all classes in English-speaking peoples.

Added to the pleasure from the output of strength or skill in sport is the general sentiment of exultation, the sense of glory. To what must that be attributed? Not to the magnitude of the strength or skill. A navvy may display greater strength or endurance in his work, a trapper or a common fisherman a finer skill in catching his prey. But the true glory of sportsmanship is denied them. Why? Because their work is useful, and they are doing it for a living. The glory of the successful sportsman is due to the fact that his deeds are futile. And this conspicuous futility is at the root of the matter. The fact that he can give time, energy, and money to sport testifies to his possession of independent means. He can afford to be an idler, and the more obviously useless and expensive the sport, the higher the prestige attaching to it. His personal glory of strength, endurance, or skill is set in this aureole of parasitism. The crucial test of this interpretation is very simple. Let it turn out that a Marathon winner, who seemed to be a gentleman, was really a professional, what a drop in his personal prestige! The professional is a man who has to earn a living, his reputation as a sportsman is damaged by that fact. Can there be any more convincing proof that the high prestige of sport is due to the evidence of financial prowess which it affords?

The hunting and the fighting instincts evidently underlie the pleasure of nearly all the exclusively male sports. Doubtless other instinctive satisfactions enter in, such as the gregarious instinct with its conscious elaboration of *esprit de corps*. Whenever any game or sport brings the sexes into relation with one another, the mating instincts are evidently involved. The crossing of war with sex in the theory and practice of chivalry was a conscious and artistic blending of these pleasure motives.

But this treatment of sport as a frivolous pursuit of pleasure ignores one important aspect. Sport, it will be urged, after all has health for its permanent utility. It is exercise for the body and diversion for the mind. It wards off the natural consequences of the purely parasitic life, which a private income renders possible, by providing work-substitutes. The primal law, 'in the sweat of thy face shalt thou eat bread,' is gracefully evaded by games that include a gentle perspiration. Golf may take the place of spade-labour to win appetite and digestion; bridge will save the brain from absolute stagnation. So Nature's self-protective cunning elaborates these modes of sham-work.

§ 3. The social condemnation of a sporting-life is two-fold. In the first place, it diverts into lower forms of activity the zests and interests intended to promote a life of work and art. The sporting-life and standards choke the finer arts. The sportsman and the gamester are baser artists choosing the lower instead of the higher modes of self-realisation in manual and intellectual skill. This maintenance of barbarian standards of values by the classes possessing social prestige is a great obstacle to the development of science, art, and literature. In the second place, sport spoils the spontaneity and liberty of play, which is a necessity of every healthy life. It spoils it for the sportsman by reason of its artificiality and its excess. For the sporting-life does not satisfy those who practise it. It carries the Nemesis of boredom. The sense of triviality and of futility gradually eats through, and the make-believe realism, when confronted with the serious values of life, shows its emptiness. A heavier social damage is the economic cost which the expensive futility imposes. For sport involves the largest diversion of unearned income into unproductive expenditure. Not only does it dedicate to extravagant waste a larger share of the land, the labour, and the enterprise of men than any other human error, unless it be war itself, but it steals the play-time of the many to make the over-leisure of the few. If the parasitic power which sustains the sporting-life were taken away, the world would not be duller or more serious. On the contrary, play would be more abundant, freer, more varied, and less artificial in its modes.

The identification of a sportsman with a gentleman has carried great weight in the unconscious settling of social values, and in England has been subtly serviceable as a sentimental safeguard against the attacks upon the economic supports not only of landlordism but of other wealth which has covered itself with the trappings of sport.

The relative prestige of other occupations is determined to a considerable extent by their association with the sporting-life or with the original activities which sport reproduces. Not only the idle landowner, but the yeoman, and in a less degree the tenant farmer, enjoy a social consideration beyond the measure of their pecuniary standing, by virtue of the opportunities for hunting and other sport which they enjoy. Part of the reputation of the military and the naval services is explained by the survival of the barbarian feeling that a life of hazard and rapine contains finer opportunities for physical prowess than a life of productive activity. Though a good deal of this prestige belongs to the glory of 'command' and extends even to a great employer of labour, the glamour of the soldier's, hunter's, sportsman's life hangs in a less degree about all whose occupations, however servile, keep them in close contact with these barbarian activities. A publican, a professional cricketer, a stud-groom, a gamekeeper, enjoy among their companions a dignity derived from their association with the sporting-life.

§ 4. If physical recreations thus carry prestige, so in a less degree and in certain grades of society do intellectual recreations. Once a sportsman alone had a claim to be regarded as a gentleman. Only in comparatively modern times did the association of 'a scholar and a gentleman' seem plausible. Even now prowess of the mind can seldom compete in glory with prowess of the body. The valuation of achievements current in our public-schools persists, though with some abatement, among all sorts and conditions of men. But as mental skill becomes more and more the means of attaining that financial power which is the modern instrument of personal glory, it rises in social esteem. As manners, address, mental ability and knowledge more and more determine personal success, intellectual studies become increasingly reputable.

It might appear at the first sight that the highest reputation would attach to those abilities and studies which had the highest immediate utility for money-making. But here the barbarian standard retains a deflecting influence. To possess money which you have not made still continues to be far more honorific than to make money. For money-making, unless it be by loot or gambling, involves addiction to a business life instead of the life of a leisured gentleman. So it comes to pass that studies are valued more highly as decorative accomplishments than as utilities. A man who can have afforded to expend long years in acquiring skill or knowledge which has no practical use, thereby announces most dramatically his possession, or his father's possession, of an income enabling him to lead the life of an independent gentleman. The scale of culture-values is largely directed by this consideration. Thus not only the choice of subjects but the mode of treatment in the education of the children of the well-to-do is, generally speaking, in inverse ratio to their presumed utility. The place of honour accorded to

dead languages is, of course, the most patent example. Great
as the merits of Greek and Latin may be for purposes of intellectual and emotional training, their predominance is not mainly
determined by their merits, but by the traditional repute which
has made them the chosen instruments for a parade of 'useless'
culture. Though some attempt is made in recent times to extract from the teaching of the 'classics' the finer qualities of the
'humanities' which they contain, this has involved a revolt
against the pure 'scholarship' which sought to exclude even such
refined utilities and to confine the study of the classics to a grace-
ful, skilful handling of linguistic forms and a purely superficial
treatment of the thought and knowledge contained in the chosen
literature. It is significant that even to-day 'culture' primarily
continues to imply knowledge of languages and literature as accomplishments, and that, though mathematics and natural
sciences enter more largely into the academic curriculum, they
continue to rank lower as studies in the education of our wealthy
classes.

Most convincing in its testimony to the formation of intellectual values is the treatment of history and modern English
literature. Although for all purposes of culture and utility, it
might have been supposed that the study of the thought, art,
and events of our own nation and our own times, would be of
prime importance, virtually no place is given to these subjects.
History and literature, so far as they figure at all, are treated not
in relation to the life of to-day, but as dead matter. Other subjects of strictly vital utility, such as physiology and hygiene,
psychology and sociology, find no place whatever in the general
education of our schools and universities, occupying a timid position as 'special' subjects in certain professional courses.

Pedagogues sometimes pretend that this exclusion of 'utility'
tests for the subjects and the treatment in our system of education rests upon sound educational principles, in that, ignoring
the short-range utilities which a commercial or other 'practical'
training desiderates, they contribute to a deeper and a purer
training of the intellectual faculties. But having regard to the
part played by tradition and ecclesiastical authority in the establishment of present-day educational systems, it cannot be

admitted that they have made a serious case for the appraisement of studies according to their human values. Probably our higher education, properly tested, would be found to contain a far larger waste of intellectual 'efficiency' than our factory system of economic efficiency. And this waste is primarily due to the acceptance and survival of barbarian standards of culture, imperfectly adjusted to the modern conditions of life, and chiefly sustained by the desire to employ the mind for decorative and recreative, rather than for productive or creative purposes. Art, literature and science suffer immeasurable losses from this misgovernment of intellectual life. The net result is that the vast majority of the sons and daughters even of our well-to-do classes grow up with an exceedingly faulty equipment of useful knowledge, no trained ability to use their intellects or judgments freely and effectively, and with no strong desire to attempt to do so. They thus remain or become the dupes of shallow traditions, or equally shallow novelties, under the guise of scientific, philosophic, economic or political principles which they have neither the energy of mind nor the desire to test, but which they permit to direct their lives and conduct in matters of supreme importance to themselves and others.

As education is coming to take a larger place as an organised occupation, and more time, money and energy are claimed for it, the necessity of a revaluation of intellectual values on a sane basis of humanism becomes more exigent than ever. For there is a danger of a new bastard culture springing up, the product of a blending of the barbarian culture, descending by imitation of the upper classes, with a too narrowly utilitarian standard improvised to convert working-class children into cheap clerks and shopmen. Our high-schools and local universities are already victims to this *mésalliance* between 'culture' and 'business', and the treatment of not a few studies, history and economics in particular, is subject to novel risks.

§ 5. Dilettantism is the intellectual equivalent of sport. What is the moral equivalent? The sporting-life has an ethics of its own, the essence of which lies in eschewing obligations with legal or other compulsory external sanctions, in favour of a voluntary code embodying the mutual feelings of members of a superior caste. In an aristocracy of true sportsmen honesty and sexual 'morality' are despised as bourgeois virtues, while justice is too compulsory and too equalitarian for acceptance. Honour takes the place of honesty, good form of morals, fair-play and charity of justice. It is the code of the barbarian super-man or chieftain, qualified, softened and complicated to suit the conditions of the modern play-life. Courage and endurance, fidelity, generosity and mercy are his virtues: temperance, modesty, humility, gratitude, have no proper place in such a code, which is indeed based upon a free exercise of the physical functions for personal pleasure and glory.

The hazard belonging to a sporting life makes for superstition. Nobody is more crudely superstitious than the gambler, and everybody to whom life is primarily a game conceives of it as proceeding by rules which may be evaded or tampered with. This aspect of the sporting character gave the priestly caste its chief opportunity to get power. So pietism was grafted on the sportsman and the fighting-man, and religion kept a hold on the ruling and possessing classes, adapting its moral teaching to his case. The wide divergence of British Christianity from the teaching of the gospels finds its chief explanation in this necessity of adaptation. Its doctrines and its discipline had to be moulded so as to fit the character and conduct of powerful men, who not only would repudiate its inner spiritual teaching, but whose lust, pride, cruelty and treachery, the natural outcome of their animal life, were constantly leading them to violate the very code of honour they professed. As industry and property, peace and order, became more settled and wide-spread, there came up from below a powerful commercial class, whose economic and social requirements evolved a morality in which the so-called puritan virtues of industry, thrift, honesty, temperance, sexual purity, prevailed, and a Christianity designed primarily to evoke and to sustain them. Just as the intellectual culture of the aristocracy came to clash with the utilitarian education of the bourgeois and to produce the confusing compromise which at present prevails, so with the differing ethics of the same two classes. The incursion of the wealthy tradesman into 'high life' and of the landed gentry into the 'city' has visibly broken down the older standards both of morals and of manners. The prestige of the sporting virtues has played havoc with the simplicity and austerity of the puritan morals and creeds, though it may fairly be maintained that the saner utilities of the latter have tempered to a perceptible degree the morals and manners of the sportsman. Luxuries and frivolities of a more varied order have largely displaced the older sporting-life, introducing into it some elements of more intellectual skill and interest, though it remains primarily devoted to the pursuit of pleasurable sensuous futilities.

But, though the modes of the leisure life are shifting, the definitely parasitic attitude and career which it embodies remain unchanged. The sense of justice and of humanity among its members is as defective as ever. This truth is sometimes concealed by the change in social areas that is taking place. Class honour and comradeship have a somewhat wider scope as the range of effective intercourse expands, and classes which formerly were wide apart come partially to fuse with one another, or are brought within the range of sympathy, as regards their more sympathetic members. So intercourse upon a fairly equal basis can take place in such a country as England between most persons who have reached a certain level of refinement of living. This certainly implies some transfusion of moral standards, the union of common sentiments regarding industry and property with the downward spread of a modified conception of a sporting life. Indeed, imitation has gone a certain way towards infecting all the stabler grades of the working-classes with this blend of barbarian and puritan valuations. While the larger pecuniary means and leisure which they possess has introduced into their standard of life sporting habits largely imitative of the fully leisured aristocracy, it has implanted habits of 'respectability' as the contribution of the bourgeois type immediately above them in the social scale.

§ 6. But when we dip down below the bourgeois and the regular working-classes which he has drilled in industry, we find a lower leisure class whose valuations and ways of living form a most instructive parody of the upper leisure class. Both in country and town life these types appear. They include 'gypsies', tramps, poachers and other vagabonds, who have never been enlisted in the army of industry, or have deserted in favour of a 'free' life of hazard, beggary and plunder. In towns natural proclivities or misfortune account for considerable groups of casual workers, professional or amateur thieves and prostitutes, street-sellers, corner-men, kept husbands, and other parasites who are a burden on the working-classes. Alike in country and in town, these men practise, so far as circumstances allow, the same habits and exhibit the same character as the leisure class at the top. The fighting, sporting, roving, generous, reckless, wasteful traits are all discernible, the same unaffected contempt for the worker, the same class camaraderie, often with a special code of honour, the same sex license and joviality of manners. Even their intelligence and humour, their very modes of speech, are the half-imitative, half-original replica of high life as it shows in the race-course, in the club smoke-room, or the flash music-hall. Often the parasites and hangers-on to upper-class sports and recreations, these form a large and growing class of our population, and their withdrawal from all industry that can be termed productive, coupled with the debased mode of consumption which they practise, count heavily in the aggregate of social waste.

§ 7. As the opportunities of leisure and of some surplus income beyond the current accepted standard of class comfort become more general, this sympathetic imitation of recreations, education and morals, undoubtedly makes for a national standardisation of life, though the enormous discrepancies in economic resources greatly limit the efficacy of such a tendency to unity. But the apparent gain in humanity thus suggested is largely counterworked by the stronger sense of national and especially of racial cleavage which has come with modern world intercourse. If class barriers of conduct, education and feeling are somewhat weakening in the foremost European nations, a clearer and intenser realisation of national and racial barriers takes their place. Every modification of class exclusiveness, and of economic plunder, upon the smaller scale, is compensated by this wider racial exclusiveness, with its accompanying parasitism. The civilised Western world is coming more consciously to mould its practical policy, political and economic, and its sentiments and theories, upon a white exploitation of the lower and the backward peoples. Imperialism is displacing, or at present is crossing, class supremacy, and is evolving an intellectualism and a morals accommodated to the needs of this new social cleavage. It is moving towards a not distant epoch in which Western white nations may, as regards their means of livelihood, be mainly dependent upon the labour of regimented lower peoples in various distant portions of the globe, all or most members of the dominant peoples enjoying a life of comparative pleasure and leisure and a collective sense of personal superiority as the rulers of the earth.

That standards of recreation, education and morals, thus formed and transformed, are likely to contain enormous 'wastes' in their direct and indirect bearing upon economic life, is obvious. How far this waste is to be imputed to imitation of the prestige-possessing habits of 'the leisured class', how far to 'original sin' or the errors or excesses natural to all sorts and conditions of men, it is not possible to ascertain. But it will be evident that in these higher satisfactions, to which an increasing 'surplus' of wealth, leisure and energy can be devoted, will be found the largest wastes. For the conventional expenditure embedded in these strata of the various class standards will be largely directed by motives which are very loosely related to any real standard of organic welfare. One need not exaggerate this expenditure of time or money, or deem it wholly unproductive. It may even be conceded that few of the pursuits of pleasure are wholly destitute of benefit, nor are prestige and the imitation it engenders wholly valueless. But such practices contain much that is obsolete, incongruous or indigestible, much that is actively injurious, both to the individual and to society. Regarded from the standpoint of pecuniary expenditure, the misdirection of the surplus income into empty or depraved modes of recreation, culture, religion and charity is the largest of all economic wastes. Could it be set forth in veracious accounts, its enormity would impress all reflective minds. How small the total yield of human welfare or even of current pleasurable satisfaction from the idle travel, racing, hunting, motoring, golfing, yachting, betting and gambling, in comparison with the human gain from the work and arts of which they are the futile substitutes! Consider the damage to agriculture, the sheer loss of human energy, the selfishness, sensuality and brutality incidental to many sports, the empty-mindedness, obtuseness of intelligence and insensate pride, the shutting of the senses and the emotions to most of the finer and nobler scenes in the spectacle of nature and the drama of humanity, that are the natural and necessary consequences of 'a sporting life.' Or could one accurately analyse the costs of dilettantism, sham culture, with its monstrous perversions of productive energy in the fields of pedagogy, art, science, and literature, in a descending scale of frivolousness or depravity, as they seize by imitation the awakening mind of ever larger strata of our populations! But even worse than sham intellectualism is the sham morality which tricks itself out in pietistic formulas and charitable practices, so as to evade obedience to the plain laws of human brotherhood and social justice in this world.

The widest and deepest implications of this parasitic life of luxury and leisure, the substitution of recreation for art and exercise, of dilettantism for the life of thought, of pietism, and charity for human fellowship, lie beyond the scope of our formal enquiry. We are concerned with them primarily as affecting economic production and consumption. Sport, dilettantism and charity are for us characteristic products of mal-distribution seizing that surplus-income which is the economic nutriment of social progress, and applying it to evolve a complicated life of futile frivolities for a small leisured class who damage by their contagious example and incitement the standards of the working members of the society in which they exercise dominion.

CHAPTER XII

§ 1. In seeking at once to establish and apply to industry a standard of human value, we have taken for our concrete subject-matter the aggregate of marketable goods and services that constitute the real income of the nation. This real wealth, distributed in income among the various members of the community, we subjected to a double analysis, tracing it backwards through the processes of its production, forward into its consumption. Some of the activities of its production we recognised as being in themselves interesting, pleasant, educative or otherwise organically useful: others we found to be uninteresting, painful, depressing or otherwise organically costly. A similar divergence of human value appeared in the consumption of those forms of wealth. Some sorts and quantities of consumption were found conducive to the maintenance and furtherance of healthy life, both pleasant and profitable. Other sorts and qualities of consumption were found wasteful or injurious to the life of the consumers and of the community.

The general result of this double analysis may be summarised in the following tabular form.

WEALTH

PRODUCTION		CONSUMPTION
Art & Exercise. ⎱	Human	⎰ Needs.
Labour. ⎰	Utility	⎱ Abundance.
Toil. ⎱	Human	⎰ Satiety.
Mal-production. ⎰	Cost	⎱ Mal-consumption.

In the ordinary economic account 'costs' appear entirely on the Production side of the account, 'utility' entirely on the Consumption side. Production is regarded not as good or desirable in itself, but only as a means towards an end, Consumption. On the other hand, all parts of Consumption are regarded as in themselves desirable and good, and are assessed as Utilities according to the worth which current desires, expressed in purchasing power, set upon them.

Our human valuation refuses to regard work as a mere means to consumption. It finds life and welfare in the healthy functioning of productive activities, as well as in the processes of repair and growth which form sound consumption.

If all production could be reduced to Art and Exercise, the creative and the re-creative functions, all consumption to the satisfaction of physical and spiritual needs, we should appear to have reached an ideal economy, in which there would be no human costs and a maximum amount of human utility. The conditions of a complete individual life would seem to be attained. But we are not concerned with a society in which completeness of the individual life is the sole end, but with a society in which the desires, purposes and welfare of the individuals are comprised in the achievement of a common life. For this reason I have included under the head of Utility on the Productive side of our account, not only the Art and Exercise which are directly conducive to individual well-being, but a quantum of Labour which represents the economic measure of the inter-dependency, or solidarity, of the so-called individuals. Such labour is the so-called 'sacrifice' required of 'individuals' in the interest of the society to which they belong. To the individualist it appears a distortion of the free full development of his nature, an interference with his perfect life. But it is, of course, neither sacrifice nor distortion. For the so-called individual is nowise, except in physical structure,[1] completely divided from his fellows. He is a social being and this social nature demands recognition and expression in economic processes. It requires him to engage in some special work which has for its direct end the wel-

---

[1] Even there he is not separated in physical functions. The sexual, philoprogenitive, and the gregarious instincts, which are rooted in physical structure, negate physical individualism. So does the structure of his brain, which in solitude decays or becomes diseased.

fare of society, in addition to the work of using his own powers for his own personal ends. How far this routine labour for society can be taken into his conception of his human nature, and so become a source of personal satisfaction, is a question we shall discuss later on. At present it will suffice to recognise that each man's fair contribution to the routine labour of the world, though irksome to him, is not injurious but serviceable to his 'human' nature. Thus interpreted, it stands on the utility, not on the cost, side of the account. It must be distinguished from its excess, which we here term 'toil', and from work, which whether from an abuse of the creative faculty or of social control, is bad and degrading in its nature and is here termed mal-production.

A similar distinction between the narrowly personal and the broader social interpretation of welfare is applicable on the consumption side. It is clearly not enough that the income which is to furnish consumption should suffice only to make provision for the satisfaction of the material and spiritual needs of the individual—or even of his family. The expenditure of every man should contain a margin—which I here call 'abundance'—from which he may contribute voluntarily to the good of others. There will be public needs or emergencies, which are not properly covered by State services but remain a call upon the public spirit of persons of discernment and humanity. There are also the calls of hospitality and comradeship, and the wider claim of charity, the willing help to those in need, a charity that is spontaneous, not organised, that degrades neither him who gives nor him who receives, because it is the natural expression of a spirit of human brotherhood. For the sting alike of condescension and of degradation would be removed from charity, when both parties feel that such acts of giving are an agreeable expression of a spirit of fellowship. From the consumption which is thus applied to the satisfaction of sound personal needs, or which overflows in 'abundance' to meet the needs of others, we distinguish sharply that excessive quantity of consumption, which in our Table ranks as 'Satiety', and those base modes of consumption which in their poisonous reactions on personal and social welfare strictly correspond to the base forms of production.

§ 2. Such are the general lines of demarcation between the

strictly business and the human valuation of the productive and consumptive processes. We now perceive how close is the resemblance of the laws of human valuation as applied to the two sides of the equation of Wealth. This similarity is, of course, no chance coincidence: it inheres in the organic nature of society and of individual life. But, in order to proceed with our main purpose, the expression of the economic income in terms of human income, we must bring the two sides of the enquiry into closer union. We can thus get a fair survey of the current life of industry from the standpoint of wealth and waste, health and disease. So far as our national income, the £2,000,000,000 of goods and services, are produced by activities, which in their nature and distribution can be classed as Art, Exercise and Social Labour, and are consumed in ways conducive to the satisfaction of individual and social Needs, our industrial society is sound.

Probably the greater part of our income is thus made and spent. The necessity of attending more closely to the defects than to the successes of the present system must not lead us to disparage the latter.

If industry were in fact the irrational, unjust and utterly inhuman anarchy it is sometimes represented to be, it would not hold together for twenty-four hours. Not merely is the individual business in its normal state a finely adjusted, accurately-working complex of human skill, industry and coöperative goodwill, but the larger and less centralised structures, which we call trades and markets, show a wonderful intricacy of order in their form and working. To feed the thousands of mills and workshops of England with a fairly regular supply of countless materials drawn from the wide world, to feed the millions of mouths of our people with their regular supply of daily food, are notable achievements of industrial order. In concentrating, as we must, our chief thought upon the disorder of the system, the places where it fails, and the damage of such failure, we gain nothing by exaggerating the industrial maladies and their social injuries.

The proportions of order and disorder, health and disease, human cost and human utility, in the working of our industrial system are best ascertained by turning once more to our concrete mass of wealth, our income, and enquiring into the quantitative method of its distribution.

In examining the human costs involved in a given output of labour-power (and of other productive energy) we recognised that very much depended upon the conditions of that output, and particularly upon the length and intensity of the working-day and working-week.

Similarly, in examining the human utility got from the consumption of a given quantity of goods, we recognised that it will depend upon the sort and the number of persons who receive it for consumption.

So from both sides of the question we approach the central issue of the distribution of Wealth.

If the £2,000,000,000 of goods were found to be so distributed in the modes of their production as to involve no burden of toil and no injury upon the producers, while they were so distributed in income as to involve no waste or damage in consumption, the human utility it represented would reach a maximum and cost would be zero.

If, on the other hand, the same goods were largely produced by ill-nourished labourers, working long hours under bad hygienic conditions, and using capital largely furnished by the painful and injurious saving of the poor, while the distribution of the goods was such as to assign the bulk of them to a small affluent class, the masses living on a bare subsistence level, the human utility of such a system would be very small, its human cost very great.   Judged indeed from any right standard of civilisation, an industrial society of the latter sort might represent a minus quantity of human welfare.

There might even be two nations of equal population and economic income, equally prosperous from the standpoint of statistics of commerce, which nevertheless, by reason of the different apportionment of work and income, stood poles asunder in every true count of human prosperity.

§ 3. Now the Human Law of Distribution, in its application to industry, aims, as we have seen, to distribute Wealth, in relation to its production on the one hand and its consumption on the other, so as to secure the minimum of Human Costs and the maximum of Human Utility. No bare rule of absolute equality, based upon the doctrine of equal rights, equal powers or equal needs, will conduce to this result. The notion that the claims of justice or humanity would be met by requiring from all persons an equal contribution to the general output of productive energy is manifestly foolish and impracticable. To require the same output of energy from a strong as from a weak man, from an old as from a young, from a woman as from a man, to ignore those actual differences of age, sex, health, strength and skill, would be rejected at once as a preposterous application of human equality. If such an equal output were required, it could only be obtained by an average task which would unduly tax the powers of the weak, and would waste much of the powers of the strong. A similar human economy holds of the provision of capital through saving. To impose saving upon working folk whose income barely maintains the family efficiency, when other folk possess surplus-incomes out of which the socially necessary capital can be provided, is a manifestly wasteful policy. Those who have no true power to save should not be called upon to undergo this 'cost': all saving should come proportionately out of higher incomes where it involves no human sacrifice. Alike, as regards labour and capital, the true social economy is expressed in the principle that each should contribute in accordance with his ability.

It should be similarly evident that exact equality of incomes in money or in goods for all persons is not less wasteful, or less socially injurious. I cannot profess to understand by what reasoning some so-called Socialists defend an ideal order in which every member of society, man, woman and child, should have an absolutely equal share of the general income. The needs of people, their capacity to get utility out of incomes by consuming it, are no more equal than their powers of production. Neither in respect of food, or clothing, or the general material standard of comfort, can any such equality of needs be alleged. To say that a big strong man, giving out a correspondingly large output of energy, needs exactly the same supply of food as a small weakly man, whose output is a third as great, would be as ridiculous as to pretend that a fifty-horse power engine needed no more fuel than a ten-horse power one. Nor will the differences in one set of needs be closely compensated in another. Mankind is not equal in the sense that all persons have the same number of faculties developed, or capable of development, to the same extent, and demanding the same aggregate amount of nutriment. To maintain certain orders of productive efficiency will demand a much larger consumption than to maintain others. Because differences of income and expenditure exist at present which are manifestly unjust and injurious, that is no reason for insisting that all differences are unwarrantable. Equality of opportunity does not imply equality but some inequality of incomes. For opportunity does not consist in the mere presence of something which a man can use, irrespective of his own desires and capacities. A banquet does not present the same amount of opportunity to a full man as to a hungry man, to an invalid as to a robust digestion. £1,000, spent in library equipment for university students, represents far more effective opportunity than the same sum spent on library equipment in a community where few can read or care to read any book worth reading. Equality of opportunity involves the distribution of income according to capacity to use it, and to assume an absolute equality of such capacity is absurd.

It may no doubt be urged that it is difficult to measure individual needs and capacities so as to apply the true organic mode of distribution. This is true and any practical rules for adjusting income, or for distribution of the product, according to needs, will be likely to involve some waste. But that is no reason for adopting a principle of distribution which must involve great waste. However difficult it may be to discover and estimate differences of needs in individuals or classes of men, to ignore all differences insures a maximum of waste. For, assuming, as it does, a single average or standard man, to which type no actual man conforms, it involves a necessary waste in each particular case. Everyone, in a word, would under this mechanical interpretation of equality possess either a larger or a smaller income than he could use. Such a doctrine, though sometimes preached by persons who call themselves socialists, is really a survival of the eighteenth-century doctrine of individual rights, grafted on to a theory of the uniformity of human nature that is contradicted by the entire trend of science.

This levelling doctrine only serves to buttress the existing forms of inequality, by presenting in the guise of reform a spurious equality, the folly and the waste of which are obvious even to the least reflecting of mankind.

§ 4. Distribution of income according to needs, or ability to use it, does not, indeed, depend for its practical validity upon the application of exact and direct measurements of needs. The limits of any sort of direct measurement even of material needs appear in any discussion of the science of dietetics. But inexact though such science is, it can furnish certain valid reasons for different standards of food in different occupations, and for other discriminations relating to race, age, sex and vigour. What holds of food will also hold of housing, leisure, modes of recreation and intellectual consumption. Nor must it be forgotten that, for expenditure, the family is the true unit. The size and age of the family is certainly a relevant factor in estimating needs, and in any distribution on a needs basis must be taken into account.

Public bodies, and less commonly private forms, in fixing salaries and wages, are consciously guided by such considerations. The idea is to ascertain the sum which will maintain a worker, with or without a family, in accordance with economic efficiency, and having regard to the accepted conventions of the class from which he will be drawn. Having determined this 'proper' salary or wage, they seek to get the best man for the work. It is true that the conventional factor looms so big in this process as often to obscure the natural economy. When it is determined by a municipality that its Town Clerk ought to have £1500 a year and its dustman 22s. a week, it appears a palpable straining of language to suggest that differences of 'needs' correspond to this discrepancy of pay. For, though it is true that in the existing state of the market for legal ability and experience the town may not be able to get a really good town clerk for less, that state of the legal market is itself the result of artificial restrictions in opportunity of education and of competition, which have no natural basis and which a society versed in sound social economy will alter. But the fact that the existing interpretation of needs is frequently artificial and exaggerated must not lead us to ignore the element of truth embodied in it. The wages of policemen, the real wages of soldiers and sailors, are determined with conscious relation to the needs of able-bodied men engaged in hard physical work, and with some regard to the existence of a wife and family. But I need not labour the point of the difference between the salary and the 'commodity' view of labour. The acceptance among all thoughtful employers of 'the economy of high wages' applied within reasonable limits is itself the plainest testimony to the actuality of the 'needs' basis of income. That unless you pay a man enough to satisfy his needs, you cannot get from him his full power of work, is a proposition which would meet with universal acceptance.

But it will commonly be added that the safest way of measuring needs is by means of output. This output, measured by work-time, or by piece, or by a combination of the two, still remains the general basis of payment. How far is this conformable to our theory of human distribution, according to needs? That there is some conformity will, I think, be easily perceived. If one docker unloads twice as much grain or timber as another docker in the same time, or if one hewer working under the same conditions 'gets' twice as much coal as another, there is a reasonable presumption that the larger actual quantity of labour has taken a good deal more 'out of him'.

Putting the comparison on its barest physical basis, there has been a larger expenditure of tissue and of energy, which must be replaced by a larger consumption of food. A strong man doing much work may not be exerting himself more than a weak man doing little work. But all the same there is some proportion between the respective values of their output of physical energy and their intake of food. This, of course, is a purely physiological application of our law of human distribution. It applies both to sorts of work and to individual cases in the same sort of work, and constitutes an 'organic' basis for difference of 'class' wages and individual wages. We urge that it is applicable to other factors of consumption than food, and throughout the whole area of production and consumption. But applied as a practical principle for determining distinctions of class or grade payment, and still more for individual payment within a class, it has a very limited validity. Rigorously applied it is the pure 'commodity' view of labour, the antithesis of the 'salary' view which best expresses the 'needs' economy. But, though output cannot be taken as an accurate measure of 'needs' for the purpose of remuneration, it clearly ought to be taken into account. The practical reformer will indeed rightly insist that it must be taken into account. For he will point out that output is a question not merely of physiological but still more of moral stimulus. A strong man *will* not put out more productive energy than his weaker fellow unless he knows he is to get more pay; a skilful man cannot be relied upon to use his full skill unless he personally gains by doing so. If the sense of social service were stronger than it is, a bonus for extra strength or skill might be unnecessary. But as human nature actually stands, this stimulus to do a 'best' that is better than the average, must be regarded as a moral 'need' to be counted for purposes of remuneration along with the physiological needs. Too much need not be made of this distinctively selfish factor. In many sorts of work, indeed, it may not be large enough to claim recognition in remuneration. But where it is important, the application of our needs economy of distribution must provide for it. This admission does not in the least invalidate our organic law. For the moral nature of a man is as 'natural' as his physical nature. Both are amenable to education, and with education will come changes which will have their just reactions upon the policy of remuneration.

§ 5. The organic law of distribution in regarding needs will, therefore, take as full an account as it can both of the unity and the diversity of human nature. The recognition of 'common' humanity will carry an adequate provision of food, shelter, health, education and other prime necessaries of life, so as to yield equal satisfaction of such requirements to all members of the community. This minimum standard of life will be substantially the same for all adult persons, and for all families of equal size and age. Upon this standard of human uniformity will be erected certain differences of distribution, adjusted to the specific needs of any class or group whose work or physical conditions marks it out as different from others. The present inequalities of income, so largely based upon conventional or traditional claims, would find little or no support under this application of the organic law. Indeed, it seems unlikely that any specific requirements of industrial or professional life would bulk so largely in interpreting human needs as to warrant any wide discrimination of incomes. There seems no reason to maintain that a lawyer's or a doctor's family would require, or could advantageously spend, a larger income than a bricklayer's, in a society where equality of educational and other opportunities obtained. But, if there were any sorts of work which, by reason of the special calls they made upon human faculties, or of the special conditions they imposed, required an expenditure out of the common, the organic law of distribution according to needs would make provision for the same as an addition to the standard minimum. So likewise the hours of labour would be varied from a standard working-day to meet the case of work unusually intense or wearing in its incidence. To what extent society would find it necessary to recognise individual differences of efficiency within each grade as a ground for particular remuneration—and how far such claims would represent, not payment according to true needs but power to extort a personal rent—is a question which can only be answered by experience. It may, however, be regarded as certain that the high individual rents which prevail at present in skilled manual and mental work, could not be maintained. For these high rates depend upon conditions of supply and of demand which would not then exist. The enormous fees which specialists of repute in the law or medicine can obtain depend, partly, upon the inequality of educational and social opportunities that limits the supply of able men in these professions; partly, upon other inequalities of income that enable certain persons to afford to pay such fees. Equality of opportunity and even an approximate equalisation of income would destroy both these sources of high rents of ability. What applies in the professions would apply in every trade. Individual 'rents' of ability might survive, but they must be brought within a narrow compass.

While, then, the selfishness of individual man might give a slight twist to the application of the social policy of distribution according to needs, it would not impair its substantial validity and practicability.

Thus we see this law of distribution, operative as a purely physical economy in the apportionment of energy for mechanical work, operative as a biological economy through the whole range of organic life, is strictly applicable as a principle of social economy. Its proper application to social industry would enable that system to function economically, so as to produce the maximum of human utility with the minimum of human cost.

§ 6. If we can get an industrial order, in which every person is induced to discover and apply to the service of society his best abilities of body and mind, while he receives from society what is required to sustain and to develop those abilities, and so to live the best and fullest life of which he is capable, we have evidently reached a formally sound solution of the social problem on its economic side. We are now in a position to approach the actual processes of economic distribution that prevail to-day, so as to consider how far they conform to this sound principle of human industry.

We are not justified at the outset in assuming that any wide discrepancy will be admitted. On the contrary, in many quarters there survives a firm conviction that our actual system of industry does work in substantial conformity with the human law of distribution.

The so-called *laissez-faire* theory of industrialism based its claims to utility and equity upon an assertion of the virtual identity of the economic and the human distribution. If every owner of capital or labour or any other factor of production were free to apply his factor in any industry and any place he chose, he would choose that industry and that place where the highest remuneration for its employment was attainable. But since all remuneration for the factors of production is derived from the product itself, which is distributed among the owners of the several factors, it follows that the highest remuneration must always imply the most productive use. Thus, by securing complete mobility of capital and labour, we ensure both a maximum production and an equitable distribution. 'Led as by an invisible hand,' every owner of capital, labour or other productive power, disposed of his factor in a manner at once most serviceable to the production of the general body of wealth and most profitable to himself. The application of this theory, of course, assumed that everybody knew or could get to know what employment he would be likely to find most profitable for his capital or labour, and would use that knowledge. It was, moreover, held that the actual conditions of industry and commerce did and must substantially conform to this hypothesis of mobility. Any circumstances, indeed, which contravened it by obstructing the mobility and liberty of employment were treated as exceptional. Such exceptions were monopolies, the exclusive owners of which forbade freedom of entry or of competition to outside capital and labour, and secured higher rates of profit than prevailed in other businesses. The harmony of perfect individualism demanded that all such monopolies, together with protective duties and other barriers to complete liberty of commerce and of industry, should be removed. All productive power would then flow like water through the various industrial channels, maintaining a uniform level of efficient employment, the product being distributed in accordance with the several costs of its production and being absorbed in the processes of productive consumption that were required to maintain the current volume of productive power or to enhance it.

There was a little difficulty in the case of rents of land. Though differential rents, measuring the superior productivity of various grades of land as compared with the least productive land in use, were necessary payments to landowners, they could not rank as costs and could not be productively consumed. So likewise with the scarcity rents, paid even for the least productive lands where the supply for certain uses was restricted. Both scarcity and differential rents were classed as surplus. But though the magnitude of this exceptional element might seem to have been a fatal flaw in the individualist harmony, a characteristic mode of escape was found in the doctrine of parsimony which prevailed. Though economic rents could not be productively consumed by their recipients, they furnished a natural fund of savings, so providing the growing volume of new capital which was necessary to set labour to productive work. So, by a somewhat liberal interpretation, it was contended that 'the simple system of natural liberty', even operating on a basis of private ownership of land, drew from each man the best and fullest use of his productive powers, and paid him what was economically necessary to maintain and to evoke those powers. Early critics of this theory, of course, pointed out that the interpretation of distribution 'according to needs' was defective from the standpoint of humanity, since the only needs taken into account were efficiency for productive work, the nourishment and stimulus to produce a larger quantity of marketable goods, not the attainment of the highest standard of human well-being. But to most economists of that day such a criticism seemed unmeaning, so dominant in their minds was the conception of economic wealth as the index and the instrument of human welfare.

§ 7. It is commonly asserted and assumed that this *laissez-faire* theory is dead, and that the attainment of a harmony of social welfare, by the free intelligent play of individual self-interest in the direction of economic forces, has been displaced by some theory of conscious coöperative or corporate direction in which the State takes a leading part. But at this very time, when the policy of every civilised nation is engaged more and more in checking monopolies and industrial privileges upon the one hand, and in placing restraints upon the havoc of unfettered competition on the other, a distinct and powerful revival of an economic theory of production and distribution undistinguishable in its essentials from the crude 18th century *laissez-faire* has set in. Largely influenced by the desire to apply mathematics, so as to secure a place for economics as an 'exact' science, many English and American economists have committed themselves to a 'marginalist' doctrine, which for its efficiency rests upon assumptions of infinite divisibility of the factors of production, and frictionless mobility of their flow into all the channels of industry and commerce. These assumptions granted, capital and labour flow into all employments until the last drop in each is equally productive, the products of the 'marginal' or final drops exchanging on a basis of absolute equality and earning

for their owners an equal payment. Among English economists
Mr. Wicksteed has set out this doctrine in all its economic ap-
plications most fully. He shows how by a delicate balance of
preferences 'at the margins' i. e. in reference to the last portion
of each supply of or demand for anything that is bought or sold,
there must be brought about an exact equivalence of utility, of
worth, and of remuneration, for the marginal increments in all
employment. 'So far as the economic forces work without friction, they secure to everyone the equivalent of his industrial
significance at the part of the industrial organism at which he
is placed.'[1] Elsewhere[2] he asseverates that, as regards the
workers in any employment, this means that 'they are already
getting as much as their work is worth,' and that if they are to
get more, this 'more' can only be got either out of 'communal
funds,' or by making their work worth more. The same application of the marginalist doctrine is made by Professor Chapman. 'The theory, then, merely declares that each person will
tend to receive as his wage *his value*—that is, the value of this
marginal product—no more and no less. In order to get more
than he actually does get, he must become more valuable,—work
harder, for instance—that is, he must add more to the product
in which he participated.'[3] This is precisely the old '*laissez-
faire, laissez-aller*' teaching, fortified by the conception that some
special virtue attaches to the equalising process which goes on
'at the margin' of each employment of the factors of production.

The 'law of distribution' which emerges is that every owner
of any factor of production 'tends to receive as remuneration'
exactly what it is 'worth'. Now this 'law' is doubly defective.
Its first defect arises from the fact that economic science assigns
no other meaning to the 'worth' or 'value' of anything than what
it actually gets in the market. To say, therefore, that anybody
'gets what he is worth', is merely an identical proposition, and
conveys no knowledge. The second defect is the reliance upon
a 'tendency' which falsely represents the normal facts and forces.
It is false in three respects. It assumes in the first place an infinite divisibility of the several factors, necessary to secure the

[1] *The Common-sense of Political Economy*, p. 698.
[2] P. 345.   [3] *Work and Wages*, Vol. I, p. 14.

accurate balance of 'preferences' at the margins. It next assumes perfect mobility or freedom of access for all capital and labour into all avenues of employment. Finally, it assumes a statical condition of industry, so that the adjustment of the factors on a basis of equal productivity and equal remuneration at the margins may remain undisturbed. All three assumptions are unwarranted. Very few sorts of real capital or labour approach the ideal of infinite divisibility which marginalism requires. An individual worker, sometimes a group, is usually the minimal 'drop' of labour, and capital is only infinitely divisible when it is expressed in terms of money, instead of plants, machines or other concrete units. Still less is it the case that capital or labour flows or 'tends' to flow with perfect accuracy and liberty of movement into every channel of employment where it is required, so as to afford equality of remuneration at the several margins. Lastly, in most industrial societies the constant changes taking place, in volume and in methods of industry, entail a corresponding diversity in the productivity and the remuneration of the capital and labour employed in the various industries 'at the margin.' [1]

§ 8. This slightly technical disquisition is rendered necessary by the wide acceptance which 'marginalism' has won in academic circles. Its expositors are able to deduce from it practical precepts very acceptable to those politicians and business men who wish to show the injustice, the damage and the final futility of all attempts of the labouring classes, by the organised pressure of trade unionism or by politics, to get higher wages or other expensive improvements of the conditions of their employment.

---

[1] Professor Pigou (*Wealth and Welfare*, p. 176), though adopting the general position of marginalism, makes a concession, as to its applicability, which is a virtual admission of its futility. For by showing that only in 'industries of constant returns' are 'supply price' and 'marginal supply price' equal, and that in industries of 'decreasing' or of 'increasing' returns there exists a tendency to exceed or to fall short of 'the marginal net product yielded in industries in general,' he virtually endorses the criticism that 'marginalism' assumes a statical condition of industry. For only in a statical condition would all industries be found conforming to constant returns: the operation of increasing or diminishing returns means nothing else than that changes in volume or methods of production are raising or lowering productivity and remuneration above or below the equal level which 'marginalism' desiderates.

For if 'marginalism' can prove that, as Professor Chapman holds, 'in order to get more than he actually does get, he must become more valuable—work harder, for example,' it has evidently re-created the defences against the attacks of the workers upon the fortresses of capital which were formerly supplied by the wage-fund theory in its most rigorous form. If wages can only rise on condition of the workers working harder or better, no divergence of interests exists between capital and labour, no injustice is done to any class of labour, however low its 'worth' may be, and no remedy exists for poverty except through improved efficiency of the workers. If our political economists can bring this gospel of marginalism home to the hearts and heads of the working-classes, they will set aside all their foolish attempt to get higher wages out of rents and property and will set themselves to producing by harder, more skilful and more careful labour an enlarged product, the whole or part of which may come to them by the inevitable operation of the economic law of equal distribution at the margin!

It is right to add that an attempt is sometimes made to bring marginalism into a measure of conformity with the notorious fact that large discrepancies exist in the rates of remuneration for capital or labour or both in various industries, by treating these inequalities as brief temporary expedients for promoting the 'free flows' of productive power from less socially productive into more socially productive channels, and for stimulating improvements in the arts of industry. Abnormal gains, of the nature of prizes or bonuses, are thus obtainable by individual employment, or by groups of employers, who are pioneers in some new industry or in the introduction of some new invention or other economy. But these rewards of special merit, it is argued, are not lasting, but disappear so soon as they have performed their socially serviceable function of drawing into the favoured employments the increased quantity of new productive power which will restore the equality of productivity and remuneration 'at the margins'.

Now, even were it possible to accept this rehabilitation of *laissez-faire* theory, accepting this equalising 'tendency' as predominant and normal, and classifying all opposing tendencies as mere friction, it would not supply a law of distribution that would satisfy the conditions of our 'human' law. It would afford no security of distribution according to 'needs', or human capacity of utilising wealth for the promotion of the highest standard of individual and social welfare. It would remain an ideally good distribution only in the sense that it would so apportion the product as to furnish to all producers a stimulus which would evoke their best productive powers, so contributing to maximise the aggregate production of marketable goods. Only so far as man was regarded as an economic being, concerned merely in the nourishment and improvement of his marketable wealth-producing faculties, would it be a sound economy.

Just as in the case of the older, cruder 'freedom of competition', it rests upon the fundamental assumption that all the product, the real income of the community, will be absorbed in 'productive consumption', defraying the bare 'costs' of maintaining and improving the productive powers of capital, labour and ability, for the further production of objective economic goods and services. It would remain open to the objection that it assumed an identity of economic wealth and human welfare which is inadmissible, and that it refused to provide that subordination of economic production and consumption to the larger conception of human welfare which sound principles of humanity require. Though all work might be most productively applied, it might still contain excessive elements of human cost, and though all products were productively consumed many of the finer needs of individual men and of society might still remain without satisfaction.

§ 9. But the full divergence between the operation of the actual economic law of distribution and the human law can best be discovered by unmasking the fundamental falsehood of all forms of the *laissez-faire* or competitive economy, viz. the assumption that the national income tends to be distributed in a just economy of costs. Is there in fact any operative law which distributes or 'tends' to distribute the £2,000,000,000 worth of goods that form our income, so that all, or even most of it, acts as a necessary food and stimulus to evoke the full and best productive work of those who receive it? Or, if there are failures in this economical distribution, are they so few, so small, and so ephemeral, that they may reasonably be treated as 'friction', or as that admixture of error or waste which is unavoidable in all human arrangements?

Now it is of course true that the national income must continually provide for the subsistence of the labour, ability and capital, required to maintain the existing structure of industry and the current output of goods and services. The brain-workers and the hand-workers of every sort and grade, from artist and inventor to routine labourer, must be continuously supplied with the material and non-material consumables sufficient to enable them to replace in their own persons, or through their offspring, the physical and psychical wear and tear involved in their work. The fertility of the soil, the raw materials, fuel, buildings, tools and machines, requisite in the various productive processes, must similarly be maintained out of the current output. These bare costs of subsistence, the wages, salaries and depreciation funds necessary to replace the wear and tear of the human and material agents of production, are a first charge upon the national dividend. To refuse the payments which provide this subsistence would be suicidal on the part of the administrators of the income. They rank, from the standpoint of society[1] as costs of production. If the product which results from the productive use of these factors exceeds what is necessary to defray these costs, the surplus may be employed in either of two ways. It may be distributed among the productive classes in extra-payments so as to evoke by a set of economically-adjusted stimuli such enlarged or improved efficiency as will provide for a larger or a better product in the future. In a society of a progressive order where the numbers or the wholesome needs, or both, are on the increase, no surplus, however large, can be excessive for such provision. A socially sound and just distribution of the surplus would be one which absorbed it entirely in what may be called the 'costs of growth'. This, however, does not by any means imply that the whole of the surplus must ad-

---

[1] From the standpoint of the individual business firm 'costs of production' may include many higher rates of payments, necessary under the actual conditions of competitive industry to secure the use of the required agents.

vantageously be distributed directly among the individual owners of labour, ability or saving power, in order to evoke from them the maximum extension of their several productive powers. A good deal of the surplus may, indeed, be thus applied in higher individual incomes of producers. But the State, politically organised society, must look to the 'surplus' for its costs, not only of upkeep but of progress. For whatever part we may assign to the State in aiding industrial production, all will agree that much of its work, in the protection and improvement of the conditions of life, is essential to the stability and progress of industry, and involves 'costs' which can only be met by a participation in the industrial dividend. It may even be urged that the claims of the State to maintenance and progress are equal to the claims of individuals upon the surplus. For it is evident that industrial progress demands that both individual and social stimuli and nutriment of progress must be provided from the surplus by some considered adjustment of their several claims. A surplus, thus properly apportioned in extra-subsistence wages and other payments to producers and in public income, would be productively expended and would thus contribute to the maximum promotion of human welfare.[1]

§ 10. But though in such a society as ours a certain part of the surplus is thus 'productively' applied, and is represented in industrial and human progress, a large part is not so expended in 'costs of progress'. A large quantity of 'surplus' is everywhere diverted into unproductive channels. The income which should go to raise the efficiency of labour, to evoke more saving, and to improve the public services, is largely taken by private owners of some factor of production who are in a position to extort from society a payment which evokes no increase of productive efficacy, but is sheer waste. This power to extort superfluous and unearned income is at the root of every social-economic malady. Indeed, it often goes beyond the diversion of surplus from productive into unproductive channels. It often encroaches upon costs of maintenance. For the vital statistics of large

[1] For it must be kept in mind that the 'productive expenditure' to which reference is here made refers ultimately to a standard not of market but of human values.

classes of labour show that the food, housing and other elements of real wages, are insufficient for the upkeep of a normal working life and for the rearing of a healthy and efficient offspring. This means that surplus is actually eating into 'costs', in that the costs of maintenance, which sound business administration automatically secures for the capital employed, are not secured for the labour. The reason why this policy, which from the social standpoint is suicidal, can nevertheless be practised, is obvious. For the capital 'belongs to' the business, in a sense in which the labour does not. A sweating economy which 'lets down' the instruments of capital is of necessity unprofitable to the individual firms: a similar sweating economy applied to the instruments of labour need not be unprofitable. To the nation as a whole, indeed, regarded merely as a goods-producing body, any such withholding of the true costs of maintenance must be unprofitable. But there are businesses, or trades, where 'sweated' labour may be profitable to the employers or the owners of capital. There are many more where such a wage-policy, though not really profitable, appears so, and is actually practised as 'sound business'. How large a proportion of the 14,000,000 wage-earners whose incomes are paid out of our £2,000,000,000 come under this category of 'sweated' workers, we cannot here profitably discuss. But, apart from the great bulk of casual workers in all less skilled trades, there are large strata of skilled and trained adult-labour in the staple trades of the country which are not paid a full subsistence wage. Such are the large bodies of women employed in factories and workshops and in retail trade, at wages varying between eight and fourteen shillings. Indeed, it may safely be asserted that the average wage of an adult working-woman in this country, not in domestic service, is a sweating wage, definitely below true economic maintenance, and still more below the decent human requirements of life. The same statement also holds of the wage of agricultural labour in most districts of the middle and southern counties of England. In such employments the true economic 'costs' of maintenance are not provided out of the present distribution of the national income. Of a far wider range of labour is it true that the true wages of progressive efficiency, which we have seen are vital to the economic progress of the nation, are withheld. Though this deprivation does not form the whole case for labour as stated from the 'human' standpoint, it constitutes the heaviest economic count against the current distribution of wealth. The full physical and spiritual nutriment, the material comforts, the education, leisure, recreation, mobility and broad experience of life, requisite for an alert, resourceful, intelligent, responsible, progressive working-class, are not provided either by the present wage-system, or by the growing supplements which the communal action of the State and the municipality are making to the individual incomes of the workers. Out of the £2,000,000,000 a wholly insufficient sum is distributed in wages of progressive efficiency for labour.

In certain other respects also the current 'costs' distribution is exceedingly defective. The saving which goes to provide for the enlargement of the capital structure of industry is very wastefully provided. A large proportion of such savings as are contributed out of working-class incomes involves an encroachment upon their costs of progressive efficiency, and represents, from the standpoint both of the individual family and of society, bad economy. Moreover, the methods of collection and of application of such capital are so wasteful and so insecure as to render working-class thrift a byword in the annals of business administration.

§ 11. But these deficiencies in the economy of 'costs' can only be understood by a study of that large section of the national income which in its distribution furnishes no food or stimulus whatever to any form of productive energy. Even in the idealist *laissez-faire* economics we saw that rent of land was distinguished from the wages, interest and profits, which constituted the 'costs of production', and was described as 'surplus'. It was recognised that, where land was required for any productive purpose, its owners would receive in payment for its use any portion of the product, or its selling value, which remained over after the competitively determined 'costs' of capital and labour had been defrayed. The payment was economically necessary because suitable land for most industrial uses was scarce, and the amount of the payment would depend upon how much was left when capital and labour had received their share. For the land-

lord would take all the surplus. There are those who still insist
that the owners of land are everywhere in this position of resid-
uary legatees. Land, they think, is always relatively scarce,
capital and labour always and everywhere relatively abundant.
Free competition then between the owners of the relatively abundant factors will keep down the price for them to bare 'costs',
leaving a maximum amount of surplus which the so-called land
'monopolists' will receive as rent. This surplus evokes no productivity from the soil or its owners; its payment does nothing
to stimulate any art of industry. But, if the landowner did not
take it, and it was kept by farmers as profits, or by labourers as
wages, it would be just as wasteful from the productive standpoint, as if it passed as rent, for, upon the hypothesis of such
economists, the full competitive wages and profits are the only
payment entitled to count as cost, and no addition to such payments would increase the productivity of capital or labour.

§ 12. Now though there have been times and countries in
which rent of land was the only considerable surplus, this is not
the case in any developed industrial community to-day. Other
factors of production, capital, ability, or even in some instances
labour, share with land the power to extort scarcity prices.

The hypothetical abundance, mobility and freedom of competition, which should prevail among all owners of capital, ability and labour, keeping down all their remuneration to a common
minimum, are everywhere falsified by industrial facts. At various points in industry capital or managerial ability is found
strongly entrenched against the competition of outsiders, and
able to set limits upon internal competition. Wherever this condition is found, the owners of the capital or the ability so advantageously placed are able to obtain a 'surplus', which, in its
origin and its economic nature and effects, nowise differs from
the economic rents of land. The fluidity and complete freedom
which appear to attach to the term capital, so long as we treat
it in its abstract financial character, disappear as soon as for
capital we substitute certain skilfully made machinery constructed under patent rights and operated by more or less secret
processes, turning out, with the assistance of carefully trained
and organised labour, goods which enjoy a half-superstitious

fame and special facilities of market. An examination of the capitalist system will disclose in every field of industry numerous instances of businesses or groups of businesses, sometimes constituting whole trades, which by reason of some advantage in obtaining raw materials, transport or marketing facilities, public contracts, legal privilege or protection, by using some superior process of manufacture, skill in advertising, established reputation, financial backing, or by sheer magnitude of operations, are screened from the full force of free competition, and are earning interest and profits far exceeding the minimum. Some such businesses or groups of businesses possess a virtual monopoly of the market, and can control output and prices, so as to secure abnormal dividends. Such control is, to be sure, never absolute, its control of prices being subject to two checks, the restriction of demand which attends every rise of prices, and the increasing probability of competition springing up if profits are too high. But qualified monopolies, earning dividends far larger than are economically necessary to support the required capital, are everywhere in evidence. Trusts, cartels, pools, combines, conferences, and trade agreements of various potency and stringency, pervade the more highly organised industries, substituting the principle of combination for that of competition. In all major branches of the transport trade by land and sea, in large sections of the mining industry, in the iron and steel industry and in many branches of machine-making, in many of the specialised textile trades, in the chemical and other manufactures where special scientific knowledge counts, in many departments of wholesale and retail distribution, and, last not least, in banking, finance and insurance, freedom of investment and of competition have virtually disappeared. To assume that fresh streams of capital, labour and business ability, have liberty to enter these fields of enterprise, and by their equal competition with the businesses already in possession so to increase the output, lower selling prices and keep interest and profits at a bare 'costs' level, is a childish travesty of the known condition of these trades. To affirm that such mobility and liberty of competition is the sole normal 'tendency', and that the monopolistic and combinative forces merely represent friction, is so grave a falsification of the facts as to put out of court the whole method of economic interpretation which is based thereon. Concrete capital has none of the qualities assigned to the abstract capital of these economists. It is neither infinitely divisible, nor absolutely mobile, nor accurately directed, nor legally and economically 'free' to dispose itself in any part of the industrial system where the current interest or profit exceeds the average. Over large tracts of industry combination is more normal and more potent than competition, and where this is not the case, the most competitive trades will be found honeycombed with obstructive clots, businesses enjoying special advantages and earning correspondingly high profits.

§ 13. Because certain qualities of business ability are requisite, to wit astuteness, keenness of judgment, calculating power, determination, capacity for organisation and executive ability, it is sometimes claimed that the high rates of profit which accrue from such businesses as we have indicated are really the creation, not of monopoly or combination, but of the talents of these *entrepreneurs*. But even though it be admitted that some such ability is essential to produce or to maintain a successful combination, can the entire profits of such a combination be imputed to this ability or regarded as its natural and proper reward? Take the common instance of the 'forestaller', who stops the supply of some commodity on its way to a market, secures the whole supply at competitive prices from the various contributors, and then sells it at a monopoly price fixed by himself. Are the profits of this corner a product of ability and a reward of ability, and not a 'surplus' representing an artificially contrived scarcity value? Or take the case of a contracting firm, which persuades all the other firms in a position to compete to come into an arrangement as to a minimum tender. Are the extra profits due to such an arrangement to be regarded as wages of ability, because some tact was needed to work the thing? But suppose we granted the whole contention, and agreed that the extra dividends paid to shareholders in favoured or protected businesses were really produced by the ability of the *entrepreneur* or manager, what then? It is not proved that these extra profits are 'costs', not 'surplus'. On the contrary, the fact that they can be taken as

extra dividends or bonuses by the owners of the capital, instead
of passing in 'wages of ability' to the *entrepreneur*, is proof positive that they are surplus. For if they were a subsistence wage
of ability, or even a 'prize', essential to evoke some special output of skill or energy, they could not be thus diverted from the
entrepreneur to the shareholders. In fact, there is no reason to
suppose that any very rare or conspicuous ability is evinced in
working a successful pool or combine, or even in organising a
successful business. Still less is there reason to suppose that the
profits attending such an enterprise are in any way proportionate to the skill or energy of the *entrepreneur*. Everyone is aware
that the contrary is the case. Indeed, so far as scientific, professional, and business ability is industrially useful and has a
claim to income, enquiry shows that there is no better security
for mobility, freedom of competition and equality of payment,
than in the case of capital. Inequalities of economic conditions
between various classes of our population, involving inequalities
of nurture and of education, and of every other sort of 'opportunity' relevant to the discovery, training, equipment and success of 'natural ability', set up a series of almost impenetrable
barriers to the free flow of natural ability throughout the industrial system, and give rise to an elaborate hierarchy of restricted employments where the rates of remuneration represent, not any inherent services of ability, but the degree of the
restriction in relation to the importance of the work. All such
advantages of opportunity are reflected in rates of payment for
'ability' which carry elements of 'surplus.'

Though some portion of the higher remuneration paid to successful professional workers may be regarded as interest upon
the capital-outlay of their education and training, there is no
reason to hold that the extra payment is adjusted to the costs
of this outlay. Still less can any such argument avail in the case
of high business profits. Though ability and expensive training
may be favouring conditions to such financial success, restricted
competition must be accounted the principal direct determinant
of all such extra payments.

§ 14. There remains one final demurrer to our doctrine of the
unproductive 'surplus'. If you take into consideration, it is

urged, all the unsuccessful as well as the successful businesses, you will find that the average return for capital and for business ability is low enough, not in fact more than represents a bare 'costs' economy. Similarly with the high incomes earned by the few successful men in the professions and in other walks of life. Set the failures fairly against the successes and there is no net 'surplus' to take account of.

But this contention is one more abuse of the method of averages. To the charge that one man is overpaid, it is no answer that another is underpaid. To the statement that surplus emerges in the payment for some orders of capital or ability it is no answer to say that other capital and ability does not even get its true 'costs' or subsistence wages. The force of this rebuttal is still further strengthened when it is realised to what extent the success of those who succeed is directly responsible for the failure of those who fail. For the economic strength of those whose superior advantages have secured for them a position of control will necessarily operate to make the competition of outsiders difficult and their failure probable. Indeed, a portion of the gains which combination yields will often be consciously applied to kill the competition of outsiders, or to restrict their trade to the less profitable or the more precarious forms of enterprise. But even where this business policy is not adopted, the very fact that strong firms and 'combines' control many markets, must, by limiting the area of free competition, intensify the competition within that area and so cause the failures to be numerous.

The contention, that the excessive profits of successful firms are balanced and in some way cancelled by the losses of those that fail, is also contradicted by the psychology of the case. If it could be shown that the chance of winning these high gains was in fact a necessary inducement to the winners to stake their capital and business capacity in an inherently risky line of enterprise, there might be some force in this plea. But to the men who achieve these successes business is not a simple game of hazard in which they have merely the same chance as the others. Success is commonly achieved by force, strategy and the possession of known advantages, and is used to strengthen these advantages and so to increase continuously the 'pull' by which they accumulate their gains and ruin their would-be competitors. Although tight forms of monopoly are very rare, loose or partial restrictions upon competition are very numerous and often very profitable. All these extra gains, issuing from various forms of natural or contrived scarcity in all sorts of industries, are rightly classed as unproductive surplus. Many of them are as constant and as certain as the economic rents of land, arise in the same way from a limitation of some productive factor, and are 'unearned' income in the same sense of that term. Other of these gains are more fluctuating, proceeding from less stable forms of privilege or combination, but while they exist they equally belong to unproductive 'surplus'.[1]

§ 15. The distinction between that portion of the social income which goes as necessary payments to support and evoke the energies of body and mind of wealth-producers, i. e. costs of production, and that which goes as unproductive 'surplus' to those who, possessing some necessary instrument of production that is relatively scarce, can exact a scarcity price, is fundamental in a valuation of industry. For this surplus not only represents sheer economic waste, regarded from the social standpoint, but it can be shown to be directly responsible, as an efficient cause, for most of those particular maladies in our current processes of production and consumption which impede the economic and the human progress of the nation.

For if our analysis of this surplus is correct, it consists in the seizure of a large portion of the fruits of individual and social productive energies, required for the full support and further

[1] Economists, following the classical distinction made by Adam Smith in the case of land-values, may break up the surplus into various species of scarcity rents on the one hand and differential rents on the other. A scarcity or 'specific' rent will occur when the whole supply of some factor of production, e. g. all the land available for some particular use, or all the capital employed in some trade, is in a position to take a payment higher than is obtainable where more land or capital is available for this particular use than is required to turn out the supply of goods that is actually sold. The worst hop land in use in England obtains a positive rent, the worst equipped ships in the Atlantic combine obtain a surplus-profit: better acres of hop land, better-equipped ships obtain a differential rent or profit in addition. Both specific gain and differential gain are surplus, and the basis of each is a scarcity of supply and a restraint of competition.

stimulation of these energies and for the wider human life which they are designed to serve, and their assignment to persons who have not helped to make them, do not need them, and cannot use them. The payment of surplus takes large sections of the income, needed to raise the economic and human efficiency of the working-classes, or to enable society to enlarge the scope and to improve the quality of the public services, and disposes them in ways that are not merely wasteful but injurious. In effect, all the excessive human costs of production and all the defective human utilities of consumption, which our separate analysis of the two processes disclosed, find their concrete and condensed expression in this 'surplus'. The chief injuries it causes may be summarised as follows:

(1) Flowing abundantly as 'unearned' income into the possession of 'wealthy' individuals and classes, it thereby causes large quantities of the national income to be consumed with little or no benefit. For much, if not most, of this surplus, being devoted to luxury, waste, extravagance and 'illth', furnishes by its expenditure not human utility but human 'cost', not an enhancement but a diminution of the sum of human welfare.

(2) By enabling its recipients to disobey the sound biological and moral precept, 'In the sweat of thy face thou shalt eat bread,' it calls into being and sustains a leisured or unemployed class whose existence represents a loss of productive energy and of wealth-production to the nation.

(3) The evil prestige and attraction of the life of sensational frivolity this idle class is disposed to lead tends by suggestion to sap the wholesome respect for work in the standards of the rest of the community, and to encourage by servile imitation injurious or wasteful methods of expenditure.

(4) The economic necessity of producing this surplus imposes excessive toil upon the productive classes, being directly responsible for the long hours and speeding-up which constitute the heaviest burden of human costs. The direction which the expenditure of the surplus gives to capital and labour degrades the character of large bodies of workers by setting them to futile, frivolous, vicious or servile tasks.

(5) The disturbing irregularity of the trades which supply

the capricious and ever-shifting consumption, upon which the 'surplus' is so largely spent, imposes upon the workers a great cost in the shape of irregularity of employment, and a considerable burden of costly saving by way of insurance against this irregularity.

(6) By stamping with the badge of irrationality and inequity the general process of apportionment of income, the surplus impairs that spirit of human confidence and that consciousness of human solidarity of interests which are the best stimuli of individual and social progress.

The surplus element in private income thus represents the human loss from defects in the current distribution of wealth, not only the loss from wasteful and injurious consumption but from wasteful and injurious production, an exaggeration of human costs and a diminution of human utilities. The primary object of all social-economic reforms should be to dissipate this surplus and to secure its apportionment partly as useful income for individual producers, partly as useful income for society, so that, instead of poisoning the social organism as it does now, it may supply fuller nourishment and stimulus to the life of that organism and its cells.

Thus directed, partly into higher wages of efficiency for workers, partly into further income for the enrichment of the common life, the 'surplus' will in effect cease to be surplus, being completely absorbed in satisfying the human requirements of individuals and society. For not only will it furnish the expenditure required to bring the standard of consumption of all grades of workers up to the level of a full satisfaction of human needs, but it will establish an entirely new conception of public income. For it will be recognised that the public revenue, taken either by taxation or as profits of public industry, is earned by public work precisely as the revenue of individuals is earned by private work, and is required for public consumption just as private income is required for private consumption. Thus the whole of what now figures as a wasteful 'surplus' would be applied in productive consumption.

The scope of the operation of this organic law, of course, widely transcends this special application to the distribution of economic income. It is the general law of order and of progress in all departments of organic activity. But for our task, that of a human valuation of industry, its worth is supreme. For in the application of the organic law of distribution all the great antagonisms which loom so big as social Problems, Luxury and Poverty, Toil and Idleness, The Individual and Society, Authority and Liberty, find their solution.[1]

1 For a detailed and more technical defence of the fundamentally important distinction between 'costs' and 'surplus' and for a closer analysis of the sources of 'unproductive surplus', readers may be referred to the author's earlier work, *The Industrial System: an enquiry into earned and unearned income.* (Longman's 2nd and revised edition, 1909).

CHAPTER XIII

THE HUMAN CLAIMS OF LABOUR

§ 1. The validity of the human law of distribution is well tested by considering the light it sheds upon the modern claims of Labour and the Movement which is endeavouring to realise these claims. For the significance of the Labour Movement will continue to be misunderstood so long as it is regarded as a mere demand for a larger quantity of wages and of leisure, important as these objects are. The real demand of Labour is at once more radical and more human. It is a demand that Labour shall no longer be bought and sold as a dead commodity subject to the fluctuations of Demand and Supply in the market, but that its remuneration shall be regulated on the basis of the human needs of a family living in a civilised country.

At present most sorts of labourers are paid according to the quantity of labour-power they give out, and according to the market-price set upon a unit of each several sort of labour-power. This means that the actual weekly earnings of some grades of labourer are much higher than those of other grades, not because the work takes more out of them, or because it involves a higher standard of living, but because some natural, some fortuitous, or some organised scarcity of supply exists in the former grades, while there is abundance of supply in the latter.[1] Moreover, the weekly earnings for any of these sorts of labour will vary from week to week, from month to month, or year to year, with the variations of Supply and Demand in the Labour Market. The income of the working family will thus vary for reasons utterly beyond its control, though its requirements for economic and human efficiency show no such variation. Thus there is no security for any class standard of living.

Within each class or grade of labour there will be variations

---

[1] The width of variations in the weekly earnings, involving in most instances a nearly corresponding variety of family income, may be illustrated by the following

of the individual family wage, based on the amount of labour-power actually given out in the week. A less effective worker,

estimate compiled by Mr. Webb, from a careful analysis of official wage returns. *New Statesman*, May 10, 1913.

TABLE SHOWING ESTIMATED EARNINGS OF EMPLOYED MANUAL WORKING WAGE-EARNERS IN THE UNITED KINGDOM IN THE YEAR 1912

MEN

Class	Numbers	Average rate of earnings in a full week (including all emoluments)	Average wages bill for a full week	Yearly wages bill (allowing 5 weeks for short time, sickness, involuntary holidays and unemployment)
Men in Situations:		s. d.	Million £	Million £
Below 15s..........	320,000.. 4%	(abt.) 13.0	0.21	10
15s. to 20s........	640,000.. 8%	(abt.) 18.0	0.58	27
20s. to 25s........	1,600,000..20%	22.6	1.80	85
25s. to 30s........	1,680,000..21%	27.6	2.31	109
30s. to 35s........	1,680,000..21%	32.6	2.73	128
35s. to 40s........	1,040,000..13%	37.6	1.95	92
40s. to 45s........	560,000.. 7%	42.6	1.20	56½
Over 45s..........	480,000.. 6%	50.0	1.20	56½
Men in Situations ..	8,000,000..100%	30.0	12.0	564
Casuals..........	700,000	12.0	0.42	18.5
Adult Males.......	8,700,000	28.4	12.42	582.5
Boys.............	1,900,000	10.0	0.95	44.0
All Males.........	10,600,000	25.3	13.38	626.5

Average Earnings per Adult Man throughout the year: ($\frac{582.5}{8.7}$) £66.95 or £1.5.9 per week.

WOMEN

Class	Numbers	Average earnings in a full week	Average weekly wages bill for a full week	Yearly wages bill (net as above)
		s. d.	Million £	Million £
Women..........	3,000,000	12.0	1.8	85.0
Girls.............	1,500,000	8.0	0.6	28.0
Casuals..........	100,000	3.6	0.015	0.5
All Females.......	4,600,000	10.6	2.415	113.5

Average Earnings per Adult Woman throughout the year: ($\frac{90}{3.1}$) £27.58, or 10s. 7d. per week.

Total Wages Bill (both sexes) for the year, net: £740,000,000.

even though he puts out as much effort, will earn less money than a more effective. This seems necessary, reasonable and even just, so long as we accept the ordinary view that labour should be bought and sold like any other commodity.

But once accept the view that to buy labour-power, like other commodities, at a price determined purely by relations of Supply and Demand, is a policy dangerous to the life and well-being of the individual whose labour-power is thus bought and sold, to those of his family and of society, your attitude towards the labour-movement in general, and even to certain demands which at first sight seem unreasonable, will undergo a great change.

The fundamental assumption of the Labour Movement, in its demands for reformed remuneration, is that the private human needs of a working family should be regularly and securely met out of weekly pay. The life and health of the family, and that sense of security which is essential to sound character and regular habits, to the exercise of reasonable foresight, and the formation and execution of reasonable plans, all hinge upon this central demand for a sufficiency and regularity of weekly income based upon the human needs of a family.

§ 2. This explains alike the working-class objections to piece-work, the demand for a minimum wage, and the policy of limitation of individual output. For piece-work, even more than time-work, is based upon a total ignoring of the human conditions which affect the giving out of labour-power. It is the plainest and most logical assertion of the commodity view of labour, the most complete denial that the human needs of the worker have any claim to determine what he should be paid.

So firmly-rooted in the breast of the ordinary non-working man, and of many working-men, is the notion that a man, who has produced twice as large an output as another man, ought, as a simple matter of right or justice, to receive a payment twice as large, that it is very difficult to dislodge it. It represents the greatest triumph of the business point of view over humanity. If a man has done twice as much, of course he ought to receive twice as much! It seems an ethical truism. And yet I venture to affirm that it has nothing ethical in it. It has assumed this moral guise because of a deep distrust of human nature which it expresses. How will you get a man to do his best unless you pay him according to the amount he does? It is this purely practical consideration that has imposed upon the piece-work system the appearance of axiomatic justice.

It is not difficult to strip off the spurious ethics of the principle. You say that piece-wages or payment by result is right because it induces men to do their best. But what do we mean by 'doing their best'? A weak man may hew one ton of coals while a strong man may hew two. Has not the former 'done his best' equally with the latter? The strength of a strong man, the natural or even the acquired skill of a skilful man, cannot be assumed as a personal merit which deserves reward in the terms of payment. If there is merit anywhere, it is in the effort, not in the achievement or product, and piece-wages measure only the latter.

No! there is nothing inherently just in the piece-wage system. Its real defence is that it is the most practical way of getting men to work as hard as they can: it is a check on skulking and sugaring. It assumes that no other effective motive can be made operative in business except quantity of payment.

§ 3. As Ruskin and many others have remarked, the lie is given to this assumption in an increasing number of kinds of work where the highest qualities of human power, the finest sorts of mental skill and responsibility, are involved. Public servants of all grades, from Cabinet Ministers and Judges down to municipal dustmen, are paid by salaries, not by piece-wages. The same is true of the more remunerative and more responsible work in private businesses. No Government, no private firm, buys the services of its most valuable employees at the lowest market-price, or attempts to apply to them a piece-work scale. It would not pay them to do so, and they know it. Nor is this merely because some sorts of work do not easily admit of being measured by the piece. It would be possible to pay Judges, as counsel are paid, by the case: Cabinet Ministers might be paid on piece-wages for Laws measured by the number or length of their clauses. The chief reason for adopting payment by fixed salary is that it is reckoned a wise mode of securing good individual services. It is recognised that each piece of work will be better done, if the workers set about it in a thoroughly disinterested manner, concentrated in their thoughts and feelings entirely on the work itself, and not entangled in the consideration of what they are to get out of it. This is supposed to be the difference between the professional man and the tradesman, that the former performs a function and incidentally receives a fee, while the latter, by the very acts of buying and selling that constitute his business, keeps his mind set upon the profit from each several transaction.

But the fixed and guaranteed salary for public servants has another ground. It may profit a business firm to practise an economy of sweating, to drive its employees and consume their health and strength by a few years' excessive toil, to take on new casual workers for brief spurts of trade, to sack employees ruthlessly, as soon as trade begins to flag, or their individual powers of work are impaired by age. A piece-work system, with no guarantee of employment or of weekly wage, may be a sound business economy for a private firm. It cannot be a sound economy for a State or a Municipality.

For a large and increasing share of the work and the expenditure of most States and Municipalities is applied in trying to mend or alleviate damages or dangers to the health, security, intelligence, and character of the workers and their families, arising from insufficiency of work and wages or other defects of private industrialism. It would obviously be bad public economy to break down the lives and homes of public employees by underpaying or overworking them, or by dismissing and leaving them to starve when work was slack. For what was saved in the wage-bill of the particular department, would be squandered in poor-law, police, hospitals, old-age pensions, invalidity and employment relief. Nor is that all. A mass of ill-paid, ill-housed workers, alternately overworked and out of work, stands as a chief barrier in every one of those paths of social progress and national development which modern statecraft sets itself to follow. The low wage of unskilled labour is to-day a source of infinite waste of the forces of national education. Still keeping our argument upon the narrowest lines of economy, we plainly realise that the financial resources, upon which the State can draw for all her services, depend in the last resort upon the general economic efficiency of the working population, and that a system of public employment which was, however indirectly, detrimental to this health, longevity and intelligence, would rank as bad business from the public standpoint.

It is possible that in this country the salary mode of payment is gaining ground. Apart from the public services, national and municipal, which now employ some 7 per cent of the total employed population, the great transport and the distributive industries are almost entirely run upon the salary basis. These departments of industry are constantly increasing, not only in absolute size, but in the proportion of the total employment they afford. To them must be added the large class of domestic service. Such great salaried services cannot, indeed, be claimed as triumphs for the organic principle of distribution, or payment according to needs. For the most part they are very unsatisfactory modifications of the piece-wage or commodity view of labour. For, except for the small higher grades of officials, they mostly retain the two chief defects of the ordinary wage-system, a payment of weekly income not based on a proper computation of human needs, and a lack of adequate security of tenure. Over a large part of the field of industry and commerce where weekly fixed salaries are paid, there exists a flagrant disregard for all considerations of human subsistence. Some of the worse, though not the worst, forms of 'sweating' are found in shops, workshops and factories where women are employed on weekly salaries.

None the less, it remains true that the salary is a more rational form of payment for labour than the time or piece wage, and that, as the humanisation of industry proceeds, it will more and more displace the wage-system. For where salaries are paid, the consideration of needs or subsistence does tend always to qualify the mere commodity view of labour.

Piece-wage or time-wage ignores the worker as a human being and the supporter of a family: it ignores him as a personality and regards him merely as an instrument for giving out units of productive power to be paid for on the same terms as the units of mechanical power used in working machinery.

§ 4. The Labour Movement insists that the personal and

human factor is fundamental as a condition in the labour bargain. If labour is treated as a mere commodity, its price affords no security of life to the labourer. It may not find a customer at all, and so he starves and with him his family, the future supply of labour. Or, left to the fluctuations of the market, it may sell at a price which is insufficient for his maintenance. The fluctuations of price in all other markets involve only the pecuniary profit or loss of those who sell, fluctuations of the price of labour involve the existence and well-being of human families and of the nation. Hence the attack of organised labour on this whole conception of the labour-market, and the demand that the remuneration of labour shall not be left to the higgling of a market.

The chief fight is for a secure weekly income, or for conditions of employment which lead up to this. A minimum or a living wage is the usual name given to this demand. Complaint is made of the vagueness of the demand. But this vagueness does not make the demand unreasonable. A living wage indeed is elastic as life itself: it expands and will continue to expand, with the development of life for the workers. But what in effect is meant at the present by a living or subsistence wage is such a regular weekly sum as suffices to maintain the ordinary working family in health and economic efficiency.

It is contended that no purchase of labour should be permitted which entails the degradation of that standard. When a minimum rate of piece-wages is demanded, the implicit understanding is that it is such as will yield under normal conditions the ordinary weekly subsistence or standard wage. Since piece-wages are so firmly established in many trades that it is impracticable to demand their immediate abolition, the actual struggle between employees and employers is as to whether these piece-wages shall be allowed to fluctuate indefinitely, being dragged at the heels of the prices of commodities, or whether an absolute limit shall be set upon their fall. The employer says, 'When trade is good and prices and profits high, labour will share the prosperity in high rates of wage and large weekly earnings: so, when trade is bad and prices and profits low, labour must share this adversity and take low pay.' Organised labour replies, 'No, there is no parity between the power of capital and of labour to bear depressions: capital is strong and can bear up against low profits without perishing, labour is weak and cannot bear up against low wages. We will only sell our labour-power on condition that a lower limit is set upon its price, such a limit as will enable the labourer to keep body and soul together, and to maintain that efficiency which constitutes his working capital. This minimum wage should be regarded as a fixed cost in your production. At present the prices of your goods oscillate without any assigned limit. You accept low contracts for work, and then adduce this low price as a reason for reducing wages. Let a minimum wage once be adopted in the trade, and contract prices cannot be accepted on so low a level. The minimum wage will thus help to steady selling prices and to regulate employment and output.'

Both the economics and the social ethics of this labour contention are in substance sound. So long as the price of labour is left to higgling in a competitive market, there is nothing to prevent the wages falling to the lowest level at which a sufficient number of workers can be induced to consent to work, and that level may involve a reduction of the standard of living in their families below the true subsistence point. The fixing of wages by so-called free competition affords no security for a family wage of efficiency or even of subsistence. There should be no mistake upon this essential matter. The doctrine of 'economy of high wages' has no such general efficacy as is sometimes suggested. Though in many cases high wages are essential to maintain and evoke the energy and efficiency required, in other cases they are not. From the standpoint of the immediate profits of employers 'sweating' often pays. But from the standpoint of society it never pays.

Therefore, the policy of the organised workers, in seeking to enforce the doctrine of a minimum wage, is not only a policy of self-preservation for the working-classes but a salutary social policy. It is for this reason that the State intervenes in favour of the practice, establishing Trade Boards to enforce its application in so-called 'sweated trades', and acknowledges, in theory at any rate, its validity in all public employments and public contracts.

§ 5. Although this minimum wage is tolerably remote from the ideal of a fixed weekly salary in most trades, it is a true step in this direction. The most controverted item in trade-union policy, the limitation of individual output, is also partly actuated by the same motive. Few things make the ordinary business man more indignant than the trade-union regulations in certain trades which restrain stronger or quicker workers from putting forth their full productive energy. They denounce alike its dishonesty and its bad economy. It is based, they say, upon the 'lump of labour' fallacy, the false notion that there exists an absolutely limited amount of employment, or work to be done, and that if the stronger or quicker men do more than their share, the others will go short. This refusal to allow each man to do his best, like the related refusal to get the full work out of new labour-saving machinery, appears monstrously perverse and wicked. But, though partly animated by short-sighted economic views, this policy is not entirely to be thus explained. The levelling down of the output of all workers to a standard has partly for its object the establishment of greater evenness of income among the workers in a trade. At any given time in a given mill, or factory town, the actual amount of available employment *is* limited, and for the time it is true that by limitation of individual output a larger number of workers are employed, and a larger number of working families are provided with a normal wage, than would have been the case if a certain number of men were encouraged to an unrestricted energy and unlimited overtime. In the long run, it may be better to encourage full individual liberty of output, even in the interest of the aggregate of employment, but the restraints to which I here allude become more intelligible when they are regarded as attempts to enforce a common class weekly wage by means of an even distribution of employment.

A minimum piece-wage, based on a moderate computation of the weekly output per worker, and accompanied by a substantial security of full regular employment, would in effect place the piece-worker in the position of a salaried employee. But, of course, a minimum piece-wage, however high, does not go far to this end, unless security of tenure at fairly full employment is obtained. The problem of un- and under-employment and of irregular employment is now beginning to be recognised in its full social gravity. A weekly wage of bare efficiency with regular employment is socially far superior to a higher average wage accompanied by great irregularity of work. The former admits stability of modes of living and ready money payments: it conduces to steadiness of character and provision for the future without anxiety. Rapid and considerable fluctuations of wages, even with full employment, are damaging to character and stability of standards: but irregularity of employment is the most destructive agency to the character, the standard of comfort, the health and sanity of wage-earners. The knowledge that he is liable at any time, from commercial or natural causes that lie entirely outside his control, to lose the opportunity to work and earn his livelihood, takes out of a man that confidence in the fundamental rationality of life which is essential to soundness of character. Religion, ethics, education, can have little hold upon workers exposed to such powerful illustrations of the unreason and injustice of industry and of society.

The regularisation of industry, so as to afford substantial guarantees of full regular employment, thus ranks with the minimum wage as the most substantial contribution towards the substitution of salary for wages, which the organic law of Distribution requires. The State is beginning to coöperate with the Labour Movement for the attainment of this social object, stimulating employers to organise their industries so as to furnish a more even volume of employment.

§ 6. This interpretation of the Labour Movement as a half-conscious manifold endeavour to rescue the remuneration of Labour from the risks and defects of the competitive labour-market, and to establish it on an economy of human needs, is not fully understood without some further reference to the action of organised society. The Labour Movement, in its endeavour to get a better distribution of the income, is not confined to trying to secure a satisfactory minimum or standard wage, fortified by greater security of work and personal insurance against unemployment. It seeks also to supplement its wages by cooperative and public provisions.

The coöperative movement is an attempt to convert into real wages some of the profits of employers and shareholders in manufacturing and commercial businesses, so enlarging the proportion of the real income of the nation which goes to the remuneration of labour. But the growing attachment of the Labour Organisations to politics is equally motived by the endeavour to secure from the State, not merely legal supports for higher wages and improved conditions of employment, but actual supplements to wages in the shape of contributions from the public services to their standard of living. Free education, old-age pensions, and public subsidies towards insurance are a direct contribution from the State to the higher standard of life which modern civilised society demands. Health, education, recreation, and provision against emergencies, are coming more and more to be recognised as proper objects of governmental action, and other important services, such as transport, credit, art, music and literature, are far on the way to becoming communal supplies. Although these modes of social provision may be chiefly motived by considerations of public health and other common goods, they nevertheless must rank as contributions to the standard of comfort and well-being of the working-class families who are the special beneficiaries. Relieving, as they do in many instances, the private incomes of the workers from expenditure which otherwise the family would find it to its private interest to incur, these growing public services form a genuine and a considerable contribution to the available real income of the working-classes. So far as by taxation direct or indirect the cost of such public services can be considered a burden upon, or a deduction from the wage-income of the workers, it forms, of course, no net addition to their share, but is only a public control over methods of expenditure. But inasmuch as the distinct tendency of modern taxation is towards an increasing taxation of the incomes and property of the non-working classes, these public services rank as supplementary income, paid in kind, and tending to equalise the standard of living of individual workers and grades of workers. The criticism sometimes directed against this State socialism, upon the ground that it tends to weaken the force of wage-bargaining and transfers to the shoulders of 'society' costs which employers would otherwise have to bear in the shape of higher money wages, would have considerable force, if the old *laissez-faire* principle of 'free contract' were allowed otherwise to work unimpeded. But this, as we see, is not the case. The growing policy of minimum and standard rates, supported by public opinion and, where necessary, by public law, and hardening into a policy of fixed salaries, is nowise inconsistent with a simultaneous development of communal supplies of goods and services which usually lie a little above the normal standard of comfort of those who are the chief beneficiaries.

The growing political activities of a labour movement which once eschewed State aids not merely attest the general growth of conscious democracy but imply a recognition of the direct contribution which the State is making towards a general distribution of the national income in accordance with an economy of human needs.

CHAPTER XIV

§ 1. No humanist treatment of modern industry can ignore the recent advances of scientific methods into the regulation both of standards of production and standards of consumption. In both arts alike the crude empiricism of the past is giving place to a more ordered, conscious rationalism. As is only natural, the advance of science is more rapid in the productive arts.

In recent years many scattered attempts have been made to apply physiology and psychology to economic processes. Business men by scientific observation and experiment have brought criticism to bear upon the traditional and empirical modes of organising and conducting businesses. The more or less hand-to-mouth methods which were possible in small businesses where the manager was owner, and could keep a close personal supervision of his employees and all their work, were found increasingly unsuitable to modern types of large capitalist business. It was necessary to devise regular methods for correlating the work of the different departments, and for enabling a single central purpose to operate by complex delegation through several grades of subordinate officials with automatic checks and registers. More accurate methods of book-keeping, especially of cost-taking, were devised; experiments were made in bonuses, profit-sharing, fines, pace-making and various modifications of the wage-systems applied to evoke more energy, skill, or care from the workers and officials; hours of labour and shift-systems were subjected to measured tests. Still more recently the detailed technology of manual and mental labour has been made material of physiological and psychological investigation. Scientific Management has become a conscious art. Business colleges in America and Germany give courses of instruction in this art, and a new profession has arisen of expert advisers who are called in as specialists to diagnose the deficiencies or wastes of industrial or financial power in particular businesses and to prescribe remedies.

Economic progress, regarded from the standpoint of the business man, consists in getting a given quantity of saleable goods turned out at a lower cost of production. That cost of production consists of the salaries and wages paid to various grades of employees for mental and manual labour, cost of materials and power, standing expenses for maintenance of plant and premises, including replacement and insurance, and interest upon capital. Anything that reduces any one of these costs, without a corresponding increase of another, is profitable from the standpoint of the individual employer, or of all employers in the trade, if it be generally adopted, or of the consuming public, if it wholly or partly goes to them in lower selling prices. Where the reduction of costs simply takes the shape of reduced wages for the same work, however, it causes no net increase of concrete wealth, but merely distributes the same amount (or less by reason of reduced efficiency of labour) in a different manner. Such a reduction cannot then be regarded as economic progress, from the national standpoint.

But every other reduction of cost carries with it *prima facie* evidence of a net increase of concrete wealth. Inventions of machinery, improved chemical or other treatment of materials, better business organisation and subdivision of labour, improved skill and energy in employees, better book-keeping, credit, marketing arrangements,—all such technical improvements promote the increase of concrete wealth. In all these ways many great advances have been made in various industries. But, alike in invention and in organisation, too much has been left to chance, or to the pressure of some emergency, too little is the result of ordered thought. Business has been conducted too much in the spirit of an art, too little in that of applied science. The modern tendency is to introduce the exacter methods of science. The modern large manufacturing or mining enterprise employs expert engineers and chemists, not only to test and control the operation of existing processes, but to invent new and cheaper ways of carrying out a process, to discover new products and new uses for by-products. It employs expert accountants to overhaul its book-keeping and finance and to suggest improvements. Initiative and economy are to be studied, evoked and applied along every path.

§ 2. But until lately the detailed organisation of labour and its utilisation for particular technical processes had received little attention in the great routine industries. Even such technical instruction as has been given to beginners in such trades as building, engineering, weaving, shoemaking, etc., has usually taken for granted the existing tools, the accepted methods of using them and the material to which they are applied. To make each sort of job the subject-matter of a close analysis and of elaborate experiment, so as to ascertain how it could be done most quickly and accurately and with the least expenditure of needless energy, comes as a novel contribution of business enterprise. To get the right man to use the right tools in the right way is a fair account of the object of Scientific Management. At present a man enters a particular trade partly by uninstructed choice, partly by chance, seldom because he is known by himself and his employer to have a natural or acquired aptitude for it. He handles the tools that are traditional and are in general use, copying the ways in which others use them, receiving chance tips or suggestions from a comrade or a foreman, and learning from personal experience how to do the particular work in a way which appears to be least troublesome, dangerous, or exhausting. Both mode of work and pace are those of prevailing usage, more or less affected by machinery or other technical conditions.

The scientific manager discovers enormous wastes in this way of working. Part of the waste he finds due to improper tools and improper modes of working, arising from mere ignorance; part he attributes to systematic or habitual slacking, more or less conscious and intentional on the part of the workers. The natural disposition of the worker to "take it easy" is supplemented by a belief that by working too hard he deprives some other worker of a job. Scientific Management, therefore, sets itself to work out by experiment the exact tool or machine appropriate to each action, the most economical and effective way by which a worker can work the tool or machine, and the best method of selecting workers for each job and of stimulating them to perform each action with the greatest accuracy and celerity. By means of strictly quantitative tests it works out standard tools, standard methods of work and standard tests for the selection, organisation, stimulation, and supervision of the workman.

In his exposition of this economy [1] Mr. Taylor takes as his simplest illustration of choice of tools the 'art' of shovelling. Left to himself, or working with a gang, the shoveller will use a shovel whose weight, size, and shape have never been considered in relation to the particular material it has to move or the sort of man who has to use it. 'By first selecting two or three first-class shovellers, and paying them extra wages for doing trustworthy work, and then gradually varying the shovel load and having all the conditions accompanying the work carefully observed for several weeks by men who were accustomed to experimenting, it was found that a first-class man would do the biggest day's work with a shovel load of about 21 pounds.' [2] As a result of this discovery, instead of allowing each shoveller to choose his own shovel, the company provided eight or ten different kinds of shovels accommodated to the weight of different materials and to other special conditions. Again, thousands of stop-watch observations were made to discover how quickly a labourer, provided with his proper shovel, could push the shovel into the materials and draw it out properly loaded. A similar study was made of 'the time required to swing the shovel backward and then throw the load for a given horizontal distance, accompanied by a given height.' With the knowledge thus obtained it was possible for the man directing shovellers, first to teach them the exact method of using their strength to the best advantage, and then to assign the daily task by which they could earn the bonus paid for the successful performance of this task. For, though the skilled director can prescribe the right tool and the right method, he cannot get the required result without the willing coöperation of the individual worker. For this purpose a bonus is applied, the size of which is itself a subject of scientific experiment. The relation of this bonus to the ordinary day or piece wage will vary with the various types of work and workers. In the Bethlehem

[1] *The Principles of Scientific Management* (Harper & Bros.).
[2] Op. cit., p. 65.

Steel Works it was found that the best effect in stimulating energy was got by a bonus of about 60 per cent, beyond the wages usually paid. 'This increase in wages tends to make them not only thrifty but better men in every way; they live rather better, begin to save money, become more sober, and work more steadily. When, on the other hand, they receive much more than a 60 per cent increase of wages, many of them will work irregularly and tend to become more or less shiftless, extravagant, and dissipated. Our experiments showed, in other words, that it does not do for most men to get rich too fast.'[1]

Considering that it was claimed that the result of this new plan of work was to raise the average daily output per man from 16 to 59 tons, and to secure an annual saving in the labour-bill amounting to between $75,000 and $80,000, it would have been interesting to follow the effects of a rapid advance of wealth upon the dividend-receivers who gained so disproportionate a share of the advantages of the new economy.

§ 3. So far as the selection and adaptation of tools to the special conditions of the work are concerned, there exists no opposition between the business and the human economy. If a shoveller can shovel more material without greater exertion by using a particular shovel, the system which ensures his using this shovel is beneficial to everybody, assuming that he gets some share of the value of the increased output. When we turn from a simple tool to more elaborate machinery, it becomes evident that quantitative testing is capable of achieving enormous technical economies. Mr. Taylor describes the gains in the output of metal-cutting machines made by means of such economies. 'Its pulling power at the various speeds, its feeding capacity, and its proper speeds were determined by means of the slide-rules, and changes were then made in the countershaft and driving pulleys so as to run it to its proper speed. Tools, made of high-speed steel and of the proper shapes, were properly dressed, treated and ground. A large special slide-rule was then made, by means of which the exact speeds and feeds were indicated at which each kind of work could be done in the shortest possible time in this particular lathe. After preparing in this way so

[1] *The Principles of Scientific Management*, p. 74.

that the workman should work according to the new method, one after another, pieces of work were finished in the lathe, corresponding to the work which had been done in our preliminary trials, and the gain in time made through running the machine according to scientific principles ranged from two and one-half times the speed in the slowest instance to nine times the speed in the highest'.[1]

This illustration, however, makes it evident that when we pass from technical improvements of tools to improved methods of working, we open possibilities of opposition between the business and the human interest. An improvement in the shape or contour of the 'cutting edge' for a particular material is an unqualified gain. So is a discovery as to the ways in which hardness or softness of metals affects the cutting rate. But when it is a question of evoking from the workman a higher pace of movement to meet the requirements of the speeded-up machine, no such consistency of interests can be assumed. The fact that by selection, instruction, and minute supervision, workmen can be got to work successfully at the higher speed, and regard themselves as sufficiently compensated by a bonus of 35 per cent, does not settle the question of human values. So far as the selective process simply chooses the men most easily capable of working at a higher speed and of eliminating those who could not easily or possibly adapt themselves to it, no net increase of human cost is involved. But so far as the bonus and the 'athletic' spirit which it is used to evoke,[2] induce workmen to give out an amount of muscular or nervous energy injurious to them in the long run, the human cost may greatly outweigh both the social value of the increased output and the utility to them of higher wages. How crucial is this question of speeding-up the human labour is well illustrated by the experiments in bricklaying, by means of which the bricklayers engaged on straight work, were raised from an average of 120 bricks per man per hour to

---

[1] *The Principles of Scientific Management*, p. 100.

[2] 'While one who is not experienced at making his men really enthusiastic in their work cannot appreciate how athletic contests will interest the men, it is the real secret of the success of our best superintendents. It not only reduces costs, but it makes for organisation and thus saves foremen's time.' F. G. Gilbreth, *Bricklaying System*, p. 13.

350. By alterations of apparatus Mr. Gilbreth dispenses with certain movements which bricklayers formerly considered necessary, while saving time in the actual process of laying by using both hands at the same time, bricks being picked up with the left hand at the same instant that a trowel of mortar is seized with the right.

'It is highly likely that many times during all of these years individual bricklayers have recognised the possibility of eliminating each of these unnecessary motions. But even if, in the past, he did invent each one of Mr. Gilbreth's improvements, no bricklayer could alone increase his speed through their adoption, because it will be remembered that in all cases several bricklayers work together in a row and that the walls all around a building must grow at the same rate of speed. No one bricklayer, then, can work much faster than the one next to him. Nor has any workman the authority to make other men coöperate with him to do faster work. It is only through *enforced* standardisation of methods, *enforced* adoption of the best implements and working conditions, and *enforced* coöperation that this faster work can be assured. And the duty of enforcing the adoption of standards and of enforcing this coöperation rests with the *management* alone. The *management* must supply continually one or more teachers to show each new man the new and simpler motions, and the slower men must be constantly watched and helped until they have risen to their proper speed. All of those who, after teaching, either will not or cannot work in accordance with the new methods and at the higher speed, must be discharged by the *management*. The *management* must also recognise the broad fact that workmen will not submit to this more rigid standardisation and will not work extra hard, unless they receive extra pay for doing it.'[1]

This makes it clear that, though part of the larger output, or increased speed, is got by improved arrangements or methods of work that need not tax the workers' powers, part of it does involve their working "extra hard." Not only a better direction but a larger amount of energy is required of them, with an increase of wear and tear and of fatigue. It is an unsettled point of great importance, how much of the enlarged output can be imputed to the former, how much to the latter. Even more important is the allusion in the passage just quoted to 'the rigid standardisation' to which workmen will not submit, unless they are well paid to do so. For this rigid standardisation of the work involves a corresponding mechanisation of the workmen. Men who formerly exercised a certain amount of personal choice in the details of their work, as regards action and time, must abandon

[1] *The Principles of Scientific Management*, p. 83.

this freedom and follow exactly the movements prescribed to them by the taskmaster with a chart and a stop-watch. He will prescribe the particular task for each, the tool he shall use, the way he shall use it, the intervals of work and rest, and will take close note of every failure to conform. The liberty, initiative, judgment, and responsibility of the individual workman are reduced to a minimum.

This is admitted by the advocates of Scientific Management, though in a qualified manner. One of the elements of success is said to be: 'An almost equal division of the work and responsibility between the workman and the management. All day long the management work almost side by side with the men, helping, encouraging and smoothing the way for them, while in the past they stood on one side, gave the men but little help, and threw on to them the entire responsibility as to methods, implements, speed, and harmonious coöperation.'[1] But in the broader discussion of the difference between the ordinary business method and Scientific Management, in relation to the numerous little problems that arise in every kind of work, we are told that, 'the underlying philosophy of this (ordinary) management necessarily leaves the solution of all these problems in the hands of each individual workman, while the philosophy of Scientific Management places their solution in the hands of the management.'[2] Elsewhere [3] it is stated that Scientific Management 'involves the establishment of many rules, laws, and formulæ which replace the judgment of the individual workman.'

§ 4. Now in endeavouring to apply to this policy of Scientific Management a standard of human welfare, we are confronted by three questions:—

(1) What is the effect of this policy upon the human costs of labour?

(2) How far will any increase of human costs of labour be offset by the greater human utility of the higher wages they receive?

(3) How far is any balance of human costs, which is imposed on special classes of producers, compensated by the increased wealth at the disposal of society at large?

[1] Taylor, p. 85.   [2] Op. cit., p. 103.   [3] Op. cit., p. 37.

There is some tendency among the advocates of Scientific Management to burke a full discussion of these issues by asserting that their policy is only a fuller and more rational application of that principle of division of labour which is by general consent the economic foundation of modern civilised society. If some sacrifice of individual freedom in industrial work is involved, it is assumed to be more than compensated by gains to society in which every individual, as a member of society, has his proper share.

But we cannot consent thus to rush the issue. For it may turn out that the new method, though but a stricter and finer application of the old, carries this economy so far that the increased human costs imposed upon the producer grow faster than the human gains which the increased productivity confers either upon him or upon society at large. In other words, the human indictment brought by the mid-Victorian humanists against the factory system of their day and rejected on a general survey of the economic situation, might be validated by the increased standardisation and specialisation of labour under scientific management. For though the division of labour under modern capitalism in all its branches has narrowed the range of productive activity for the great bulk of workers, a survey of those activities shows that within their narrowing range there may and does survive a certain scope for skill, judgment, and initiative, a certain limited amount of liberty in detailed modes of workmanship. Moreover, the conditions of most organised work form a certain education in discipline and responsibility. It is only a small proportion of the workers who are converted into mere servants of the machine. Though large classes are engaged in monotonous routine, the paces and the detailed movements are not rigidly enforced upon them. Different workmen will be doing the same work in a slightly different way.

Now the standardisation under the new method is expressly designed so as to extirpate these little personal equations of liberty and to reduce the labour of the ordinary employee to an automatic perfection of routine. It is, indeed, contended by Mr. Taylor that the knowledge of each man that he is working at his highest personal efficiency will be a satisfaction to him, that the attention he must pay to the detailed orders of the task-master will evoke intelligence and responsibility, and that his initiative in the way of suggesting improvements, which has hitherto been prized as an element of liberty and a source of industrial progress, can be conserved under scientific management. But a careful examination of the illustrations of the method compels our rejection of these claims. The knowledge of a routine worker that he is speeded up to his highest pitch by a method whose efficiency is prescribed by others, does not yield a sense of personal efficiency. Mere meticulous obedience is not a proper training in the discipline of a 'person', and a workman operating under these conditions will not have the practical liberty for those little experiments in trial and error on his own account which makes his suggestions of improvement fruitful.

Mr. Taylor, however, carries his defence so far as to deny all narrowing effects of subdivision of labour on the worker. Admitting that the workmen frequently say when they first come under the system, 'Why, I am not allowed to think or move without someone interfering or doing it for me,' he seems to think the following answer satisfactory:—

'The same criticism and objection, however, can be raised against any other modern sub-division of labour. It does not follow, for example, that the modern surgeon is any more narrow or wooden a man than the early settler in this country. The frontiersman, however, had to be not only a surgeon, but also an architect, house-builder, lumber-man, farmer, soldier, and doctor, and he had to settle his lawsuits with a gun. You would hardly say that the life of the modern surgeon is any more narrowing or that he is more of a wooden man than the frontiersman. The many problems to be met and solved by the surgeon are just as intricate and difficult and as developing and broadening in their way as were those of the frontiersman.' [1]

Now as to this we can only reply, first that it is untrue that the surgeon's life on its productive side (the issue under discussion) is as broad and as varied as that of the frontiersman. In the second place, even if we accepted the view that a narrow field of activity admitted of as much variety and interest as a wider field, provided liberty of action were equal in the two, that view is quite inapplicable to the case at issue. For there all liberty of action in the subdivided field of labour is excluded.

[1] Taylor, p. 126.

§ 5. So far, then, as initiative, interest, variation, experiment, and personal responsibility are factors of human value, qualifying the human costs of labour, it seems evident that Scientific Management involves a loss or injury to the workers. Are there, however, any personal considerations, apart from wages, that may be taken as an offset? Suppose that workers can be found of a dully docile character with a large supply of brute muscular energy, will any harm be done them by utilising them to carry pig-iron or to shovel earth under "scientific" supervision? Mr. Taylor has an interesting passage bearing on this question: 'Now one of the very first requirements for a man who is fit to handle pig-iron as a regular occupation is that he shall be so stupid and so phlegmatic that he more nearly resembles in his mental make-up the ox than any other type.' [1] These ox-like men, it may be held, do not really suffer any injury, undergo any human cost, by having no opportunity furnished them for exercising faculties and activities of mind which they do not possess and are unlikely to acquire. If then, in every grade of workers, there are to be found enough men who appear destined by nature for a rigidly mechanical task conducted under servile conditions, it may be thoroughly sound social economy to put them to perform all labour of such kind as is required for the supply of human needs.

This is a problem of applied psychology, or of psycho-physiology. Professor Münsterberg, in a recent volume,[2] makes a contribution towards its solution, and towards a finer art of Scientific Management than that which has been evolved by business men. For since all industry primarily involves the voluntary ordered application of human faculties to manual and mental actions, the psychologist must be in a position to give important advice in all economic operations. For he alone is qualified by scientific tests to discover and estimate the various mental capacities which count for success in industry, to ascertain how they coöperate and conflict, and how they may be best applied to the performance of the various operations in each process. Attention, memory, ideas, imagination, feeling, volition, suggestibility, ability to learn, ability to discriminate, judgment,

[1] Taylor, p. 59.　　　　[2] *Psychology and Industrial Efficiency.*

space-sense, time-sense, and other mental qualities, enter in varying measures as factors of industrial ability. Economic psychology may, it is contended, increase the efficiency of industry in three ways.

'We ask how we can find the men whose mental qualities make them best fitted for the work they have to do; secondly, under what psychological conditions we can secure the greatest and most satisfactory output of work from every man; and finally, how we can produce most completely the influences on human minds which are desired in the interests of business. In other words, we ask how to find the best possible man, how to produce the best possible work, and how to secure the best possible effects.' [1]

The first of these services, fitting the man to the job, involves a double psychological enquiry, first into the vocational needs, and secondly into the personal ability of each applicant to meet these needs. We must examine the task to learn what combination of mental qualities in the employee is required to do it well, and we must examine each applicant for such work to learn whether he possesses the requisite qualities.

Two illustrations will serve to indicate what is meant. The problem of selecting fit motor-men for electric railways was brought to Professor Münsterberg's attention. To drive fast and at the same time avoid accidents were the requirements of the companies. Fitness for this purpose he found to centre in a single mental process:—

'I found this to be a particular complicated act of attention by which the manifoldness of objects, the pedestrians, the carriages, and the automobiles, are continuously observed with reference to their rapidity and direction in the quickly-changing panorama of the streets. Moving figures come from the right and from the left towards and across the track, and are embedded in a stream of men and vehicles which moves parallel to the track. In the face of such manifoldness there are men whose impulses are almost inhibited and who instinctively desire to wait for the movement of the nearest objects; they would evidently be unfit for service, as they would drive the electric car far too slowly. There are others who, even with the car at full speed, can adjust themselves for a time to the complex moving situation, but whose attention soon lapses, and while they are fixating a rather distant carriage, may overlook a pedestrian who carelessly crosses the track immediately in front of this car. In short, we have a great variety of mental types of this characteristic unified variety, which may be understood as a particular combination of attention and imagination.' [2]

[1] Op. cit., p. 23.   [2] Op. cit., p. 66.

An apparatus was devised, representing the psychological conditions involved in the actual problem, not a mere miniature, but an adaptation which should call out and test the same mental qualities. A number of actual motor-men were then carefully examined in the working of this apparatus so as to test the amounts of speed and accuracy and the relation between the two. Quantitative estimates were thus reached of fitness in working the apparatus, values being assigned respectively to speed and accuracy. In this way a psychological standard of fitness was attained, such as would be available for selecting applicants for the motor service. So in ship-service, where everything may turn upon prompt and accurate handling of a sudden complicated emergency. Ship officers are found whom a sudden danger paralyses, or keeps vacillating until it is too late. Others, feeling only the urgency of prompt action, jump to a too hasty decision. The desirable type is 'the men who in the unexpected situation quickly review the totality of the factors in their relative importance and with almost instinctive certainty immediately come to the same decision to which they would have arrived after great thought.'[1] Here again it was possible to conduct a series of experiments, testing the mental processes and measuring the degrees of rapidity, correctness, and constancy.

Other tests can be applied for the qualities desirable in such work as the telephone service, in which memory, attention, intelligence, exactitude, and rapidity are involved. Sometimes the mental qualities can be separately tested, sometimes their inter-relation is such as to require a simultaneous testing.

§ 6. It is equally obvious that a good deal can be done to increase the productive efficiency of those who have been selected for any work, by methods of teaching that involve psychological guidance. In learning such processes as typewriting and telegraphy, for instance, much can be achieved by technical adjustments of movement such as we have already described, and by considered adaptations of machine and materials to suit human faculties. But methods of improving memory and securing a more regular and accurate attention, of increasing

[1] Op. cit., p. 85.

the rapidity of repeated actions with the least nervous wear and tear, of educating delicacy of touch and sight for specific purposes, the utilisation of rhythmic tendencies, the proper balance of intervals of work and rest, the influence of imitation and social coöperation in gang labour, and finally the effects of different quantities and modes of remuneration in evoking and maintaining the various factors of efficiency—all such considerations offer a fruitful field for psychological investigation.

Hence psychology, it is urged, can contribute greatly to productivity by finding the best man for each job and adjusting his mental equipment to conditions of work which in their turn can be modified to fit his powers. But, regarding production as designed to satisfy human demands, psychology can be utilised also to assist in getting the right quantities and qualities of goods to the right persons. Commercial organisation exists for this purpose. It does study the wants and demands of consumers. But it might do so with more 'science'. Professor Münsterberg makes an exceedingly interesting study of the arts of advertising and of selling over the counter, to illustrate how much might be done by substituting experimental laws for instinctive and traditional practices. One comment upon this application of his science, however, is called for. Though the social-economic view would oblige the psychologist to approach the subject specifically from the standpoint of the consumer and the psychology of satisfactions in his standard of comfort, Professor Münsterberg virtually confines himself to the psychology of commerce and of marketing regarded from the standpoint of the manufacturer or merchant.

Thus psychology can be made to devise and prescribe economies of human power in industry, which, like the technical improvements of Scientific Management, would seem to increase greatly the productivity of industry, turning out larger quantities, and perhaps better qualities, of goods, with the same amount of labour.

§ 7. What would be the human valuation of these processes of scientific economy? Assuming that this economy fructifies in an enlarging volume of wealth, it would appear to be accompanied by an increase of welfare, unless the human costs of labour were correspondingly increased, or the distribution of the larger volume of wealth were made so much more unequal that it furnished a smaller volume of utility in its consumption. Neither of these qualifications is, indeed, excluded by the terms of the economy. For each stroke of Scientific Management is primarily justified as a profit-making device, advantageous to the capitalist-employer in a particular business. It enables him to turn out goods at a lower labour-cost and so to make a larger margin of profit on their sale. If we suppose this economy to be of wide or general adoption, it would be equivalent to an all-round increase in the technical efficiency of labour. Unless we suppose the aggregate quantity of production to be a fixed quantity (a supposition not in accordance with experience), it would seem to follow that at least as large a quantity of this more efficient labour would be employed in turning out an increased volume of goods. In that event, it would be possible that the workers, as well as the capitalist employers, should enjoy a higher rate of remuneration. Whether they would do so, however, and to what extent, seems quite uncertain. For though the payment of a considerable bonus in addition to current wages was necessary in the experiments described by Mr. Taylor, in order to evoke from a particular group of workers submission to the new terms of work, it does not follow that, once adopted by all employers in the trade, the method would entail or even permit a continuance of this higher pay. For the pioneer firm admittedly pays the bonus partly in order to overcome the pains and scruples of workers subjected to a speeding-up system. If it did not pay a bonus, the workers would quit this employment for some other that was open to them. But if no other employment upon the old terms were open, this part of the bonus might be unnecessary as an inducement. Even that part of the bonus which seems to be directed to stimulate the ambition and energy of the individual worker, and to break up the habitual slackness of the group and its regulation stroke, would seem to stand on a precarious footing, when the new method of work was once well established and itself became a habit. Only that part, if any, of the bonus, or higher wage, which was necessary to replace the greater muscular or nervous wear and tear of the speeded-up and more automatic work, would necessarily survive. It would stand as a necessary cost of production. If, however, as Mr. Taylor and Professor Münsterberg appear to hold, the scientific management need entail no such additional wear and tear, there seems no ground for holding that, after the method became general, any bonus to the workers would be necessary. And if it were unnecessary, it would not, indeed under competitive terms could not, be paid. On this hypothesis, the additional wealth created by the improved efficiency of the system might go entirely to capital. Indeed, so far as the determination were left to individual bargaining, this result would appear almost inevitable. For the greater average efficiency of labour would be equivalent to a larger supply of labour (though it might also mean a better quality), and since no immediate or corresponding increase of demand for labour need accrue, the price per unit of labour would fall. This would mean that the labourer would get no higher payment for his higher productivity. Even if the increasing rate and amount of profits brought increased saving and larger masses of competing capital, it would still seem doubtful whether the aggregate demand for labour would be found to keep pace with the growth of the supply which scientific management plus psychological selection would yield.

Though, therefore, the aggregate product increased, it remains doubtful whether any considerable share of the increase must or would go to labour. But suppose that organisation of labour or social intervention were able to secure some considerable rise of real wages from the enlarged product, so that as consumers the workers were better off, the human value of the process is not yet established. Two related questions still remain for settlement. First, that already tentatively raised, the question whether the workers may not suffer more from increased human costs of production under the new scientific *régime* than they gain in human utilities of consumption. Some of the 'science' in its application would indeed appear to be wholly beneficial. The improved methods of selecting and of training labour, so as to get the best man for each job, and to enable him to do his work in the best way, is pure gain, provided that best way does not unduly strain his energy or dull his mind. Other elements of applied psychology are more doubtful in their net effect. The practices of scientific advertising and of suggestive selling have very little proved utility and are nearly as likely to be applied to force the wrong articles on the wrong purchasers as to distribute wealth along the lines of its maximum utility for consumption. The persons engaged for a livelihood in palming off goods on a public irrespective of any intrinsic merits they contain, pay a heavy toll in character for the work they are called upon to do.

§ 8. But, turning to the main problem, there remains the issue of the increased mechanisation, or standardisation, of the worker under Scientific Management. Admitting that a certain amount of subdivision of labour, and of diminishing variety, interest and initiative, accruing therefrom, is justified in a human sense by the benefits of enhanced production, is there any limit to this economy, and if there be, is that limit transgressed under Scientific Management? The question does not admit perhaps of any general or certain answer. Suppose it be admitted, as I think it must, that every application of this Scientific Management does squeeze out of the labour-day some human interest, some call upon initiative, reason, judgment, responsibility, surviving under previous conditions even in the most routine and subdivided toil, must we necessarily regard this loss as a heavy increased human cost of labour? Surely it depends upon the particular labour in question. In some, perhaps most, branches of heavy routine toil, the shreds of human interest, the calls on personality, are usually so trifling that it seems absurd to take them into much account. The work of carrying pig-iron, or of shovelling continually the same material, contains so little scope for the play of initiative, responsibility, etc., that any such regimentation as is described can hardly be said to damage the quality of the work or the character of the worker as affected by his work. If a higher efficiency and a larger output can enable a smaller number of workmen to be kept on labour of so low a grade, there ought to be a net social gain. But there is another compensation possible for any loss of liberty, or increase of monotony, involved in Scientific Management. If it be accompanied by a shortening of the hours of labour, the damage inflicted by the rigour of mechanical discipline may be compensated by a larger leisure. This compensation, of course, is reduced or even nullified, if the greater intensity of labour in the shorter day takes more out of the man, as often happens, than was taken out before. But, assuming that this is not the case, and that for a longer dull routine work-day is substituted a shorter but even more mechanical day, a net gain for labour is still possible. I am disposed to hold that a good case might be made out for Scientific Management as regards those orders of routine labour which, as ordinarily carried on, contain very little interest or humanity. Even then, however, there is a danger that deserves attention. If this regimentation can reduce the cost per unit of dull, heavy muscular toil, as is likely, it may prevent the discovery and application of wholly mechanical substitutes for this work.

But the human economy is far more doubtful in the case of labour which, though subdivided and mainly of a routine character, still contains a margin for the display of skill, initiative and judgment. To remove these qualities altogether from such work and to vest them, as is proposed, not even in the overseers, but in a little clique of scientific experts, would mean the conversion of large bodies of skilled, intelligent workers into automatic drudges. The life and character of these men would suffer as an inevitable reaction of this drudgery, and it is doubtful whether a somewhat shortened work-day and somewhat higher wages would compensate such damage. While we may recognise the general desirability of division and specialisation of labour, some detailed liberty and flexibility should be left to the worker.

§ 9. Indeed, were the full rigour of Scientific Management to be applied throughout the staple industries, not only would the human costs of labour appear to be enhanced, but progress in the industrial arts itself would probably be damaged. For the whole strain of progress would be thrown upon the Scientific Management and the consulting psychologist. The large assistance given to technical invention by the observation and experiments of intelligent workmen, the constant flow of suggestion for detailed improvements, would cease. The elements of creative work still surviving in most routine labour would disappear. On the one hand, there would be small bodies of efficient taskmasters carefully administering the orders of expert managers, on the other, large masses of physically efficient but mentally inert executive machines. Though the productivity of existing industrial processes might be greatly increased by this economy, the future of industrial progress might be imperilled. For not only would the arts of invention and improvement be confined to the few, but the mechanisation of the great mass of workmen would render them less capable of adapting their labour to any other method than that to which they had been drilled. Again, such automatism in the workers would react injuriously upon their character as consumers, damaging their capacity to get full human gain out of any higher remuneration that they might obtain. It would also injure them as citizens, disabling them from taking an intelligent part in the arts of political self-government. For industrial servitude is inimical to political liberty. It would become even more difficult than now for a majority of men, accustomed in their work-day to mechanical obedience, to stand up in their capacity of citizens against their industrial rulers when, as often happens upon critical occasions, political interests correspond with economic cleavages.

I would not dogmatise upon the necessity of these human disadvantages of Scientific Management. The more rigorous routine of the work-day might be adequately compensated by shorter hours, higher wages, increased opportunities for education, recreation, and home life. But there can be no security for adequate compensations of these orders under a scientific management directed primarily by private profit-making motives. For there is no guarantee that the larger profits to a business firm do not entail a damage to its employees, not offset by the bonus which they may obtain. Nor have we the required security that any social gain in the way of increased product and lower prices may not be cancelled by the human injury inflicted upon large bodies of workers and citizens by the more mechanical and servile conditions of their labour.

* * *

§ 10. A little reflection will make it clear that the complete success of such a business economy would involve a corresponding 'science' on the side of consumption. The standardised worker ought also to be a standardised consumer. For the regular reliable conformity of work must involve a similar conformity in diet and in other habits of life. If the 'scientific manager' were the full owner of his workmen, it would evidently be a function of his science to work out experimentally, with the assistance of the bio-psychologist, the cheapest and best way of living for each particular trade and type of worker. He would discover and prescribe the precise combination of foods, the most hygienic clothing and housing, the most appropriate recreations and the 'best books' for each class, with a view to the productive efficiency of its members. He would encourage by bonuses eugenic, and discourage by fines dysgenesic marriages among his employees. So far as intelligent employers are in a position to determine or to influence the expenditure of the wages they pay and the general conduct of the lives of their employees outside the working hours, they are disposed to practice this policy. Where they are the owners of the town or village in which the workers find it most convenient to live, they can often do so with considerable effect. Philanthropic motives are often combined with business motives, and the combination may often be genuinely conducive to the human welfare of the community. Temperance, sanitation, and hygiene, educational and recreative opportunities may be made available. Certain regulations, chiefly of a prohibitory nature, regarding the use of alcohol, betting, or marriage, are imposed by some employers as conditions of employment. Such interferences outside the hours of labour are, however, exceptional and are generally justified on special grounds of economic safety and efficiency.

§ 11. But an altogether wider issue is opened up in the claims, not of the particular employer but of industrial society to impose or evoke standards of consumption scientifically adjusted to the various grades of industrial efficiency. If we regard a nation as an economic society, putting out productive energy in wealth-creation, it becomes evident that science has much to say, and can have more, regarding the expenditure of incomes and the consequent consumption of wealth. The science of scientific management, with all its psycho-physical apparatus for measuring results, can be applied to standards of living for individuals and families. The beginnings of this idea are found in the distinction which figured so largely in the classical Political Economy between productive and unproductive consumption. The discussions of Arthur Young, Eden and others, regarding the respective merits of wheat and oatmeal, beer and tea, as ingredients of working-class diet, were directed avowedly by this conception of economy. A good food was one that yielded more muscular energy or endurance per penny of expenditure. The more enlightened doctrine known as 'the economy of high wages' was early recomended by philanthropists like Robert Owen, or business men like Mr. Brassey, on the score of experiments relating to the larger output of labour-power which higher wages with better feeding rendered possible. But there was no 'science' worth mention in these crude experiments. Only within recent years, with the advance of organic chemistry and physiology, has the 'science' of dietetics begun to emerge, analysing the various foods and assigning them their values as producers of tissue and of energy. We are now told the quantities of proteids, carbohydrates and fats contained in various foods, and dietaries based upon these analyses are prescribed for different sorts of workers, and for different ages of members of a family. At present the science does not pretend to any large amount of accuracy, indeed wide divergences still exist in its very foundations. But there is no reason to doubt that further analysis and experimentation may be able to reach food standards which on the consumption side will correspond to the economy of standard methods of work under scientific management. It may be quite possible to lay down with considerable exactitude the amounts and combinations and intervals of food for coal-miners, weavers, clerks, motor-men, etc., together with estimates of the amount of expenditure required to maintain the different forms of industrial efficiency. The productive value of other elements of the wage-earner's expenditure will not indeed admit of so much exactitude, partly because his own 'utility' obtained from such expenditure will not easily be separable from that of his family. But though family expenditure cannot thus be regarded as exclusively directed by productive considerations, the physical efficiency which is its chief test may be regarded primarily as an industrial asset. Indeed, this view is implicit in most talk of standards of comfort and in most discussions of a 'minimum' or 'living' or 'subsistence' wage. It means such wage as, economically expended, will enable a wage-earner to rear an average family in that measure and kind of efficiency required to do work of a sort similar to that by which he earns the wage. No doubt this notion is tempered by some slight considerations of education and of betterment. But productive efficiency is always the basic factor. Food and housing, by far the most important elements in working-class expenditure, are clearly in process of being standardised by hygienics in the service of a science of productive consumption.

§ 12. Two other sciences, by which society may seek to standardise the lives of workers, are eugenics and education. In both of these the humanists may have a fierce battle to fight against the dominion of the industrialists. Eugenics, if it can get recognition as a social art, will regulate marriage for the purposes of good stock. But good for what? Perhaps for industry and war, if some specialists should have their way. So too with education. Primary education has already been ear-marked in our towns for the production of cheap clerks, and technical and professional training under various guises invade our citadels of higher learning. All is part of the same great claim of society to economise and standardise the body and the mind of its citizen, primarily in order that he may do more efficiently the social or routine services it requires of him.

This economic standardisation, as we recognise, is not identical in motives or in operation as it bears respectively upon the productive and consumptive functions. On its productive side it is regulated by considerations of private business profits. Its primary aim is to get men to work in such a way as to produce the largest margin between the wage necessary to evoke full efficiency under 'scientific management' and the market value of the output. Indirectly, it is claimed, this policy redounds to the advantage of industrial society in an increase of the body of consumable wealth, some considerable share of which will pass into the general store. On its consumptive side the scientific standardisation works differently. It is plied more directly as a social-economic art, working out for the family, as well as for the individual workman, a standard of living, physical, intellectual, and moral, conducive to the interests of society regarded as an economic or wealth-producing entity.[1] But though society, in thus seeking to secure standards of economic efficiency for its family units, is not directly concerned in furthering the profit-seeking ends of private business firms, indirectly it is doing so. For, so long as expenditure of income, or family budgets, are estimated strictly in accordance with the economic efficiency they yield to the present and prospective working members, the process is in reality supplementary to the science of business management. For the better birth, better rearing, better health and education which it furnishes, will all eventually be translated into larger quantity and better quality of labour-power for scientific management to handle in its various profit-making processes.

Now the thoughtful members of the working-classes have always half-instinctively regarded with some suspicion the endeavours of social reformers to make them use cheaper foods yielding more nutriment for the money, temperance movements to keep down their conventional necessaries, and technical education to make their labour-power more productive. For they have doubted whether the cheaper living or the increased productivity would necessarily come home to them in improved conditions of life. Nor has their suspicion been wholly groundless. Though in the long run, it might seem to follow that as consumers and even perhaps, though less surely, as wage-earners, they would get some gain from the more economical use of their labour-powers, the bulk of the visible gains might very well

---

[1] This rationalisation of life for distinctively economic purposes, alike on its productive and expenditure side, has been carried further by the Jews than by any other people, i. e., their religion, politics, eugenics and education have been directed more exclusively and more rationalistically towards the business arts in which they excel, those of the financier, undertaker, trader, than in the case of other peoples. See Sombart, *The Jews and Modern Capitalism*, Chs. IX and X.

pass into the hands of the employing classes in higher profits or salaries of management.

This consideration opens the deeper criticism which humanism and Sociology are entitled and required to press upon the policy of the industrial economists. Every improvement in the technique of the arts of industry or of consumption may be considered as conducive to economic progress, yielding an increase of marketable wealth. But, if such improvements increase the human costs of production, or diminish the human utilities of consumption, as may happen if they consist largely in the standardising of productive and consumptive processes, they may bring no increase, possibly may bring a decrease, of human welfare. Proposals for scientific management or for standardised dietaries are not indeed to be condemned, upon the general application of such criticism. For it is agreed that such standardisation within certain limits is socially advantageous. The question, therefore, is partly one of degree, partly as to the security there exists that the economic gains of the improved economy shall be properly apportioned.

§ 13. But the final test would not consist in determining whether increased costs and diminished utilities did or did not offset the *prima facie* advantages of the economic improvements. The art of social welfare, humanism, will insist upon considering the reactions of the standardisation of work and consumption upon other faculties and functions than the economic, and in considering prospective as well as present gains. A scientific rigour in economy of work and of expenditure, which should remove, both from the industry and the lives of the great masses of a population, all opportunities for initiative, experiment, risk-taking and the display of personality, might reduce the human value of life for the average man, and so impair the worth of the society. Humanism, therefore, while approving the application of science to the arts of production and consumption, insists that it shall be shown to be the servant not the master of humanity. Such proof is sought, because the assumption, so often made, that all such economic progress must be humanly profitable, is seen to be unwarranted.

A 'scientific' view of human industry would establish the following lines of investigation.

(1) The productive ability of each producer would be considered in relation to its technical efficiency, i. e., the *best way* for him to do his job.

(2) His special productive function would be considered in its reactions (a) upon his general standard of life on its economic side, i. e., in relation to his productive and consumptive functions; (b) upon his individual human life.

(3) The standard of consumption of each consumer would be considered in relation to its technical efficiency (a) for purposes of production; (b) for purposes of individual welfare.

(4) Industry as a social function would be subjected to criticism from the wider standpoint of social welfare, i. e., as one element contributing to the life of a nation.

Finally, an analysis of the human worth of existing industry on its productive and consumptive sides would not suffice. For such an analysis merely accepts the existing system of industry and enquires into the best human methods of working it.

But humanist criticism must, of course, go behind this acceptance. The problem of industry which it will envisage will be one that takes as its data the existing resources of the nation, natural and human, and considers how these resources may, in accordance with present knowledge, be best applied for the provision of organic welfare according to the best accepted interpretation of that term. However difficult it may be to secure, to justify and to apply that standpoint, this is the form in which the economic problem must present itself to the statesman, the publicist, and the social reformer, so far as they are clear-sighted, rational and disinterested in their work.

So regarded, each individual would be considered as a complex of activities and wants, whose specialised work for society must be harmonised with that freedom and exercise of his non-specialised functions needed to enable him to realise himself as a human personality. Due consideration would be given to the interplay of his productive and consumptive functions within his economic life. His economic life must, however, be kept in due subordination to his wider human life, consisting, as the latter does, mainly of non-economic functions.

Finally, his economic and human life as a personality must be harmonised with the economic and human life of the society of which he is a member.

Such are the main implications of what might be termed the human scientific calculus of industrial values.

CHAPTER XV

§ 1. Leisure, regarded as an economic good, comes under the general law of distribution of wealth. But the notorious defects of its distribution, and their human consequences, are such as to claim for it a separate place in our enquiry. Modern industrialism by its large unearned surplus has greatly increased the size of the leisure classes. For wherever such surplus goes, there is the possibility and probability of a life of leisure. In our study of Consumption we traced the part played by conspicuous leisure as an element of pride and power in the economy of the rich. In Great Britain the size of this leisure class is by no means measured by the number of those who stand in the census as 'unoccupied.' In the top stratum of the business world we find considerable numbers of the directing and managerial class who are seldom or ever 'busy.' Their office hours are short and irregular, their week-ends extend from Friday to Tuesday, their holidays are long and frequent.

Most of their leisure is accompanied by profuse consumption, involving thus from the standpoint of society a double waste, a waste of time and of substance. Where does all this leisure come from? The answer to this question seems tolerably simple. It has often been observed that labour-saving machinery and other devices for abridging human toil have done very little to lighten or shorten the work-day for the workers. What then has become of the labour that is saved? Most of it has gone to enlarge the leisure of the leisured class, or perhaps we should say, of the leisured classes. For we saw that there existed a lower as well as an upper leisure class, a necessary product of the same mal-distribution of resources as sustains the latter. For an industrial system that grinds out unproductive surplus breaks down the physical and moral efficiency of large numbers of actual or potential workers as a by-product of the overdriving and underfeeding process. The reckless breeding of the class thus broken down furnishes a horde of weaklings, shirkers and nomads, unassimilated, unassimilable by the industrial system. These beings, kept alive by charity and poor-laws, have grown with modern industrialism and constitute the class known as 'unemployables.' They are often described as a 'standing menace to civilisation,' and are in fact the most pitiable product of the mal-distribution of wealth.

§ 2. But the irregularities of modern production and consumption are also responsible for a vast amount of involuntary and injurious leisure among the genuine working-classes. That leisure is commonly termed 'unemployment.' It is not true leisure, in the sense of time for recreation or enjoyment, though it might become so. For the most part it is at present wasteful and demoralising idleness.

A certain amount of unemployment is of course unavoidable in any organisation of industry. There will be some leakage of time between jobs and unpredictable irregularities of weather and climate will involve some idleness. Expansions and contractions of special trades, changes in methods of production and of consumption, the necessary elasticity of economic life, will continue to account for the temporary displacement of groups of workers. There is, of course, no social wastage in this process, if it is properly safeguarded. But hitherto it has been a great source of individual and social waste. Society is only beginning to realise the duty, or indeed the possibility, of taking active steps to reduce the quantity of this unemployment and to utilise what is unavoidable for the benefit of the unemployed and of society. The cultivation of these spare plots of time in the normal life of the workers may become a highly serviceable art.

If all unemployment could be spread evenly over the working year, taken out in a shortening of the ordinary working-day and in the provision of periodic and sufficient holidays, an immense addition would be made to the sum of industrial welfare. Thus, without any reduction in the aggregate of labour-time, a sensible reduction in the human cost of labour might be achieved, if law, custom, or organised labour policy made it impossible for employers to vary violently or suddenly the volume of employment and to sandwich periods of over-time with periods of short-time. These baneful irregularities of employment appear inevitable so long as they remain permissible, as do sweating wages and other bad conditions of labour. When they are no longer permissible, the organised intelligence of the trade will adjust itself to the new conditions, generally with little or no loss, often with positive gain.

If there are trades upon which season, fashion, or other uncontrollable factors impose great irregularity of employment, a sound social policy will have close regard to the nature of this irregularity. Where an essentially irregular trade is engaged in supplying some necessary or convenience of life, as, for instance, in gas-works and certain branches of transport, alternative trades may be found whose fluctuations tend to vary inversely with those of the former trades, and which can furnish work suitable in kind and place to those who are out.

Statistics of employment show that the aggregate of employment during any given year does not vary much. It would vary less, if every man engaged in an essentially irregular trade had an alternative, in which he was qualified to earn a living when employment in the other trade was short. For there is little truth in the contention that specialisation for most manual trades is carried so far that an alternative or subsidiary employment spoils a worker for efficiency in his prime trade. If there are any necessary trades for whose unavoidable unemployment no such effective provision can be made, society must either saddle the trade with the obligation of keeping the 'reserve' of labour while it stands in waiting, or it must itself undertake the administration of the trade as one which cannot safely be left in private hands. In the case of fashion or luxury trades, which furnish many instances of greatest irregularity, legal prohibition of over-time will often operate most beneficially. Where much unemployment still remains, a high contribution to an unemployed insurance fund would stimulate advantageous readjustments. Finally, if there are trades incapable of bearing the true costs of maintenance of the labour they employ, it would still be right to place on them the obligation to do so, for their destruction will be a gain not a loss to a society that understands its human interests.

But the main problem of leisure would still remain unsolved. For the normal burden of industrial toil, imposed by our present economic system upon most workers, is excessive. That excess consists primarily in duration of the work-day, though aggravated in many cases by intensity or pace of working. Great numbers of workers, especially among women, are employed in occupations where neither law, custom, nor trade organisation, imposes any limits. No factory day affects the employees in shops or offices or most warehouses, or in most transport trades, or in domestic service—departments of employment which absorb a rapidly increasing number and proportion of the employed population. There are vast numbers of domestic workshops and home trades in which men and women are employed, where all hours are worked. No legal restrictions of hours are set upon adult male labour in manufacturing and other industrial work in most of the metal and other trades which are exclusively or predominantly men's employments, though in trades where women also are employed restrictions are often imposed which in fact extend to men the factory day.

But there is a generally recognised feeling that the length of the factory day is gravely excessive, that 10½, or even 9 hours per diem, under modern conditions of speeded-up machinery and nervous tension, involve too heavy a human cost.

§ 3. It is this growing volume of feeling that has crystallised in the demand for an eight-hours day. This is no immoderate demand. A regular contribution of eight hours' working energy of hand, or brain, or nerves, to some narrow routine process, is as much as, or more than, the ordinary man or woman can afford, in the wholesome interest of his personality, to give up to society. For we have recognised quite clearly that a specialisation of function, a division of labour, growing ever finer, is required of the individual in the interests of society. He must make this apparent sacrifice of his private tastes, feelings and interests, for the good of the society of which he is a member. It is not, as we perceive, a real sacrifice, unless the demand made upon him is excessive, for the good of the society he serves is his good, and what he gives out comes back to him in participation of the common life. But, when the task imposed is too long or too hard, the sacrifice becomes an injury, the encroachment upon the human life of the worker inflicts grave damage, which damage again reacts upon society.

The stress of the Labour Movement upon the urgency of shortening the work-day to-day is extremely significant. It testifies to two advances in the actual condition of the labouring classes. In the first place, it indicates that some substantial progress has been made towards a higher level of material standard of consumption. For workers on the lower levels of poverty dare not ask for reduced hours of labour, involving, as may well occur, a reduction of pay. Workers struggling for a bare physical subsistence cannot afford to purchase leisure.

Of course I know that even the better-to-do workers who voice a demand for an eight-hours day are not ready to proclaim their willingness to pay for it in diminished wages. Nor need they in all cases. Where the shorter day is attended by improved efficiency or increased intensity of labour, or merely by better organisation of the business, there may be nothing to pay. More leisure has been squeezed out of the working-day. There are many cases where this can be done, for the working-day in many instances is wastefully prolonged. But, though in certain trades a ten-hours day may be reduced to nine, or even eight, without any reduction of output, this is not the case in other trades, nor even in the former trades could the process be carried far without a loss of output. In a great many employments a short working-day will involve a larger economic cost of labour, and where, as is usual in competitive trade, this larger cost cannot be made good out of profits, labour will have to buy this leisure, in part at any rate, by reduced wages. For even if he can get it shifted on to the consumer in the shape of higher prices, as consumer he will in his turn have to bear a part of it.

Where the demand for shorter hours is genuine, and is not a mere cover for extended over-time, to be paid for at a higher rate, it must be taken as indicative of the workers' willingness to take part of his share of industrial progress in leisure instead of wages.

§ 4. But leisure, as an economic asset, is not a mere question of hours. A shorter work-day might be dearly bought at the cost of an intensification of labour which left body and mind exhausted at the end of each day. The opposition of workers to a policy of speeding-up, or the use of pace-setters, is usually a sane act of self-defence, and not the fractious obstruction to industrial progress it is sometimes represented. No considerations of human endurance limit the pace at which machinery driven by mechanical power may be worked. Unless, therefore, restraints are put by law, custom or bargaining, upon the speed of machines, or the number which a worker is called upon to serve, competition may impose a work-day which, though not unduly long in hours, habitually exhausts the ordinary worker. It is not always realised how great a change took place when the weaver, the shoemaker, the smith, passed from the workshops, where the pace and other conditions of work were mostly regulated by their voluntary action, to the steam-driven factory. The shoemaker and the tailor under the old conditions had time, energy and liberty for thought while carrying on their work: they could slacken, break off or speed up, their work, according to their inclination. The clicker or heeler in a shoe factory, the cutter-out in a clothing factory, have no such measure of freedom. This is, of course, a normal effect of modern industrialism. Closer and more continuous attention is demanded during the working hours.

Thus the real question of leisure is a question of spare human energy rather than of spare hours. The shorter working-day is chiefly needed as a condition favourable to spare energy. Though therefore, an eight-hours day may not unreasonably be taken as a proximate reform, for labour in general, there is no reason why the work-day in all occupations should be cut to this or any other exact measure. Such arithmetical equality would evidently work out most inequitably, as between trade and trade, or process and process in the same trade. In many large departments of industry, the transport and distributive trades in particular, numerous interstices of leisure are inserted in a day's work, easing the burden of the day, and sometimes affording opportunity for recreation and intercourse. In the more arduous processes of manufacture, mining, or in clerical and other routine brain work, there is little or no scope for such relaxation.

But while such considerations evidently affect the detailed policy of the shorter day in its pressure on the several occupations, they do not affect the general policy.

There can be no doubt that an excessive and injurious amount of specialised labour is exacted from the workers by the ordinary industrial conditions of to-day in nearly all industrial processes.

§ 5. The first plea for a shorter day is one which our analysis has made self-evident.

It will greatly reduce the human cost of production in most processes. For, as we recognise, the strain of muscular and nervous fatigue, both conscious and unconscious, gathers force and grows with great rapidity during the later hours of the workday. Though the curve representing the variations of the human cost will of course differ in every sort of work and for different workers, their age, sex, strength, health and other personal conditions affecting it, the last hours of each shift will contain a disproportionate amount of fatigue, pain and other 'costs,' while the quality and quantity of the work done in these last hours will be inferior.

If out of any stock of material goods, we were able to separate the product of the last hour's work from that of the earlier hours in the work-day, and could subject it to the analysis of human cost and utility, which we have endeavoured to apply to the general income, what should we find? This last increment of the product would contain a heavier burden of human cost of production than any of the earlier increments. Again, turning to the consumption side, what should we find? This last increment must be considered as furnishing the smallest amount of human utility in its consumption. Indeed, if we are right in holding that a considerable fraction of each supply, even of what are commonly classed as material necessaries of life, such as foods, clothings, etc., is wastefully or even detrimentally consumed by the well-to-do, there is reason to hold that this last increment of product, involving the largest human cost in its production, contains no utility but some amount of human disutility in its consumption.

If this analysis be true, the last hour's work may be doubly wasteful from the standpoint of human welfare.

Of the £2,000,000,000 which constitutes our income it may very likely be the case that £200,000,000 of it represents wealth, which, from the human standpoint, is 'illth,' alike in the mode of its production and of its consumption. If it had not been produced at all, the nation might have been far better off, for by abstaining from the production of this sham wealth, it would have produced a substantial amount of leisure.

It is of course true that the particular groups of producers, who by their last hour's labour made these goods, may not have been losers by doing so; their heavy toil may have been compensated by the enhanced wage which they could not otherwise have got, and the loss of which would have injured their standard of life. It is, indeed, the operation of competition upon wages that actually forces into existence this sham-wealth. Drawn out of over-wrought workers by the unequal conditions of the wage-bargain, it passes into wasteful consumption by the back-stroke of the same law of distribution, which pays it away as 'surplus' or 'unearned' wealth.

It is only the clear consideration of its production and consumption from the social standpoint that exhibits the waste of the last hour's product.

But from the standpoint of the individual worker the economy of a shorter work-day has a double significance. We have seen that it more than proportionately diminishes his personal cost, by cancelling the last and most costly portion of his work-day. But it also increases the human utility which he can get out of his wages. A day of exhausting toil entails the expenditure of a large portion of his wage in mere replacement of physical wear and tear, or incites to expenditure on physical excesses, while the leisure hours are hours of idleness and torpor. A reduction of the work-day will, by the larger leisure and spare energy it secures, reduce the expenditure upon mere wear and tear, and increase the expenditure upon the higher and more varied strata of the standard of comfort. More leisure will in general so alter the mode of living as to enable the worker to get more and better utility out of the expenditure of his wages. Take an extreme case. A man who toils all day long at some exhausting work, and goes home at night too tired for anything but food and sleep, so as to enable him to continue the same round to-morrow, though he may earn good wages from this toil, can get little out of them. If he were induced to work less and leave himself some time and energy for relaxation and enjoyment, he would get a larger utility out of less money income.

The matter, however, does not need labouring. It is evident that many modes of consumption depend in part, for the pleasure and gain they yield, upon the amount of time given to the consuming processes. It would be mere foolishness for a tired worker to spend money upon improving books which he had not the time and energy to digest. Shorten his hours, leave him more energy, such expenditure may be extremely profitable. Even the enjoyment and good of his meals will be increased, if he has more time and energy for wholesome processes of digestion and for the exercise which facilitates digestion. And what is true of his food will hold also of most other items in his standard of consumption. No consumption is purely passive: to get the best utility or enjoyment out of any sort of wealth, time and energy are requisite. The greater part of a workman's income goes to the upkeep of his home and family. Does the normal work-day in our strenuous age permit the bread-winner to get the full enjoyment out of home and family? He belongs perhaps to a club or a coöperative society. Can he make the most of these opportunities of education and of comradeship, if his daily toil leaves him little margin of vitality? Most of the growing public expenditure which the modern State or City lays out upon the amenities of social life, the apparatus of libraries, museums, parks, music and recreation, is half wasted because industry has trenched too much upon humanity.

§ 6. More leisure means an increased fund of utility or welfare got out of the income at the disposal of each worker.

This introduces us to the fuller economy of leisure regarded as the opportunity of opportunities—the condition of all effective social reconstruction and progress.

Consider it first in relation to industrial welfare. We have seen how society enforces its claims upon the worker by division of labour and specialisation of functions. This specialisation is usually justified by the variety of consumption which it yields. But will not this more complex and refined consumption in large part be wasted or perverted to base ends, if the producer becomes ever narrower in his productive function?

The Organic Law presses here insistently. It would be going too far, doubtless, to assert that he who can produce one thing can only consume one thing. But everyone familiar with the finer arts of Consumption will admit that a consumer who is utterly unskilled in the production of these goods cannot extract from their consumption the full enjoyment or utility which they contain. A true connoisseur of pictures must, in training and in study, be a good deal of an artist: the exquisite *gourmet* must be something of a cook.

In other words, our industrial civilisation offers a dangerous paradox, if it merely presents man exposed to two opposed forces, tending on the one hand to greater narrowness of production, on the other, to greater width and complexity of consumption. To solve this paradox is the first service of the large new fund of leisure which, for the first time in history, the new economies of industry render available not for a little class but for whole peoples.

The first use of leisure, then, is that it supplies a counterpoise to specialisation by the opportunity it gives for the exercise of the neglected faculties, the cultivation of neglected tastes. As the specialisation grows closer, this urgency increases. More leisure is required for the routine worker to keep him human.

In the first place, it must afford him relaxation or recreation by occupations in which the spontaneity, the liberty, the elements of novelty, increasingly precluded from his work-day, shall find expression. It must liberate him from automatism, and afford him opportunity for the creative and interesting work required to preserve in him humanity.

An eight-hours day would mean that thousands of men, who at present leave the factory or furnace, the office or the shop, in a state of physical and mental lassitude, would take a turn at gardening, or home carpentry, would read some serious and stimulating book, or take part in some invigorating game.

Thus each man would not merely get more out of each item of his economic consumption, but he would add to the net sum of his humanity, and incidentally of his economic utility, by cultivating those neglected faculties of production which yield him a positive fund of interest and human benefit.

§ 7. So far I have set forth the economy of leisure from the standpoint of physical and moral health: the order and harmony of human powers. This, however, is in the main a statical economy. Now, Order is chiefly valuable as the means of Progress, Health as the means of Growth. The dynámic economy of Progress demands leisure even more insistently.

Everyone will formally admit that Education is impossible without leisure. It is often pointed out that the Greek word which has been converted into our word 'School' means Leisure. One might, therefore, suppose that the utmost care would be taken to get the fullest use out of the leisure which child-life affords, and to ensure that throughout life there should remain a sufficient supply of this raw material of progress—the surplus energy beyond the bare needs of existence needed for organic growth.

The prodigal waste of this sacred store of leisure for child-life in the processes of our Elementary Education is only too familiar to all of us. Mr. Stephen Reynolds [1] hardly overstates the case when he says, 'It gives to the children about three years' worth of second-rate education in exchange for eight or nine years of their life.' [2]

I believe that the trained educationalist of the next generation, examining the expensive education given even in the best-equipped of our secondary schools and our universities, in the light of a more rational conception of human progress, will find

[1] (Times, 23 Dec. 1912.)

[2] The best that can be said for this education has recently been said by Mr. George Peel, who writes of London children (*The Future of England*, p. 96):

'They spend 28 hours a week continuously during nine years under fairly satisfactory conditions of air, warmth and light, engaged in wholesome and stimulating pursuits. Considering what their homes often are, this itself must be reckoned an immense benefit.'

at least as large a waste of opportunity in these seats of learning as in our elementary schools. Not until educational standards and methods are better adjusted to true conditions of the vital progress of individuals and of societies, will the chief significance of leisure be realised.

§ 8. But the value of leisure is by no means exhausted by these considerations. The finest fruits of human life come not by observation. To lay out all our spare time and energy to the very best advantage by a scrupulous seizure of opportunities is in reality a false economy. Industrialism has undoubtedly done much both to discipline and to educate the powers of man. But it has preached too arrogantly the gospel of economy and industry. It is not good for any man to account for his time either to himself or to another, with too great exactitude, or to seek to make a mosaic of his days. The Smilesian philosophy of thrift and industry imparts more calculation into life than is good for man. We should not be so terribly afraid of idleness. Dr. Watts held that 'Satan finds some mischief still for idle hands to do.' But far saner is Wordsworth's view, 'that we can feed this mind of ours in a wise passiveness,' and Thoreau's demand for a 'broad margin of life.'

We are not yet sufficiently advanced in psychology to know much of the processes within the mind by which novel thoughts and feelings seem to enter of their own accord, starting new impulses to action, or by which the unchecked imagination works along some rapid line of intuition. But that such seasons of vacancy and reverie are essential to many of the finest processes of the intellect and heart, is indisputable. To deny this to any man is to deprive him of a part of his rightful heritage of human opportunity. The inventor, the poet, the artist, are readily allowed such free disposal of time. Everyone allows that genius must have ample periods of incubation. But the implication that common men ought to have their faces kept to the grindstone is quite false. Everybody wants leisure for his soul to move about in and to grow, not by some closely prescribed plan of education, but by free experimentation of its secret powers. A very slender harvest of happy thoughts and feelings will justify much apparent idleness.

In the narrower investigation of methods of industry which we essayed, we realised the critical part played by leisure in the art of invention. The lack of leisure for the great majority of workers is assuredly a waste of inventive power. We think our society prolific in inventions, especially in the age we are living in, but it is likely that the pace of progress through industrial inventions would be greatly quickened if the proper play-time of the mind were not denied to the great majority of men and women.

Biologists and psychologists have made many interesting enquiries into the motives that prompt animals and human beings to play. The forms of play, the rhythm or patterns into which the organic cooperations of muscular and nervous tensions and discharges cast themselves, are found to have some direct relation to the serious pursuits of adult life, the protection against enemies, the pursuit of prey and other food, courtship, mating and the care of the young, and the corporate movements necessary for the protection of the horde or tribe. So interpreted, play is an instinctive education for life. Nature is full of indirectness, and a great deal of this play is not closely imitative of any particular sort of useful activity but is directed to general fitness. This applies particularly to the higher animals who are less exclusively directed by separate particular instincts and are liable to have to meet novel and irregular emergencies that call for general adaptability of body and of mind. The play of higher animals and especially of human young will thus run largely into forms in which the intellectual and emotional powers will have large scope, where spontaneous variation and free imagination will express themselves, and where the more or less routine rhythms of the primitive dance or song or mock fight will pass into higher forms of individual cunning and competitive exploit, having as their main biological and social 'meaning' the practice of an efficient mental and emotional equipment. Play thus considered is an experimentation of vital powers. Its utility for child-life is commonly admitted. In fact, there is a grave danger lest the spontaneity and instinctive direction which nature has implanted should be damaged by the attempts of educationalists to force the vital utility of play by organising it into 'set games.' Though we need not rudely rule out reasonable regulation from this, as from any other department of life, it would be well to remember that play has powerful directive instincts behind it in child-life which adult notions of economy may gravely misconceive and injure by over-regulation. Hasty endeavours to displace instinct by reason in child-life are likely to prove costly to human welfare in the long run. The spontaneous joy of those activities of childhood that seem most 'wasteful' is probably a far better index to welfare than any pedagogic calculations.

But because the human utility of play is great for children, it does not follow that it is small for men and women. Even the physiological and much more the psychological utility of play lasts through life, though doubtless in diminishing value. For adult workers mere repose never exhausts the use of leisure. The biological or the social utility of his play may be much smaller than in the case of the young. But it will remain considerable. Nor is this utility chiefly expressed in the relation between play and invention. The chief justification for leisure does not consist in its contribution to the arts of industry but rather in raising the banner of revolt against the tyranny of industry over human life.

§ 9. We have grown so accustomed to regard business as the absorbing occupation of man, that which necessarily and rightly claims the major part of his waking hours, that a society based on any other scale of values seems inconceivable. Though history has made us familiar with civilisations, such as those of Athens and of Rome, where a large body of free citizens regarded politics, art, literature and physical recreations as far more important occupations, we know that such civilisations rested on a basis of slave labour. We do not seem to realise that for the first time in history two conditions are substantially attained which make it technically possible for a whole people to throw off the dominion of toil. Machinery and Democracy are these two conditions. If they can be brought into effective coördination, so that the full economics of machine production can be rendered available for the people as a whole, the domination of Industry over the lives, the thoughts, and the hearts of men, can be overthrown. This is the great problem of social-economic reconstruction, to make industry the servant of all men, not the servants of the few, the masters of the many. Its solution demands, of course, that after the wholesome organic needs are satisfied, the stimulation of new material wants shall be kept in check. For if every class continues constantly to develop new complicated demands, which strain the sinews of industry even under a socially-ordered machine-economy, taking the whole of its increased control of Nature in new demands upon Nature for economic satisfaction, the total burden of Industry on Man is nowise lightened. If we are to secure adequate leisure for all men, and so to displace the tyranny of the business life by the due assertion of other higher and more varied types of life, we must manage to check the lust of competitive materialism which Industrialism has implanted in our hearts.

I am aware how difficult it is to translate these handsome aspirations into practical achievement. To urge the working-classes of this country, or even considerable sections of the middle-classes engaged in the trades and professions, to sacrifice some immediately attainable rise in their material and intellectual standard of comfort, in order thereby to purchase more leisure, will be taken to indicate a blank ignorance of the actual conditions of their lives. I shall be reminded that recent statistics of wages in this country show that about one-third of our working-class families are living upon precarious weekly incomes amounting to less than 25s. a week, and that this computation does not take into account a large body of the population living upon casual earnings indefinitely lower than this sum. Now Mr. Rowntree and other searchers into working-class expenditure have shown that 25s. will hardly purchase for an ordinary family in any English town a sufficiency of food, clothing, housing, fuel and other requisites to maintain its members in full physical efficiency. It will seem idle to contend that working-people in this case would do well to prefer a shortening of their working day, however long it be, to an increase of their wages. None of the considerations I have urged relating to the better utilisation of their consumption will be held to justify so obviously wasteful a policy. These workers simply cannot afford to buy more leisure at so high a price. They dare not sacrifice any fraction of their current wages to procure a reduction of hours from ten hours to eight, even if the conditions of their trade otherwise admitted such a change; and if increasing prosperity in their trade presents them with the option of obtaining higher wages or shorter hours, their pressing demands for better food and housing will rightly compel them to choose the former of the two alternatives.

Nor is this reasoning refuted by dwelling upon the undeniable facts, that most standards of working-class comfort contain elements of conventional consumption which might be cut out with positive advantage, and that, apart from this, a more intelligent housekeeping would enable most of them to do much better with their actual incomes than they do. For when a due allowance has been made for such errors or extravagance, the ordinary labourer's wage in town and in country still remains below the margin of family efficiency. Of course, in almost every occupation there will be a considerable number of workers who, having no family dependent on them, will have some means at their disposal for comforts, luxuries, saving or leisure. But the normal standard wage for unskilled or low-skilled labour in this country does not appear to have attained a height at which the purchase of a shorter working day is sound economy. We must always bear in mind, besides, that the existence in a trade of even a considerable minority of workers who could afford to take in increased leisure what they might take in enhanced wages, would not make this step practicable or desirable. For most trades are now so organised that a common standard working day is even more essential than a uniform rate of wages.

These facts enable us to realise why it is that so much elasticity or ambiguity attends the actual labour movement for a shorter working day. The demand is seldom framed in such a way as to preclude the common use of over-time, though such a use of course defeats the aim for leisure, converting it into an aim for higher wages, the time and a half rate usually paid for over-time.

But, though this open or secret competition between more leisure and more wages continues to take place in trades where general conditions of labour are improving, the relative strength of the claim for leisure is advancing. There comes a point in the improved conditions of each working-class when the demand for liberty and ease and recreation begins to assert itself with so much insistence that it outweighs some part of the chronic demand for higher wages. Though workers are usually reluctant to admit the economic necessity of making a wage-sacrifice in order to purchase leisure, and will hardly ever claim a shorter day, if they know it to involve an actual fall of wages, they will sometimes risk this fall, and more often they will forego a portion of a contemplated rise of wage, so as to get a shorter day. The strength and effectiveness of this demand for leisure in comparison with wages must, of course, vary with the actual standard of comfort that obtains, the onerousness or irksomeness of the work, the age, sex and intelligence of the workers, and the variety and sorts of opportunities which increased leisure will place at their disposal. In the ordinary English feudal village, or even in the small country town, leisure commonly means torpor qualified by the public-house. The price of such leisure, in terms of sacrifice of wage, would be very low, for the utility in the sensational enjoyment of the leisure would be slight as compared with the substantial addition to the material standard of family comfort which even a shilling would afford. On the other hand, to the better-paid mechanic, compositor, or skilled factory worker, where the family wage was relatively high, and where organised city life presented many opportunities for the use and enjoyment of leisure, it might seem well worth while to pay something in cash for the advantage of a longer evening.

§ 10. This problem, of course, is merely one illustration of the complicated issues which arise in any orderly study of the human economics of class and individual standards of consumption. Even such a merely cursory glance at this delicate organic problem will serve to expose the fatuity of so much of the crude dogmatic criticism lavished upon working-class economy by well-to-do reformers who have not sufficient imagination or discretion to abstain from applying the standards of valuation appropriate to an income of £1,000 a year to a family living upon £60 a year. The exact income-point where a West Ham worker can afford to observe the legal requirements against overcrowding by hiring another room, where he can join a Club with a reasonable chance of keeping up the subscriptions, where he can afford to keep the boys or girls at school beyond the legal age-limit, such questions cannot be settled by general maxims as to the duty of thrift or the advantages of education, or even the dangers of bad sanitation. It must be remembered that even in this highly-civilised and Christian land there are still some millions of people who cannot afford to set aside anything for a rainy day, or to let their children enjoy the education which the State freely provides, or even to obey some of the fundamental laws of health. As the family wage rises beyond a bare minimum of current subsistence, a point will emerge where each of these and many other sound practices becomes economically feasible: the particular income-point, of course, will differ with each family according to its composition, its needs, and the opportunities of meeting them.

What applies so evidently to the narrow incomes of the wage-earners is, of course, equally applicable to the higher incomes of other classes. The well-to-do professional man recognises that an annual expenditure of five or even ten per cent of his income on holidays may be a sound economy, just as he calculates that he is doing better for his son by spending £1,000 on his professional training than by putting him to business at sixteen with the same sum for capital. Not only is it impossible to generalise for a whole people, or for all families in a given trade or of a given income, but there will be no two cases where a rising income ought to be laid out precisely in the same way. This is of course nothing else than saying that, as no two persons, or families, are precisely alike in physical and moral make-up, in tastes, needs, opportunities, their expenditure cannot rightly be the same.

Though this belongs to the most obvious of common-places, none is more habitually ignored. And that neglect is largely due to the fact that the platitudinarian moralist has always been allowed to have a free run in the region of commentary on expenditure.

Eulogia of thrift and industry have been as indiscriminate

and as unprofitable as diatribes against luxury and idleness. What is needed is a flow of orderly investigation into the real needs and capacities of the individuals and groups who constitute industrial society, not confined to the hard facts which can be tabulated and plotted in curves but taking count of those softer and more plastic facts which a closer study of human life will always show as the main determinants of any art of conduct.

The place of leisure in the organic standard of a group or class or nation will be one of the most delicate problems in such a study. Its delicacy for the individual economy may, indeed, be deduced from the expression which we used at the outset of this treatment, in describing it as 'the opportunity of opportunities.' In other words, its human utility to any man, and, therefore, its importance, relative to his wages or any other good he gets from them, will depend upon the nature of all the opportunities it opens up, and that in its turn depends upon the entire sum of those conditions which we name his Nature and his Environment.

The progressive achievement of this economy of leisure is closely linked with a gradual reorganisation of industry so as to eliminate the large waste of time and energy which present productive methods involve. With science and humanity coöperating in the art of social organisation it ought to be possible to effect such economies as would place all Englishmen in private possession of the greater part of their waking day for their own purposes in life. It requires, however, a genuine faith in the organic progress of Human Nature to urge with confidence the fuller measure of such a reform. We need at least to assume that the normal tendency will be towards the use, not the abuse, of more leisure, as of higher wages. That some waste will be incurred in learning to use leisure, as also in building up each stage in a rising standard of expenditure, is of course inevitable. Much might be said about the conditions which facilitate the assimilation both of leisure and of wages to nourish a higher human life. Race, climate, social traditions and surroundings, the nature of the work, age, sex and, indeed, many other conditions, must help to determine how a given shortening of hours, or enhancement of wages, will affect the standard of life. Some crude distinctions of great significance have been observed. The Bantu and most other Africans, new to processes of wage-labour and to the needs of civilised life, will take the whole of a sudden rise of wages in increased leisure, but that leisure will be spent almost wholly in idleness. Pushful German traders in tropical countries commonly complain of the 'verdammte Bedürfnislösigkeit' (accursed wantlessness) of the inhabitants. This low conservative standard of living impedes economic processes of exchange. It also precludes the fruitful use of leisure, the satisfaction of the non-economic needs. Though there is no reason to hold that any race or type of man is unprogressive, in the sense that his mind is impervious to new wants and is incapable of inciting him to new efforts for their satisfaction, the extent and pace of such progress vary greatly with the economic environment and with the degree of conscious culture hitherto attained. The stimuli of economic needs and of non-economic needs will normally proceed together, and in the masses of a working population will manifest themselves in a simultaneous demand for higher wages and more leisure. But as wages reach a tolerably high standard of economic comfort, it might be expected that the relatively stronger pressure of the non-economic needs would give increasing emphasis to the demand for a shorter and easier working day. This, indeed, will seem to accord with the general claim which socialists as well as individualists make for progressive industrialism, that it shall make larger provision for personal liberty and self-development. As specialised and regimented industry represents the direct economic service each must render to society, the demands of expanding personality are held to require that an increasing proportion of each man's time and energy shall be put at his disposal.

§ 11. No abstract considerations indeed, can be adduced to support an indefinite reduction of the work-day. As a high level of civilisation is attained in any community, the proportion of energy devoted to material, as compared with non-material commodities and services, will doubtless be reduced. But that does not necessarily imply a corresponding reduction of economic time and activity. For among economic goods themselves, those which are wholly or mainly non-material will form an increasing proportion of the whole. A community like that of Great Britain, with a population declining in its growth, will tend to take a continually increasing share of its real income in the shape of intellectual, moral, æsthetic, recreative, and other non-material services. These will absorb an ever-growing share of the productive energy of the people. This demand for the satisfaction of higher economic needs will be likely to put a check upon the tendency towards an illimitable reduction of the work-day. For most of these higher non-material goods do not admit the application of those economies of capitalist production available in the making of material goods. Take one example, that of education. Here is a service which will probably absorb a continually increasing percentage of the total time and energy devoted to economic services. The same is probably true of hygienic services. Though portions of these and other activities may pass from the economic into the non-economic sphere, being undertaken by individuals as private occupations, for their leisure, as public services they will certainly furnish employment to an increasing number of employees.

Thus the claims of a growing progressive social organisation will impose some necessary limits upon the demands of the individual for larger liberty and leisure.

There is, however, no final conflict between the claims of personal liberty and the social order. Even though the process of readjustment between the claims of industry and leisure should incline generally in favour of more leisure, with the prime purpose of nourishing more fully the private personality and affording larger scope for home life and recreation, society is not thereby the loser. For some of the finest and most profitable uses of leisure will consist of the voluntary rendering of social services of a non-economic order. I allude in particular to a fuller participation in the active functions of citizenship, a more intelligent interest in local and national politics, in local administration and in the numerous forms of voluntary association which are generally social in the services they render. More leisure is a prime essential of democratic government. There can be no really operative system of popular self-government so long as the bulk of the people do not possess the spare time and energy to equip themselves for effective participation in politics and to take a regular part in deliberative and administrative work. This is equally applicable to other modes of corporate activity, the life of the churches, friendly societies, trade unions, coöperative societies, clubs, musical and educational associations, which go to make up the social life and institutions of a country. Leisure, demanded primarily in the interests of the individual for his personal enjoyment, will thus yield rich nutriment to the organic life of society, because the individual will find himself drawn by the social needs and desires embedded in his personality to devote portions of his leisure to social activities which contribute to the commonwealth as surely as do the economic tasks imposed upon him in his daily industry.

CHAPTER XVI

THE RECONSTRUCTION OF INDUSTRY

PART I

CAPITAL AND LABOUR

§ 1. Since industry is a great coöperative process for the mutual aid of members of society, it is well that the fact should be held in the consciousness and will of individuals as clearly as possible. For this conscious realisation of the meaning of industry will have a helpful influence on their intelligence and feelings.

Now there are general related tendencies in modern industry which are powerful obstacles to this realisation of the social meaning of industry.

The first is the growing subdivision of labour with the related expansion of markets. When a man made a watch or a pair of shoes and sold them to a neighbour, or known customer, his work had for him a distinct human significance. For, making the whole of a thing, he realised its nature and utility, while, seeing the man who wore his watch or shoes, he realised the human value of his work. Now he performs one of some ninety processes which go to make many watches, or he trims the heels of innumerable shoes. The other processes he cannot do, and does not accurately know how they are done. His separate contribution has no clear utility, and yet it solely occupies his attention. Not only does he thus lose grasp of the meaning of his work, but he has no opportunity of realising its consumptive utility. For he cannot know or care anything about the unknown person in some distant part of the world who shall wear the boots or watch he helped to make. The social sympathy of coöperative industry is thus atrophied by the conditions of his work. Division of labour, in its first intent, thus divides each worker into a section of a producer, and separates each set of producers from the consumers of their products.

Though, therefore, this division of labour is in itself a finer mode of coöperation, it is not realised as such by those who are subjected to it.

§ 2. The second dehumanising and derationalising influence is the stress which the operations of modern industry lay on competition between trade and trade, business and business, worker and worker. No graver injury has been inflicted on the mind of man, in the name of science, than the prepotence which the early science of Political Economy assigned to the competitive and combative aspects of industrial life. To represent commerce between individuals and nations as a 'competitive system,' mainly dependent for its sucessful operation upon the absorption of each man in seeking his own gain, and in getting the better of others in his trade, was an error of the first magnitude. Nor was this error sufficiently corrected by the qualifying theory that from this pursuit by each of his separate gains the greatest good for all would somehow emerge. For, by laying the stress upon the competitive aspect of industry, this teaching stifled the growth of intellectual and moral sympathy between the various human centres of the industrial system, and impaired the sense of human solidarity which, apart from its spiritual value, is the mainspring of efficient economic organisation. The presentation of industry as competition with attendant coöperation, instead of as coöperation with attendant competition, has greatly contributed to the popular misunderstanding of commerce, alike upon its domestic and its international scales.[1]

Competition, if defended as a socially useful method of industry, must, like division of labour, be proved to contribute to coöperative ends. The general underlying assumption, that it will do so, we have seen to be false. Equally unjustified have been the accounts of actual industry which assume the general

---

[1] Adam Smith, by opening his *Wealth of Nations* with a dissertation upon the economy of division of labour, without explaining that this economy rests upon a prior conception of coöperation, unwittingly assisted to set English Political Economy upon a wrong foundation.

prevalence of free competition. At all times the area and liberty of effective competition between business and business, worker and worker, have been limited, and tend in recent times to closer limitation.

But if division of labour and competition, apart from a realisation of their coôperative values, are dehumanising and antisocial, so likewise is the growing anonymity of modern business. 'Compagnie Anonyme' is the significant French name for a Jointstock Company with its unknown shareholders. But this depersonalising process is everywhere inseparable from the magnitude and intricacy of modern businesses and modern markets. The capital belonging to a crowd of persons, who are strangers to one another, is massed into an effective productive aggregate, and is set to coôperate with masses of labour power whose owners are divorced from all direct contact, either with the owners of the tools and material, or with the purchasers of the product. An effective comradeship among large numbers of workers, distributed over diverse processes and often severed widely in their places of work, is also difficult to maintain. A great modern business is in its structure less effectively human than was the small workshop which it displaced. One effect of this weaker humanity of the business, especially in the relations between capital and labour, employer and employee, has been to shift the sentimental attachment of the worker from his business to his trade-union. He is less a member of a business firm, serving some directly productive function, than a member of a labour-group extending over the area of a local or even a national trade.

§ 3. This consideration brings to the front the antagonism between capital and labour which has in modern times assumed ever graver dimensions and clearer consciousness. In considering the industrial system as an effective economic harmony it is not easy to determine whether the coôperative or the competitive forces are gaining ground. On the one hand, the competition between businesses in the same trade is in all great staple trades giving place to combinations, which not only unite the formerly conflicting businesses, but weld into close unity the capital of various related trades. Trusts, cartels, pools, conferences and various experiments in federal compacts, for regulating output and selling prices, are everywhere engaged in substituting industrial peace for war. Direct and conscious harmony thus grows among formerly antagonistic capitalists and employers. The organisation of labour in the several trades, on the basis of a standard wage upheld by collective bargaining, marks a similar though less close harmony on the side of labour.

But these advances towards conscious harmony among hitherto competing capitalists and labourers have been attended by a widening and intensification of the conscious antagonism between capital and labour within the several trades. Indeed, there are signs of a growing extension of combination for definitely hostile purposes, a ranging of capital on the one side, labour on the other, animated by a broad class consciousness which is new in the history of industry.

In fact, it has all along been inevitable that the combinatory forces, which appeared to make for social solidarity in industry, should be brought up at what appears to be an impenetrable barrier, the class hostility between the owners of instruments of production and the workers. For this hostility is inherent in the distribution which evokes an Unproductive Surplus. So long as economic advantages permit some groups of capitalists, landowners and owners of organising power, to take for themselves large masses of unearned income, which might have gone to improve the conditions of the workers, had they been able to divert it into wages, no false platitudes about the harmony of capital and labour will secure industrial peace.

For that harmony, as we have seen, only extends to the portion of the product distributed as costs. Now, the enormously increased productivity of modern industry has resulted in an increase of the size and relative importance of the surplus, and the large proportion of that surplus which is distributed unproductively in 'unearned' income represents a growing element of discord.

This real divergence of economic interests between capital and labour is not then to be bridged by an economy of costs based upon the fact that, since each factor needs the other, it is interested in its proper remuneration. The complaints of the existing system made by the workers not merely testify to a growing realisation of their economic weakness and a growing sensitiveness to the inequitable modes of distribution. They are founded on the belief that upon the whole distribution is becoming more inequitable and more wasteful. For though the absolute share of the workers and the standard of real wages have been rising in most countries,[1] that rise has not been commensurate with the aggregate increase of wealth. In other words, a larger proportion of the total is passing into unproductive surplus, the factor of discord, a smaller into costs, the factor of harmony. If this is true, it implies inevitably a worsening of the relations between capital and labour. For, so long as the owners of strong or scarce factors of production are rewarded according to their strength or scarcity, no peace is possible. The absorption of the unassimilated mass of wealth in a higher standard of life for the workers and an enlargement and improvement of the public services is essential to secure the substance and the sense of social harmony in industry.

§ 4. Leaving out for the moment the claim of the State for public services, this socially sound distribution of the product could only be achieved by a recasting of the governmental structure of the Business, the Trade and Industry. Towards this governmental reform many different experiments are afoot. Various modifications of the ordinary wage-system, by way of bonuses upon individual and departmental efficiency of labour, are tried. More direct attempts to harmonise the interests of capital and labour within the business take shape in schemes of profit-sharing, which are sometimes carried further into the closer form of co-partnership, by which the workers own a share of the capital and, by virtue of this ownership may be admitted to a share of the administration.

Regarded as methods of harmonising capital and labour in the business structure, most of these schemes appear to be of dubious worth, when we apply the proper test, viz, the ability to divert

[1] Even this measure of working-class progress has been checked during the last decade. Recent statistics show that in Great Britain and in most other Western civilised countries, the rise of prices since 1896 and still more since 1905 has not been attended by a corresponding rise of wages, though profits and rate of interest have risen at least equally with prices.

into wages a portion of the unproductive surplus. For, though the stimulus of a 'bonus' or a so-called [1] share of profit may increase the absolute wage of the workers in the business, if at the same time it proportionately increases the dividend or profit, it does nothing to reduce either the aggregate or the proportion of unproductive surplus. Moreover, if the increased productivity of labour under such a stimulus is attended by enhanced intensification of effort in muscle or in nerve, with accompanying exhaustion, the total utility of the process to the worker may be a negative quantity, when the increased human cost of production has been set against the utility of the higher income, less advantageously consumed by reason of the exhaustion. Again, though many of these schemes expressly induce the workers to become small shareholders in the business, by applying the 'bonus' or 'profit' to the purchase of shares, nowhere has this ownership by the workers been permitted to go so far as to give them any determinant voice in the administration of the business. Finally, many of these schemes by express intention, nearly all of them in actual tendency, weaken the attachment of the work-

[1] The ordinary profit-sharing scheme is vitiated, alike in theory and in practice, by the erroneous attribution of the concept 'profit' to that which is 'shared.' This is recognised at once when the experiment is properly described. For the ordinary profit-sharing scheme begins by laying down a normal rate of wages and of profits, based upon current facts of commerce. The provision for this standard wage and standard profit constitutes a first charge upon the takings of the business. Under normal conditions this would absorb the whole. But the workers are now told that, if they produce an additional income, they shall have in extra wages half of it. Now the whole of this additional income is due to the increased efficiency of labour under the new stimulus. For if any more capital than before is required, provision for its payment at the normal rate is made before account is taken of the so-called profit that is shared. No more ability or effort of superintendence is required; in fact it is usually contended that the greater care taken by the workers renders less supervision necessary. Thus 'profit' is a misnomer for what is 'shared.' For this so-called 'profit' is entirely produced by greater intensity, skill or care on the part of labour. The fact that labour gets only half, and that only after the whole of what should be called the deferred 'wage-fund' has served to meet any deficiency in the sum required to pay the normal dividends, explains why most of these schemes fail after a short trial. The proportion of the extra-product (evoked entirely by the increased stimulus applied to labour), that is actually paid to labour, is too small to maintain the efficiency of the stimulus. When these profit-sharing schemes succeed, the success is nearly always traceable to the fact that in the original agreement, the benevolent employer has fixed his rate of interest or salary, or both, upon a lower scale than is current in the trade, so that the stimulus to labour is effective.

ers in these businesses to their fellow-workers in other businesses belonging to the trade. So, whatever power proceeds from collective bargaining, for raising wages and improving the other conditions of employment, is diminished by these attempts to harmonise the capital and labour within the area of the single business.

It is significant that nearly all the businesses where co-partnership shows signs of enduring success are legal monopolies, or are otherwise protected from free competition, so that the prices for the commodities or services they sell contain a considerable element of surplus. A fraction of this surplus is diverted from unproductive into productive purposes by a subsidy to wages. In the case of gas-works, the most conspicuous example, this process is furthered by the fact that legal restrictions upon dividends make what at first sight appears a policy of generosity to labour, costless to capital.

§ 5. This criticism of the defects of these private experiments in industrial peace is reinforced by the experience of coöperative movements. Of the completely self-governing workshop or other business in which the whole body of the workers are sole owners of the whole capital they employ, there have been too few examples to enable any conclusion to be drawn. But nearly all the cases where the actual full administration of a business has been in the hands of those employed have been signal failures, save in rare instances where the possession of some skill or situation endowed with a scarcity value has assisted them. Experiments in the self-governing workshop make it evident that direct government by the workers in their capacity of producers is technically worse than government by the owners of the capital. The selection and the remuneration of ability of management are always found defective, and the employees are often unwilling to submit to proper discipline, even when they have elected the persons who shall exercise it. A few successful experiments conducted in favourable circumstances, i. e., where a special market is available, or where only a section of the employees wield the power of administration, afford no considerable grounds of hope for this mode of coöperative settlement.

Thus there seems no ground for holding that any really satisfactory settlement of the conflicts between capital and labour can be got by private arrangements of a profit-sharing or a coöperative character.

PART II

PRODUCER AND CONSUMER

§ 6. Before considering more definitely 'socialistic' remedies, it is best, however, to open out the other conflict of interest, between producer and consumer. It is, of course, often held, even by those who recognise some reality in the opposition between capital and labour, that the supposed opposition between producer and consumer has no real foundation.

When producers compete, the gains of such competition in lower prices, better quality, etc., drop into the consumer's lap. Even where producers combine, or a single business holds the market, it is supposed that the monopolist will generally find it most profitable to furnish a sound article at a moderate price.

But this natural harmony between producer and consumer is subject to precisely the same qualification as that between capital and labour. Producer and consumer are necessary to one another, there is community of interests up to a limit. But beyond that limit there is an equally natural conflict. It is true that where producers compete freely prices are cut down for the consumer. But it is by no means true that he tends to get the cheapest goods which current arts of production render possible. For the expenses of competition, which are enormous, are defrayed by him in the price he pays. Nor does free competition secure quality of product. It stimulates the arts of adulteration and deceit, and sets the cunning of the skilled producer against the simplicity of the unskilled purchaser. While, therefore, it may be urged that where competition of producers is effective, comparatively little 'surplus' passes into their hands, the waste of industrial power through the maintenance of excessive machinery of production and of distribution is a grave social loss.

Still less can it be admitted, that where combination has displaced competition, the consumer's interests are safe. On the contrary, it is recognised by all economists that where any effective monopoly is established, the selling prices to consumers will always be such as to secure a surplus profit to the producer. Prices may not always be as high as, or higher than, they would have been if a wasteful competition were maintained, but they will always be such as to extract a higher profit than is needed for the remuneration of capital and ability. Where the articles sold are necessaries or prime conveniences of life, and do not admit of effective substitutes, the prices will be indefinitely higher than under competition, and the conflict between producer and consumer more acute. Since under modern capitalism an ever-increasing number of 'routine' requirements, covering the chief necessaries of large populations, are passing under some form or other of effective combination, it is clear that the problem of industrial peace must come to concern itself more and more with the conflicts of producer and consumer. At present the consumer, at any rate in England, largely realises this conflict as a by-product of the struggle between capital and labour. Though the strikes and lock-outs, which express that struggle, disastrously affect his welfare, he is told that they are not his business, and he has no right to interfere. Where a settlement has taken place between capital and labour on a basis of higher wages or shorter hours, he finds the cost of this settlement is usually passed on to him in higher rates or prices.

As joint-agreements between employers' federations and trade unions become more common and more effective, as methods of conciliation and arbitration receive legal sanction and assistance, as wage-boards extend to new fields of industry, the falsehood and the social wrong which underlie the maxim '*caveat emptor*' become more manifest. The consumer will become increasingly more impotent to protect himself against the depredations of organised groups of producers. Indeed, experience proves that even where combinations are subject to the sanction and control of the State, which theoretically is dedicated to the service of the public as a whole, and might at least be expected to hold the balance even between producer and consumer, producers' interests are preferred. In the present policy of state control of Railways, and in the various schemes for the extension of Wage Board legislation, there is no proper recognition of the interests of the consumer. An ill-devised lopsided Socialism is springing up, the likely result of which appears to be to set up groups of selected and preferred employments, whose higher wage-bill will in reality be defrayed not out of rents, surplus profits or any other unearned income, but in large measure out of the reduction of real wages which arbitrary rises of consumers' prices will impose upon other wage-earners. A flagrant instance of this defective social policy is supplied by the recent arrangement by which the railways of this country have been empowered by Government to raise the wages of their employees by reducing the real wages of the general body of the wage-earners, who are called upon to bear a large part of the cost in the higher prices of commodities which follows upon the rise of railway rates.

§ 7. Now, admitting, as we must, that a real divergence of interests between producers and consumers may and must arise in the ordinary course of industry, what remedy is possible?

There is one large working-class movement which seems expressly designed for the protection of the consuming public. I allude of course to the great Coöperative Movement on the Rochdale plan, in which the supreme control is vested in the consumers and their representatives. How far does this scheme represent a true reconcilement of producers' and consumers' interests? A very little investigation will show that, however excellent the other services it renders to the working-classes, its conduct of business affords no complete harmony of the interests of the several factors.

For its entire structure and working are motived by the intention to absorb in real wages (by means of dividends on purchases) the 'profits' to which in ordinary trade most of the unproductive surplus seems to adhere. By dispensing with the profits of various grades of middlemen, by reducing the expenses of management, by saving most of the costs of advertising and other incidental costs of distribution, much surplus is diverted into real wages. But, regarding this scheme from the standpoint which immediately concerns us, as a reconcilement of capital and labour within the business, we find an obvious defect. There is nothing in the theory, or commonly in the practice, of the coöperative store or workshop, to evoke from the employees any special interest in its successful conduct. If they are members, they do indeed get in this capacity a gain equal to that enjoyed by other members not employed in the business. But, as employees, they have no voice in the administration and no share in the gains. Where, as in the Scottish Wholesale, a profit-sharing scheme is attached, this scheme is exposed to the same criticism that we have applied to other profit-sharing schemes. There is no security afforded by this coöperative form of business for the full reconcilement of the claims of capital and labour within the business. But, after all, it might be objected, that does not really matter. For, if the worker in a coöperative mill or store is also a coöperative consumer, he will, as such, enjoy a collective gain as great as he could hope to gain if he were assigned a special lien upon the surplus that emerged from the successful conduct of the particular business in which he worked. It will be his intelligent interest, as consumer, to help to elect and to maintain an effective administration in all the various productive and distributive businesses from which are derived the half-yearly dividend on purchases which he receives.

Now if the working-classes of the nation made all their purchases through coöperative stores, and if these stores, in their turn, bought what they sell exclusively from coöperative productive businesses, and if all working-class consumers were employed in these coöperative businesses, a solution of the social problem on coöperative lines might be plausible. For any surplus made at any stage would flow in the ordinary course of events into consumers' dividends, forming an addition to the real wages which they earned as producers. Nor need it matter that the coöperative consumers were not full owners of all the capital they needed to employ, provided they could borrow it in a free market. If the agricultural and mining lands, whose produce they required, did not belong to them, there would indeed remain a large leakage in the shape of economic rent. But the nature of the so-called land monopoly is not such as to prevent the coöperative consumers from taking in real wages the great bulk of the surplus which otherwise would have gone to capitalists and *entrepreneurs* in unearned income.

Unfortunately, large and important as is this Coöperative Movement, it falls far short of the full conditions here laid down. The majority of the wage-earners are not members of Coöperative Stores: those who are members only purchase certain sorts of goods at the store: owing to the slighter development of productive coöperation, a large proportion of the goods sold in the stores are bought in the ordinary markets: comparatively few of the coöperative consumers are employed in coöperative businesses. There are large tracts of industry, such as agriculture, mining, transport, building,[1] metal-working and machine-making, which the Coöperative Movement has hardly touched, nor are there signs of any rapid extension in these fields of enterprise. In point of fact, coöperation has almost entirely confined itself to trades and industries where competition is normally free, and where the object of coöperation has rather been to save and secure as 'divi' certain ordinary expenses of competitive businesses than to invade the strongholds of highly profitable capitalism where unearned surpluses are large. While, then, a considerable proportion of the total working-class income is expended upon articles bought in the stores [2] and valuable economies are affected, only a small proportion of the eleven millions paid in dividends and interest to consumers can be taken to represent unproductive surplus absorbed into wages. While, therefore, the advance of the Coöperative Movement in recent years, alike in membership, in volume of trade and in profits, has been rapid, a careful examination of the field of coöperative progress does not indicate any solution of the main problem of distribution along these lines. The areas of really profitable private enterprise are to all appearance unassailable by the Coöperative Movement.

§ 8. But we find within the Coöperative Movement some experiences which shed light upon the problem of business administration. If the truly social nature of the 'business' is to be expressed in its government, the Rochdale plan, upon which the

---

[1] Building Societies are only in a very restricted sense coöperative.

[2] In 1909 the aggregate sales at the Retail Stores amounted to £70, 423,359, or about 10% of the working-class income, and the profit (including interest paid on shares) was £10,851,739.

main coöperative structure has been erected, contributes an element of really vital importance. It asserts that a business exists, not to furnish profit to the capitalist employer or wages to the workers, but commodities to consumers. The consumer, being the end and furnishing by his purchase-power the stimulus, should hold the reins of government. He is the owner, he shall rule, he shall receive the whole gain. This is a complete reversal of the ordinary idea of the business world, to which a business exists to secure profits to business men, the worker and the market (consumer) being mere instruments in profit-making. Hardly less does it counterwork the ordinary ideas and feelings of the working-man, for whom the business exists merely as a means of remunerative employment, and whose sole idea of reform is to secure in higher wages and improved conditions of labour as much of the profits as possible. To neither does it for one moment seem reasonable that the consumer should interfere in the administration of the business, or take any share in its gains, save such as must come to him in the ordinary course of trade.

Thus the success of the Rochdale plan is a dramatic assertion of a revolutionary idea in the organisation of business. It is proved that large numbers of routine businesses can be conducted by and for consumers. But it cannot be assumed that this concentration of the meaning, the utility and the government of industry in the consumer, has complete validity. It may be called consumers' socialism, as distinguished from the sort of producers' socialism which prevails among trade unionists. As the latter aims at controlling businesses in order to divert directly into wages all surplus profit, so the former aims at controlling businesses in order to divert the same fund into consumers' dividends. Now, if the producers and the consumers of the goods produced in any business were the same, it might seem a matter of indifference in which capacity they took the gain. But they are not. The workers in a particular mill or store buy for their own use a very minute fraction of the goods there produced. Even if the workers, by means of their unions or their coöperative societies, could capture the whole industrial machinery, it would still remain a matter of importance how far they paid themselves in higher wages, how far in consumers' dividends. For unless their claims as producers and as consumers were properly adjusted in the control of the several businesses, there would be little or nothing to distribute. Few thoughtful coöperators will claim finality and all-sufficiency for the coöperative idea as embodied in the present movement.

The persistent struggles in the movement itself to temper the absolutism of the consumer by the assertion of coöperative employees to a higher rate of pay than obtains in the outside labour market and to a share of the profits, is an interesting commentary on the problem of social administration of the business. It is widely felt that the view that a business exists in order to supply utilities to consumers is defective as a principle of business government. The claim of the owners of the factors of production employed in the business to some voice in the conduct of that business is not lightly to be set aside by asserting that the factors of production are mere means to the consumer's end. If the consumers themselves own the share-capital or borrow other capital at market rates with good security, the issue of the control of capital need not arise. But the labour employed in a coöperative business has a human interest in the conduct of the business separate from that of the consumers. In virtue of this human interest, these workers impugn the doctrine that the business exists solely for the consumers, and insist that their human interest shall be adequately represented in the conduct of the business and the distribution of its gains.

§ 9. Those who have followed and accept the general principles of our analysis of industry into human costs of production and human utilities of consumption will be disposed *a priori* to accept the view that, in the equitable control of every business, the interests of the worker as well as of the consumers should be represented. Regarded from the social standpoint, it is as important that good conditions of employment shall prevail in a business, as that good articles shall be furnished cheaply to consumers. Nor, as we recognise, can we assume that an enlightened business government by consumers, any more than by capitalists, will necessarily secure these good conditions for employees. Definite and not inconsiderable instances of sweating inside the coöperative movement itself testify to the reality of this need. But it is urged not merely on grounds of equity, as a protection against possible abuses of power by consumers or their representatives, but on grounds of sound economy. For if it be admitted that the employees in a coöperative business have a special human interest, it is idle to argue that it is socially advantageous to leave this interest without representation in the conduct of the business.

The coöperation which assigns all power and all gain to the consumer is in fact vitiated by the same social fallacy as the syndicalism which would assign the same monopoly to the employee, or as the capitalism which does assign it to the profitmonger. Equity and economy alike demand that the interests of all three shall be adequately represented. Social remuneration in its application to the business unit must proceed upon this fundamental principle. A business consists of capital, labour, and the market. To place unlimited control in the hands of any of those factors is wasteful and dangerous. The human defects of uncontrolled capitalism have been made sufficiently apparent. Any adequate experiment in uncontrolled trade-unionism or in syndicalism would disclose similar abuses. The idea of the miners running the mine, or the factory-hands the factory, the railway workers the railway, is not so much unsound in the sense that they must fail to run it properly. For though unlikely, it is at least conceivable that they might have enough intelligence and character to buy competent managers and carry out their detailed instructions. Its fundamental vice consists in ignoring the factor of the market, and in building up a number of separate industrial structures in which the consumers' interests are unrepresented. It may appear plausible to argue that the control of each process of production should be left to the producers who may be presumed to know it best. But it becomes evident, even to the syndicalist, that no business could be conducted upon this policy unmodified. No housebuilding could proceed, if the plasterers, the bricklayers, the carpenters, had each full power to determine when they would work, at what pace they would work, and what remuneration they should exact.

There must be a definite arrangement between the groups of workers in the several processes within each business, which will qualify the control of plastering by the plasterers, bricklaying by the bricklayers, by a wider control that represents the common interests of the business. Not merely does the syndicalist idea recognise this coöperation of the processes within a business, but it extends the coöperative character of the control to the trade as a whole. Under syndicalism the building trade would not be broken into a number of businesses in each of which would be made a separate arrangement between the carpenters, bricklayers, etc., employed in it. The arrangements as to hours and pace and remuneration, etc., would be determined by representatives of the various crafts on a trade basis, and would be the same for all businesses and all jobs. But the organisation of producers could not stop there. Each trade could no more be entirely self-governing than each business or each process in a business. The trade-organisation of the miners could not, having regard to the interests and needs of other trades, be safely entrusted with the absolute control of mining, or the railway workers with the absolute control of the railways. There must be some power to prevent the miners reducing their amount of work and their output to an extent which will cripple the other trades which need coal, and to compel the railway workers to afford reasonable facilities of transport on reasonable terms to shippers and travellers. For, otherwise, there would be substituted for the conflict of capital and labour within each business or each trade, a conflict of trades, each striving to do as little and to get as much as possible out of the aggregate wealth. Nor can it be assumed that the intelligent self-interest or social sympathy of the miners, or railwaymen, or other trades, would be adequate safeguards against such abuses. This is evident when we bear in mind the central concrete problem before us, the social distribution and utilisation of the surplus. For it will be technically possible for any strongly-placed special group of workers, such as the miners or railway workers, to take to themselves, in remuneration or in leisure, an excessive proportion of this surplus, leaving very little for any other group of workers. The guild-feeling, upon which syndicalism mainly relies, not merely supplies no safeguard against this abuse of power, but would almost certainly evoke it, unless a potent control, representing industry in general, were established over the individual trades or guilds. Experience of cases where local trade-unions are occasionally placed in a position of tyranny shows that they will play for their own hand with a disregard to the interests of their fellow-workers in other trades as callous as is displayed by any trust of capitalists. Assuming, then, that it were possible for guild-societies to develop to the point that the workers in each trade were in possession of all the instruments of production, and were able to conduct the processes efficiently, the problem of distributing the 'surplus' among the several trades or guilds, in the shape of pay or leisure, would still remain unsolved. Among the groups of producers, in a word, there would remain divergencies of interest, which would be incapable, upon a producers' policy, of solution. Syndicalists, confronted with this phase of their problem, plunge into vague assurances that the process of agreement which had taken place between the workers in the several processes and the several businesses in a trade, could be extended to the workers grouped in the larger trade-units, and that the real solidarity of working-class interests would somehow instinctively express itself in equitable and durable arrangements. But the moment one passes from the region of phrases to that of concrete facts the difficulties thicken. An elected council of national workers would have to devise some practicable method of comparing units of railway service with units of mining, bricklaying, doctoring, acting, waiting, etc., so as to apply to each productive process the support and stimulus needed to induce the workers engaged in it to do their share of work and to receive their share of wealth. No mere time basis for such competition would be practicable. It would be necessary to induce a body of labour and capital to apply itself to each process of each occupation, sufficient in quantity and in efficiency to supply the requirements of the working community as a whole, and to devise a mode of remuneration, or distribution of products, which would satisfy this requirement.

It is quite evident that all this adjustment of the claims and needs of individuals within a process in a business, of businesses in a trade, of trades in industry, would need an elaborate hierachy of representative government, with a supreme legislature and executive, whose will must over-rule the will of the national or local groups within the several trades, as to the quantity and method of work to be done in each concrete process, and as to the remuneration of each sort of work. In other words, society, as a whole, would have imposed its final control upon each group of workers, diminishing to that extent their power to determine the conditions under which they would work, and their effective separate ownership of the instruments of production. The ideal of the self-governing mine, or factory, or railway, would thus be over-ridden by the superior ideal of a self-governing society. But that self-government by society, the supreme legislation of industry, could not perform its work by confining its attention to the various productive processes, and the businesses and trades in which they were conducted. It would be compelled to study the wants and will of the consumers, or, if it be preferred, of the workers in their capacity of consumers. For, only by the study of the consumer, or the market, could the work of adjusting the application of productive power at the different productive points, and the process of remuneration by which that distribution was achieved, possibly be accomplished. Thus, although the whole body of this syndicalist legislature might have been elected to represent the interests of separate groups of producers, or trades, it would be compelled to give equal attention to the wants and the will of the consuming public. But it would discover that, just in proportion as it was accurately representative of the separate interests of groups of producers, to that extent was it disqualified for safeguarding the interests of the consuming public, which in each concrete problem would be liable to cut across the interests of special groups of producers. In other words, it would be impossible properly to regulate the railway service without direct regard to the interests of the travelling and trading public as a whole, to regulate the mining industry without regard to the local, seasonal and other needs of coal consumers. But these consumers' interests could not be properly considered in a legislature chosen entirely by separate groups of producers, with the object of promoting the special interests of these groups. The impossibility of syndicalism thus turns upon ignoring in the control of business the will of the consumer.

§ 10. Thus we are compelled to recognise that in a sound social organisation of the industrial system, and of each part of it, the business, the trade, (or the group of trades) and the consumer or market must be introduced as integral factors of government. We cannot content ourselves with the view that a producer, or any composite body of producers, is necessarily impelled by its self-interest to safeguard the interests of the consumer. Nor can the consumer safeguard his interests adequately through the guidance or stimulus he brings to bear through his separate individual acts of demand. He is incapable of protecting himself properly, even when producers are not combined but are competing. When they are combined he is helpless. The cleavages of immediate economic interest between the worker and the consumer are so numerous that no abstract identity of interests in a community where all consumers were also workers, all parasites being excluded, would suffice to secure the requisite economy and harmony. This economy and harmony can only be secured by giving the consumer a direct voice in the government of industry.

Syndicalism is in large measure a reaction against forms of state socialism which are vitiated by a defect similar to that which we find in the Rochdale coöperative plan. So far as the public services are honestly and efficiently administered by public officials, the public which these officials represent is primarily the citizen in his capacity of consumer. The municipal services are run, either to give him cheap transport or lighting of sound standard quality, or else to enable him to get police, street-cleaning or some other service which he could not otherwise have got. But this bureaucratic socialism is apt to neglect or to ignore the interests of its employees, and to deny them any influence in determining the conditions of their employment, other than that which they can bring to bear as citizen-consumers. Thus are found cases where public departments, or the contractors they employ, are allowed to pay wages so low or to offer such irregular employment, as to contribute to that inefficiency and destitution for which the same public is subsequently called upon to make financial and administrative provision. This is an inevitable defect of a one-sided or consumers' socialism. Nor is it likely to be remedied by any general perfunctory recognition of the duty of the public employer to observe standard conditions. For in most cases public employment will, by virtue of its monopolistic character, contain features that have no precise analogy in the outside business world, so that some separate method of determining the application of standard conditions is necessary. Unless that method admits direct representation of the interests of the employees, there can be no sufficient security that these interests shall receive proper consideration. This is not a demand that the employees shall 'interfere' with the public management, or 'dictate' the terms of their employment. On the contrary, it is clear that the official managers must, in the ordinary course of business, secure the execution of their orders. But, considering that their standpoint must always be biassed towards a special interpretation of the public interest in the sense of efficiency and economy of a particular output, this narrower public interest must be checked by reference to a wider public interest in which the human costs of production shall be represented. An accumulating weight of recent experience in various countries makes it evident that state-socialism must fail unless adequate provision is made for safeguarding the interest of particular groups of public employees. This safeguard cannot, of course, be given by any mere concession of the right of combination and of collective bargaining. For while collective bargaining may enable the employees to secure fair terms where they are dealing with competing private businesses, it cannot where the sole employer is the State or Municipality. The latter is technically able to impose its terms upon any group of workers who are specialised for the work it offers. Recognition of the Union, and an admission by the management of the right of union-officials to consultation and discussion of conditions of employment, do not really furnish any basis of settlement, though they may often ease a difficulty and remove misunderstanding. What is required is a statutory right of appeal to a public authority, outside of and independent of the particular department, competent to take that wider view of public interest from which the departmental public official is, by the necessity of his situation, precluded. That claim of the public employee is frequently misunderstood. It does not arise from any real or pretended opposition of interests between the public and a group of its employees, and a claim on the part of the latter that the public shall make some concession or sacrifice to their particular group interest. There is no such real opposition of interests. The valid claim for an appeal from the arbitrary decisions of the public departmental managers is based upon the fact that the latter are disqualified for a full impartial view of the public interest, so far as that public interest is affected by the conditions of employment of the employees under them. The fact that the employees are often likely to make unreasonable demands and to claim in wages, hours and other conditions, an excessive share of the public revenue, does not affect the validity of this contention. For practical convenience official departmentalism exists. But this departmentalism involves a business management essentially defective from the standpoint of public welfare, inasmuch as it tends to depreciate or overlook the interest which the public has in the total welfare of that section of the public which is in its direct employment.

§ 11. Of course, in treating the issue of a public business as if it consisted simply in reconciling the immediate interests of the consuming public with those of the public employees, we have intentionally excluded another view which may often be more important. State socialism may be run primarily in the interests, neither of the citizen-consumer nor of the employer, but of the bureaucracy, who here occupy the place of the capitalist-managers under private enterprise. The official may be held to be naturally disposed to magnify his office and to abuse any power which can be made to subserve his personal or class interests. Practical permanency of tenure of his office, and the special knowledge which it brings, enable him, with safety, either to neglect his public duties, or to encroach upon the liberties of citizens, according as he is lethargic or self-assertive. He may squander the resources of the public upon ill-considered projects, or in serving the private interests of his friends. Or, he may practice a tyrannical or a niggardly policy towards his employees, not through a narrow interpretation of public economy, but from sheer carelessness or from defective sympathy. These charges against officialism are too familiar to need expansion here. However carefully the public service is recruited, such abuses will be liable frequently to occur, and the structure of Government should be such as to supply effective checks and remedies.

CHAPTER XVII

THE NATION AND THE WORLD

§ 1. We have examined the chief defects in the structure of a business and a trade, regarded in the light of instruments of human welfare, and we have considered some of the remedies, applied sometimes for purposes of distinctively industrial economy, sometimes as devices of social therapeutics.

There remains, however, one other mode of economic antagonism deserving of consideration. Until modern times a nation was to all intents and purposes not only a political but an economic area, in the sense that almost all trade and other economic relations were confined within the national limit. The small dimensions of foreign, as compared with domestic trade, and the nature of that trade, confined to articles not produced at home, had little tendency to generate a feeling of international rivalry. Foreign trade was almost wholly complementary and not competitive. With the modern changes, which have altered this condition and made nations appear to be hostile competitors in world commerce, we are all familiar. The development of capitalist production to a common level and along similar lines in a number of Western nations, the tendency towards an increase of output of manufactured goods at a price exceeding the demands of the existing markets, the consequent invasion of the markets of each industrial country by the goods of other countries, and the growing competition of the groups of traders in each nation to secure and develop new markets in the backward countries, with the assistance of the physical and military forces of their respective governments, have imposed upon the popular mind a powerful impression of economic opposition between nations. No falser and more disastrous delusion prevails in our time. The only facts which seem to give support to it are the Tariffs, Commercial Treaties and the occasional uses of political pressure and military force by States for the benefit of financiers, investors, traders or settlers belonging to their nationality. This intervention of Governments for the supposed advantage of their citizens has had the unfortunate effect of presenting nations in the wholly false position of rival business firms. Groups of private manufacturers, traders and financiers, using their government to secure their private profitable ends, have thus produced grave conflicts of international policy. The worst instrument of this antagonism, because the most obvious and the most vexatious, is the protective Tariff, and the most singular proof of its derationalising efficacy is found in the conduct of our recent fiscal controversy. The fiercest fight in all that controversy has raged round the relative size, growth and profitable character of the foreign trade of Great Britain, Germany, America, etc. These States are actually treated, not merely by Protectionists but by many Free Traders, as if they were great trading firms, engaged in struggling against one another for the exclusive possession of some limited economic territory, the success of one being attended by a loss to the others. Now, Great Britain, Germany and America are not economic entities at all; they are not engaged in world commerce, either as competitors or as coöperators; the respective advances or declines made by certain groups of merchants within their confines in overseas trade have no net national significance at all. Finally, overseas trade, by itself, furnishes no index of the collective prosperity of each nation.

§ 2. The whole presentation of the case under the head of Nations is irrelevant and deceptive, conveying, as it is designed to do, the false suggestion that Englishmen, grouped together as a people, are somehow competing with Germans grouped together as another nation, and Americans as a third nation. Now no such collective competition exists at all. So far as trade involves competition, that competition takes place, not between nations, but between trading firms, and it is much keener and more persistent between trading firms belonging to the same nation than between those belonging to different nations. Birmingham or Sheffield firms compete with one another for machinery and metal contracts far more fiercely than they compete with Germans or Americans in the same trade, and so it is in every other industry. The production of import and export figures, and of balances of trade, under national headings, is a mischievous pandering to the most dangerous delusion of the age. It has done more than anything else to hide the great and beneficent truth, that the harmony and solidarity of economic interests among mankind have at last definitely transcended national limits, and are rapidly binding members of different nations in an ever-growing network of coöperation. Within the last generation a more solid and abiding foundation for this coöperation than ordinary exchange of goods has been laid in the shape of international finance. Though certain dangerous abuses have attended its beginnings, this coöperation of the citizens of various countries in business enterprises in all parts of the world is the most potent of forces making for peace and progress. More rapidly than is commonly conceived, it is bringing into existence a single economic world-state with an order and a government which are hardly the less authoritative because, as yet, they possess a slender political support. That economic world-state consists of all that huge area of industrially developed countries in regular and steady intercourse, linked to one another by systems of railroads and steamship routes, by postal and telegraphic services, administered by common arrangements, by regular commerce, common markets and reliable modes of monetary payment, and by partnerships of capital and labour in common business transactions.

§ 3. The actuality of this world-system has preceded its conscious realisation. But the growing fact is educating the idea and the accompanying sentiment in the minds of the more enlightened members of all civilised nations. We hear more of internationalism from the side of labour. But, in point of fact, the corporate unity of labour lags far behind that of capital. For the mobility of capital is much greater, and its distribution is far better organised. But, as the financial machinery for the collection and distribution of industrial power over the whole economic world is further perfected and unified, it will be attended by a loosening of those local and national bonds which have hitherto limited the free movement of labour. As the centre of gravity in the economic system shifts from land, which is immovable, to money, the most mobile of economic factors, so the old local attachment which kept most labour fastened to some small plot of the earth, its native village, will yield place to liberty of movement accommodated to the needs and opportunities of modern profitable business. Within the limits of each country the increased mobility has long been evident: it has helped to break up parochialism and provincialism of ideas and feelings, and to evolve a stronger sense of national unity. But there is to be no halting at the limits of the nation. Already large forces of international labour exist. Not merely do vast numbers of workers migrate with increased ease from Belgium into France, from Russia into the United States, from Germany into South America, for settlement in these countries, but large bodies of wage-earners are being organised as a cosmopolitan labour force following the currents of industrial development about the world. So far as unskilled labour is concerned, large tracts of China, India and the Straits Settlements, form a recruiting ground in Asia; while Italy and Austro-Hungary furnish a large European contingent. But not less significant are the higher ranks of cosmopolitan labour, the British and American managers, overseers and workmen in the engineering, railroad, electrical and mining industries, who to-day are moving so freely over the newly developing countries of three continents, placing their business and technical ability at the service of the economic world. The new movements in the economic development of Asia and of South America will enormously accelerate this free flow of business ability and technical skill from the more advanced Western nations over the relatively backward countries, and will also bring into closer coöperation at a larger number of points the capital and management of Western peoples.

My object in referring to these concrete economic movements of our time is to illustrate the powerful tendencies which are counteracting the old false realisation of industry in terms of human competition and antagonism, and are making for a conscious recognition of its coöperative and harmonious character.

CHAPTER XVIII

SOCIAL HARMONY IN ECONOMIC LIFE

§ 1. A brief summary of the actual tendencies towards harmony and discord at present visible in the economic world may be conveniently presented here.

We see among the fundamental industries the transformation of the structure of the single business; large numbers of little rivulets of savings from innumerable separate personal sources merging to form a single body of effective capital; large numbers of workers closely welded into a single body of effective labour-power; both operating in normal harmony under the direction of a common central management, and engaged in the continuous work of turning out a product, the price of which forms the common income alike for capitalists and workers. So far as that portion of the dividend is concerned which forms the economically necessary costs of these masses of capital and labour, there exists a harmony of interests between the two groups of claimants, which is more clearly recognised with every improvement of the general standard of intelligence and information. In most businesses that common area of interest covers by far the larger part of the business dividend. Where a surplus emerges in excess of these economic costs, an initial discord arises between the claims of the capital and labour. But this discord may be resolved in two ways, in each of which important experiments, attended by a growing measure of success, are being carried on. Large patches of the area of discord are being reclaimed to order by the modern State, whose policy is more and more directed to absorbing by taxation, and applying to the use of the community, great shares of these business surpluses, as they emerge in incomes and inherited properties. As regards the surplus which is not so absorbed, the grouped forces of capital and labour within the business are constantly engaged in seeking to discover pacific and equitable modes of division which shall reconcile, or at least mitigate, the remaining opposition. Though this remains at present the sharpest field of conflict, pacific forces are making more gain than perhaps appears upon the surface. Some of those industries, where such discords have been most rife and most wasteful, have been taken over by the State or the Municipality. In these cases such quarrels as may still arise in connection with the claims of labour admit of settlement by other means than economic force. In others, the State intervenes on behalf of public order by assisting to promote processes of arbitration or conciliation. In others, again, the organisation of the forces of capital on the one hand, labour on the other, over the whole range of businesses comprising a national trade, has tended to make actual conflicts rarer, and presents a machinery capable of application to pacific settlements. Grave as are the defects in the working of this machinery of Joint Boards, Sliding Scales, Conciliation and the like, and terrible as are the injuries these defects cause, they ought not to blind us to a recognition of the fact that the number of actual conflicts between capital and labour is constantly diminishing.

§ 2. This truth is better realised when we turn from the structure of the business to that of the trade or market. There, though keen and even cut-throat competition still survives, the tendency is more and more, especially in the great staple industries where large aggregates of capital and labour are employed, towards coöperation, combination and trade agreements. If, for the moment, we ignore the dangers which such combinations often threaten to consumers, and regard them from the standpoint of trade structure, we cannot fail to recognise the enormous advance they represent in the cause of industrial harmony. For whatever the degree of unity attained by such a Trust, Cartel, Conference, Trade Agreement, Federation, it means *pro tanto* a saving of the energy of capital and labour formerly expended upon conflict, and a concentration of the thoughts and purposes of business men upon the best performance of the useful functions of production which constitute the social value of their trade. So long as a trade remains in a distinctively competitive condition, an enormous part of the actual energy is consumed not in production but in warfare. The thoughts and wills of the controllers of the several businesses are deflected from the economical fulfilment of their social function to conscious rivalry. Neither the capital nor the labour in each several business enjoys a reasonable measure of security; and not only the profits but the wages of each firm are jeopardised by the success of a stronger competing firm. The growing displacement of this condition of a trade by the principle and practice of combination is perhaps the most conspicuous movement towards industrial peace. I am aware that, in itself, this concentration and combination of businesses within a trade afford no sure settlement for the differences between capital and labour. They may even aggravate those differences in several ways. For, in the first place, such combinations are expressly and chiefly designed to produce a larger quantity of surplus profits, thus stimulating conflict by offering a larger object of attack to labour. In the second place, such combinations, if at all complete, may prove more clearly than in any other way the superiority of organised capital over organised labour in the determination of wages and conditions of labour. Finally, private ownership of natural resources, producing for its owners economic rent, remains an unsolved antagonism. Though the extent to which the 'surplus', which monopolistic, protected or otherwise well-placed businesses obtain, as open or concealed 'rent', is not capable of exact estimate, many, if not most, profitable businesses derive some of their surplus from the possession or control of natural resources. Such natural resources are to all intents and purposes capital, so far as relates to issues of conflict between capital and labour. The amount and possibly the proportion of surplus (taking the whole industrial world into consideration) which is plain or disguised rent, is probably upon the increase. Even in Great Britain, though aggregate rents do not keep pace with profits and other incomes derived from business capital, they probably form an increasing proportion of that income which, according to our definition, ranks as 'unproductive surplus.' Though these rents, like other 'unproductive surplus,' could be advantageously diverted into wages on the one hand, public revenue upon the other, they are kept on the side of capital by the full force of combination.

Thus the labour in any trade may be confronted by a larger body of wealth which it would like to secure for higher wages, while at the same time it finds itself less able to achieve this object.

§ 3. Equally sharp may be the antagonism of interests set up between such a combine and the general body of consumers, by means of the control of prices which the former possesses. For the large surplus, which we see to be an object of desire to the workers in a combination or trust, represents to the consumer an excess of prices. So it comes to pass that the consumer, unable to combine in his economic capacity, as the workers do in their trade unions, combines as citizen and calls upon the Government to safeguard him against monopolies. His first instinctive demand is, that such combinations shall be declared illegal bodies, acting in restraint of trade, and broken up. But nothing proves more plainly the inherent strength of the cohesive unifying tendencies than the completeness of the failure to achieve this object. When business men desire to combine, it is impossible to force them to compete. The alternatives are, either to leave the consuming public to the tender mercies of a monopoly, which, from mere considerations of profit, may not be able to raise its prices beyond a certain limit, or else to impose legal regulations, or, finally, to buy out the business, transferring it from a private into a public monopoly.

Wherever the modern State is driven to confront this problem, it is compelled, in proportion as public opinion is articulate and politically organised, to fasten an increasing measure of public control upon such powerful combinations, and to take over into the sphere of State enterprises those which cannot effectively be controlled. In such ways does modern society seek to heal the new discords generated by the very processes employed by the several businesses and trades in their search after an internal harmony.

But the largest forms of capitalistic enterprise will tend more and more to transcend the limits of any single state, not only in their composition but in the powers they exercise upon subsidiary industries, and upon the general body of consumers throughout the industrial world.[1] The privately organised apparatus of

[1] The foremost example of such organisation in a great staple industry is the In-

economic machinery, which constitutes the fabric of this economic world-state, has been described as a striking example of the expansion of industrial solidarity and harmony. But here again the possibilities, nay, certainties, of new discord between capital and labour, producer and consumer, cannot be ignored. Hence the great social problems of the future will to a less and less extent lie within the political competence of single states or be soluble by the separate action of the Governments of those states. The vast currents of international capital and labour cannot flow without great disturbances of order and of economic interests often affecting several nations. The safe, successful, profitable, pursuit of large foreign enterprises by the capital and labour of persons belonging to many nationalities, will more and more involve common political action.

§ 4. We are already beginning to recognise that our State is disabled for the fully satisfactory solution of some of the most pressing of our social problems. The immigration of foreign labour complicates our treatment of sweated industries. The improvement of conditions of labour in our trades may be rendered more difficult by the admission of sweated imports, or our feelings may be shocked by the influx of the products of slave labour. The policy of taxing interests and profits may be thwarted by our inability to trace the incomes derived from foreign investment and trade. A financial crisis in America or Germany may deplete our gold reserve and work havoc on our credit. As these movements gather force and frequency, the impotence of any single State to exercise an effective control over the primary economic interests of its people will grow more apparent. The gravest social-economic problems will be found insoluble except by international arrangement. An era of free conferences and of more or less loose agreements between States will lay the foundation for what in time must amount to international regulation of industry. In other words, the economic internationalism, which I have traced, will weave for itself the

ternational Iron & Steel Association, formed in July 1911 by representatives of Austria, Belgium, Canada, France, Germany, Great Britain, Hungary, Russia, Spain, United States. The objects of this organisation were to regulate production, so as to control profitable prices and to prevent undercutting in times of depression. (Cf. Chiozza-Money, *Things that Matter*, Ch. XI).

necessary apparel of political institutions. The true germ of
world-federation is perhaps to be traced to-day less clearly at the
Hague than at Bern, where the representatives of the leading
industrial nations have already met to set the seal of their respective governments upon undertakings to promote common
policies of legislation in such matters as the regulation of night
labour for women, and the disuse of poisonous ingredients in the
match trade. In such agreements, as in the better-known Postal
Union (which also has its offices at Bern), one finds the earliest
contributions made by modern industrialism to the federal government of the world.

These facts I cite, partly to enforce the thesis that the tendencies of modern industry which make for harmony and coöperation are gaining, both in the smaller and the larger areas, over
those which make for discord and for competition. This growing harmony of fact must tend to evoke a corresponding harmony
of thought and feeling. But here we are retarded by a set of
psychological obstacles which pervert or disguise the truth. I
have alluded to the damage due to the false representation of nations as rival traders, contending for a limited market upon terms
which signify that the gain of one is the loss of another. But the
whole intellectual and moral atmosphere is thick with similar mistakes of fact and fallacies of reasoning, chiefly sustained by false
phrases which evoke false images and arouse injurious desires
and passions. Ordinary business language is filled with selfish,
separatist and combative phrases, representing trade as a warfare,
in which every man must fight for his own hand, must force his
wares upon the public, outwit or bludgeon his competitors, con-
quer new markets, beat down the prices of the goods he buys,
or in finance become a 'bull' or a 'bear.' In certain large departments of the business world there still remains so much disorder, insecurity and competition as to afford support to these
combative views and feelings. But they are no longer representative of the main normal activities of industry, and they
ought and must by degrees be displaced by views and feelings
accommodated to the more organic conception. It is an important task of economic science to enforce conceptions of
the operation of economic laws which will support these newer

and sounder views and feelings. For only with this growing recognition of the social harmony represented by industry can the social will be nourished that is necessary to support and further it. So long as the ordinary business man or worker has his eyes, his mind, his heart and will, glued to the tiny patch of industry to which his own directly personal effort is applied, the pulse of humanity beats feebly through the system of industry. But let the ordinary education of every man and woman impose clear images of this economic order as a great human coöperation in which each bears an essential part, as producer, consumer and citizen, the quickened intelligence and sympathy will respond, so that the blind processes of coöperation will become infused and strengthened by the current of a conscious will.

CHAPTER XIX

INDIVIDUAL MOTIVES TO SOCIAL SERVICE

§ 1. Our examination of the existing industrial system discloses certain discords of interest and desire between the owners of the several factors of production, on the one hand, between producers and consumers on the other. Among the owners of factors of production the sharpest antagonisms are those between the capitalist employer and the wage-earner, and between the landowner and the owners of all other factors. Except as regards the ownership of land, these antagonisms are not absolute but qualified. The interests of capital and labour, of producer and consumer, march together up to a certain point. There they diverge. These discords of interest materialise in what we term 'the surplus,' that portion of the product which, though not essential to the performance of the economic process, passes to capital, labour or the consumer, according to the economic strength which natural or artificial conditions assign to each. The humanisation and rationalisation of industry depend, as we recognise, upon reforming the structure of businesses and industries, so as to resolve these discords, to evoke the most effective coöperation, in fact and will, between the several parties, and to distribute the whole product, costs and surplus, among them upon terms which secure for it the largest aggregate utility in consumption. The operation of industry upon this truly and consciously coöperative basis, would, it is contended, evoke increased productive powers, by bringing into play those instincts of mutual aid that are largely inhibited by present methods, and by distributing the increased product so as to evoke the highest personal efficiency of life and character.

But it would be foolish to ignore the doubts and objections which are raised against the spiritual assumption upon which this ideal of human industry is based. It is often urged that man is by nature so strongly endowed with selfish and com-

bative feelings, so feebly with social and coöperative, that he
will not work efficiently under the reformed economic structures
that are proposed. He must be allowed free scope to play for
his own hand, to exercise his fighting instincts, to triumph over
his competitors, and to appropriate the prizes of hazard and
adventure, the spoils attesting personal force and prowess, or
else he will withhold the finest and most useful modes of his
economic energy.

The distinctively spiritual issue thus raised is exceedingly
momentous. Suppose that the business life can be set upon
what appears to be a sound and equitable basis, is human nature
capable of responding satisfactorily to such an environment?
Putting it more concretely, are the actual powers of human
sympathy and coöperation capable of being organised into an
effective social will? This issue is seen to underlie all the doubts
and difficulties that beset the proposals to apply our organic
Law of Distribution for purposes of practical reform. All proposals by organised public effort to abolish destitution give rise
to fears lest by so doing we should sap the incentives to personal
effort, and so impair the character of the poor. Among such
critics there is entertained no corresponding hope or conviction
that such a policy may, by the better and securer conditions of
life and employment it affords, sow the seeds of civic feeling and
of social solidarity among large sections of our population whose
life hitherto had been little else than a sordid and unmeaning
struggle. Proposals to secure for public use by process of taxation larger shares of surplus wealth are met by similar apprehen-
sions lest such encroachments upon private property should
impair the application of high qualities of business and professional ability. The growing tendency of States and Municipalities to engage in various business operations is strongly and
persistently attacked upon the ground that sufficient public
spirit cannot be evoked to secure the able, honest management
and efficient working of such public concerns.

Finally, the whole basic policy of the Minimum Wage and the
Maximum Working-day is assailed on the same ground as a
levelling down process which will reduce the net productivity
of industry and stop all economic progress.

§ 2. To such criticism two replies are possible, each valid within its limits. The first consists in showing that the existing business arrangements are extremely ill-adapted for offering the best and most economically effective stimuli to individual productivity. They are not well-directed to discover, apply, and improve the best and most profitable sorts of human ability and labour. In other words, the actual system for utilising selfishness for industrial purposes is wofully defective: nine-tenths of the power remains unextracted or runs to waste.

Those who rely upon this criticism base their reform policy upon the provision of better economic opportunities and better personal stimuli to individuals. But such reforms will not suffice. What is needed above all is a social soul to inhabit the social body in our industrial system. A conscious coördinating principle—an industrial government, in which the consent of the governed shall be represented in their several wills and consciousness as well as in some central organic control—is to be desiderated. Now is this condition of thought and of desire really attainable? Can we really suppose that any sort of education is likely to arouse and maintain in the rank-and-file of employees either in the public services or in the great private industries a sense of public duty and a realisation of the larger industrial harmony, which will compensate in any appreciable measure for the dulness and drudgery of their particular job, and furnish an effective check upon shirking or slacking? Suppose that a salary basis of payment, a shortened work-day and security of tenure, with adequate insurance against economic mishaps, had been obtained in all regular occupations, would the quickened sense of coöperation yield a productive energy adequate to the requirements?

To this question it must, I think, be frankly answered, that we cannot tell. We have no sufficient data for a confident reply. The general reply of business men and of economists would, I think, be in the negative. It would be urged that the greater part of the routine work of industry will always remain so dull and tiresome, the sense of public duty so weak and intermittent, that the fixed salary basis of remuneration will not prove an adequate incentive for the required amount of human effort.

The experience of existing social services would be adduced in support of this judgment. Public employees, it is complained, work with less energy than private employees; there is more slacking and scamping and more malingering; the 'government stroke' has become a by-word. The dignity of social service does not evoke any clear response in the breast of the employee. Such is the complaint. It is probably not ill-founded. The great mass of public employees are certainly not animated by much conscious pride and satisfaction in rendering social service. But, before registering a final judgment upon such evidence, certain qualifying considerations must be taken into account.

The attitude of a worker towards his work will be strongly affected by the prevailing attitude of those around him. So long as the general economic environment is one in which the interests of employer and employed are represented as antagonistic, similar ideas and sentiments will continue to affect the feelings of public servants. They will not realise that they are working for themselves in working for society of which they are members: they will treat the department for which they work rather as an alien or a hostile body, bent upon getting as much out of them and giving as little as possible. It is just here that we touch the most sensitive spot in the psychology of government, the best recognised defect of bureaucracy. The higher officials, who control and manage public businesses, evoke in the rank-and-file of the public employees very much the same sentiments of estrangement or opposition that prevail in most private businesses between employer and employee. For in point of fact, the temper and mental attitude of higher officials are those of a master in his own business, not those of a public servant. That affects their dealings not only with the rank-and-file in their department, but with the outside public. In a so-called democracy, where the highest as well as the lowest officers of state are paid by the people to do work for the people, no method of effective popular control over the official services has yet been devised. The absence of any such control is clearly recognised by all high officials, and it powerfully influences their mind and their behaviour. Uncontrolled, or insufficiently controlled power, of course, affects differently different types of men. It induces slackness and the adoption of a slow conservative routine in those of torpid disposition. Men of arbitrary temper will be led to despotic treatment of their staff. Men of brains and enterprise will be free to embark upon expensive enterprises, to the gain or loss of their paymasters. But in no case does the actual situation favour the permeation of the public service by a full sense of social coöperation and joint responsibility. High officials may and often do exhibit great energy and disinterested zeal in the public service. But the sense of mastery, both in relation to the lower grades of employee and to the public, is always discernible. They have this power and they know it. Until, therefore, the sense of public service can be made a reality among the higher public officers, no true test of the efficacy of the general will is to be obtained. This reformation of Bureaucracy is the chief crux of modern democracy. For unless some mode is found of expelling from the higher public servants the pride of caste, and of keeping them in sympathetic contact with the general current of popular feeling, the mass of the subordinate employees will not respond to the social claim upon their economic energies.

Finally, the familiar criticism of the inefficiency of public employees in this country does not take proper account of conditions of employment. For while the top grade of officials is paid more handsomely and enjoys more dignity and security than in other countries, the lower grades are often subject to conditions of pay, hours and tenure, not appreciably better than those prevailing in the ordinary labour-market. Until these conditions are improved, it may reasonably be contended that the dignity of public service cannot be expected to furnish an effective economic motive.

If, however, increased security of life and livelihood could be obtained for the people, with such improvement of our educational system as provided adequate opportunities for enabling the children of the poorer classes to enter all grades of the public services, the beginnings of a great change in the spirit of those services might be attained. For, if the wide gaps of dignity and of emoluments, which divide at present the higher from the lower grades, could be reduced, while at the same time effective publicity and criticism could be brought to bear upon all departments of public work, the 'bureaucratic state' might be transformed into something more nearly approaching a self-governing society.

§ 3. The cool practical business men will, however, probably insist that none of these devices for improving education and for stimulating public spirit will enable a public department to get out of its employees so large an output of productive energy as can be secured by the stimuli of private profit-seeking enterprise. And this may possibly be true. But those who have accepted the general lines of our analysis will recognise that such an admission is not fatal to the case for salaried employment and public service. For the private business is primarily concerned with one side of the human equation, the product, and is able in large measure to ignore the human costs involved in getting it. But the State, as representing the human welfare of its members, must take the costs into account as well. An intelligent Society would regard it as a foolish policy to attempt to get out of its employees the amount of daily toil imposed under the conditions of most profit-making businesses. While, therefore, it is true that a public service, run upon an adequate basis of fixed salary and short work-day, would stand condemned, if the output of effective energy per man fell *greatly* below that furnished under the drive of ordinary capitalism, a slight reduction of that output might be welcomed as involving an actual gain in human welfare. The diminished utility of the product might be more than compensated in terms of human welfare by the diminished human cost of the productive process.

It is not, therefore, incumbent upon the advocates of a new industrial order, based upon a closer application of the organic law, to show that such an order will yield at least as large an output of economic energy and economic product as can be got out of the mixed competition and combination which prevail at present. Applying this standard of human valuation, they are entitled to set off against any reduction of purely economic stimuli that may ensue from their reforms, not only the relief in human costs which accompanies such reduction but the enlargement of other human gains.

For, though in this endeavour to value industrial activities and products in terms of human welfare, we have for the most part confined ourselves to the human costs and utilities directly connected with the processes of economic production and consumption, we cannot ignore the wider meaning of these processes. Man lives not by bread, or economic goods, alone, but by 'admiration, hope and love.' Though the various non-economic goods and activities do not directly enter into our human valuation of industry, we cannot neglect the interactions between the economic and the other human interests involved in the organic nature of man and of society.

§ 4. The wider problem of human economy, the employment of all human powers for human welfare, must in fact involve a continual readjustment between the respective claims of the economic and the non-economic activities upon our lives. Most thoughtful critics of our age complain that this adjustment is defective in that business bulks too largely in our lives. They consider that our modern command over the resources of nature for the satisfaction of our wants ought to issue not so much in the larger supply of old, and the constant addition of new economic wants, as in the increased liberation of human powers for other modes of energy and satisfaction. There exist whole countries even in our time, such as China, where population lies so thick upon the earth, and where the arts of industry remain so primitive, that virtually the whole vital energy of the people must be absorbed in the economic processes. This is not our case. With our improving arts of industry and our dwindling growth of population, we can afford to give an increasing share of our interests and energies to the cultivation and enjoyment of intellectual and moral goods. The gradual realisation of this human economy is the best measure of our civilisation. Our greatest impediment in this progress is the superstitious and excessive value put by all classes of our people upon industry and property. This is almost identical with a charge of materialism, for economic values centre round material forms of property. 'Getting and spending we lay waste our powers.' This is a literal statement of our bad economy. Until we can, as a nation, throw off the dominion of the economic spirit, we cannot win the spiritual liberty needed for the ascent of man. So long as we stand, for full six-sevenths of our time and more, with hands and eyes, intelligence and will, dedicated to the service of industrialism, we cannot see, much less realise, better ideals of humanity. Absorbed in earning a livelihood, we have no time or energy to live.

Such sentences as these, I am well aware, have become commonplaces, and such wisdom as they contain has so become almost impotent. This drawing of the fangs of truth by reducing it to truisms is one of the most serious obstacles to intellectual and moral progress. From the time of Wordsworth to the present day our wisest teachers have demanded that industry and property shall be put in their right places as servants, not masters, of men, and that our conquest over nature shall be attended by a liberation of all sorts and conditions of men from the tyranny of matter. In no adequate degree has this liberation been achieved. The iron of industrialism has entered so deeply into our souls that we are loth to use our liberty. Why is this so?

Man is a spiritual as well as a material being. His ascent in civilisation implies an increasing satisfaction of his spiritual needs. In this higher life economic processes and market values play a diminishing part. How comes it, then, that the vast economies of modern industry have done so little to release us from the bondage of the economic system? Why have industry and property retained so dominant a grasp upon our thoughts and feelings, continually checking our aspirations to the higher life, continually encroaching on the time and energy which by rights would seem to belong to that life?

§ 5. The true answer to these questions is not difficult to find. We have sketched a growing order, harmony and unity, of industrial life, concerned with the regular supply of economic needs for mankind. Were such an order effectively achieved, in accordance with the rational and equitable application of our human law of distribution, the economy of industrial processes would be accompanied by a corresponding economy of thought and emotion among the human beings engaged in this common coöperation. This social economy demands, as we have seen, the substitution of social welfare for private profit as the directing motive throughout industry. But it does not imply a completely socialistic system in which each productive process is under the direct and exclusive control of Society. For that assertion of absolute unity would contain a denial of the manifoldness of desire and purpose involved in the very concept coöperation. Scope must remain, in the interests of society itself, for the legitimate play of individuality. The well-ordered society will utilise the energies of egoism in fruitful fields of individual activity. The human ego will always seek a directly personal self-expression in the free exercise of artistic instincts and other creative or adventurous activities that yield the glory of achievement.

These primarily self-regarding impulses are made socially profitable by allowing them free expression in these fields. The attempt to regulate and direct these impulses and their productive activities would be disastrous. This play of unfettered personality in the fine arts, in literature, in the unsettled and experimental section of each profession and each trade, must be conserved, not as an inherent right of individuals but as a sound social economy. For the distinction between these free creative activities and the ordinary run of routine work in the trade and professions is fundamental. It is not that the former, the free unorganised activities, are not as truly social as the latter in their ultimate significance and worth. But their social value is best secured by leaving them to the stimuli of personal interests. The creative activities, including all work which pleasure, interest, surprise or personal pride, cause to be desired upon its own account, need no social compulsion to evoke them. Their product is the free gift which the individual makes to the commonwealth out of the riches of his active personality. As their cost to him is more than compensated by the pleasures of creation, he will contribute them freely to the service of mankind. But even if a coarser streak of selfishness causes the creative artist, poet, inventor, discoverer, to claim some large share of the marketable value of his product for himself, it will better serve society to pay him his price, than to attempt to 'organise' creation on a public basis. Such sufficient material rewards of genius or high talent, if they are really necessary to evoke the creative activity, must rightly be considered 'costs' rather than 'surplus.' There will remain a margin of such unfettered private enterprise, not only in the fine arts and the learned professions, where the creative mind seems most in evidence, but at the growing point of every living industry. For the distinction between creation and imitation or routine, as we have seen, cannot be applied in a wholesale way to entire trades and occupations. Budding and experimental industries, involving large application of inventive and constructive energy, appealing to new and uncertain tastes, carrying heavy risks of capital and reputation, are better left to individual enterprise. The same industries, settled on established lines, with smaller risks and smaller opportunities of useful change, will properly pass under direct social control. It is hardly conceivable that the development of the motor-car and the aëroplane could have been so rapid, if these industries had been at the outset claimed as State monopolies and official experts had alone been set to operate them. The injurious retardation of electric lighting and transport in this country by the legal shackles imposed upon them has been a striking testimony to the social harm done by premature application of social control to an industry in its early experimental stage.

On the other hand, it is equally foolish to exclude from effective social regulation or state organisation entire professions, such as teaching, law, or medicine, on the ground that they are essentially 'creative.' For they are not. The very name profession implies the adoption of prescribed and accepted methods for dealing with large ordinary classes of cases, that is to say routine procedure. Though, as we recognise, such procedure may never reach the same degree of mechanical routine as prevails in ordinary processes of manufacture, the common factors may be so predominant as to bring them properly under the same public regimen. Though, for example, class-teaching will always carry some element of originality and personal skill, a true regard for public interests establishes close public control of curriculum and method in those branches of instruction in which it is convenient to give the same teaching to large numbers of children at the same time. In education, as in medicine and in every other skilled calling, there are grades of practice rightly classed as regular or routine. Where it is important for members of the public to be able to obtain such services, in reliable qualities upon known and reasonable terms, effective social control of them must be secured. For, otherwise, a power of private tyranny or of extortion or neglect is vested in the producers of such services. The inadequate public control over the medical and legal services in this country is raising a crop of grave practical problems for early solution.

So in every industry or occupation the relatively routine work requires direct social organisation while the preponderantly creative work should be left to 'private' enterprise. The former class contains the great bulk of those industries which, concentrated in large businesses for the profitable supply of the prime needs and conveniences of ordinary men and women, breed combinations and monopolies. Whereas in the creative industries there exists a natural harmony of interests between producer and consumer that will secure to society the best fruits of individual effort, this is not the case in the routine industries. There the operation of the human law of distribution can only be secured by direct social organisation. Only thus can excessive private surplus, involving a tyranny over labour on the one hand, the consumer on the other, be prevented. In no other way can the main organs of industry be infused with the human feelings of solidarity and coöperation essential to the stability and progress of social industries.

§ 6. For to this vital point we must return. The substitution of direct social control for the private profit-seeking motive in the normal processes of our industries is essential to any sound scheme of social reconstruction. For not otherwise can we get the social meaning of industry represented consciously in the coöperative will of the human factors of production. It is not too much to say that the pace of civilisation for nations, of moral progress for individuals, depends upon this radical reconstruction of common industry. For the existing structure of ordinary business life inhibits the realisation of its social meaning by the stress it lays upon the discordant and the separatist interests. The struggle to keep or to improve one's hold upon some place in the industrial system, to win a livelihood, to make some gain that involves a loss to someone else, derationalises the intelligence and demoralises the character of all of us.

This derationalisation and demoralisation are seen to be rooted in the defective structure and working of industrialism itself.

If Industry were fairly apportioned among all, according to the capability of each, if Property were allotted to each according to his needs, by some natural process of distribution as regular and certain as the process of the planets, persons would not need to think or feel very keenly about such things as Industry and Property: their intellects and hearts would be free for other interests and activities.

But the insecurity, irregularity and injustice of economic distribution keep Industry and Property continually in the foreground of the personal consciousness.

Here comes into terrible relief the moral significance of the unearned Surplus—the term which gathers all the bad origins of Property into the focus of a single concept.

At present much Industry is conducted, much Property is acquired, by modes which are unjust, irrational and socially injurious. Legal privilege, economic force, natural or contrived scarcity, luck, personal favour, inheritance—such are the means by which large quantities of property come to be possessed by persons who have not contributed any considerable productive effort to their making.

Such property stands in the eye of the law, and in the popular regard, upon precisely the same footing as that owned by those who have earned it by the sweat of their brow, or the effort of their brain. The failure of so many thoughtful men and women to appreciate the vital bearing of the issue of origins upon the validity of property is the supreme evidence of the injurious reactions of the present property system upon the human mind. The crucial moral fallacy which it evokes is the contention, seriously put forth by certain social philosophers, as well as by social reformers, that property acquired in the ways I have just indicated is validated in reason and morality by the good uses to which it may be put by its owners. Mr. Carnegie and Mr. Rockefeller have seriously propounded the theory that certain individuals are endowed by nature or by circumstances with the opportunity and power of accumulating great wealth, but that their wealth, though legally their private property, is rightly to be regarded by them as a 'social trust' to be administered by them for the benefit of their fellow-men. It seems to them a matter of indifference that this wealth is 'unearned,' provided that it is productively expended. So fragments of profits, earned by sweating labour or by rack renting tenants, are spent on pensions, public hospitals or housing reform. Fractions of the excessive prices the consuming public pays to privileged transport companies or 'protected' manufacturers are given back in parks or universities. Great inheritances, passing on the death of rich bankers, contractors or company promoters, drop heavy tears of charity to soften the fate of those who have failed in the business struggle. Fortunes, gained by setting nation against nation, are applied to promote the cause of international peace. This humor is inevitable. Unearned property can find no social uses more exigent than the application of charitable remedies to the very diseases to which it owes its origin. So everywhere we find the beneficiaries of economic force, luck, favour and privilege, trying to pour balm and oil into the wounds which they have made. The effect of the process, and what may be called its unconscious intention, is to defend the irrationality and injustice of these unearned properties by buying off clear scrutiny into their origins. Sometimes, indeed, the intention attains a measure of clear consciousness, as in the cases where rich men or firms regard the subscriptions given to public purposes as sound business expenditure, applying one fraction of their gross profits to a propitiation fund as they apply another to an insurance fund.

§ 7. The radical defect of this doctrine and practice of the 'social trust' is its false severance of origin from use. The organic law of industry has joined origin and use, work and wealth, production and consumption. It affirms a natural and necessary relation between getting and spending. A man who puts no effort into getting, a rent-receiver, cannot put well-directed effort into spending. He is by natural proclivity a wastrel. A man who is purely selfish in his getting, as the sweater, gambler, or monopolist, cannot be social in his spending. The recipient

of unearned income is impelled by the conditions of his being to
a life of idleness and luxury: this is the life he is fitted for. He is
unfitted for the administration of a social trust.

These obvious truths, so fatally neglected, are no vague
maxims of revolutionary ethics, but are firmly rooted in physical
and moral fact. We have seen that there is throughout organic
life a quantitative and a qualitative relation between function
and nutrition, each being the condition of the other. He who
does not eat cannot work: he who does not work cannot eat.
It is true that the latter law works less directly and less immediately than the former. Parasitism, individual or social, continues to exist in many walks of life. But it never thrives, it
always tends to degeneration, atrophy and decay. Normally,
and in the long run, it remains true that 'Whosoever will not
work, neither *can* he eat.' If then the recipiency of unearned
wealth, parasitism, disables the recipient from putting his 'property' to sound personal uses, is it likely that he can put it to
sound social uses? Though abnormal instances may seem, here
as elsewhere, to contravene the natural law, it remains true that
the power of individual earning, not merely involves no power
of social spending, but negates that power. It might even be
contended that there will be a natural disposition in the recipient
of unearned wealth to spend that wealth in precisely those ways
in which it injures most the society he seeks to serve. This is
probably the case. It is more socially injurious for the mil-
lionaire to spend his surplus wealth in charity than in luxury.
For by spending it on luxury, he chiefly injures himself and his
immediate circle, but by spending it in charity he inflicts a
graver injury upon society. For every act of charity, applied to
heal suffering arising from defective arrangements of society,
serves to weaken the personal springs of social reform, alike by
the 'miraculous' relief it brings to the individual 'case' that is
relieved, and by the softening influence it exercises on the hearts
and heads of those who witness it. It substitutes the idea and
the desire of individual reform for those of social reform, and so
weakens the capacity for collective self-help in society. The
most striking testimony to the justice of this analysis is furnished
by the tendency of 'model millionaires' to direct all their charity

to wholesale and what they deem social purposes, rather than to individual cases. In order to avoid the errors of indiscriminate charity, they fasten their munificence upon society in the shape of universities, hospitals, parks, libraries and other general benefits. Realising quite clearly, as they think, that the character of an individual is weakened and demoralised by a charitable donation which enables him to get what otherwise he could only have got by his personal exertion, they proceed to weaken and demoralise whole cities and entire nations, by doing for these social bodies what they are quite capable of doing for themselves by their own collective exertions. These public gifts of millionaires debauch the character of cities and states more effectively than the private gifts of unreflecting donors the character of individuals. For, whereas many, if not most, of the private recipients of charity are victims of misfortune or of lack of opportunity, and are not fully responsible for the evil plight in which they stand, this is not the case with an organised self-governing community, a City or a State. Such a society is able, out of its own resources, if it chooses to secure and use them, to supply for itself all its own legitimate needs. It has a far larger self-sufficiency for meeting all ordinary emergencies and for following an economy of self-development and progress, than has the individual citizen. For it can supply its needs out of the social income which its collective life is constantly assisting to produce, out of that very surplus which, wrongly allowed to flow, unearned, into the coffers of rich individuals, is the very fund used for this debasing public charity.

§ 8. The clear recognition of these truths is closely germane to our central consideration in this chapter, viz., the question whether there can be evoked in the common consciousness a flow of true social or coöperative feeling strong and steady enough to evoke from individual citizens a sufficient voluntary efficiency in production. No absolutely convincing answer to the question is at present possible. But, if any such experiment is to be tried hopefully, it can only be done by setting Property upon an intelligible moral and social basis, so that it passes into the possession of him to whom it is really 'proper,' in the sense that he has put something of himself into its making. Only by resolving unearned into earned income, so that all Property is duly earned either by individuals or by societies, can an ethical basis be laid for social industry. So long as property appears to come miraculously or capriciously, irrespective of efforts or requirements, and so long as it is withheld as irrationally, it is idle to preach 'the dignity of labour' or to inculcate sentiments of individual self-help.

When all Property is visibly justified, alike in origin and use, the rights of property will for the first time be respected, for they will be for the first time respectable. To steal, to cheat, to sweat, to cadge or beg, will be considered shameful, not because the law forbids, but because such acts will be felt by all to be assaults upon the personality of another. For the first time in history, also, the tax-dodger, the contractor who puts up his price for public works, the sinecurist, the jobber, the protectionist and other parasites upon the public purse, will receive the general reprobation due to robbery. For when the State is recognised as having rights of property identical in origin and use with those of individual citizens, that property will claim and may receive a similar respect. Property, in a word, becomes a really sacred institution when the human law of distribution is applied to the whole income, surplus as well as costs. Such inequalities in income as survive will be plainly justified as the counterpart of inequality of efforts and of needs. The wide contrasts of rich and poor, of luxury and penury, of idleness and toil, will no longer stagger the reason and offend the heart.

So the standard of sentimental values which affects the conventional modes of living of all classes—largely by snobbish imitation and rivalry—will be transformed.

Ostentatious waste and conspicuous leisure, with all their injurious reactions upon our Education, Recreation, Morals, and Æsthetics, will tend to disappear. The illusory factor of Prestige will be undermined, so that the valuations, both of productive activities and of consumption, will shift towards a natural, or rational, standard.

§ 9. Not merely will the wide gulf which severs mental from manual workers disappear, but all the elaborate scale of values for different sorts of intellectual and manual work would undergo a radical revision.

The effect of setting on a human basis the industry of the country would, of course, react upon all other departments of life, Religion, Family and Civic Morality, Politics, Literature, Art and Science. For though economics alone cannot mould or interpret history, the distinctively economic institutions of Industry and Property have always exercised a powerful, sometimes a dominant influence, upon other institutions. The reformation of economic life must, therefore, produce equally beneficent effects upon all other departments—transforming their standards and feeding the streams of their activities with new thoughts and feelings, drawn no longer from the minds of a little class or a few original natures, but from the whole tide of human life flowing freely along every channel of individual and social endeavour.

The security and rationality of the economic order will give to all that confidence in man, and that faith in his future, which are the prime, conditions of safe and rapid progress. For the brutal and crushing pressure of the economic problem in its coarsest shape—how to secure a material basis of livelihood— has of necessity hitherto absorbed nearly all the energy of man, so that his powers of body, soul and spirit have been mainly spent on an unsatisfactory and precarious solution of this personal economic problem. Religion, politics, the disinterested pursuits of truth or beauty, have had to live upon the leavings of the economic life.

An economic reformation which, by applying the human law of distribution, absorbs the unproductive surplus, would thus furnish a social environment which was stronger and better in the nourishment and education it afforded to man. Every organ of society would function more effectively, supplying richer opportunities for healthy all-round self-development to all. So far as the economic activities can be taken into separate consideration, it is evident that this justly-ordered environment would do much to raise the physical, and more to raise the moral efficiency of the individual as a wealth-producer and consumer. But its most important contribution to the value and the growth of human welfare would lie in other fields of personality than the distinctively economic, in the liberation, realisation and improved condition of other intellectual and spiritual energies at present thwarted by or subordinated to industrialism.

CHAPTER XX

THE SOCIAL WILL AS AN ECONOMIC FORCE

§ 1. To secure by education and reflection such a revaluation of human activities, aims and achievements, as will set economic processes and products in a definitely lower place than that which they occupy at present, is, I think, essential to safe and rapid progress. For the early steps towards a better industrial order will very likely involve some economic sacrifice, in the sense of a reduced output of personal energy and of wealth-production on the part of the average member of society. Although this loss may be more than compensated by the elimination of large wastes of competition and by improved organisation, we are not warranted in assuming that this will at once take place.

We need not assume it. For even if we do not, our analysis has shown that an economic system, thus working at a lower rate of human costs, and turning out a smaller quantity of goods, may nevertheless yield a larger quantity of human welfare, by a better distribution of work and product. But the great gain, of course, will consist in the increased amount of time, interest and energy, available for the cultivation of other human arts outside the economic field. Upon the capacity to utilise these enlarged opportunities the actual pace of human progress in the art of living will depend. At present this capacity may seem small. The increased opportunities of leisure, travel, recreation, culture, and comradeship, which have come in widely different degrees to all classes, have often been put to disappointing uses. But a great deal of such waste is evidently attributable to that prevailing vice of thought and feeling which the domination of industrialism has stamped upon our minds, the crude desires for physical sensations and external display. Not until a far larger measure of release from our economic bonds has been acquired, shall we enjoy the detachment of mind requisite for the larger processes of revaluation and realisation.

§ 2. One word remains, however, to be said upon the all-important subject of motives and incentives. We have seen that, in so far as it is possible to displace the competitive system of industry, with its stimulation of individual greed and combativeness, by a more consciously coöperative system, the will of the individual engaged upon industrial processes will be affected in some measure by the social meaning of the work he is doing, and will desire to forward it. The efficacy of this social will is not, however, adequately realised so long as it is regarded merely as a feeling for the public good originating from a number of separate centres of enlightened personality. The growing recognition on the part of individual workers, that the structure of society establishes a strong community of interests, will no doubt supply some incentive to each to do his fair share to the necessary work. But this personal incentive may not go very far towards overcoming the selfishness or sluggishness of feebler personalities. If, then, the social will be taken merely to mean the aggregate of feeling for the public good thus generated in the separate wills, it may not suffice to support the commonweal. But if our organic conception of society has any validity, the social will means more than this addition of separately stimulated individual wills. The individual soldier may have a patriotic feeling expressing his individual love of his country, which has a certain fighting value. But, as his attachment to his profession grows, another feeling of wider origin and more enduring force fuses with the narrower feeling, enhancing greatly its effectiveness. That feeling is *esprit de corps*, a corporate spirit of the service, capable of overcoming personal defects, the cowardice, apathy or greed of the individual, and of evoking an enormous volume of united effort. I have no intention of suggesting that the routine of ordinary industry can yield scope for displays of this *esprit de corps* comparable in intensity with the dramatic examples of great military achievements. But I do affirm that every conscious corporate life is accompanied and nourished by some common consciousness of will and purpose which feeds and fortifies the personal centres, stimulating those that are weaker and raising them to a decent level of effort, reducing dissension, and imparting conscious unity of action into complex processes of coöperation. The power of this social will as an economic motive-force ought not to be ignored. As the processes of industrial coöperation grow closer, more numerous, more regular in their operation, this coöperation and coördination, representing a unity of will and purpose far transcending the vision and the purpose even of the most enlightened and altruistic member, will form a powerful current of industrial consciousness, influencing and moulding the will and purposes of individuals.

Such a force, emanating from the social whole, will of necessity not be clearly comprehensible to the individuals who feel its influence and respond to it. They are the many, while it flows from their union, which must always be imperfectly mirrored in the mind of each. Yet this direct social will only works through its power to stimulate and direct the will of each, so as to produce a more effective harmony. Vague theory this will seem to some, utterly remote from the hard facts of life! The problem is how to induce public or other salaried employees to do a fair day's work, when they might shirk it without loss of pay. Well, we suggest that when that fair day's work is not unduly long or onerous, when it is fairly paid, and when each sees that all the others are called upon to do their proper share, the general sense of fairness in the arrangement will come to exercise a compelling influence on each man to keep his output up to a decent level. This power of the social will has never yet been tested. For a society with arrangements based on manifest principles of justice and reason has never yet been set in operation. But though our organic law of distribution may never attain a perfect application, so far as it is applied it may surely be expected to act in the way here described, appealing to the springs of honour, equity, comradeship and respect for public opinion, with a force immeasurably greater than is possible in a system of industry and property where reason and fair play in the apportionment of work and its rewards are so imperfectly apparent.

§ 3. These conditions of organic welfare in the apportionment of work and wealth do not imply a conception of industrial society in which the individual and his personal desires and ends are impaired or sacrificed to the interests of the community. They do imply a growth of the social-economic structure in which the impulses of mutual aid, which from the earliest times have been civilising mankind, shall work with a clearer consciousness of their human value. As the individual perceives more clearly how intimately his personal efforts and effects are, in process and in product, linked with those of all the other members of society, that perception must powerfully influence his feelings. He will come consciously to realise his personal freedom in actions that are a willing contribution to the common good. This consciousness will make it more difficult for him to defend in himself or others economic conduct or institutions in which individual, class or national conflicts are involved. Thus a better social consciousness and a better economic environment will react on one another for further mutual betterment. The unity of this social-industrial life is not a unity of mere fusion in which the individual virtually disappears, but a federal unity in which the rights and interests of the individual shall be conserved for him by the federation. The federal government, however, conserves these individual rights, not, as the individualist maintains, because it exists for no other purpose than to do so. It conserves them because it also recognises that an area of individual liberty is conducive to the health of the collective life. Its federal nature rests on a recognition alike of individual and social ends, or, speaking more accurately, of social ends that are directly attained by social action and of those that are realised in individuals. I regard such a federation as an organic union because none of the individual rights or interests is absolute in its sanction. Society in its economic as in its other relations is a federal state not a federation of states. The rights and interests of society are paramount: they override all claims of individuals to liberties that contravene them.

§ 4. So far as industry is concerned, we perceive how this harmony between individual and social rights and interests is realised in the primary division of productive activities into Art and Routine. The impulses and desires which initiate, sustain and direct what we term art, including all the creative activities in industry, flow freely from the individual nature. We recognise that productive activities in which these elements are of paramount importance form an economic field which society, guided by its intelligent self-interest, will safely and profitably leave to individuals and private enterprise. Industries which are essentially of a routine character, affording little scope for creative activities of individuals, must pass under direct social administration. For free individual initiative and desires will not support them. They can only be worked under private enterprise on condition that great gains are procurable for the *entrepreneurs* and an unfree body of proletarian labour is available for compulsory service. The routine services of society cannot properly be secured by appeals to the separate self-interests of individuals. So administered, they involve the waste of vast unearned gains accruing to a private caste of masters, the injury and degradation of economic servitude in the workers, and a growing insecurity and irregularity of service to the consumers. The only volume of free-will and voluntary enterprise that can support those routine industries is the free-will and enterprise of Society. If we can bring ourselves to regard the great normal currents of routine industry, engaged in supplying the common daily needs, from the standpoint of a real live Society, we shall recognise that to that Society this industrial activity and its achievements are full of interest and variety. What to the individual is dull routine is to Society creative art, the natural employment of social productive energies for the progressive satisfaction of social needs. Though the individual will soon flags before demands for work so irksome and repellent to its nature, the social will gladly responds to work in which that will finds its free natural expression.

This is the ultimate argument in favour of the socialisation of the routine industries, viz., the release of the individual will from work that is costly, repellent and ill-done, in order to enable the social will to find in that work its healthy, interesting, educative self-realisation. For once conceive Society as a being capable of thought and feeling, these processes have an interest for it. They are social art, part of the collective life in which Society realises itself, just as the individual realises himself in individual art. Once accept the view of Society not as a mere set of social institutions, or a network of relations, but as a collective personality, the great routine industrial processes become the vital functions of this collective being, interesting to that being alike in their performance and their product. That subdivision of labour and that apparent contradiction of interests between producer and consumer which seem designed to feed personal antagonisms and to thwart individuality, now acquire rational justification as the complex adaptive play of healthy vital functions in Society.

§ 5. Labour, thus interpreted, becomes a truly social function, the orderly half-instinctive half-rational activity by which society helps itself and satisfies its wants, a common tide of productive energy which pulses through the veins of humanity, impelling the individual members of society to perform their part as contributors to the general life. Whether those individual actions are strictly voluntary, pleasurable and interesting in themselves to those who perform them, as in the finer arts, or are compulsory in their main incidence upon the individual, and accompanied by little interest or social feeling on his part, is a matter of quite secondary importance as viewed from the social standpoint. As labour is social, so is capital. The other apparent discrepancy, that between the interests of present and future, spending and saving, also disappears when we consider the social significance of saving. For society secretes capital by the same half-instinctive half-rational process by which it generates, directs and distributes, its supply of labour. Only by a hypothesis which thus assigns a central industrial purpose to society can we possibly understand the life of industry and the complex coöperation it displays.

Take for a single instance the wheat supply of the world—or the cotton industry of Lancashire. We see large rhythmic actions, elaborate in their complicated flows, responsive to innumerable stimuli of world-markets,—a nervous system of affluent and effluent currents, directed by the desires and beliefs of innumerable producers and consumers, each consciously actuated by his own particular motives and yet coöperating towards large social ends.

We can neither grasp, intellectually or emotionally, the human or social significance of these processes, if we persist in resolving them into the ideas, feelings and actions of individual persons. The harmony becomes either fortuitous or purely mystical. But, if we regard Society as having a large life of its own, the coöperative harmony of individual aims and activities becomes a corporate organic process. The social life does not suffer from division of labour and specialisation of function, but gains, as in the animal organism. The social life is not oppressed, degraded or injured by the routine of the smaller working lives, any more than the animal organism by the regularity and repetition of the respiratory, circulating and other routine operations of its organs and their cells.

§ 6. "But," it will be objected, "even if we are justified in pushing the organic analogy so far as to claim the existence of a real social life with a meaning and end of its own, superior to that of the individual, as the life of every organism is superior to that of its organs and cells, that larger social being can only remain a shadowy or hypothetical being to actual men and women. And it is the aims, ideas, feelings and activities of these little units that, after all, will always absorb our attention and occupy our hearts and minds."

Here is the final quintessence of individualism surviving in many professing socialists, the denial of the existence of a rational moral society. Yet such a society exists. The earliest beginnings of animal gregariousness, sexual feelings, and other primary instincts of association, with the mutual aid they give rise to, are a first testimony to the existence, even at the opening of the human era, of a real though rudimentary society, physical and psychical in its nature. Civilisation has its chief meaning in the extension and growing realisation of this unity of Society, by utilising these secret threads of social feeling for the weaving of the fabric of social institutions. Thus, through these instruments of common social life, language, art, science, industry, politics, religion, society gathers a larger, more solid and various life. Race, Nationality, Church, the bond of some common interest in a science, an art, a philanthropic purpose, often present intense examples of genuinely common life and purpose. These are not mere social contracts of free individuals, seeking by coöperation to forward their individual ends. Such a conception of mutual aid is as false for religion, science, art or industry, as for politics. The statement that 'man is a social animal' cannot merely signify that among man's equipment of feelings and ideas there exists a feeling and idea of sympathy with other men. That is only how it looks *from the standpoint of the cell*. It means that humanity in all its various aggregations is a social stuff, and that whatever forms of coalescence it assumes, i. e. a nation, caste, church, party, etc., there will exist a genuinely organic unity, a central or general life, strong or weak, but, so far as it goes, to be considered as distinct from and dominant over the life and aim of its members.

This central life, though distinguishable from the lives of its members, as an object of thought and will, is yet only lived in and through the life of the organs and cells. This is the subtle nature of the organic bond.

We are told indeed that "Society only exists in individuals." This, however, is only true in the same restricted sense in which it is true that an animal organism only exists in the life of its cells. There is nothing but the cells *plus* their organic coöperation. But I should rather say that the organism exists in the coöperation of the cells. So I should say that Society exists in the coöperation of individuals.

This is not a matter of theoretic accuracy of statement, but of immense practical significance. For the future progress of the arts of social conduct, especially of industry and politics, must largely depend upon the measure and manner of acceptance of this view of the nature of Society. It must, indeed, to the individual mind always remain as a hypothesis, incapable of full and exact verification. For such verification would imply an absolute merging of individual personality in the social unity. Such a public spirit can never absorb and displace private spirits. But the hypothesis may, for all that, possess both intellectual and emotional validity. Its clear provisional acceptance will not only explain many of the difficulties and reconcile many of the discrepancies in those tendencies, industrial and political, which are generally accepted as making for human progress, but will afford increased economy of direction and of motive. For once let us realise Society as possessing a unity and a life of its own, to the furtherance of which each of us contributes in the pursuance of the particular life we call 'our own,' the so-called sacrifices we are called upon to make for that larger life will be considered no longer encroachments on but enlargements of our personality. We shall come in larger measure to identify our aims and ends willingly with the aims and ends we impute to society, and every step in that public conduct will enrich or strengthen that social sympathy which we shall recognise to be the very life of society flowing in our veins. This is the spirit of social reform, as distinguished from the concrete measures of reform. Upon the creation and recognition of this spirit the possibility, the usefulness, the durability of every one of the institutions and policies, which are evolved by modern civilisation, depend. It is, therefore, of supreme and critical importance to obtain the widest possible acceptance of the conception of Society as a living being to which each of us 'belongs,' a being capable of thinking and feeling through us for itself, and of desiring, pursuing and attaining ends which are its ends, and which we are capable of helping to realise. So long as Society is spoken of and thought of as an abstraction, no social conduct can be sound or safe. For an abstraction is incapable of calling forth our reverence, regard or love. And until we attribute to Society such a form and degree of 'personality' as can evoke in us those interests and emotions which personality alone can win, the social will will not be able to perform great works.

The final claim we make for the human valuation of industry presented here is that it helps to bring into clear relief a set of human problems which, from the conception of society as a mere arrangement for securing individual ends, are perceived to be insoluble, but for which reason and emotion alike demand a satisfactory solution. Only by substituting for the attainment of individual welfare the ideal and the standard of social welfare, are we able to obtain a method of analysis and valuation which furnishes satisfactory solutions to the problems that industry presents.

CHAPTER XXI

PERSONAL AND SOCIAL EFFICIENCY

§ 1. What light does our human valuation of economic processes throw upon the conditions of individual and social progress? Our examination of industry has shown us the ways in which the actual production and consumption of wealth affect the personal efficiency and welfare of individuals. The organic law of distribution clearly indicates personal efficiency, alike for purposes of economic productivity and for the wider art of life, to depend primarily upon the maintenance of sound relations between the output of economic activities and the income of economic satisfactions. A healthy system of industry will demand from each producer an amount and kind of 'costly' labour accommodated to his natural and acquired powers. By such a distribution of the socially useful work which is not in itself agreeable to its performers, the common economic needs of society are supplied with the smallest aggregate amount of human cost. Similarly, we see how, by a distribution of wealth according to the needs of each member, i. e. according to his 'power' as consumer, the largest aggregate amount of human utility is got out of the wealth distributed.

But this burden of 'costly' work, required of the producer and adjusted to his powers, is not the only work that he can do. The main object of the shorter work-day and the better apportionment of 'costly' labour, as we have already recognised, is to liberate the individual so that he has time and energy for the voluntary performance of 'productive' activities that are 'costless,' interesting and beneficial to his personal life. Some of these voluntary activities will be 'economic' in the sense that they may produce goods or services which have an exchange value. Such is the gardening or the wood-carving which a man may do in his spare time. Though it may bring him a direct return of personal gain and satisfaction that is non-economic, it may also be a supplementary means of income. There is no reason why a man whose hobby is his garden should not be able to exchange some of the fruit and flowers, which it has been a pleasure for for him to grow, for the photographs or the book-bindings on which his neighbours may prefer to spend a portion of their leisure. Most of the spare energy or leisure, however, won for the worker by a fair distribution of 'costly' labour, will, of course, usually be applied to personal employments, to the arts of home life and of society, which, though highly conducive to personal efficiency, lie outside the range of 'economics.' Each person would apply this free time and energy differently, his voluntary work having some natural relation as 'relief' or 'variety' to the sort of 'costly' or routine labour which earned his livelihood. Thus on this true equalitarian basis there would arise an immense variety of freely active personalities. Each person would have what may be called a personal standard of production, an orderly application of his productive energies, which, though partly imposed by his status as a member of society bound to do his share in social work, would largely represent his personal tastes, choices and interests, selfish or altruistic, according to his temperament.

§ 2. Turning to the other side of industry, the distribution of wealth to each according to his needs, i. e. capacities of use, personality would impress itself similarly upon an immense variety of actual standards of consumption, or modes of applying income to the satisfaction of desires. There is, however, an important distinction to be noted between standards of consumption and of production. Whereas in modern industry the earning of income is normally an individual art, its consumption is normally a family act. While the family, except in some agricultural societies, is very rarely a unit of production, it remains usually a unit of consumption. It would appear, then, that our human distribution would affect personal efficiency differently upon the two sides of its application. As producer his standard of production, or of use of productive activities, would appear to be directed by a balance between the social requirements of labour and his personal proclivities, whereas on the side of consumption the balance would be between the social requirements and the family. Society must secure for the standard of family comfort such an expenditure as will sustain the working numbers of the family in full economic efficiency, i. e. a proper economy of what the classical economists called 'productive consumption' must take place. But, outside this limit, the particular requirements and conditions, not of the earner alone, but of the family as a whole, must determine the expenditure that makes for efficiency. This discrepancy, however, is not really so great as it appears at first sight. The direct interest of society in the productive and consumptive life of its individual members lies in their performance of this proper share of 'costly' or social service and their use of a proper portion of their income for consumption adjusted to maintain their efficiency for this social service. The rest of their productive energy, the rest of their consumptive wealth, lie under their own control for their personal life. The fact that this personal life may be more narrowly personal on the productive side, more of a family life on the consumptive side, does not seriously affect the issue. Indeed, the discrepancy almost wholly disappears when we look a little closer at the liberties which a better social economy of production secures for the worker. The better life which a slackening of the industrial strain will bring to the producer will consist in the cultivation of interests and activities which, precisely because they are voluntary and in themselves desired, cannot rightly be classified as either production or consumption but unite the qualities of both. We have seen that this is the characteristic of all art, or all work which is good and pleasant in itself. Any activity that carries a surplus of human utility over human cost is at once function and nutrition, production and consumption. In a word, it is an increase of life. So it comes about that the 'human distribution' feeds personal efficiency equally on its productive and consumptive sides. A healthy application of productive activities will contribute as much to individual progress as a healthy standard of consumption.

§ 3. It remains to recognise that the organic treatment of our problem does not permit society to adopt a separatist view of the distribution of work and its product. A distribution of work 'according to the powers' of workers is conceivable on terms which would cause heavy damage to society through ignoring the reactions of work upon consumption. It might appear superficially a sound human economy to place all the burden of the heaviest and most repellent muscular toil upon classes or races of men whose powerful bodies and insensitive minds seemed to indicate that they were best fitted by nature for such work.[1] But if the effect of such an economy were, as it would be, to keep considerable bodies of population in a low grade of animalism, as represented in coarse modes of living and brutal recreations, this one-sided view, by neglecting these organic reactions, would injure the personality of these lower grades of citizens, and through them damage the efficiency of the society of which they were members. Or, taking an opposite instance, a Society which enabled classes of artistic or literary folk to escape all share of 'costly' social labour, so as to cultivate exclusively their individual activities and tastes, would incur a similar social danger through the presence of highly stimulating personalities, unchecked by any adequate sense of social responsibilities, who by their example and influence might undermine the routine activities which are the feeders of social life.

So far, then, as economic reforms are aiming at personal efficiency, they must take simultaneously into consideration the effects which each reform will have upon the production and the consumption of wealth. For example, a shortening of the workday ought to be accompanied by improved opportunities of education and of recreation as an integral part of the reform.

§ 4. Our setting of the problem, which brings into contrast the routine social production that is 'costly' to individuals and the creative or individual production which is 'costless,' might seem to involve the view that social progress, as distinct from individual, would involve an increasing total burden of routine work under direct social control. Thus an antagonism between the conscious interests of the individual and the social interests might appear to remain. For, though a better social will, operating upon the individual, might dispose him to accept his duty of serving society in the performance of his share of routine work, it

[1] Ruskin had a curious notion of this sort (cf. *Time and Tide*, par. 107, *Munera Pulveris*, par. 109, *Fors Clavigera*, Letter lxxxii), and the recent American 'Scientific Management' appears to endorse it.

would still be true that such service was less desirable to him and less nourished his personal life than the free personal activities upon which it encroached. This opens up an exceedingly important issue in social economy. It has been assumed that a really enlightened society will so administer industry that a light day's labour shared among all will suffice to win the wealth necessary for the support of society and the satisfaction of the common material needs of its members. Thus an increasing proportion of human energy will be liberated for the performance of those activities which are pleasant and interesting to those who engage in them. A diminishing amount of time and energy will be applied to the mechanical processes of getting food and other materials from the earth, and of fashioning them and carrying them about. Thus there will be more time and energy for the fine arts and crafts, which depend less upon quantity of materials and more upon the skilled application of personal powers. From the standpoint of human welfare such an economy is obvious. It means, on the productive side, a progressive increase of activity that is humanly 'costless' and pleasurable, a progressive decrease of that which is costly and unpleasurable. On the consumptive side, it means the substitution of non-material wealth, such as books, pictures, poetry, science, which are virtually infinite in the human utility that they are capable of yielding, for material wealth which is mostly consumed in a single act of appropriation. The higher kind of goods thus brings a minimum of costs and a maximum of utilities, and that upon each side of the organic equation.

In most advanced nations of our time this gain in the relative importance of the arts and professions engaged in artistic, professional, recreative, educational, scientific and other creative activities, is recognised as being an evidence and a measure of advancing civilisation, and some offset to the advance of material luxury.

§ 5. If, however, there is to be a continuous increase in the proportion of time and energy available for the production and consumption of the higher grades of non-material economic goods and for other activities of a non-economic nature, some limitation must take place of the demand and supply of material economic goods. If in any country, or throughout the industrial world, the growth of population were such as, in the old phrase, to press 'upon the means of subsistence,' the amount of productive energy needed for the arts of agriculture, mining, and the staple branches of manufacture and transport would be such as to defeat the economy of social progress just indicated. Even if the population did not advance, but were chiefly engaged in seeking fuller satisfaction of an increasing number of distinctively physical wants, the same result would follow. Larger drafts must continually be made upon the natural resources of the soil, by means of industries subject to what political economy calls "the law of diminishing returns," and an increasing proportion of labour must be engaged in these industries. Though mechanics and the division of labour in the manufactures, and even in agriculture, temper the tyranny of matter, enabling a given amount of routine toil to achieve an increasing output of goods, this policy of human liberation is impeded and may be entirely frustrated by a constant preference among large populations for a strictly quantitative satisfaction of new material wants. The root issue of social progress from the economic standpoint is here disclosed. It is the question of the relative importance of quantity of matter in the satisfaction of wants. In urging that social progress requires a progressive diminution of the part played by matter and the industries in which quantity of matter is a chief determinant factor, I do not merely mean that civilisation implies an increasing valuation of the intellectual and moral faculties and of their activities. Most of the fine arts require some matter for their manipulation and for their instruments; every branch of the intellectual life needs some material equipment. But in these occupations and in their products quantity of matter is of an importance that is slight, often wholly negligible. A fine art, a skilled craft, a machine industry, may each handle the same sort of material, metal, stone or wood, but the quantity of this material will have a rapidly increasing importance, as one descends from the manipulation of the artist to the craftsman and from the craftsman to the manufacturer.

If, then, we are to secure an economy of social progress in which relatively less importance is to be given to those industries which are less humanly desirable, alike in the work they involve and in the satisfaction their products yield, we must have a society which becomes increasingly qualitative in its tastes and interests and in its human constitution. A larger proportion of its real income must take shape in non-material goods, or in material goods which depend more for the satisfaction they yield upon their quality. In a word, there must be a tendency to keep life simple in regard to material consumption.

But when one says that society itself must grow more qualitative in its constitution, a more difficult consideration emerges. In the discussion regarding the bearing of the growth of population upon general welfare too much attention was formerly accorded to the merely quantitative question. Too little is now accorded. Under the title of eugenics the population question threatens to become entirely qualitative. Now this is evidently a mistake. For whatever interpretation we accord to social welfare, some consideration as to the desirable number and rate of growth of the population is evidently of importance. Though it may be agreed that vital values in their spiritual and even in the physical meanings are distinctly qualitative, and that, as far as possible, a society should set itself to maintain conditions of sex selection favourable to admittedly finer and healthier types, this issue of quality must not be detached from the issue of quantity. As in the economy of the individual life a proper allowance of attention must be secured for physical wants and for the material production and consumption they involve, so in a society the size of its physical structure, the number of coöperating human cells through which it lives, is a consideration that inheres in the art of social life. Ruskin was surely right in his general setting of the social question 'How can society consciously order the lives of its members so as to maintain the largest number of noble and happy human beings?'[1] How much consciousness or calculation can advantageously be brought to bear upon the regulation of the play of the sexual and related instincts and desires, is a highly controversial question into which we need not enter here. But so far as social reform can make good any claim to regulate the growth of the population, its regulation should clearly have re-

[1] *Time and Tide*, par. 123.

gard to quantity as well as quality. A large number of physically sound and happy human beings must be taken as a prime condition of social welfare. It is not easy to defend the prosperity of a people who shall seem to purchase a fuller and even a more spiritually complex life for some or all their members by a continuous reduction of their numbers. Where life is valued and valuable the natural disposition to extend its values as widely as is consistent with their maintenance is a natural instinct difficult to impugn. If it be contended that this is in some sense an admission of the social validity of the tendency to multiply so as to 'press on the means of subsistence,' I might admit the interpretation, provided it were understood that 'means of subsistence' included all the essentials of spiritual as well as of physical life. I do not, however, wish to dogmatise upon a difficult and exceedingly debateable matter, but only to insist that a conscious art of social progress can no more ignore quantity than quality of population in any general calculus of human welfare.

§ 6. The greater equalisation of incomes which would follow from the absorption of unproductive surplus into public income and into remuneration of labour, would be favourable to the two conditions of social progress here laid down, a restriction upon the growth of material consumption and a reasonable regulation of the growth of population. For, as luxury and material waste are seen largely to arise as instruments for the display of individual prowess in competitive industry, the removal of that competition from fields which yield large means for such display would necessarily quench the zest which it exhibits, as well as stop the sources of such extravagant expenditure. For when profuse display of material apparatus is no longer possible, the natural desire for personal distinction, which is the deepest-rooted of all personal desires, will tend more and more to find expression in those arts of refined living which are more truly personal in that they cause the more intellectual and spiritual qualities of personality to shine forth. If, for the quantitative display of material goods, there can gradually be substituted a qualitative display of spiritual goods, this change will be attended by a corresponding change in economic activities. There will be a reduction in the coarser forms of productive energy making large drafts upon the material resources of nature, and an increase of the higher forms of energy whose drafts on these material resources are relatively small.

The proportion of non-material to material wealth will increase, and there will be a corresponding increase in the proportion of productive activities that contain large factors of creative interest. Every enlargement of the scope for free individual expression through economic demand, even for purely material goods, will have a necessary effect in curbing the dominion of machinery and of routine labour. For social arrangements which enable and incite each consumer to seek a more personal satisfaction of his individual needs will force producers to study these individual needs and satisfy them. This cannot be done by mere machine-economy, which rests upon the opposite hypothesis that large numbers of consumers will consent to sink their individual differences of need and taste accepting certain routine forms of goods which do not exactly meet the requirements of any one of them. It is, therefore, reasonable to expect that a more equal and equitable distribution of income will evoke in the masses of population, who now consent to consume common 'routine' goods because they cannot afford to consult their particular tastes and preferences, a more personal and discriminative demand, which will set strict limits upon the machine economy and call for a larger application of individual skill in the various crafts. Or if, valuing more highly as fields for personal expression the less material elements in their standard of living, they still consent to utilise routine industry for the satisfaction of their common physical needs, they will apply an increasing proportion of their interests and their incomes to the acquisition and enjoyment of those goods, artistic, intellectual, emotional, which are more ennobling alike in their production and their consumption.

§ 7. A final word upon population. Is there not reason to believe and hope that this sounder distribution of work and wealth will contribute to a satisfactory solution both of the quantitative and the qualitative population question? If women were no longer forced by economic pressure into marriages for which they had no natural inclination, much unfit parentage and much incompetent nurture would be averted. If they were free to live unmarried, or to choose the father of their children and the size of their family, the normal current of those instincts making for the preservation and instinct of the race, obstructed by artificial barriers of economic circumstances, would be restored to their natural course. If the support of a young family were no longer a heavy and injurious strain upon the economic resources of the parents and their future career a grave anxiety, the human love of children and the attractions of a complete home life would probably check that rapid decline of the birth-rate which to many is one of the darkest features of our present order. It would not, indeed, restore the reckless propagation of former times which imposed on parents, and chiefly upon the mother, a burden injurious in its private incidence and detrimental to society. But while the better economic order would stop compulsory marriages and undesired and therefore undesirable offspring, it would restore the play of the normal philoprogenitive instincts. The net effect would seem to be some retardation of the decline of birth-rate in those types of families where the conditions, physical and psychical, appear favourable to good nature and good nurture for children, and a positive elimination of certain types of union unfavourable to sound offspring. The total effect upon the quantitative issue would of course depend upon the balance between this freer play of the philoprogenitive instinct and the other influences, not directly affected by economic causes, which make for smaller families. But that the quality or character of the population must be improved by the more natural play of the rejective and selective influences here indicated can hardly admit of controversy. Indeed, it may well be urged that the crowning testimony to the validity of the human law of distribution will consist in the higher quality of human life it will evoke by liberating and nourishing the natural art of eugenics in society.

CHAPTER XXII

SOCIAL SCIENCE AND SOCIAL ART

§ 1. The task of a human valuation of industry involved at the outset the arbitrary assumption of a standard of value. That standard consisted in a conception of human well-being applicable to the various forms of human life, man as individual, as group or nation, as humanity. Starting from that conception of the health, physical and spiritual, of the individual human organism, which is of widest acceptance, we proceeded to apply the organic metaphor to the larger groupings, so as to build up an intelligible standard of social well-being. This standard, at once physical and spiritual, static and progressive, was assumed to be of such a kind as to provide a harmony of individual welfares when the growing social nature of man was taken into due account.

With the standard of human well-being we then proceeded to assign values to the productive and the consumptive processes of which industry consists, examining them in their bearing upon the welfare of the individuals and the societies engaging in them.

Now this mode of procedure, the only possible, of course involved an immense *petitio principii*. The assumption of any close agreement as to the nature of individual well-being, still more of social well-being, was logically quite unwarranted.

Economic values have, indeed, an agreed, exact and measurable meaning, derived from the nature of the monetary standard in which they are expressed. Now, no such standard of the human value of economic goods or processes can be established. Yet we pretended to set up a standard of social value and to apply a calculus based upon it, claiming to assess the human worth which underlies the economic costs and utilities that enter into economic values.

Has this procedure proved utterly illicit? I venture to think not. Though at the outset our standard was only a general phrase

committing nobody to anything, the process of concrete application, in testing the actual forms of work and wealth which make
up industry, gave to it a continual increase of meaning. While
the widest divergence would be found in the formal definitions of
such terms as "human welfare" or "social progress," a large and
growing body of agreement would emerge, when a sufficient number of practical issues had been brought up for consideration. The
truth of our standard and the validity of our calculus are established by this working test. It is not wonderful that this should
be so, for the nature and circumstances of mankind have so much
in common, and the processes of civilisation are so powerfully assimilating them, as to furnish a continually increasing community
of experience and feeling. It is, of course, this fund of 'common sense' that constitutes the true criterion. The assumption
that 'common sense' is adequate for a task at once so grave and
delicate may, indeed, appear very disputable. Granting that
human experience has so much in common, can it be claimed that
the reasoning and the feeling based on this experience will be so
congruous and so sound as to furnish any reliable guide for conduct? Surely 'common sense' in its broadest popular sense can
go a very little way towards such a task as a human interpretation of industry.

There is no doubt a good deal of force in this objection. If we
are to invoke 'common sense' for the purposes of an interpretation. or a valuation, it must evidently be what is termed an
'enlightened common sense.' And here at once we are brought
into danger lest enlightenment should not supply what is required, viz., a clearer or more fully conscious mode of common
sense, but a distorted or sophisticated mode. How real this
danger is, especially in the conduct of public affairs, may be recognised from the excessive part played by certain highly conscious and over-vocal interests of the commercial and intellectual classes in the art of government. The most pressing task of
civilisation in the self-governing nations of our time is so to spread
the area of effective enlightenment as to substitute the common
sense of the many for that of the few, and to make it prevail. It
is this common sense, more or less enlightened, that the disinterested statesman takes for the sanction of his reading of the

general will which he endeavours to express in the conduct of public affairs. That it is never at any time a certain, a perfectly coherent, a precise criterion, will be readily admitted. But that it is sufficiently intelligible, sufficiently sound, is the necessary presupposition of all democratic statecraft. And, so far as it is thus serviceable, it supplies a valid standard and a valid calculus of social values. Though the reading of this standard and the application of this calculus will always be subject to some bias of personal idiosyncrasy, the weight of the general judgment commonly prevails in the more important processes of social valuation.

But, in pinning our faith to enlightened common sense for an interpretation or valuation of industry, we must not allow ourselves to be deceived as to the amount of 'scientific accuracy' which attends such a procedure. While this standard can and must supply the rules and measurements which we apply in the processes of detailed analysis and comparison by which we estimate the costs and utilities and the net human values of the various industrial activities and products, we must not put into this standard a stability it does not possess, or into the quantitative methods it uses an authority for social conduct which they are inherently disqualified from yielding.

§ 2. The science and art of society have suffered so much from want of exact and measured information that it is only right and natural for immense importance to be attached to the collection of masses of ordered and measured social facts. If a sufficient number of trained investigators could be set to work to gather, measure, sift and tabulate, the various orders of crude fact relating to the employment, wages, housing, expenditure, health, thrift, education, and other concrete conditions of the poorer grades of town and country dwellers, it seems as if a number of accurate and valid generalisations would emerge by clear induction upon which could be constructed an absolutely scientific treatment of poverty. Or, again, to take a narrower and more distinctively economic issue, that of the shorter working day. If a careful series of observations and experiments could be made in a number of representative businesses, as to the effect upon the size, cost and quality of output produced by given reductions in the hours of labour among various classes of workers, it might appear as if an accurately graded social economy of the working day could be attained by calculations.

But though statesmen, philanthropists and reformers are more and more influenced in their judgments and policies by these measured facts, no safe mechanical rules for the guidance of their conduct in any social problem can be based upon them. The facts and figures which appear so hard and so reliable are often very soft and ineffective tools for the social practitioner. There are several defects in them regarded as instruments of social progress.

It is hardly ever possible to prove causation by means of them. You may obtain the most exact statistics of housing conditions and of death-rates for the population of a group of towns, but you cannot prove to what extent 'back to back' houses affect infant mortality. No figures professing to measure the causal connection between drink and crime or insanity, income and birth-rate, or any other two social phenomena, possess the degree of validity they claim. Why? Because you can never isolate the factors completely in any organic or social problem, and you can never know how far you have failed to isolate them. You may, indeed, by varying the conditions of your experiments or observations sufficiently, obtain practical proof of organic causation, but you can seldom express this causation in terms of any quantitative accuracy. Still more is this true of psychological and social problems. A purely descriptive science of society may attain a considerable degree of quantitative accuracy, but the laws expressing the causal relations of these measured facts will always lack the certainty of operation and the measurability of action belonging to the laws of chemistry and physics.

Now the chief facts with which the statesman and the social reformer are concerned in forming judgments and policies are these laws of causal relation, and not the crude measured facts that constitute the raw material of statistics. This comparative inexactitude or lack of rigidity in the laws of social science constitutes the first difficulty in applying the science to the art of social conduct with the same amount of confidence with which the laws of physics and chemistry are applied to the mechanical arts. But another difficulty quite as grave as this want of rigidity in social facts is the instability of the standard. In all processes of physical measurement it is customary to make allowances for errors due to what is called 'the personal equation,' abnormalities of observation in the experimenter. But the standard of human valuation, the enlightened common sense of a community, applied to interpret social phenomena in terms of 'utility' or 'welfare,' will evidently be subject to much wider variations, and the interpretation of this standard by statesmen, or other individual agents of society, will be subject again to wide errors of personal bias.

Illustrating from the economic sphere which is our concern, that specialisation of industrial life which has made three quarters of our population town-dwellers and is making our nation continually more dependent upon foreign supplies of food, will have a very different value set on it by the narrower nationalism which believes the interests and ambitions of nations to be irreconcilable, and by the wider political outlook which conceives the economic·interdependence of nations as in itself desirable and as the best guarantee of national security. Or again, a difference of view or sentiment regarding the relative worth of the personal qualities of enterprise and self-reliance on the one hand, of plodding industry and sociality upon the other, must materially affect the values given to such phenomena as emigration, public provision against unemployment, copartnership, taxation of high incomes or inheritances. Indeed it is quite manifest that with every difference of the range of sympathy and imagination the meaning which enlightened common sense will give to social welfare, and to every fact submitted to this test, will vary.

These considerations may seem at first sight to invalidate the entire purpose of this book, the endeavour to apply a social calculus for the valuation of industry. So long as the cost and utility of economic material and process is expressed in terms of money, you have a fixed standard capable of yielding exact valuations. Endeavour to resolve this cost and utility into terms of human welfare or desirability, you appear to have adopted a fluctuating standard that can give no serviceable information.

§ 3. The truth, of course, is that a scientific valuation of anything can only proceed by way of quantitative analysis. A standard of valuation which should regard qualitative differences as ultimate would not be scientific at all. It might be æsthetic or hygienic or ethical, according to the nature of the qualitative differences involved. A strictly scientific valuation of wealth, or of cost or of utility, or of life itself, must apply a single standard of measurement to all the various objects it seeks to value, i. e. it must reduce all the different objects to terms of this common denominator. It can measure and value all forms of purchasable goods or services, however various in nature, through the market processes which reduce them to a single monetary equivalent. It can measure and value labour-costs of different sorts, either by a monetary standard or by some measure of fatigue or vital expenditure. It can measure the utility of various sorts of food or of fuel, by comparing the quantities of working-power or output which upon an average they yield. It can ascertain the vital values of different towns and occupations, incomes, races, in terms of longevity, fertility, susceptibility to diseases, etc.

This method, essential to scientific analysis, rests on an assumption that £1 worth of bad books is of the same value as £1 worth of good books. This assumption is true for the purpose to which it is applied, that of a market valuation. It assumes that a year's life of an imbecile or a loafer is worth the same as a year's life of a saint or a genius, and so it is for the purpose of vital statistics.

This is of course universally admitted. Science proceeds by abstraction: it does not pretend to describe or explain the individuality or particular qualities of individual cases, but to discover common attributes of structure or composition or behaviour among numbers of cases, and to explain them in terms of these common characters.

So far, then, as the so-called value of anything, or any happening, consists in its uniqueness or idiosyncrasy, this value necessarily evades scientific analysis. It is only the common properties, the regularities, the conformities, that count for scientific valuation. Nay, more. So far as science takes account of individual qualities, it is in the capacity of eccentricities, i. e. it measures *the amount* of their variation from the average or normal. It cannot entertain the notion that there is any sort of difference which is inherently immeasurable, i. e. that there is difference in kind as well as in degree.[1]

§ 4. A scientific analysis treats all differences as differences of degree. So-called difference of quality or kind it either ignores, or it seeks to reduce them to and express them in differences of quantity. This endeavour to reduce qualitative to quantitative difference is the great stumbling-block in all organic science, but particularly in the departments of psychology and sociology. The difficulty is best illustrated in the recent extension of quantitative analysis into economics by the method of marginal preferences. Not content with the assumption that the particular costs, consumable qualities, etc., of any two articles selling for £1 each may be disregarded, and the single property of their market value abstracted for consideration, the mathematical economists now insist that the study of marginal preferences discloses important laws of the psychology of individuals and societies.

The whole process of expenditure of income appears to be replete with instances of the capacity of the human mind to measure and apply a quantitative comparison to things which seem to be different in kind. It might seem as if my desire to help the starving population of India in a famine, and my desire to attend a Queen's Hall concert this evening were feelings, not merely of different intensity, but of such widely different nature that they could not be accurately measured against each other. And yet this miracle is said to be actually performed, when I decide upon due consideration to divide the 7s 6d in my purse so as to give 5s to the Famine Fund and to buy a 2s 6d ticket for the concert, instead of the more expensive ticket I should have bought had I not been lured to the Famine meeting. I might have given the whole 7s 6d to the Famine Fund, and missed the concert. Why did I not? I must have performed the very delicate spiritual operation of reducing my humanitarian feeling to common terms with my love of music, and to have struck a balance which can only mean that I consider the additional satis-

[1] It was precisely on this rock that J. S. Mill's utilitarianism split. He tried to incorporate in the quantitative calculus of Benthamite pleasure and pain distinctions of the quality or worth of different sorts of pleasure and pain, and failed to furnish any method of reducing them to common terms.

faction I would have got from giving another 2s 6d to the Famine Fund to be a little less than the satisfaction I would get from the concert. But this, of course, is a single crude instance of a far more elaborate process of comparison which underlies the whole expenditure of my income. After the routine expenditure upon necessaries and comforts, which may be said to represent my habitual standard of consumption, has been defrayed, there are various attractive uses to which every other sovereign and shilling may be put. All sorts of different appeals of pleasure, duty, pride, press their claims through a thousand different channels. In order to apportion my expenditure as I do, I must be conceived as reducing all these claims to some common standard of desirability, and deciding how much to lay out on this, how much on that. That physical satisfactions can be compared with one another, by the application of some standard of pleasure may appear intelligible enough. But that a sense of moral duty can be brought into direct comparison with a physical pleasure, or that various duties can be compared in size or strength with one another, would seem almost impossible. Yet this is done incessantly and quickly, if not easily. Even when it is claimed that some duties are so paramount that a good man will refuse to 'weigh' any other claim against them, assigning them a value which, he says, is 'infinite,' the marginal economist will not admit the claim to exemption. 'This only means that to him the total difference between the command of things in the circle of exchange that he already enjoys, and an indefinite, or unlimited command of them, *does not weigh as heavy in his mind* as the dishonour or the discomfort of the specific thing he is required to do. It does not mean that his objection is "infinite." It merely means that it is larger than his estimate of all the satisfaction that he could derive from unlimited command of articles in the circle of exchange, and this is a strictly, perhaps narrowly, limited quantity.'[1]

But though there are men whose honour is so incorruptible as always to 'outweigh' other considerations, the ethics of bribery make it clear that a weaker sense of honour can be measured against material satisfaction, and that is all that seems necessary

[1] Wicksteed, *Common Sense of Political Economy*, p. 405. The italics are mine.

to support the view that such qualitative distinctions can ' be reduced to questions of quantity.' Nor is it merely a matter of the monetary valuation through expenditure of incomes. Precisely the same problem arises in the disposal of one's time or energy. How much shall be given to the performance of this or that personal or family duty, to recreation, or to study? In what proportions shall we combine these activities? If a curtailment of money or of time is necessary, how much shall be taken from this, how much from that employment?

But it is needless to multiply examples. When any scientific valuation is taken, all qualities are abstracted and quantities only are compared and estimated. As in economics, so in ethics. The moral struggle to resist a temptation is nearly always set in scientific psychology as a mechanical problem, for when the ethicist professes to introduce some imponderable 'freedom of the will' he has to throw overboard his science. A 'conflict of duties,' as Mr. Wicksteed recognises, implies that 'duty itself is a quantitative conception.' [1]

§ 5. Similarly with the scientific politician who seeks to make full use of quantitative analysis. He too is compelled to visualise and represent the psychological operation through which a political judgment is reached as a mechanical one, conceived in terms of size, weight, strain or intensity. In his *Human Nature in Politics* Mr. Graham Wallas gives a very interesting example of the scientific valuation of a process of political thinking, viz. the process by which Mr. Gladstone, in the autumn and winter of 1885–6, must be conceived to have arrived at his Home Rule policy, ' thinking incessantly about the matter' and 'preparing myself by study and reflection.'

After describing, with the aid of Lord Morley's *Life*, the various studies and courses of reflection employed, the 'calculations' of the state of feeling in England and Ireland, the examination of various types of federation, as found in past and current history, the statistical reports upon finance, law and other concrete issues, considerations of the time and opportunity, the play of the emotional valuations, 'the irresistible attraction for him of all the grand and external commonplaces of liberty and

[1] P. 409.

self-government,' Mr. Wallas sees the results of all this acquisition of knowledge and reflection gathering and being coördinated into a problem in which the factors are quantities and the solution 'a quantitative solution,' 'a delicate adjustment between many varying forces.'[1] 'A large part of this work of complex coördination was apparently in Mr. Gladstone's case unconscious,' an operation he declares, 'rather of art than of science.' Now, since 'the history of human progress consists in the gradual and partial substitution of science for art,' it is desirable to bring out with clearer consciousness, and fortify with greater accuracy of knowledge, the processes of political thinking. 'Quantitative method must spread in politics and must transform the vocabulary and the associations of that mental world into which the young politician enters. Fortunately, such a change seems at least to be beginning. Every year larger and more exact collections of detached political facts are being accumulated; and collections of detached facts, if they are to be used at all in political reasoning, must be used quantitatively.'[2] Since the problems of political conduct are thus essentially quantitative, they can, in theory at any rate, be 'solved' by science. 'The final decisions which will be taken either by the Commons—or by Parliament in questions of administrative policy and electoral machinery must therefore *involve* the balancing of all these and many more considerations by an essentially quantitative process.[3]

§ 6. Now how far is it true that any political problem is essentially quantitative and soluble by a quantitative process? It is of course to be admitted at once that the science of statistics will feed a statesman's mind with a variety of ordered and measured facts. But will this mind, working either scientifically or artistically, consciously or subconsciously, go through a distinctively mechanical process of balancing and measuring and register a quantitative judgment? A scientific setting of the process must indeed so present it. But, then, a scientific setting of any process whatsoever sets it thus in purely quantitative form. The real issue is how far this scientific setting is competent to interpret and explain the facts, and to deliver a judgment

[1] P. 153.   [2] P. 156.   [3] P. 159. The italics are mine.

which shall be authoritative for the conduct of an individual or a society.

In order to test the scientific claim let us take what seems to be a very different sort of action from that of the politician or the business man, that of the artist. Follow the mind of the painter as he plies his art. Each of his operations too *involves* considerations of quantity and measurement, scope and focus, adjustment, coördination, balance, the application of definite blends of colours: optics, anatomy, and other sciences feed his mind with exact knowledge. A delicate adjustment of quantities in line and colour is *involved* in every part of his artistic operations. But does the operation consist of these quantitative arrangements and can it be understood or 'appreciated' by analysing them? Evidently not. Why not? Because in such an analysis or explanation the essentially qualitative or creative action of the artist, which gives unity and artistic value to the whole operation, escapes notice. Science kills in order to dissect. So in the case of every other art. A poem *involves* certain ordered arrangements of sound which may be expressed in quantitative terms of rhythm and prosody. But any attempt to 'resolve' it into these forms loses its spirit, its unity, its value as a poem. Students of the drama have sometimes explained or interpreted a tragedy of Sophocles or Shakespeare in terms of the gradation of intensity of the various emotions involved, the length of pauses of suspense, the balancing, relief and interlacing of the plots or episodes, the relative strength or height of the climaxes and subclimaxes, the growing rapidity of movement towards the catastrophe. But can it be pretended that this 'mechanics' of the drama can furnish a standard of appreciation, or supply laws according to which a 'good' drama may be constructed or appreciated? No. An artistic operation is essentially organic, creative and qualitative. None of these characters can really be reduced to quantity. Science by quantitative analysis can only deal with the skeleton not with the life that informs it.

I think this eternal inability of science adequately to interpret value, or explain a work of art, will be generally admitted. It is due to the fact that this work and its value are inherently incapable of being reduced to quantities. The difference between one picture and another, one poem and another is a difference of quality. It is of course true that by a merely linguistic necessity we often speak of a picture as being 'much' finer than another, and compare the 'greatness' of one poet with that of another. But we are aware all the time that we are really comparing unlikes, dealing with qualitative differences. On no other supposition indeed can we understand the valuation set upon a work of genius as compared with one of talent.

> "Oh the little more, how much it is,
> And the little less what worlds away."

What then do economists mean when they insist that qualitative differences, the desires and satisfactions which have such widely diverse origins and natures, can be weighed and measured against one another, and that problems of industry are essentially and ultimately quantitative? Our examination of artistic activities has shown that in each case quantities are involved, but that in no case do quantities constitute the problem of action. But how, it may be said, do you dispose of the admitted facts that by means of monetary valuations these diverse desires and satisfactions are reduced to a common standard, are compared, and that a course of conduct is apparently based upon these quantitative considerations?

The answer is that this is an entirely illusory account of the psychical process by which a man lays out his money, or his time, or his energy. He does not take the several uses to which he might apply the means at his disposal, reduce them, in thought or in feeling, to some common term, and so measure the amount he will expend upon each object that the 'marginal' or 'final' portion of each use shall be exactly equal in the utility it yields. The 'marginalist' [1] is correct in saying that the utility imputed to the last sovereign I expend on bread during the year must be

---

[1] This older doctrine of marginalism, concerned with the comparison of marginal utilities, or marginal costs, in the application of expenditure of productive energy, must not be confused with the novel doctrine which we discussed in Chapter XI in relation to wages. In the newer doctrine any unit of a supply may be regarded as the marginal unit and every unit as equally productive or useful. According to the older doctrine each unit has a different cost or utility.

considered to be neither greater nor less than that imputed to the last sovereign's worth of tobacco, or books, holiday or charitable subscriptions.   In precisely the same sense it is true that the last brushful of green and brown and Turkey red expended on a picture has the same art-value to the painter.

Perhaps the issue can be made clearer by reference to an art usually considered less 'fine' and more closely affected by quantitative considerations than painting, the culinary art. The composition of a dish is here expressed in proportions of its various ingredients, so much flour, so many ounces of raisins, so many eggs, so much sugar, etc. The marginalist would dwell upon the crucial fact that the last pennyworth of the flour, raisins, eggs and sugar, taken severally, had an equal value for the pudding, and that these marginal or final increments were in some way causal determinants of the composition of the pudding, because in using the ingredients the cook took care to use just so much of each, and neither more nor less. And it is quite true that the delicacy of the culinary art will in fact be displayed in deciding whether to put in another handful of raisins, another egg, or a spoonful more sugar. But, from the standpoint of trying to appreciate the virtue or worth of the dish as a culinary creation, it cannot be admitted that any special importance or causal determination attaches to the last increments of the several ingredients. For it is evident that the 'how much' and therefore the 'margin' of each ingredient is itself determined by the conception of the *tout ensemble* in the mind of the creator or inventor.

And this evidently applies to every form of composition embodying some unity of design or purpose, whether the treatment of a subject in pictorial or dramatic art, the making of a new dish, the construction of a machine, the arrangement of a business, or the laying out of a garden or a fortune. So far as an economical use is made of materials or means of any kind for the attainment of any end this marginal equivalence is *implied*. The scientific analysis of any composite arrangement, mechanical, organic, conscious, *involves* this marginal assumption. It is an axiom of all 'economy' whatsoever.

But it explains nothing. Nay, in dealing with any organic being on any plane of action, it darkens counsel. It does so in several ways. First by assuming or asserting that the human mind can and does get rid of qualitative differences by referring them to a quantitative standard: secondly, by assuming or asserting that organic unity can be broken up into its constituent parts and explained in terms of these measured parts; thirdly, by assuming or asserting a uniformity of nature which conflicts with the 'novelties' in which creative energy expresses itself. All these fallacies are just as much involved in the attempt to explain the expenditure of an income as a purely quantitative problem, as in the attempt to explain the art-value of a picture in terms of the respective quantities of line and colour. In each case the root-fallacy is the same, the illicit substitution of the abstract 'quantity' for the actual stuff, which is always qualitative and is never identical in any two cases, or at any two times.

§ 7. In laying out my income, I do not in fact compare all my several needs or tastes, and having assigned so much utility or desirability to each, plan my expenditure so as to spend on each just as much as it is worth, equalising all expenditure at the margins so as to maximise the aggregate. Even Benjamin Franklin or Samuel Smiles would not really do this, though they might think they did, and perhaps draw up schedules to enforce the notion. So far as I act like a free, rational being, not a creature of blind custom or routine, I employ all my personal resources of knowledge, taste, affection, energy, time, and command of material resources, in trying to realise my ideal of a good or desirable life. In the execution of this design, however it be regarded, self-realisation or career, I utilise my various resources in a manner strictly analogous to that in which the artist employs the materials and instruments of his art. Upon the canvas of time I paint myself, using all the means at my disposal to realise my ideal. Among these means is my money income. Its expenditure goes into the execution of my design. So far as I am justified in separating my expenditure of money from the expenditure of my time and other resources, and in regarding the design as an 'economic picture,' I can readily perceive that the unity of my artistic purpose involves and determines the expenditure of my income in definite proportions upon the various objects whose 'consumption' contributes to the design. But these proportions are not determined by a calculation of the separate values of the various items. For, strictly speaking, they have no separate value, any more than have the lines or colours in a picture. Only by consideration of what we may term indifferently the artistic or organic purpose of the whole can a true appreciation or valuation be attained. The full absurdity of suggesting that anything is learned, either in the way of valuation or of guidance, by the quantitative analysis, or the wonderful discovery of equivalence of value at the margins, will now be apparent. This mathematical analysis can do no more towards explaining the expenditure of income than explaining the expenditure of paint. Of course, the expenditure at the margins appears to produce an equal utility: that truth is obviously contained in the very logic of the quantitative analysis. But that quantitative analysis, necessarily ignoring, as it does, the qualitative character which the organic unity of the whole confers upon its parts, fails to perform the psychological interpretation claimed for it.

So far as it is true that the last sovereign of my expenditure in bread equals in utility the last sovereign of my expenditure in books, that fact proceeds not from a comparison, conscious or unconscious, of these separate items at this margin, but from the parts assigned respectively to bread and books in the organic plan of my life. Quantitative analysis, inherently incapable of comprehending qualitative unity or qualitative differences, can only pretend to reduce the latter to quantitative differences. What it actually does is to ignore alike the unity of the whole and the qualitativeness of the parts.

Nor is this all. It is not even true that an application of quantitative analysis does find exact equivalence of values at the margins. Taking a concrete instance, it is not true that the last sovereign of my expenditure in books equals, or even tends exactly to equal, in utility, that of my last sovereign's expenditure on bread. This would be the case if the future tended precisely to repeat the past. In that event my experience of the economy of last year's expenditure would progressively correct any errors, and I should come to employ my resources with greater economy or exactitude to the attainment of the same design. But I am not the same this year as last, my environment is not the same, my resources are not the same, and the plan of life I make will not be the same. This awkward factor of Novelty, involved in organic nature, belongs to every creative art, being indeed of the very essence alike of art and of creation, and impairs to an incalculable extent the quantitative calculus and its marginal interpretation. An addition of £100 to my income this year cannot be laid out by calculation so as to increase each sort of expenditure to an extent which will secure marginal equivalence of utility. That is to say, I cannot tell what will be the best employment of my larger income, until I have tried. The larger income will produce nowhere a strictly proportionate increase of expenditure on a number of several objects. It would shift my economic plan of life, making a new kind of life, and involving all sorts of changes in the items, which follow as consequences from the changed organic plan. This new plan I cannot accurately calculate or forecast. It will work itself out as I proceed. Its execution involves no doubt elements of forethought and even calculation, but the central and essential change will proceed from some novelty of conception, some qualitative change of purpose. In a word, it is the creative power of man, the artist, that is ever at work, and the art faculties of inspiration, faith and adventure will lead him to experiment anew with his resources. As a man gains more intelligence, undergoes some new critical experience of his outer or his inner life, encounters some new personal influence, his entire mode of living will change, and innumerable alterations in the outlay of his income will take place. Some articles of earlier expenditure will disappear, new articles will take their place, and the respective importance of many articles remaining in the expenditure will be shifted. A change of residence from country to town, a 'conversion,' religious or dietetic, a transfer from an outdoor manual to an indoor sedentary employment, marriage, or any other critical event, must bring about some such large complex organic alteration. A comparison of the items of expenditure before and after will shed interesting light upon the results of the psycho-economic change of which they afford a quantitative register, but it cannot be regarded as an explanation of the change of heart or of outlook which is the determinant act from which these shifts of values flow.

§ 8. The life of a society presents this same problem on a larger scale. On the plane of economic conduct which directly concerns us, every one of the innumerable and incessant alterations in methods of production and consumption ranks as an organic novelty, and, in so far as it is novel, necessarily baffles quantitative analysis and scientific prediction. It would, of course, be incorrect, either in the case of an individual or of a society, to represent any change as entirely novel. Organic growth itself is largely a quantitative conception: the changes are proportionate in size to former changes, and are in definite quantitative relations to one another. The doctrine of continuity thus enables us to go far in calculating the character of future changes. So far the scientific interpretation of uniformity of nature carries us. But quantitative growth, or any other set of quantitative changes, however calculable, always carries some qualitative and essentially incalculable elements of change. These are what we signify by novelty. It is their occurrence in evolution that baffles the clean logic of the geologist, still more of the biologist, and far more of the psychologist. Whether they show themselves as 'faults' or 'sports' or 'mutations,' they represent the disability of past experience to furnish 'laws' for their calculation, and the practical importance which attaches to these incalculable or qualitative changes is very considerable. Though they may be comparatively infrequent and may appear on first inspection almost negligible breaks in the otherwise calculable continuity of the evolutionary process, their determinant importance is receiving ever greater recognition. In human conduct, individual or social, these mutations seem to play a larger part, chiefly by reason of the operation of the so-called 'freedom' of the human will. For whatever philosophic view be held regarding the determination of the acts of the will, its operation scatters mutations thickly over the realm of human conduct. Hence it remains true that science can do so much less in explaining and predicting human history than in any other department of nature. No doubt here, as elsewhere, science hopes to apply quantitative analysis of such increasing accuracy as to enable it to determine and predict a larger number of such mutations. Since there doubtless exist quantitative conditions for every qualitative change, it may seem theoretically possible for science some day to catch up with 'the art of creation.' This supposition, however, assumes that the number of permutations and combinations in 'nature' is limited, and that, therefore, in some extensive run history does repeat itself. The final victory of science thus seems to depend upon the adoption of a cyclical view of the history of the universe. But, for all present practical purposes of social processes, science is so far removed from this perfection that the economist and the sociologist are continually compelled to allow for unpredictable changes of such frequency and of such determinant importance that their claim to direct 'the general will' and to mould the conscious policy of a society must be very modestly expressed.

Such laws of causation as they derive from past observation and experiment must usually be conceived as laws of tendencies, seldom endowed with any rigorous authority of close determination, and still more seldom with accuracy of quantitative prediction.

§ 9. It is sometimes supposed that this hampering effect of the uniqueness, irregularity, novelty and freedom of the individual and social organisms can be got rid of by a process of multiplication in which particular eccentricities will cancel. To economists, in particular, there is a strong temptation to fall back upon the average man, in the belief that scientific determinism justifies itself through averages. Now the radical defect of measurement by averages, as a mode of social valuation, has already been disclosed. The ascertained fact that the average money income, or even the average real income, of the British people may have risen 10% within the last decade, disables itself, *by the very process of averaging*, from informing us as to the effect of this increase of national wealth upon national welfare. For this effect depends upon the distribution of the increase, and the process of averaging consists in ignoring this vital fact of distribution.

This defect of averages for purposes of interpretation, of course, involves a consequent defect for purposes of guidance in economic conduct. The calculation that a given course of national conduct, e. g., the expenditure of so many millions upon improved transport, will raise the national or average income by so much, loses all the worth of its superficial exactitude unless we know how much of the increase is going to the landlord in rising rent, how much to the labourer in rising wages.

This, of course, involves no repudiation of the true utility of averages, but only of the spurious accuracy which their forms suggest. The exact statement that the average income of an English family has risen 10% in the last decade does imply a reasonable probability that an increase of total national welfare has taken place.[1] But it gives no information as to the amount of that increase, and is consistent with the fact that there may have been a decrease, owing to a worsening of the distribution of the growing income, or of the labour and other costs involved in its production.

§ 10. So far upon the supposition that welfare is a quantity. It will occur to statisticians that the information to be got from averages of income may be justified by nicer discrimination. If, in addition to learning that the average income of all families has risen 10%, we discovered the different percentages which had been added to rent, interest, profits and wages, or, better still, the ratio of increase for the different income levels, we should surely then, by this extended use of averages, get nearer towards a quantitative estimate of the increase of welfare that had been achieved!

This must certainly be admitted. By the nicer and more complex application of these measures, we should approach a more accurate account of welfare, so far as it is ultimately expressible in terms of quantity. If we discovered that a proposed course of national policy would not only increase the average income by 10% but would increase the lower incomes of the population in a higher ratio, we should seem to have got a scientific warrant for the policy. But even this degree of scientific authority would be purchased to some extent by an artificial simplification of the actual problem of social-economy. To the statesman no problem of actual finance is capable of being set in such distinctively quantitative terms. Not merely cannot an earthly Chancellor of the Exchequer know how much can be added to the incomes

---

[1] Professor Pigou in his *Wealth and Welfare* discusses with skill and precision the measurable influences of an increase of the general dividend upon general welfare, but omits to take into consideration the 'cost' factors which enter into 'welfare,' however that term be defined.

of the several classes by the expenditure of so many millions upon transport, or upon any other single service, but, if he could, he would not be much nearer to the standard he requires. There are many different ways of raising the revenue in question and an infinite number of combinations of these ways. The same holds of expenditure. To take the simplest case; the ten millions that he raises may be applied to transport, or to education, or to defence, all the sum or any proportion, to each. Each expenditure claims to be beneficial, an outlay for public welfare. But the benefit in the several outlays is not equally presentable in terms of money income, and, so far as definitely economic gains accrue, they are not equally immediate or equally assured. It is evident that no amount of possession of statistical knowledge can possibly reduce the problem entirely, or even mainly, to one of quantitative calculation. It is equally true that when the problem is solved, its solution will appear in quantitative shape, i. e. so much money for transport, so much for education, so much for defence. It will seem to have been worked out by reducing the three forms of desired benefits to common terms, and then dividing the ten millions among them so as to secure an equivalence of gains at the margins. Economists will point out triumphantly the alleged fact that the last £100 spent on education produces a national return of welfare exactly equal to that obtained by the last £100 spent on gunboats, though his assertion remains inherently insusceptible of proof. In truth, the Chancellor's mind does not work in this way. So far as his statecraft is disinterested, or even allowing for every form of bias, his mind forms an ideal of social progress, of a happier or better state of things, and allots the outlay of his ten millions in an endeavour to assist in realising this ideal. Now the ideal itself is not chiefly a product of quantitative calculus, but of his more or less informed imagination, and his more or less wholesome sympathies. His views as to the means of realising this ideal can never be purely scientific, though science may here be of considerable assistance.

If, treating expenditure more widely as an act of public policy, we consider it as an operation of the general will of the community, a true act of political economy, the problem remains essentially the same. When looked at through scientific spectacles, it is a purely quantitative and mechanically ordered act, because the scientific method by its very *modus operandi* ignores the qualitative factors. So the nation is supposed to balance this gain against another, and to lay out its revenue so as to get the largest aggregate of some common homogeneous stuff called 'welfare', in such a way that the last £100 spent on education is equivalent in its yield of this 'welfare' to the last £100 spent on the latest super-dreadnaught, or the last lot of old-age pensions. In truth, the common will no more functions in this fashion than the personal will of the Chancellor. In each case Statecraft is an Art, and the financial policy is an artistic or creative work in which quantities are used but do not direct or dominate.

By this line of argument it may appear as if we had repudiated the entire utility of a scientific calculus. This, however, is not the case. For though all the determinant acts of policy or welfare, performed by an individual or a society, involve organic unity of design, and the qualitative considerations appertaining thereto, important and indeed necessary assistance is rendered by the quantitative analysis of past acts expressed in the form of scientific generalisations. A clearer understanding of the nature and extent of this coöperation between science and art in the conduct of life enforces this truth.

§ 11. Science takes its stand upon a twofold application of the assumption of the uniformity of Nature, first, that all differences of composition can be treated as differences of quantity or degree, secondly, that history repeats itself. Now, just so far as these assumptions fit the facts, Science is valid for interpretation and for guidance. This explains why astronomy, physics and chemistry are more 'exact' sciences than biology or psychology, and why they are able to give more reliable and authoritative rules for the arts of navigation, engineering and drug-making, than the latter can for medicine, for breeding or for education. Edward Carpenter has remarked that astronomy is the most exact of the applied sciences, because we know least about it, i. e. because we treat its subject-matter almost entirely from the single quantitative standpoint of space relations. In all arts dealing entirely or mainly with inorganic matter science occupies a seat of high authority, because of the high relative uniformity of this matter and the comparative regularity of its behaviour. In physics or in inorganic chemistry the individual differences or eccentricities of the material are so trivial that they can usually be disregarded, and history repeats itself with so much regularity that quantitative laws apply.

The passage from the inorganic to the organic involves, as we recognise, a double assertion of the qualitative: first, in respect of the unity and uniqueness of the organic structure, and secondly, by reason of the novelty that attends each act of organic change, vital movement, assimilation, growth, reproduction or decay. The uniqueness of the individual organism and the novelty of each of its changes are an assertion of the qualitative nature of the subject-matter. So far as this qualitative nature prevails and counts for 'conduct,' scientific analysis is impotent for interpretation and advice. When organic matter attains the character of consciousness and the still higher character of self-consciousness, the qualitative considerations reach a maximum, and the interpretation and directive power of science a minimum. But that minimum must not be disparaged. It is not inconsiderable. The assistance which scientific laws can render to the finest arts of human conduct is very important and is capable of constant augmentation. For so far as human nature is uniform and stable among the units which constitute the life whose conduct and welfare are in question, the interpretation and direction of science has validity. To this extent a utilitarian calculus, based upon analysis of past experience, can aid the statesman or the philanthropist in working out his design. In the region of industry the extent of this scientific service will be even greater than in the arts of conduct whose material is more exclusively organic or psychical. For industry, considered as an art of human welfare, will consist largely in the orderly and progressive adaptation of inorganic matter, or of organic matter whose organic differences can be ignored, to the satisfaction of those needs of mankind in which men are similar. That is to say, in industry there exists and will remain a great deal of work and of consumption which is essentially of a uniform or routine character, requiring to be done by measured rules, and depending for its utility upon the exclusion of all individuality or quality. This applies, not only to those industrial processes which we term strictly mechanical, but to a great many others where quality is a matter of comparative indifference. In the progressive economy of human welfare mechanical or routine production will even frequently displace an art in which quality was once displayed. So home-baking, into which no small degree of culinary skill could go, has given way to machine-baking in which the element of personal skill plays a diminished part, and on which the individual taste of the consumer exerts little directive influence. This may be taken as a typical example of the displacement of qualitative art by quantitative mechanism. It is, of course, of very wide extension, being, in fact, commensurate with the application of scientific methods in the world of industry. Indeed, the sciences of chemistry and physics, botany and biology, are everywhere invading the 'arts' of industry and imposing 'rules' upon industrial processes. Even more significant is the application of the still infantile science of psychology to the arts of business organisation and enterprise and of marketing. How can psychology assist in the delicate art of recommending goods to possible purchasers? Only on the supposition that there is sufficient uniformity and stability in human nature to enable the measured rules of past experiment upon other men to hold of this man. Only so far as men are really the same sort of stuff, or so far as any differences are measurable and calculable. Novelty alone can baffle applied science.

If it were true, as some appear to think, that machinery and routine method were destined continually to absorb a larger and larger proportion of human work, and to direct a larger and larger share of human life, economic science with its quantitative calculus would acquire a continual increase of exactitude, and a growing capacity for direction in the art of social conduct. But if, as seems more reasonable, progressive industry must serve to feed a richer liberty and novelty of individual and social life, the domain of quantitative calculus, though absolutely enlarging, may be relatively shrinking.

We now seem able to get a more accurate understanding of what a scientific calculus can do for the assistance of the art of social welfare. It can do for that art what it can do for every other art, viz. furnish rules for the regular. So far as the stuff which constitutes or composes human welfare is uniform, i. e. so far as men are alike in their needs, and the material for the satisfaction of these needs is similar, it can supply rules of social economy which will have a high degree of validity. Though no two human organisms are identical in structure, all human organisms within a wide range of environment are so similar in the kinds of food, air and other material goods which they require, that it is sound 'social policy' to ignore their differences and to treat them as identical in the qualities of their demands and dissimilar only in the quantities. The practical economy of 'markets' stands upon this basis, and the quantitative treatment finds its true justification in the utility of markets. There can be no market for the single or 'singular' consumer. A market, i. e. a practical instrument for measurement of economic wants, implies a standardisation of the desires of buyers and sellers. Just so far as the members of an economic community are thus standardised in their preferences, are economic laws applicable. Thus, for the scientific interpretation of such a community, much depends upon the relative strength and importance of the standardising and the individualising forces. In a society where the so-called 'arts' of industry and of consumption have alike passed by imitation or tradition into firm conventions from which the least transgression is branded as an impiety or a wickedness, economic laws, based upon a sufficient study of the past and present, will enable one to predict the future with considerable accuracy. Primitive or backward communities are usually in this conservative condition. Moreover, as they advance and become economically progressive, it is observable that the most conservative and most calculable wants and activities are those relating to the satisfaction of the primary material needs. Hence it is evident that scientific predictions, based either upon general considerations of human nature or upon past measurements, will come nearest to fulfilment, according as they relate to the production and consumption of those articles most deeply embedded in the standard of living. Conveniences and comforts are more changeable than necessaries, and luxuries most changeable of all. Now the marginal or least useful portion of those supplies, which in the earlier or most useful increments satisfy some prime need, are often luxuries. The marginal portion of the wheat supply goes for cakes, or is thrown into the dust-bin as waste bread: the marginal oil goes into motor rides. Taking expenditure in general, we find the last ten per cent of every income most incalculable in its outlay, because it represents those purchases in which custom is weakest and individual taste or opportunity the strongest. In a word, it is precisely in those economic actions which express marginal preferences, the pivot of the mechanical calculus, that we find the maximum of instability and incalculability. For each of these nice marginal preferences proceeds directly from the changing nature of the organic personality. Whereas fifty per cent of a man's expenditure may express the common satisfaction of the fixed physical needs which custom has embedded in a standard of subsistence, thirty per cent the lighter but fairly stable comforts belonging to his class, the last twenty per cent is the part in which he expresses his individual character and his cravings for personal distinction and variety of enjoyment.

The formal invalidity of the 'marginalist' method has already been disclosed. The considerations just adduced indicate its practical futility as a means of guidance for economic art. Neither as a deductive nor as an inductive science can Economics furnish accurate rules for calculating or directing future economic events. It can only prophesy within such limits as are set by the assumptions of the stability of human nature and of its environment. Its rules or 'laws' will best interpret and predict those economic actions which are most remote from the margin, i. e. those which are most conservative or regular. Marginal preferences will therefore be precisely those which it is precluded from interpreting or predicting by the necessary defect of the intellectual instrument.

§ 12. Thus the final futility of the mechanical method of marginalism lies in its insistence upon applying a quantitative method of interpretation to the most qualitative portion of the subject-matter, that portion where the organic conditions of **personality** and novelty are of paramount significance.

Indeed, it is for this reason that economic science, though able to supply relevant and important evidence, can never solve conclusively any social-economic problem, even in that field of action where her authority is most strongly asserted. A given rise or fall of price can never produce the same effect upon demand twice running. Why? Because the desires and beliefs of the more unsettled section of buyers, the 'marginal' buyers, will have changed. Nor can this alteration in effect upon demand be calculated. Why not? Because the changes in desires and beliefs are organic qualitative changes. Observations of past price-movements and laws based upon them are not thereby rendered useless. For these organic changes will often be negligible so far as the bulk of the market is concerned. But they negate the possibilities of exact prediction, and often of approximate predictions on the margin.

This is why the 'great' business man often prefers to act by intuition than by express calculation. He recognises that, so far as the more delicate judgments are concerned, his 'feeling' of 'how things will go' is more trustworthy than any estimate. He does not act blindly. He feeds and fortifies his mind with facts and figures, until he is steeped in familiarity with the subject-matter. But he does not deliberately balance against one another these measured forces and commit himself to the resultant. For he is aware that the problem is not one of mere mechanics, a counting-house proposition, but one involving for its solution sympathy and imagination.

But the crucial instance of the organic and spiritual nature of a distinctly economic problem is in the case of credit. The mathematical mechanical treatment claims to find its supreme justification in the part played by money, the most abstract of economic phenomena. Credit, in its objective sense, is the economic plenipotentiary, the absolute representative of economic power. For he who has credit has the command of land, capital, labour, ability of every sort, at any time and in any place. Credit *is* productive power and purchasing power, for he who possesses it can convert it into any sort of supply or demand he chooses. It is absolutely quantitative, fluid, divisible and measurable. Such is credit, treated objectively by economic science. But credit

is also the heart and brains of the industrial system. Subjec-
tively regarded, it is an essentially spiritual thing, a delicate,
sensitive creature of human beliefs and desires. Its volume and
its power for practical work are affected by this spiritual nature.
For its springs are fear, hope, prestige, superstition, sympathy
and understanding. Its true basis is neither gold, nor goods,
but credibility. And that quality of credibility is fluctuating
all the time for every individual, every business, every state.
New unpredictable events are constantly affecting it. No one
can therefore say with any assurance of correctness "a Bank
should keep 20% of its resources in reserve or at call," or put
any such rigid limit for the operations of any Bank. If we do
set any such quantitative limit, we should realise that it is only a
rough practical rule, which, if interpreted with automatic rigour,
leads to waste and error in the actual working of finance. For by
no plotting of curves can you reckon the future flow of human
credibility, or the application of a given amount of concrete
credit to the ever-changing gains and risks of human industry.
Take the critical case of a collapse of credit and the run upon a
Bank. To predict with even approximate accuracy the course of
such a run, or to check it by calculations, based upon past experience of similar crises applied to the records of present assets and
liabilities, would be impossible. Why? Chiefly because of the
psycho-physical factors, the play of organic forces. You can
calculate with close exactitude the strain imposed upon a bridge
of a given size, material and structure by a given weight, distribution and pace of traffic. You cannot calculate with equal
exactitude the strain which a given quantity of liabilities, however carefully analysed and graded, will impose upon a Bank reserve of a given size.

The incalculable element consists of organic novelty, the
changes due to having to deal with matter not dead and homogeneous but living and organised. The citation of such instances
is not designed to prove that monetary and other statistics are
practically useless for the prediction and solution of social-
economic problems. On the contrary, they are exceedingly useful. But the formal exactitude which they carry in their method
can never be conveyed into the work they are required to assist

in doing. The most abundant supply of the most accurate statistics, utilised by the most approved methods of economic science, can only afford results of a rude approximate validity, expressed in tendencies. The practical man in business, in politics, in every mode of social conduct, will supplement and correct the application of the scientific rule by the play of private judgment and intuition.

* * *

§ 13. If this is true as regards all predictions of future economic happenings, it is still more true of the conscious purposive guidance of these happenings by the application of a human standard of values. The practical statesman or social reformer, confronted with a concrete social problem, e. g. the demand for a state enforcement of a national minimum of wages, local option for the closure of public houses, or a referendum for constitutional changes, will find himself 'paying attention' and 'giving weight' to a number of diverse and opposing considerations. How will the selection and the 'weighing' of these considerations be brought about? Not directly and consciously by the application of what may be termed his social ideal, the image in his soul of the society which seems to him absolutely the most desirable. The relation of that ultimate ideal to the particular scheme under consideration, e. g. a national minimum wage, may be too distant and too dubious to afford valuation and direction. The operative ideal will be derivative, one of a related set of possible-desirables, limited and practicable ideals which form the most potent instruments of his statecraft. Such an operative ideal for an Englishman at the present time might be the vision of the State, as the collective will, securing by law a clearly conceived standard of sound efficient life for the ordinary working-class family. This present practical ideal, derived from a wider conception of the duty of the State in relation to the individual members of a civilised society, would itself be a far wider scheme than the particular proposal, that of national minimum wage, which it was invoked to assess. The statesman, enlightened by this derivative ideal, would apply it as a test and standard to the particular proposal. He would consider it, not merely 'upon its own merits' but as incorporated in the more complex organic plan of his national minimum. This organic plan and purpose would determine the 'value' he gave to the various 'pros' and 'cons,' as for instance to the consideration how far legal intervention might weaken the private organisation of workmen in their trade-unions, so damaging other benefits of trade-unionism, or the consideration how far it was better to wait and secure a more democratically administered State before entrusting it with the delicate function of adjusting pecuniary arrangements between workmen and employers. This plan or purpose of a national minimum, as a possible desirable, will of course not remain quite stable in his mind, will not be a rigid standard. It will change somewhat in pattern, and in definiteness of outline, as some fresh outer or inner experience makes any part of it, or the whole, seem more or less desirable, or more or less possible, than formerly.

§ 14. But the important point to note is that it is this larger organic plan or vision, the character and changes of which are essentially qualitative, that furnishes the standard and stamps with their respective 'values' the various considerations which are said to 'determine' the practical value of the proposal and its acceptance or rejection. No social-economic proposal, however distinctively quantitative it appears, can be humanly valued in any other way. It is for this reason that a mere economist is always disabled from giving practical advice in any course of conduct. Take two examples. Political economy can legitimately apply laws of value so as to show that, under competitive conditions, a nation must produce a larger quantity of marketable goods under a policy of free imports than under any sort of Tariff. But that proof in itself can never be sufficient ground for rejecting either a Tariff for revenue, or even a Tariff for protection. For the Statesman can never take the maximum of marketable values as his final and sufficient test. If it could be shown that national security were involved in a protective system which kept all necessary industries within the national limits, he might plead 'defence is more than opulence.' Or, if it could be shown that a protective tariff could be operated so as to distribute a slightly reduced aggregate of wealth in a manner more conducive to the popular welfare and that this consideration was not offset by fear of corruption or of impaired industrial efficiency, or other disadvantages, the Statesman might rightly adopt a Tariff in the teeth of 'economic laws.' [1]

Or, take another example, the proposal for an eight hours day, secured by law. A purely economic enquiry might, by considering the elasticity of labour in various employments, arrive at the conclusion that a general shortening of the work-day would involve a present reduction of the product by so much percentage in different trades, and that it might involve a reduction of profits and of wages and a probable loss of so much export trade in various industries. It might even present some tentative estimates as to the effects of the pressure of this new cost of production in stimulating improved economies in mines, factories or railways. Such information would be useful and relevant, but not authoritative upon the judgment of the Statesman. For the social value of a shorter work-day would depend mainly upon the organic reactions of increased leisure upon the whole standard of life of the working family, how it affected his expenditure of his wages, its effect upon his health, education and recreations, the cultivation of family affection, the better performance of neighbourly and civic duties, and all that is involved in more liberty and a larger outlook upon life. It is evident, in the first place, that these essential considerations lie outside the calculations of the economist, and, secondly, that the actual value set on each of them will depend upon and be derived from the whole faith and social vision of the statesman in question.

This social or human valuation of a so-called economic process or good, involves then two departures from a quantitative calculus; first, the reduction of the particular economic factors themselves from financial or other quantitative terms to vital or subjective terms; secondly, the restoration of this artificially severed economic process to the larger integrated process of human life from which it was abstracted by the scientific specialism of the economist. The economist can find the facts, but he cannot find their human importance or value, because assigning human value

[1] Protectionists can seldom, if ever, plead successfully either of these cases. By reducing the community of economic interests between nations Protection normally increases the chances of war, while lessening the national resources which are the sinews of war. So, likewise, its normal tendency is to worsen the distribution of wealth within the nation.

means referring to an extra-economic standard. It means more than this. It means a reference to an extra-scientific standard, one whose distinctive character consists in its being the expression and operation of the organic complex of forces composing the social personality as mirrored in the conscious or unconscious efforts of the individuals and of the Society who make the valuations and frame their conduct upon them.

§ 15. In conclusion it is necessary to enforce an exceedingly important distinction in the conception of social or human valuation. The term means two things, the attribution of human or social value by an individual and by a society. In most of our illustrations we have taken the standpoint of the Statesman or the reformer, or of some other person, and regarded social values from his eyes. We have taken his ideal as a social ideal. So it is in the sense of being his ideal of a society. But it is essential also to consider society as seeking to realise its own ideal. 'The whole succession of men during many ages,' said Pascal, 'should be considered as one Man, ever living and constantly learning.' This is the true organic view of humanity, regarded either as a single whole or in its several races, nations or communities. The apophthegm is not primarily of political or of ethical significance, but a statement of natural history. It is corroborated in a striking manner by modern biological teaching, with its continuity of the germ-plasm, its embryonic recapitulation and its specific evolution. But not until natural history is rescued from the excessive domination of a purely physical biology, and is read in the language of collective psycho-physics, do we grasp the full bearing of the organic conception in its application to a society. For this conception of mankind as working out the human career by the operation of its original supply of faculties and feelings, in which instinctive physical motives take an increasing admixture of conscious rational guidance, is the key to an understanding of the ascent of man. There is no clear evidence of the continuous ascent of man regarded as individual, at any rate within 'historic' times. There is evidence of the ascent of human society towards a larger and closer complexity of human relations and a clearer intellectual and moral consciousness. This means that mankind, as a whole, and its several societies, is becoming more capable of a human valuation and of a collective conduct of affairs guided by this conscious process. In politics, regarded in its wider meaning, this truth has taken shape in the modern conception of the general will, which in popularly-governed States functions through public opinion and representative institutions. Following our examination of the limits of science or 'rationalism' in the processes of valuation and of conduct on the part of individuals, we shall expect to find some corresponding limits in collective man. In other words, the general will of a people cannot be regarded, either in its estimates or its determinations, as a merely or a mainly calculative process, working out the respective values of existing circumstances, or proposed changes, in terms of clearly-defined utility. It does not even with fuller information, wider education and firmer self-control, tend towards this scientific politics. Collective self-government, like individual self-government, will always remain essentially an art, its direction and determinant motives being creative, qualitative, and rooted in the primal instincts of man.

§ 16. It is upon this conception of the collective instincts of society regarded as an organism that a rational faith in democracy is based. The animal organism, itself a society of cells, is endowed with energy of body and mind, operating through an equipment of instinctive channels towards its own survival and development and the survival and development of its species. Where there is danger lest too much of this energy should be consumed upon individual ends, too little on specific ends, the social or self-sacrificing instincts are strengthened in the individual, and are reinforced by the herd or specific feelings of other individuals, as where plunderers of the common stock or shirkers in the common tasks are destroyed by the hive or herd. The instinct for the survival and development of the hive, herd or species, cannot be satisfactorily explained as belonging only to the psycho-physical equipment of the individual members. On this basis, viz. that of attributing a social nature only to the individual members of a society, the acts of devotion and self-sacrifice, and still more the acts of preparatory skill, the elaborate performance of deeds that are means to the survival and well-being of a future generation, become mere haphazard miracles. Take the familiar example of the Hunting Wasp.

'The larvae of the various Hunting Wasps demand a motionless prey who will not, by defensive movements, endanger the delicate egg and, afterwards, the tiny grub fixed to a part of the prey. In addition, it is necessary that this inert prey shall be nevertheless alive; for the grub would not accept a corpse as food. Its victuals must be fresh meat and not preserved provisions. These two antagonistic conditions of immobility and life the Hymenoptera realises by means of paralysis, which destroys movement and leaves the organic principle of life intact. With a skill which our most famous vivisectors would envy, the insect drives its poison sting into the nerve centres, the seat of muscular stimulation. The operator either confines himself to a single stroke of the lancet, or else gives two, or three or more, according to the structure of the particular nervous system and the number and grouping of the nerve centres. The exact anatomy of the victim guides the needle.' [1]

Such conduct is not made intelligible by any other hypothesis than that of a collective life of the species, the individual lives being, in fact, parts of a common specific life towards which they contribute in a manner similar to that in which the cells, with their particular lives, contribute to the life of their organism. Only by this application or extension of the 'organic metaphor' to the relations between members of an existing generation, and between successive generations, can we construct an intelligible sequence of causation between these preparatory acts of individual insects of one generation and the results accruing to other individuals of another generation.

This 'general will' (may we not call it so?), urging the individuals to the fulfilment of a purpose which is but slightly theirs, and is not mainly that of the existing generation, but which embodies the general purpose of the species or some wider purpose of a still larger organic whole, can only be realised for thought and feeling as a single current of will implying and conferring unity of life upon the species or the larger unity.

In 'lower' animal spheres we recognise this fact. But there is a tendency to hold that man, subject to some such specific urge or instincts in his primitive stages, has become more and more individualised and has done so largely by becoming more rational. The gradual displacement of instinct by reason, it is contended, has made man more self-sufficient, his life more of the nature of an

[1] Henri Fabre, The Eng. Review, Dec., 1912, *The Modern Theory of Instincts.*

end, less of a means towards the life of his tribe or nation, or even towards that of humanity as a whole. Is this so? There are two issues that open here. In the process of civilisation a man certainly becomes more individual. He differs in character more from his fellows than in earlier times; he is able to devote, and does devote, a larger share of his energies of body and mind to activities which are primarily self-regarding. Moreover, he tends to rely less exclusively or predominantly upon what would be called his instincts and more upon his reason.

§ 17. The 'general will', which through forms of tribal custom and of gregarious instinct pulsed so vigorously and so insistently in tribal life, seems to have weakened with every expansion of social area and with the advancing complexity of social relations. The economy of human energy allows individuals to apply a larger share of the life-force that flows through them to what appear to them their private purposes, a smaller to the protection and development of the society or species. If we were to assign any final validity to the opposition of individual and society, this change might be regarded as a shrinkage of the dominion of the 'general will,' the specific as contrasted with the individual purpose. But though the narrow intense tribal will may thus appear to have yielded to a broader, feebler and less imperative form of national or social will, it by no means follows that this latter works less effectively for the common good. As man becomes more intelligent and more reflective, and has fortified himself with larger and more reliable records and better methods of controlling his environment, the instinctive operations of the will of groups of tribal animals give place to more conscious, more rational, purposes.

The change must not indeed be overstressed. The validity of the general will does not depend upon the degree of conscious rational purpose it has attained. It remains to-day in the most highly civilised communities what it was in primitive tribal life, an organic instinct. The rationalisation of this blind faculty of organic self-protection and advancement has not yet gone very far. Indeed, it is exceedingly important to recognise that an organic instinct of conservation and of progress underlies the wisdom of the people. Those who consider politics a rightful monopoly of the educated classes doubly err; first, in ignoring the instinctive wisdom of the people, secondly in claiming for education a higher value for political direction than it possesses. The political wisdom of the Roman or the Germanic peoples partakes far more of a natural sagacity than of a reasoned process. If this applies to the great statesman, it is still more applicable to the body of the people whose consent or active coöperation contributes to the evolution of a stable and a progressive state. It is impossible to understand or to explain any long and complex movement in national history by piecing together the conscious rational designs of the individuals or groups of men who executed the several moves of which the movement seemed to consist. Such a structure as the British Constitution, such an episode as the French Revolution, cannot be otherwise regarded, in its organic unity, than as a product of energies of common will and purpose, wider, deeper and obscurer in their working than the particular intelligible motives and aims which appeared on the stage of parliamentary debates, military campaigns or mob violence. Every student of the 'spirit' of one of these great national dramas is driven to recognise some moulding or directing influence, some urge of events, by which they seem to unfold themselves in a larger and more complex pattern or consistency than is perceived by any of the agents. There is sometimes a tendency to give a mystical interpretation to this truth. So Victor Hugo writes of the French Revolution:

'Être un membre de la Convention, c'était être une vague de l'Ocean. Et ceci était vrai des plus grands. La force d'impulsion venait d'en haut. Il y avait dans la Convention une volonté qui était celle de tous et n'était celle de personne. Cette volonté était une idée, idée indomptable et démesurée qui soufflait dans l'ombre du haut du ciel. Nous appelons cela la Révolution. Quand cette idée passait elle abattait l'un et soulevait l'autre; elle emportait celui-ci en écume et brisait celui-là aux écueils. Cette idée savait où elle allait, et poussait le gouffre devant elle. Imputer la révolution aux hommes, c'est imputer la marée aux flots.' [1]

The explanation of our colonial empire as the result of a career of conquest and expansion conducted 'in a fit of absence of mind' is an exact statement of the truth. For though a few great empire-builders, such as Warren Hastings, Molesworth, Elgin, Grey and

[1] *Quatre-vingt-treize*, Livre III, Chapter XI.

Rhodes, may have played their parts with some measure of conscious design, the individual channels of this current of adventurous and constructive energy embodied in the general process had as little an idea of the imperial edifice as any working bee of the great symmetrical structure of the hive.

§ 18. This sense of 'manifest destiny' is surely no illusion. It is the evolutionary method by which all organic process is achieved, whether in the growth of an oak tree from its acorn, of a motor car from the earliest hand-barrow, a musical symphony from a savage tom-tom, or a modern federal state from the primitive tribal order. In every case a number of what seem separately motived actions are seen to carry and express the continuity of some common tendency which brings them under the control of a single collective design. This wider purpose is seen operating upon the larger organic stage of conduct in ways closely analogous to the operations of the poet or the artist in any human fine art. It exhibits the urge of an inner flow of psycho-physical energy seeking ever finer modes of expression by moulding the materials at its disposal. As soon as we grasp this idea of the collective artistry of a species or any other organic group, we recognise how lacking in logical finality is the accepted antithesis of instinct and reason. The reason of the organism will appear as a blind instinctive drive to the cell whose conduct it directs. So the specific purpose will show itself as instinct in the individual organism, though it may be neither blind nor unconscious to the species taken as the organic unit. Nay, we may go further and suggest that advancing reason in the individual animal may consist in a growing sympathy and syn-noesis with the operations of the wider organism. Must not this be what happens when what we term reason endorses and reinforces the instinctive actions of specific preservation and well-being, substituting reflection for impulse, plans for customs, orderly and changing institutions for blind ordinances whose authority is gregarious imitation or superstitious prestige? Are we wrong when we trace an instinct of obedience to a chief transformed into a reasoned submission to the law? May not then the whole process of the rationalisation of man be regarded as a bringing of the individual man into vital communion of thought and feeling with the thoughts and feelings of the race, of humanity, perhaps of the larger organic being of the kosmos? For a man only becomes rational so far as he takes a disinterested view of himself, his fellow-men and of the world he lives in, and the wider, closer, keener that view the more rational he becomes. Thus the evolution of the mind of man into a fuller rationality means the strengthening and clarifying of those relations of feeling and thought which bind him to his fellows and to his world and which are rooted in the 'blind' instincts of gregarious, superstitious, curious man.

§ 19. The upshot of these considerations is to break down the abruptness of the contrast between reason and instinct and to recognise in reason itself the subtlest play of the creative instinct. The 'disinterested' nature of the search for truth has been a subject of derision among some thinkers, who see no way by which man the individual can disengage himself from the selfish motives which seem to rule him and to dispose alike of his emotional and intellectual energies. In man regarded as individual it is very difficult to recognise any possibility of a disinterested motive, because all such motives are ruled out *ex hypothesi*. But regard the individual man as subject to the dominant control of some wider life than his, that of race, society, humanity or kosmos, and the difficulty disappears. He becomes capable of 'disinterested' curiosity, 'disinterested' love, 'self-sacrifices' of various kinds, because he is a centre of wider interests than those of his own particular self. The action of a Japanese who throws himself upon the Russian bayonets at the word of command, of a doctor who inoculates himself with a deadly poison for the sake of science, the steady lifelong toil of millions of peasants growing the food supply for unknown millions of town-dwellers, are no longer 'disinterested' when they are looked at from the standpoint of the interests of humanity as a whole. This collective will and intelligence can never be considered wholly 'blind' when regarded from the collective standpoint. Every directive instinct of an organism, at any rate in the animal world, must be accredited with some related emotion[1], and this emotion, regarded as a fact in consciousness, must be accredited with some measure of intelligence. The creature

[1] Cf. McDougall, *Social Psychology*.

subject to the drive of an emotion must have some idea of what he is about, though the full psycho-biological 'purpose' of his action may be hidden from him. This organic standpoint gives an intelligible meaning to what we may call the 'natural wisdom of the people.' The herd, the tribe, the nation is endowed with instincts of self-protection and of growth. These instincts are accompanied by corresponding emotions which, according to the degree of intelligence they contain, impel it to a right or economical use of the physical and spiritual environment for survival and 'progress.' The instinctive and emotional stream of this common life becomes more 'rational' as the factors of intelligence accompanying the emotions become clearer, better coördinated and endowed with larger capacity of central direction. In the evolution of animal organisms this growth of rationality implies, and is compassed by, a decline of the special instincts with a consequent weakening of the special emotions attached to them, and the substitution of a flexible general instinct operating through a centralised nervous system and coordinating the special organic emotions and activities to serve a more clearly conceived organic purpose of the individual or the race. Reason, regarded as a motive power and not as a mere intellectual organ, must be considered as this general instinct of survival and growth, having its roots in the apparently separate instincts of hunger, procreation, shelter, pugnacity, flight, gregariousness, protection of young, curiosity, constructiveness, acquisitiveness and the like, and utilising the emotions proper to these several instincts for the economy of some more general plan of life. Reasoning, as an 'intellectual process,' will probably derive its emotional food and impetus principally from the emotions carried by the instincts of flight and pursuit, which involve quick judgment in the use of means, and by the curiosity and constructiveness which impel the more reflective study and adaptation of material environment.

It is, however, no purpose of mine to enter into the particulars of this theory of the natural origins of reason. It is sufficient to recognise; first that prior to the dawn of 'reason' in organic evolution, the instincts carry and apply a wisdom of direction of their own; secondly that when reason takes over much of this directing power it operates by coördinating, not by creating, motive power.

So when we substitute for the individual organism the herd, the tribe, the nation, ascending to larger collective wholes, sustained by a clearer consciousness of unity and a fuller use of central conscious purpose, we follow the same economy of government. If, as is often urged, a nation, regarded as an organism, must be classed as a comparatively primitive type, on a level rather with the sponges or algae than with the higher animals, we shall expect to find that a very large measure of such 'wisdom' as it possesses will be instinctive rather than 'rational.' The evolution of a general will, whether operative by public opinion or governmental institutions, will on such a hypothesis possess no great degree of centrality or clear consciousness. Good government in such a society could not be compassed by an oligarchy or even a representative assembly assuming a measure of detailed and far-sighted policy for which the collective life was not yet ripe. A large measure of what from the rational standpoint would rank as 'opportunism' would be the true policy at such a stage of social evolution, and the wise statesman would keep his ear to the ground so as to learn the instinctive movements of the popular mind which would yield the best freight of political wisdom at his disposal. Only as education and closer and more reliable communications elevated the organic structure of Society, imparting higher spirituality, more centrality and clearer consciousness to its life, should we expect any considerable rationalisation of the general will. Meanwhile arise the temptation and danger of the formal instruments of government falling into the hands of a little highly self-conscious group or class, who may seek to impose upon the conduct of the nation its clearer plans and far-sighted purposes "under the name and pretext of the commonwealth." The absolute or actual wisdom of their will they will be apt to represent as embodying the reality of the general will. It is what *they* think 'the people' *ought* to will and therefore what the people will come to will as soon as they are really capable of willing intelligently!

It is, however, exceedingly important to try and recognise the instinctive wisdom of the people, in order that a misrepresentative government may be prevented from ignoring it and substituting the rationalism of some little conscious class.

This does not mean that a Government must always govern and adapt its laws to the level of the current feelings, desires and aspirations of the average man, giving him no lead or stimulus to higher rationality. Such a course would be to ignore that capacity for progress and that susceptibility to proximate ideals which are themselves implanted in the instincts of mankind. But it does require that a Government shall keep itself in the closest sympathy with the concrete feelings and ideas of the people, maintaining such contacts as shall enable its acts of policy to rank as substantially correct interpretations of the general will, not as the designs of a supreme governing caste or group of interests, pumped down through some artfully contrived electoral machinery so as to receive the false formal impress of 'the general will.'

These reflections upon the nature of popular government may appear to have carried us far afield. But they have been no irrelevant excursion. For upon our view of the nature and measure of rationality to be imputed to the processes of reform or progress in national life must depend our view of the part which can be played by the social sciences which are invoked as the chief instruments of conscious collective conduct.

Recognising that social progress in all its departments remains always a collective art, inspired and sustained by creative impulses which owe neither their origin or their validity to science, we shall regard the social sciences as servants rather than directors of social progress. We shall be concerned to ask, What are the proper and particular services such sciences can render? How can they assist a people in utilising its human and natural resources for the attainment of the best conditions of human life, individual and social?

This work is written as a partial and illustrative answer to these questions. Taking industry, that department of social conduct most susceptible of the quantitative measurement which is the instrument of science, we have endeavored to construct and apply an organon of human valuation to its activities and achievements. Recognising that industry, regarded from the individual or the social standpoint, was an organic activity, involving continual reactions upon the whole life of the individual and the society, we insisted that the standard of valuation must be constructed in terms of organic well-being. In other words, industry, both from its productive and its consumptive side, must be valued in terms of individual and social health, that term being selected as the one which best expresses the conditions of conservation and of progress universally recognised as the essentials of a 'valuable' life. In the actual interpretation of this organic welfare, we took for our valuer 'enlightened' common-sense. The roots of this common-sense we find laid in the silent, instinctive organic strivings of mankind. It is the business of science, or organised knowledge, to direct these strivings so as to enable them to attain their ends more economically. It does this by interpreting experience and supplying the interpretation in the shape of 'laws' to enlighten common-sense and so enable it to choose its paths. For the economy of blind instincts is only accommodated to simple activities in a stable environment, and is even then subject to enormous vital wastes. For complicated activities in a rapidly changing and complex environment, a general instinct of adaptability of means to ends, involving conscious reflection, is required. Reason is this general instinct and science is its instrument. Society, as its processes of evolution become more conscious, will be able to use more profitably the services of science. Those services consist not in authoritative legislation for social conduct, for laws based upon experience of the past can have no full authority to bind the future. Faith and risk-taking, involving large elements of the incalculable, are inherent in organic processes, and are the very sap of spiritual interest in life. They can never be brought under the dominion of a scientific economy.

But the main staple in every art of conduct is repetition and considered adaptation, resting upon a continuity of conditions. For this part of social conduct science, when sufficiently equipped, can and will offer authoritative advice. Throughout all nature the arts of conservation and creation run together. The art of conservation is the practical function of science: the art of creation ever remains a region of beckoning liberty, continually

.nnexed by science, and yet undiminished in its size and
ts appeal.

> ' For all experience is an arch where through
> Gleams that untravelled land whose margin fades
> For ever and for ever as we move.'

INDEX

363